Vietnam

0
0
100 km
100 miles

page 266-67

page 271

page 281

page 288

Qui Nhon
Mui Ong Dien
Tuy Hoa
Mui Nay
Nha Trang
Cam Ranh
Vinh Cam Ranh
Phan Rang
Cu Lao Thu
Da Lat (Dalat)
Mui Ne
Phan Thiet
Duc Trong
Bao Loc
Long Det
Ho Tri An
Vung Tau
Bien Hoa
Ho Chi Minh
My Tho
Tan An
Can Tho
Tra Vinh
Binh Long
Bac Lieu
Tay Ninh
Soc Trang
Ca Mau
Han Giang
Hau Giang
Mui Ca Mau
Con Dao

Quang Ngai
Vuc Linh
2598
Kon Tum
14
Play Cu (Pleiku)
19
Virochei
Buon Ma Thuot
Srepok
14
Kracheh
13
Kampong Cham
Mekong
22
Binh Long
Prey Veng
Phnum Penh (Phnom Penh)
Kampong Chhnang
Kampong Thum
Stoeng Sen
CAMBODIA
Kong
Stoeng Treng
Phumi Mlu Pley
Muang Khong
Pakxe
Champasak
Attapu
Sisaket
Surin
Buriram
Nakhon Ratchasima
Chuor Phnum Dangrek
Anlong Veng
Phumi Samraong
Siemreab
Tonle Sab
Pouthisat
Sisophon
Battambang
Pailin
Chuor Phnum Kravanh
Kreng Kaon Kong
Kampong Saom
Dao Phu Quoc
Kampot
Chau Doc
Long Xuyen
Rach Gia
Hon Tre
Hon Rai
Hon Nai
Trat
Ko Kut
Ko Chang
Chanthaburi

N

ABOUT THIS BOOK

Editorial

Editor
Scott Rutherford
Editorial Director
Brian Bell

Distribution

UK & Ireland
GeoCenter International Ltd
Meridian House, Churchill Way West
Basingstoke, Hampshire RG21 6YR
Fax: (44) 1256 817988

United States
Langenscheidt Publishers, Inc.
36–36 33rd Street 4th Floor
Long Island City, NY 11106
Fax: (1) 718 784-0640

Australia
Universal Publishers
1 Waterloo Road
Macquarie Park, NSW 2113
Fax: (61) 2 9888-9074

New Zealand
Hema Maps New Zealand Ltd (HNZ)
Unit D, 24 Ra ORA Drive
East Tamaki, Auckland
Fax: (64) 9 273-6479

Worldwide
**Apa Publications GmbH & Co.
Verlag KG (Singapore branch)**
38 Joo Koon Road, Singapore 628990
Tel: (65) 6865-1600. Fax: (65) 6861-6438

Printing

Insight Print Services (Pte) Ltd
38 Joo Koon Road, Singapore 628990
Tel: (65) 6865-1600. Fax: (65) 6861-6438

©2007 Apa Publications GmbH & Co.
Verlag KG (Singapore branch)
All Rights Reserved
First Edition 1992
Fourth Edition 1999
Updated 2006 (Reprinted 2007)

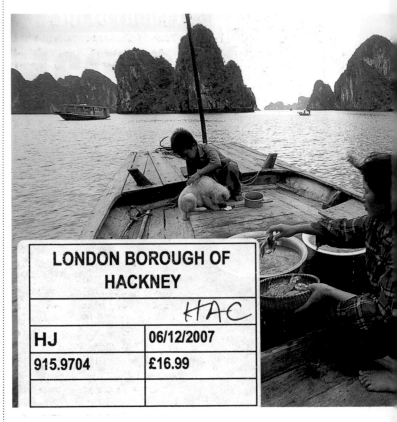

CONTACTING THE EDITORS
We would appreciate it if readers
would alert us to errors or out-
dated information by writing to:
**Insight Guides, P.O. Box 7910,
London SE1 1WE, England.
Fax: (44) 20 7403-0290.**
insight@apaguide.co.uk

www.insightguides.com

The first Insight Guide pioneered the use of creative full-colour photography in travel guides in 1970. Since then, we have expanded our range to cater for our readers' need not only for reliable information about their chosen destination but also for a real understanding of that destination. Now, when the Internet can supply inexhaustible – but not always reliable – facts, our books marry text and pictures to provide those much more elusive qualities: knowledge and discernment. To achieve this, they rely heavily on the authority of locally based writers and photographers.

In this, the fourth edition of *Insight Guide: Vietnam*, our writers and photographers travel the length and breadth of this simultaneously enchanting and confounding nation. Outside of the cities of Ha Noi and Ho Chi Minh, much of the country is not for those looking for ease of travel. But for the traveller seeking an extraordinary experience, Vietnam awaits.

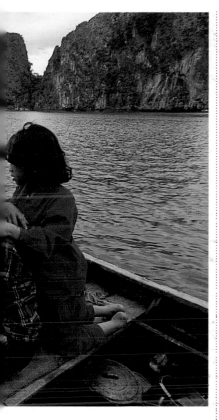

How to use this book

The book is carefully structured to convey an understanding of Vietnam and its culture and to guide readers through its sights and attractions:

◆ The Features section, with a yellow colour bar, covers the country's history and culture in lively authoritative essays written by specialists.

◆ The Places section, with a blue bar, provides full details of all the sights and areas worth seeing. The chief places of interest are coordinated by number with specially drawn maps.

◆ The Travel Tips listings sec-

tion, with an orange bar, at the back of the book, offers a convenient point of reference for information on travel, accommodation, restaurants, and other practical aspects of the country. Information can be located quickly using the index printed on the back cover flap, which also serves as a handy bookmark.

The contributors

This new edition, which builds on the first edition edited by **Helen West**, was managed and edited by **Scott Rutherford**.

Contributing to this edition, with updated material and new information on Hanoi and northern Vietnam was Bangkok-based **Susan Cunningham**. The southern part of the country, including Ho Chi Minh (Saigon), was covered by **Sharon Owyang**, a frequent contributor who worked on *Insight Guide: China*. The central region, including Hue and Da Nang, was updated by Chiang Mai-based **Andrew Forbes** and **David Henley**, who have helped with several Insight Guides.

Catherine Karnow and **Jim Holmes** provided much of the photography, while **Mariko Fujinaka** tidied up the text.

Previous contributors to the guide include **Tim Larimer, Andy Soloman, Diana Reid, Tran Van Dinh, Tim Page, Kim Naylor, Nguyen Tan Dac, Jean-Leo Dugast, Bill Wassman, Alain Evrard, Joseph Lynch**, and **Zdenek Thoma**. In 2006, this guide was updated with the help of Hanoi-based **Linda Mazur**, supervised by **Jocelyn Lau** at Insight's Singapore office.

Map Legend

▬ ▪ ▪	International Boundary
▬ ▪ ▬	National Park/Reser
▬ ▬ ▬ ▬	Ferry Route
✈ ✈	Airport: Internationa Regional
🚌	Bus Station
℗	Parking
❶	Tourist Information
✉	Post Office
✝ ✝ ✝	Church/Ruins
✝	Monastery
☾	Mosque
✡	Synagogue
🏰 🏛	Castle/Ruins
∴	Archaeological Site
∩	Cave
🗿	Statue/Monument
★	Place of Interest

The main places of interest in the Places section are coordinated by number with a full-colour map (e.g. ❶), and a symbol at the top of every right-hand page tells you where to find the map.

Left: Ha Long Bay

CONTENTS

Maps

Hill-tribe harvest in northern Vietnam.

A RESILIENT PLACE

The Vietnamese are an adaptable and pragmatic people,
with a national sense of being that has humbled great powers

In the early 1400s, the Chinese invaded Vietnam, one of many such invasions over the centuries. The Chinese were soundly defeated by the Vietnamese. Le Loi, emperor of Vietnam, might have had the Chinese prisoners killed. He chose otherwise. Le Loi apologised to the Chinese court for defeating its army, made peace with China, and then provided the defeated Chinese troops with horses and ships for their return north. Le Loi knew that, although momentarily defeated, China would never, ever disappear from Vietnam's future or memory.

Perhaps more than anything else, the presence of its leviathan neighbour to the north has shaped the nature and outlook of the Vietnamese mind. Centuries of fending off China's invasions, while at the same time not making China *too* angry, has given the Vietnamese a pragmatism, patience, and solid sense of national identity. In fact, the Vietnamese have an uncanny and unusually deep feeling of national identity and of nation-building. Had the French and Americans seriously pondered Vietnamese history, the inevitable futility of their military efforts in the 1950s and 1960s would have been more self-evident and at an earlier stage.

Vietnamese offer a modern slogan: *Vietnam is a country, not a war.* But for much of the post-World War II years, until 1975, Vietnam was nearly synonymous with war, first with the French and later the Americans. Vestiges of the war remain in the bomb craters, old military hardware, and labyrinths of tunnels where entire villages endured the fighting. The craters have been converted into fish ponds and the tunnels turned into tourist traps. Memories of the war are fading. More than 60 percent of Vietnamese today are less than 30 years old, born after the Vietnam War's end. They are the first generation in many not to know war in their homeland.

"All men are created equal. They are endowed by their creator with certain inalienable rights, among these are life, liberty and the pursuit of happiness". The meaning is familiar to every American as the foundation of the American constitution. But the words above are in the Declaration of the Democratic Republic of Vietnam, written in 1945 by Ho Chi Minh, a Communist revolutionary who was influenced by the American constitution and its ambitions.

The Vietnamese government is unabashedly Communist. It is a Leninist regime, nevertheless, that sometimes transcends the Cold War stereotype of grey, static, and anchored by a cult-of-personality leadership. While it has been at times harshly oppressive, Vietnam's Communism is occasionally, though hesitatingly, pragmatic.

PRECEDING PAGES: temple detail from Ha Tien, southern Vietnam; boats on Vinh Ha Long, northern Vietnam; Hanoi religious shop; Song Huong (Perfume River), Hue.
LEFT: vendor at a Mekong Delta market, southern Vietnam.

"Vietnam's Communist Party... voiced a common yearning for equality and betterment" reported a typically lucid article in *The Economist* in 1995. "Few communist parties so harnessed themselves to national ideals. Its cruelty might have been feared, but its daring and tenacity for a cause most Vietnamese supported – national independence – was admired".

The struggling pragmatism of Vietnam's government comes against great odds. When the Americans pulled out and the South was reunified ("liberated" has passed from pragmatic usage) with the North, the Hanoi government immediately turned southern Vietnam into a Soviet-style economy. The result nearly left a carcass of a nation. By the mid-1980s, the country's economy was destitute. Inflation exceeded 800 percent. Large parts of the rural population were starving or nearly so. Earlier, in December 1978, cross-border attacks into southern Vietnam by Cambodian troops resulted in the Ba Chuc massacre, leaving 2,000 civilians dead. Vietnam responded by attacking Cambodia and overthrowing the government of Pol Pot, an action that resulted in the former country being internationally ostracised. Also, in retaliation, Chinese troops invaded Vietnam's northern provinces, although they withdrew after 17 days. Fortunately, unlike elsewhere in Asia, saving face is not an obsessive concern of the Vietnamese. Admitting that their socialisation of the South was in error, the government shifted course towards a free-market economy with its *doi moi,* or new reform policy. The latest phase of *doi moi* involves sweeping steps to liberalise the economy and attract more foreign investment. The country is also working towards being recognised as a mature trading nation and acceptance into the World Trade Organisation (WTO) by the end of 2005.

Vietnam remains one of the poorest countries in the world, with a per capita annual income of about US$500. Yet on the streets of Hanoi or Ho Chi Minh one does not sense a wretchedness or fatalism of poverty often encountered elsewhere in the Third World. Everywhere there is the hum of activity, of a hard-working people anxious to build their country and lives. There is a future to be made and the Vietnamese intend to make it, corruption and the reactionary impediments of the central government notwithstanding. And the Vietnamese drive like they work: looking only ahead, ignoring traffic to the sides, and stopping for nothing.

For even as the country repeats its mantra – a country, not a war – its long history of conflict has left the people with a natural tendency to be wary of foreigners, to value self-reliance, and to do things their own way with an innate pride and a national awareness that this impoverished land was able to defeat great powers and superior technology. And, too, throughout Vietnam's history is a thread of victimisation – that it was foreigners who caused all of Vietnam's problems. Yet, with the pragmatism of Emperor Le Loi more than half a millennium ago, the Vietnamese will define their future, perhaps with resounding finesse. ❑

RIGHT: young girl in Ho Chi Minh, the former Saigon, in southern Vietnam.

Decisive Dates

BEGINNINGS

2879 BC: Legendary founding of the Van Lang Kingdom by the first Hung Vuong.

2879–258 BC: Hung dynasty.

1800–1400 BC: Phung Nguyen culture, the Early Bronze Age.

200 BC–AD 938: Chinese rule.

210 BC: Kingdom of Au Lac established. Chinese general Chao Tuo founds Nan Yueh (Nam Viet).

AD 39: Trung sisters lead a rebellion against Chinese.

AD 43: Trung sisters' rebellion is crushed by the Chi-

nese general Ma Yuan, and the Viet people are placed under direct Chinese administration for the first time.

542–544: Ly Bi leads uprising against China's Liang dynasty to create independent kingdom of Van Xuan.

939–967: Ngo dynasty.

968–980: Dinh dynasty.

970–975: Dinh Bo Linh gains Chinese recognition of Nam Viet's independence by establishing a tributary relationship with China's Song dynasty.

980–1009: Tien Le dynasty.

1010: Hanoi established.

1009–1225: Ly dynasty.

1225–1400: Tran dynasty.

1400–1428: Ho dynasty.

1428–1776: Le dynasty.

DIVISION AND REUNIFICATION

16th century: Decadence of Le dynasty leads to the country's division into two rival principalities.

1543: Descendants of the Le dynasty occupy the country's southern capital after a series of fierce battles. The southern court is founded near Thanh Hoa.

1592: The death of Mac dynasty's last king, Mac Mau Hop, ends the war.

1672: Lord Trinh consents to partition the country at the Linh River.

early 1770s: Struggle between French and Chinese factions begin with the court.

1776–92: Tay Son Uprising.

1792–1883: Nguyen dynasty.

1861: French capture Saigon and later defeat the Vietnamese army, gaining control of Gia Dinh and surrounding provinces. Six years later, the entire southern part of the country is annexed as a French colony.

1862: The Treaty of Saigon cedes three southern provinces to the French.

1893: Emperor Ham Nghi and Phan Dinh Phung organise a royalist movement and stage an unsuccessful uprising at Ha Tinh.

1904: Japanese victory over Russia convinces Vietnamese that Western power is no longer invincible.

1907: Eastward Movement is established by Phan Boi Chau and Cuong De, but is discovered and crushed by the French.

1919: Nguyen Ai Quoc (later known as Ho Chi Minh) attempts to present a programme for Vietnamese rights and sovereignty at the Versailles Peace conference but is turned away.

1920: Ho Chi Minh participates in the founding of the French Communist Party.

1923: Ho Chi Minh goes to Moscow to be trained as an agent of the Communist International.

1930: Ho Chi Minh successfully rallies several Communist groups and becomes the founder of the Indochinese Communist Party.

WORLD WAR II AND AFTER

1939: World War II begins.

1945: Japan overthrow the French and renders Vietnam "independent" but under Japanese "protection". Japanese surrender to the Allies some months later.

1942–43: Ho Chi Minh imprisoned in China.

1943: Ho Chi Minh is released and recognised as the chief of the Viet Minh.

1945: Japan surrenders and the Viet Minh commences the August Revolution, gaining effective control over much of Vietnam. In September Ho Chi Minh declares Vietnam's independence in Hanoi.

1946: Ho Chi Minh visits Paris during negotiations

with France; hostilities begin following violation of agreements.

1951: Ho merges Viet Minh with the Lien Viet and announces the formation of the Workers Party (Lao Dong).

NORTH-SOUTH DIVIDE

1954: The French are defeated at Dien Bien Phu on May 7. Geneva Accord divides Vietnam at the 17th parallel. South Vietnam is led by Prime Minister Ngo Dinh Diem, and North Vietnam under the Communist Ho Chi Minh.

1955: Diem refuses to hold general elections. Start of Second Indochina War. Direct US aid to South Vietnam begins.

1959: Group 559 established to infiltrate South Vietnam via the Ho Chi Minh Trail.

1960: National Liberation Front of South Vietnam (NLF) is formed. During the 1960s, the southern Communist movement – the Viet Cong – grows stronger.

1962: US military personnel in Vietnam total about 3,200.

1963: Ngo Dinh Diem, president of South Vietnam, is overthrown and assassinated.

1965: US bomb military targets in North Vietnam. First US ground combat troops land in Vietnam at Da Nang.

1968: My Lai massacre. Tet Offensive includes a raid on the American embassy that stuns and embarrasses the US. Peace negotiations begin in Paris.

1969: Ho Chi Minh dies aged 79.

1973: Paris Peace Agreement aims ends the hostilities. Last US troops depart from Vietnam in March.

1975: In April, North Vietnamese troops enter Saigon. The South Vietnamese government surrenders.

A UNIFIED VIETNAM

1976: Vietnam is officially reunified.

1977: Vietnam is admitted to the United Nations.

1978: Vietnam signs friendship treaty with the Soviet Union. Cambodian border troops launch cross-border attacks into southern Vietnam, resulting in the Ba Chuc massacre. Vietnam retaliates and the Cambodian government of Pol Pot is overthrown.

1979: China retaliates by invading Vietnam, but withdraw after 17 days.

1982: Fifth National Party Congress.

ECONOMIC SHIFTS

1986: Sixth Party Congress. Programme of socio-economic renovation called *doi moi* is launched.

LEFT: dragon motif on Nguyen mausoleum, Hue.
RIGHT: the legendary Ho Chi Minh in the 1950s.

1987: Law on Foreign Investment is passed.

1988: New contract system is implemented to encourage Vietnamese farmers to cultivate their land.

1989: Vietnamese troops leave Cambodia.

1990: Vietnam adopts a new course in foreign affairs, and peace talks in China take place. Diplomatic relations established with the European Union.

1991: China relations normalised and Soviets discontinue aid.

1993: Restrictions on Vietnam borrowing from IMF and Asian Development Bank are lifted.

1994: Trade embargo lifted by the United States.

1995: Diplomatic ties are restored with the US, and a US embassy opens in Hanoi. In the same year, Viet-

nam is admitted to the Association of Southeast Asian Nations (ASEAN).

1997: The Asian Economic Crisis forces many investors to leave Vietnam.

2000: Bill Clinton becomes the first US President to visit Vietnam since the war.

2001: The US and Vietnam implement an agreement normalising trade relations.

2002: The Vietnamese economy continues to improve.

2003: Vietnam hosts the 22nd Southeast Asian (SEA) Games.

2002: Foreign investors make a tentative return.

2005: The Hanoi Securities Trading Centre opens. Prime Minister Pham Van Khai makes a historic visit to the USA and Canada. ❑

THE FIRST 4,000 YEARS

*Dynasties rose and fell as Vietnam coalesced into a nation constantly
tempered by the ancient weight of the Middle Kingdom – China – to the north*

Vietnam's ancient history reads like a book of legend, but with many of the pages torn or missing due to a lack of early historical records. And like any ancient nation, Vietnam's earliest history has been generously embellished with legend and fairy tales. However, by melding Chinese and Vietnamese historical records together with Vietnamese folklore and recent archaeological discoveries, some of the missing pages have come to light.

The first threads of Vietnam's history are inextricably intertwined with the history of the country that looms to the north and is the most significant in the psyche of the Vietnamese people: China. Indeed, the outside force Vietnamese fear today is this most ancient of kingdoms that threatened Vietnam's existence repeatedly throughout history.

From the earliest records of civilisation, what is now Vietnam faced repeated incursions from China, even as late as 1979 when Chinese forces crossed the border in retaliation for Vietnam's earlier invasion into Cambodia. This history has left Vietnamese people with a suspicion of foreigners and perhaps with something of a martyr complex. Even today, when discussing poverty in the Vietnamese countryside, many people lay blame with America, or the French colonialists, or the centuries of fighting off the Chinese.

The Vietnamese have not been without their own territorial ambitions, however. Vietnamese history books tend to ignore the country's own invasions of neighbouring lands. Over the years, the country has had designs on what are now Cambodia and Laos, and there were early and lengthy conflicts between the northern and southern parts of Vietnam. Long before Ho Chi Minh sought to unify the country under the banner of Communism, the Viet people of what is now northern Vietnam had their eyes on – and eventually conquered – the Champa kingdom in the southern part of Vietnam. Interestingly enough, the ancient historical and geographical divisions of north and south – of Tonkin and Champa – were geographically similar to the United Nations-defined demilitarised zone that divided North and South Vietnam after World War II until reunification in 1975.

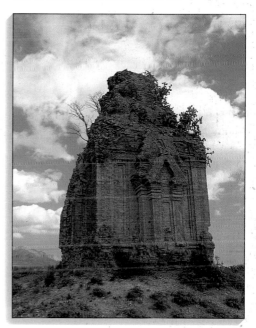

DONG SON CULTURE

Extending from northern Victnam into Cambodia, Laos, and even Indonesia, the Dong Son culture, named after a small village in northern Vietnam, produced exquisite bronze works as early as 300 BC. Often decorated with human and animal figures, Dong Son bronze was cast using wax models. Most exemplary were ceremonial "kettle" drums (the largest was found in Bali; *see photo on page 26*) and elaborate axes. Spirals are a notable motif in Dong Son bronze. The Dong Son were seafarers who ventured throughout Southeast Asia, but they also turned northern Vietnam's Song Hong, or Red River, region into a rice-growing region.

PRECEDING PAGES: pagoda of Thien Mu, Hue.
LEFT: dancing Cham *uma* stone image.
RIGHT: ancient Cham tower near Cam Ranh.

Hung Vuong dynasty

Nearly 5,000 years ago, if the stories are correct, the southern Viet kingdom of Xich Qui was divided into 100 principalities, each governed by one of the 100 sons. The eldest son was crowned as king of Lac Viet, naming himself Hung Vuong, while Lac Viet was renamed Van Lang. His kingdom of Van Lang was the most powerful around, encompassing most of present-day northern and central Vietnam. The kingdom of Van Lang prospered under the rule of 18 successive Hung kings during the 1st millennium BC – the dynasty of Hung Vuong, founded in the present-day dynasty in 208 BC. His capital was located near present-day Guangzhou (Canton).

China's influence

Nam Viet progressively entered the Chinese sphere of influence. In exchange for periodic tributes to the court of the Han emperor, Nam Viet received protection against foreign invasion. Less than a century later, however, the Han emperor Wudi sent his mighty armies to conquer Nam Viet. Despite the defending Nam Viet army's fierce resistance – a quality that continued through to the 20th century – Nam Viet yielded to the Han invaders.

province of Vinh. But like all kingdoms, this one eventually fell to another, that of Thuc Phan, king of neighbouring Au Viet, in 258 BC.

Thuc Phan (calling himself An Duong Vuong), established the new kingdom of Au Lac, putting his capital at Phuc An, where a spiral citadel was built. The remains of the citadel are in the present-day village of Co Loa, to the north of Hanoi.

Fifty years later, the kingdom fell to the northern hordes of an ambitious general, Trieu Da, who was from the south of China. Trieu Da founded the independent kingdom of Nam Viet, which included much of present-day southern China, and established the Trieu

THE TRUNG SISTERS

Heroes of Vietnam's first independence movement, sisters Trung Trac and Trung Nhi were of northern Vietnamese aristocracy. The husband of Trung Trac, the elder sister, was killed by the Chinese for plotting to overthrow them. Trung Trac took over leadership of the movement, and she and her sister led other nobles to Lien Lau and forced the Chinese to flee. They proclaimed themselves queens of a nation extending north from Hue into southern China. The sisters and their modest army were overwhelmed by Chinese forces near present-day Hanoi. Facing defeat, they committed suicide by drowning in the Song Hong (Red River), in AD 43.

The first Chinese occupation lasted half a century, until AD 42. After Trieu Dau's defeat, the country became a Chinese protectorate under the new name of Giao Chi. Highly qualified administrators were appointed as governors to rule the country, but their efforts to introduce Chinese literature, arts and agricultural techniques met with fierce resistance from the Viet people. Greatly frustrated by long decades of Chinese influence and culture, the Vietnamese not only guarded their existing national identity but fought fiercely to preserve it. Finally, in AD 39, the oppressive rule and injustices of a cruel

governor, To Dinh, provoked a victorious armed revolt against the Chinese authorities led by two sisters, Trung Trac and Trung Nhi, heroines known as Hai Ba Trung. Their reign, however, was short-lived (see box at left). Three years later, the superior strategies and arms of the Chinese armies brought the country again under Chinese control.

The fall of the Trung sisters marked the second period of Chinese occupation. Nam Viet was administered as a Chinese province and a campaign was launched against the kingdom

LEFT: an example of a large, Dong Son-era drum.
ABOVE: traditional theme of simple pleasures.

THE DRAGON AND THE IMMORTAL

Both the Chinese and Viet cosmology viewed the world through the concept of the Five Elements: metal, wood, water, fire and earth, sometimes represented by the Five Regions of Centre, South, North, East, and West. The Centre was represented by the earth and the colour yellow, the South by fire and the colour red, the North by water and the colour black, the East by wood and the colour green, the West by metal and the colour white.

From ancient times, a kingdom controlled the heart of the Asian continent, its rulers basing their power on these concepts of the Five Elements and Five Regions. Known as the Middle Kingdom, or Chung Hoa, its power centre was located in the territory of Five Mounts (Ngu Linh) and was peopled by many races but dominated by the Han and the Viet. While the Han were ethnically homogeneous, the Viets incorporated hundreds of tribes. The Viets settled south of the Yellow River and developed an agricultural culture, whereas the Han, in the northwest, became expert in hunting and battle skills.

The Viet chief ruled the Five Mounts territory, and there were three consecutive rulers: Toai Nhan, who discovered fire; Phuc Hi, who discovered the I Ching and domesticated wild animals; and Shen Nong, who cultivated wild plants for domestic use and taught his people to grow rice. The Viets regarded themselves as descendants of these three. The last ruler, Shen Nong, is the direct link to the Viet.

By the end of Shen Nong's era, the Han had invaded the Five Mounts territory. Their chief proclaimed himself Huangdi, the Yellow Emperor of the centre, in accordance with the Five Elements concept, and China's first true emperor. His son, Sung Lam, succeeded his father to become Lac Long Quan, Dragon Lord of the Mighty Seas. He married the beautiful Princess Au Co, descendant of the Immortals of the High Mountains. Their union gave birth to 100 sons and the Kingdom of Bach Viet, whose 100 principalities extended from the lower Yangzi to the north of Indochina. The kingdom prospered. But the Lord of the Dragon and the Princess of the Mountains, convinced that the difference in their origins would always deny them earthly happiness, separated. Half of the children returned with their mother to the mountains, the others followed their father to the eastern sea.

The symbolism of Lac Long Quan's descendance from the Dragon Lord and Au Co from the Immortals holds significance for the Vietnamese, as the Dragon symbolises the *yang* and Immortal the *yin*. Thus, the Vietnamese believe they are descendants of Tien Rong, the Immortal and the Dragon, and these symbols constitute the Vietnamese people's earliest totems.

of Champa, in the south. This period of Chinese occupation ended abruptly when a scholar named Ly Bon led an armed revolt and succeeded in chasing out the Chinese. Ly Bon took control of the territory, naming it Van Xuan and founding the Ly dynasty, which lasted until the Chinese once again regained supremacy in 545.

The particularly troubled era that followed was marked by frequent outbreaks of violent battles between Chinese and Vietnamese. It ended with the third period of Chinese occupation from 603 until 938. The Chinese made concerted efforts to establish their culture

transferred the capital to Co Loa, which had been the capital of the Au Lac kingdom, thus affirming continuity of the traditions of the Lac Viet people. Ngo Quyen spent the six years of his reign fighting revolts. After his death in 967, the kingdom fell into chaos. For more than 20 years, the country remained fragmented and the external threat from China's Song dynasty loomed large to the north on the border.

Dinh dynasty (968–980)

The most powerful of the feudal lords, Dinh Bo Linh, reunified the fragmented country under the name of Dai Co Viet and took the

and civilisation in Nam Viet, which they renamed An Nam. Still, numerous insurrections broke out despite the solid administrative structure imposed by the Chinese government of the Tang dynasty.

Ngo dynasty (939–967)

Disorder accompanied the decline of the Tang dynasty in China, giving the Vietnamese the chance for which they had long waited. In a protracted war that ended with the celebrated naval battle of Bach Dang, east of Hai Phong, Ngo Quyen vanquished the Chinese invaders and founded the first Vietnamese dynasty in 939. He named the country Dai Viet and

imperial title of Dinh Tien Hoang De (The First August Emperor Dinh). Well aware of the Chinese Song dynasty's military might, Dinh Bo Linh negotiated a non-aggression treaty in exchange for tributes payable to the Chinese every three years. This set the foundation of future relations with China that were to last for many centuries.

Dinh Tien Hoang established a royal court and a hierarchy of civil and military servants. He instated a rigorous justice system and introduced the death penalty to serve as a deterrent to all who threatened the new order in the kingdom. He organised a regular army divided into 10 *dao,* or military corps. Security and order were progressively re-established, inaugurating a new era of *thai binh* (peace).

However, Tien Hoang's reign was not to last long. He was assassinated in 979 by a palace guard, who saw "a star falling into his mouth" – a celestial omen heralding promotion. But the heir to the throne was only six years old and would not survive the mounting and pernicious intrigues of the court.

Tien Le dynasty (980–1009)

Le Hoan dethroned the throne's heir and proclaimed himself king as Le Dai Hanh. He retained the capital in Hoa Lu and succeeded

to consolidate the Viet nation. He developed the road network in order to better administer the country's regions. However, a succession of local revolts assured 24 years of difficult rule until Le Dai Hanh died. In the ensuing period, the monk Khuong Viet managed to establish Buddhism as a long-overdue stabilising pillar of the kingdom.

Ly dynasty (1009–1225)

The Ly dynasty, which reigned over the country for more than two centuries, was the first of the enduring national dynasties. Ly Cong Uan was a disciple of a monk, Van Hanh, who helped

in warding off several Chinese invasions by the Song court but continued paying them tributes every three years in exchange for friendly relations. With peace finally assured on the northern border, he sought to pacify the south. In 982, Le Dai Hanh launched a military expedition against the Champa kingdom. The conquest of this northern part of the Champa kingdom brought about a marked Cham influence on Vietnamese culture, particularly in the fields of music and dance.

Le Dai Hanh's reign marked the first attempt

LEFT: depicting the big cat (China) receiving tribute from servile mice (Vietnam). **ABOVE:** men of letters.

TEMPLE OF LITERATURE

In 1070, a national college was founded by King Ly Thanh Tong to educate future mandarins based in large part on Confucian ideals. The college, known as Van Mieu and designated the Temple of Literature when the capital was transferred to Hue at the beginning of the 18th century, has been restored and still stands in Hanoi. Knowledge of the Confucian classics, as well as the mastery of literary composition and poetry, were the main requirements of the rigorous three-year course, which culminated in a very competitive diploma examination. Architecturally, Van Mieu reflects Chinese influence and contains ritual bronzes in Chinese styles.

him rise to power. Assuming the name Ly Thai To, the new sovereign inaugurated his dynasty with a change of capital. Ly Thai To had seen the apparition of an ascending dragon on the site of the future capital and so decided to name it Thang Long (Ascending Dragon), near present-day Hanoi (Ha Noi). In 1054, one of his successors, King Ly Thanh Ton, renamed the country Dai Viet.

During the Ly dynasty, Buddhism flourished as the national religion. Buddhist masters, who acted as supreme advisors, assisted the Ly

MILITARY WIZARDS

The Tran dynasty is known for its many brilliant military victories, especially a notable one against Kublai Khan's much larger Mongol armies from the north.

Tran dynasty (1225–1400)

An ambitious commoner, Tran Canh, married the Ly dynasty's last queen and shrewdly manoeuvered his way to power to found the Tran dynasty. Buddhism, which had become predominant under the Ly dynasty, continued to play an important role, but it was subsequently weakened by co-existence with Confucianism, Daoism and various other popular beliefs. The century-old competitive examination system introduced during the first period of Chinese

kings in their rule. Several Ly kings led Buddhist sects and founded some 150 monasteries in the region of Thang Long. The Ly dynasty consolidated the monarchy by setting up a centralised government and establishing a tax system, a judiciary system, and a professional army. Important public works, including the building of dykes and canals, were undertaken in order to develop agriculture and settle the population.

The monarchist centralisation – influenced by Confucian notions – endowed the king with three roles: absolute monarch and religious chief of the empire; mediator between the people and heaven; and father of the nation.

occupation underwent draconian revisions. An administration incorporating both the reigning king and the heir to the title of the previous reign was adopted to ensure its continuity. The country's territorial ambitions to the south continued. The king's sister married the king of Champa in 1307, thus extending territory southward with the peaceful annexation of the Hue region and at the same time inaugurated the politics of diplomatic marriage.

Ho dynasty (1400–1428)

The king's marriage to the aunt of a minister, Le Qui Ly, was to prove a fatal move for the Tran dynasty. Taking full advantage of his aunt's union, Le Qui Ly shrewdly manoeuvered his way to power. He eventually assumed control of the kingdom and founded a dynasty under his ancestral name of Ho.

During his reign, the army was reorganised and reinforced. Taxes were revised and ports opened to trading ships, which were obliged to pay duties. Under a new fiscal system, coins were taken out of circulation and replaced with bank notes. Restrictions were imposed on land ownership. The exam system for administrators was modified to demand more practical knowledge of the peasant life, mathematics, history, Confucian classics, and literature.

Vietnamese national identity – Vietnamese literature, artistic and historical works were either burned or taken to China and replaced by the Chinese classics in all the schools.

The Chinese style of dress and hair were imposed on Vietnamese women. Most local religious rites, festivals and costumes were replaced or banished by the Chinese. Moreover, private fortunes were confiscated and taken to the Chinese court.

Le dynasty (1428–1776)

The Vietnamese found a new leader in the person of Le Loi, a man renowned for his

Legal reforms were undertaken and a medical service established.

His reign prompted yet another attack from China. Well aware that Ho had usurped the throne, the Chinese Ming-dynasty emperor sent 5,000 soldiers under the pretext of helping the movement faithful to the deposed Tran dynasty. The Ming intervention led to the fall of the Ho dynasty in 1407. During the short period of Chinese occupation that followed, the Vietnamese suffered inhumane exploitation. The Chinese resolutely strove to destroy the

courage and generosity. Under the title Prince of Pacification, he organised a resistance movement from his village and waged a guerrilla war against the enemy. By employing a strategy of surprise attacks targeting his adversary's weakest points, Le Loi managed to further weaken the enemy and at the same time avoid combat with the superior Chinese forces. His enforcement of strict military discipline ensured that no pillaging was carried out by his troops in the regions under his control, making him a very popular hero.

Le Loi founded the Le dynasty in 1428 and became king under the name of Le Thai To. He renamed the country Dai Viet and immediately

---

LEFT: Chinese influence, and the Tonkin royal court.
ABOVE: old print of traditional village in the Hue area.

began the task of its reconstruction after the devastation caused by the war. He reduced his army from 250,000 to 10,000 men and adopted a rotation system that enabled soldiers to return to the countryside to work and help boost food production. The legal system was reorganised and the penal system revised. A new college was founded to educate future administrators, with admission based entirely on merit and not on social or family status.

Le Thai To died in 1443, leaving the throne to his son, Le Thai Tong, whose sudden death not long after was followed by a decade of confusion and plots within the royal court. This troubled period ceased when Le Thanh Tong began his 36-year reign and the country prospered as never before. He revised the fiscal system, encouraged agriculture, and placed great emphasis on customs and moral principles. A writer himself, he wrote the first volume of Vietnamese history.

Le Thanh Tong was by no means only a recorder of history, nor was the dynasty solely one of pacification. His reorganised army won an easy victory over the southern Champa army in 1471. His farmer-soldiers excelled not only on the battlefields but also in the fields by setting up militarised agricultural communities wherever they went. In this way the national territory was gradually expanded southward, until finally the Champa kingdom was completely absorbed and assimilated.

Secession wars

The increasing decadence of the Le dynasty in the late 16th century led to the country's division into two rival principalities as corrupt and useless kings succeeded Le Thanh Tong. Mac Dang Dung, a shrewd and scheming adviser at the court, seized control of the country and founded the Mac dynasty. Descendants of the Le dynasty rallied around Nguyen Kim and Trinh Kiem, looking for a way to overthrow Mac Dang Dung. After fierce battles, they succeeded in occupying the country's southern capital, and in 1543 they founded the southern court near Thanh Hoa, 120 km (75 miles) south of Hanoi. The war continued indecisively until the death of the dynasty's last king, Mac Mau Hop, in 1592.

In an effort to restore law and order to the territory controlled by the Macs, Trinh left the southern court under the temporary control of Nguyen Kim's nephew, Nguyen Hoang, and set out for the north. After pacifying the north and re-establishing the Le authority in Hanoi, Lord Trinh returned to find Nguyen Hoang well entrenched in the southern court as lord and master of all, and liking where he was.

In 1672, after repeated tentative attempts failed to remove Nguyen Hoang, Trinh finally consented to the partition of the country at the Linh River. It was not, however, until after half a century of civil war that the Trinh and Nguyen lords eventually agreed to a period of co-existence. This respite lasted for more than a century, during which time the Le emperors

TAY SON UPRISING

The Tay Son brothers – Nguyen Nhac, Nguyen Lu and Nguyen Hue – led an insurrection that was initially local in scope but became country-wide in the 1770s. Provoked by the corruption rife within the disintegrating imperial court, the uprising was a peasant insurrection that grew into a force against the leading Le lords, easily defeating them. By the mid-1780s, the brothers had gained control of much of the country. From 1788 until 1793, they each ruled part of Vietnam. But they failed to ease the fundamental land issues that brought them to power and were unseated by the future emperor Gia Long in 1793.

played no more than a passive and ceremonial role. But rebellion formented in the country, including the Tay Son uprising *(see box on opposite page)*.

Nguyen Hue pronounced himself Emperor Quang Trung and overran the Chinese troops in a swift campaign. He then pacified the northern part of the country, from the Chinese border to Hai Van Pass in the country's centre, north of Da Nang, and devoted his energies to national rehabilitation, administrative reorganisation, and economic

NEW SCRIPT

The 17th century saw the phasing out of Chinese and *nom* scripts and the introduction of Romanised *quoc ngu*. The *quoc ngu* script remains in use today.

Behaine, Bishop of Adran. The Ming Chinese, who had fled the Qing takeover of the Chinese imperial court and settled in the Mekong Delta region, regarded Nguyen Anh as the leader who could safeguard their settlement in the newly annexed territory of Dai Viet. The Tay Son suspected the Ming were Nguyen Anh's sympathisers, and this suspicion intensified after the leading Tay Son generals, Tap Dinh and Ly Tai, fled to Nguyen Anh's camp. After suffering defeat at the hands of their former

development. Unfortunately, his promising reign was cut short by his premature death not long after, in 1792.

Nguyen dynasty (1792–1883)

Nguyen's successor, Nguyen Anh, was supported by Nguyen royalists who saw him as the legitimate heir in the south. With their backing, Nguyen Anh took up the fight against the Tay Son brothers and after Quang Trung's death extended control over the country with the aid of a French missionary, Pigneau de

LEFT: early European residences in old Saigon.
ABOVE: French officers in Da Nang, 1830s.

generals in the Mekong region, the Tay Son army exacted their revenge and massacred thousands of the Chinese settlers.

De Behaine saw an opportunity to expand the Catholic Church's influence and negotiated a promise of military aid for Nguyen Anh from the French government in exchange for territorial and commercial rights in the country. However, the French were busy with their own internal disputes and the promised aid never materialised. Undaunted, the bishop organised funds and recruited troops himself. Training in Western military techniques proved invaluable to Nguyen Anh and his army, and it probably facilitated victory in 1801 when he subdued the Tay Son and proclaimed himself emperor. A power struggle between French and Chinese factions began within the court.

Although Nguyen Anh owed his accession to power to the French, he was nevertheless very suspicious of France's designs on his country, and so under his reign the court's Chinese faction took precedence. He came to rely more on the assistance of Confucian mandarins than the Catholic missionaries in the consolidation of his empire, not the last time national pride would win.

The reunified and newly renamed Viet Nam extended from the Chinese frontier to the Ca

Mau Peninsula at the country's southernmost tip. Serious efforts were made to codify the law and develop the national administration along Confucian principles. Hue became the country's new administrative capital.

The Nguyen dynasty's absolutism was reflected in the extraordinary development of Hue as the most beautiful city of Vietnam. Elaborate palaces, mausoleums, temples and pagodas were successively built here, all in keeping with the harmony of cosmic order. The Nguyen kings also extended Vietnam's border into Laos and Cambodia, incorporating parts of these two kingdoms as new vassal states of their empire. Conversely, they closed

the country to Western penetration from the seas, fearing that the opening of the kingdom and the expansion of trade links would undermine the structure of the monarchy.

Meanwhile, Prince Canh, Nguyen Anh's eldest son, accompanied de Behaine to France during his negotiations with the French government. The prince was later educated at a missionary school in Malacca and converted to Catholicism. This made Canh the first Viet prince to be educated under Western ideas and teachers. Military leaders within Nguyen Anh's army realised the superiority of modern Western military technology and so wished to utilise Canh's knowledge to rebuild the country after the war. The prince was regarded by many as the one who could modernise Dai Viet and bring it into industrialisation.

While the issue of Gia Long's successor was being discussed in the imperial court before his death, the power struggle between the French and Chinese factions resumed. Military generals, including Nguyen Thanh, the governor of Thang Long, and Le Van Duyet, the governor of Gia Dinh (Saigon), supported the French and wanted Canh as the heir. However, most of the court ministers belonged to the Chinese faction and supported Canh's younger brother, Mien Tong.

Again, it was the conservative Chinese faction that triumphed. Prince Canh reportedly died of measles at the age of 21. This prognosis was refuted by missionaries close to the court, who reported to the French mission that he had died of poisoning.

Once Mien Tong was crowned as Emperor Minh Mang, the French–Chinese divide officially ended. Most of Canh's followers were either demoted or executed. Gen. Nguyen Thanh was forcefully administered poison and Gen. Le Van Duyet's tomb was desecrated.

In the meantime, the Catholic missions had accelerated their proselytising, provoking Minh Mang into an anti-Catholic policy.

An opportunity for peace, and with it, a chance to modernise and industrialise the country, was lost. It would not be the last time. Religious rivalries, political factions and foreign intervention would embroil Vietnam in tragic war once again. ❏

LEFT: the young Prince Canh. **RIGHT:** map of Tonkin Gulf and northern Vietnam dated 1653.

By Many Names

The name Vietnam has become as synonymous with war as Agincourt, Waterloo, Gettysburg, Normandy and Bosnia. Yet few know the significance of the name. The country has been known as Vietnam (in the Vietnamese language, it is spelled in two words, Viet Nam) for only about 200 years. The first national name of Van Lang was given to the country by the Hung, or Lac, ethnic group, inventors of the wet-rice cultivation technique and the bronze drums still used today by the Muong minority. The Lac were followed by the Au, or Tay Au, who arrived from China. The two people integrated and formed the new kingdom of Au Lac. Then came the Viet, or Yue, an ethnic group emigrating from the coast of China around 2,500 years ago. They came with other ethnic groups of the Bach Viet (the 100 Viet principalities of ancient China) on a long southward march towards the Indochinese peninsula, a migration from the north that would continue for more than 15 centuries.

The name Vietnam first appeared when Emperor Gia Long wanted to rename the country Nam Viet in the early 19th century. Seeking the Chinese emperor's approval of the new national name, Gia Long sent his ambassador to China. He pleaded for the reunification of the old land of An Nam and the new land of Viet Thuong, and for permission to change the ancient name of An Nam to Nam Viet.

After consulting his court, the Chinese emperor decided that the name Nam Viet would bring to mind the ancient kingdom of Nam Viet Dong, which had included the two Chinese provinces. The proposed name of Nam Viet might lead to misunderstandings or even conceal territorial ambitions.

The problem was solved by simply reversing the order of the two words to Viet Nam: the people (viet) of the South (nam).

Etymologists and anthropologists have defined the origins of the Viet people by separating the components of the original Chinese character for Viet. On the left side of this ideogram is a character pronounced tau in Vietnamese, meaning to run. On the right is the complementary component pronounced viet, with the meaning and profile of an axe. This component carries with it the particle qua, which signifies a lance or javelin, the tools of a hunter. This ideographic analysis depicts the Viet as a race known since antiquity as a migratory, hunting people. The word viet is the Vietnamese pronunciation of a Chinese character meaning

beyond or far, and with the sense of crossing or going through. The character nam, meaning south, probably served to differentiate between the Viets in the north who remained in China and those who had left and headed south.

A long history of foreign invaders branded Vietnam with different names. Marco Polo skirted the coast of Vietnam in 1292. In his writings appears the name Caugigu, which corresponds to Giao Chi Quan, Vietnam's name under the Han dynasty, from 111 BC to AD 203. This name was transformed to Kutchi by the Malays and later to Kotchi by the Japanese. The Portuguese in turn named it Cauchi Chine, to distinguish it from Cauchi or

Kutchi in India, also known as Cochin. This name was again summoned by French colonialists who called southern Vietnam Cochin China. These names, when written or pronounced in the occidental manner, evoked a far more ancient name, Cattigara, which first appeared on a map drawn by Ptolemy, the Greek mathematician and geographer.

Since the earliest antiquity, the Indochinese peninsula has played a major role in international trade relations and migrations, forming the link between India and China. This connection between the two ancient civilisations explains the name Indochina, first coined by the Danish geographer Konrad Malte-Burn (1775–1826) and still used today by some to refer to the region. ❑

THE ANTI-COLONIAL STRUGGLE

The Vietnamese fight against Western powers for over a century helped to
prop up Marxist arguments for the revolutionary struggle in Communism

Emperor Minh Mang's anti-Catholic policy gave the French a pretext to intervene in Vietnam. The old cycle of invasion-and-occupation began anew, but this time from afar. The landing of a French party in Da Nang (called Tourane by the French) in 1858 heralded the beginning of colonial occupation that would last almost a century. The French government wanted to establish a strategic and religious sphere of influence in Indochina (present-day Vietnam, Laos, and Cambodia), but their demands to install a French consulate and commercial attache in Da Nang were rejected by the Vietnamese imperial court in Hue. The French responded to the slap by occupying Da Nang.

In 1861, the French took Saigon. Six years later the entire southern part of the country, rechristened by the French as Cochin China, was annexed as a French colony. The French later extended control to the north in 1883. The central part of Vietnam, renamed by the French as Annam, and the north, or Tonkin, became French protectorates.

Of course, the Vietnamese were no happier living under French domination than they had been under the Chinese. In 1893, Emperor Ham Nghi and Phan Dinh Phung organised a royalist movement – Can Vuong – and staged an unsuccessful uprising at Ha Tinh, about midway between Hanoi and Da Nang. The Can Vuong movement survived until one of its leaders was killed by a Vietnamese traitor. Emperor Duy Tan's abortive attempt in 1916 to form a revolutionary movement resulted in his replacement as sovereign by Khai Dinh.

By the beginning of the 20th century, various nationalist resistance movements had formed. One was composed almost entirely of aristocrats, intellectuals, and young people led by radical Confucian scholars such as Phan Boi Chau, Phan Chau Trinh, and Cuong De, Prince

Canh's great-grandson. In an effort to break from royalist thinking, they embraced the idea of democracy. This resistance movement was greatly influenced by the Japanese victory over Russia in 1904, for it convinced the Vietnamese that Western power was no longer invincible. Phan Boi Chau and Cuong De established the

Eastward Movement in 1907 and secretly sent students to study in Japan. French authorities, discovering the scheme, negotiated with Japan to extradite all Vietnamese students, but Japanese officials helped some of them escape to China.

When the exiled Vietnamese in China witnessed the 1911 revolution led by Sun Yat-sen in China, some were convinced Vietnam was ready for the same kind of coup. They formed the Vietnam Quoc Dan Dang Party, which later became the leading revolutionary party in the struggle against the French. The revolutionaries were not yet united, however. A rift widened between the Westernised reformer Phan Chu Trinh and the nationalist Phan Boi

PRECEDING PAGES: young Emperor Duy Tan and court.
LEFT: French troops entering Hung Hoa in 1884.
RIGHT: the child-emperor of Annam, Duy Tan.

Chau. Phan Chu Trinh opposed appealing for foreign help to unseat the French colonialists: he believed Vietnam could regain independence through the democratic process. In 1915 he went to Paris to rally Vietnamese exiles and radical French politicians to support the Vietnamese struggle against colonial rule.

Nationalism intensified in Vietnam, especially after World War I, but tentative uprisings failed to obtain any concessions from the French. The Russian Revolution of 1917, while

ALUMNI

Vo Nguyen Giap, professor of history and the general who defeated both France and the United States after World War II, attended the same high school as Ho Chi Minh.

agent of the Communist International. He enjoyed the special privileges afforded him by his Soviet mentors and wholeheartedly espoused Stalin statesmanship.

In 1924, Ho Chi Minh was sent to China as a delegate to the Communist Party of China, where he contacted young Vietnamese revolutionaries and founded the Association of Vietnamese Youth, a group that would compete with other organisations for the liberation of the country. Some recruits were sent to Moscow for

not provoking anything similar in Vietnam at the time, nonetheless had a tremendous impact on shaping Vietnamese history, primarily because of its influence on a young revolutionary, Nguyen That Thanh, later to be known as Ho Chi Minh. (Although he changed his name much later, we shall use the more familiar Ho Chi Minh throughout.)

Ho Chi Minh, under the alias Nguyen Ai Quoc, was working with Phan Chu Trinh on an anti-colonial petition put forward at the Versailles Conference in 1919. Ho became involved with French intellectuals who formed the French Communist Party in 1920. He went to Moscow to be trained as a *kominternshik,* an

training, and others became affiliated with the Chinese Communist party. This situation fostered internal conflict within Vietnam's Communist party, between the pro-Chinese and pro-Soviet factions, for many decades.

In the same year, Emperor Khai Dinh died, and his son Bao Dai, then aged 12, ascended to the throne. Bao Dai was sent to France for his education and returned to Vietnam in 1932. The Vietnamese waited to see if the French would adopt more liberal politics, but it became clear they would make no real concessions.

In 1930, on the Comintern's instruction, Ho Chi Minh successfully rallied several communist groups and founded the

Indochinese Communist Party. For the first time in history, a revolutionary party was systematically formed with the unlimited financial and ideological support of an aspiring superpower. Also in 1930, under the leadership of Nguyen Thai Hoc, the Quoc Dan Dang, inspired by the Chinese Kuomintang, launched a military revolt. Later, communist groups following the same path of armed revolt, known as the Nghe Tinh Soviets movement, staged a series of peasant uprisings.

Unhappy with the instability, the French retaliated by taking severe measures against the fledgling movements. The apparent calm that

allowed to continue administering Vietnam. In 1945, realising that allied victory was inevitable, Japan overthrew the French, imprisoned their civil servants, and rendered Vietnam "independent" under Japanese "protection", with Bao Dai as chief of state.

The Japanese surrender later in the year was the opening that Ho Chi Minh had eagerly anticipated. Earlier, the Central Committee of the Indochinese Communist Party had met in southern China and announced the formation of the Revolutionary League for the Independence of Vietnam, which later became known as the Viet Minh. Ho Chi Minh used the Viet

reigned after the reprisals shattered with the first battles of World War II. In Asia, most coastal cities of China fell under the advancing Japanese forces, and in Vietnam, the Japanese rapidly occupied key regions in 1940.

World War II

For Vietnam, the explosion of World War II in 1939 was an event as significant as the French occupation of Da Nang in 1858. The pro-Nazi Vichy government of France accepted the Japanese occupation of Indochina, but it was

Minh as an instrument to apply his revolutionary strategy. In its creation he finally achieved "the union of diverse Vietnamese nationalist groups under communist direction", a goal that he had been working towards since announcing it as his immediate task to the Comintern in 1924.

At first, the Chinese Nationalist authorities supported the Viet Minh, but they later got wise to Ho's new political affiliation and imprisoned him and created a rival organisation. However, they soon realised that Ho's organisation was in fact needed and so released him in 1943. Moreover, they recognised Ho as the chief of the Viet Minh, and it was around this time that he adopted the name of Ho Chi Minh.

LEFT: Tonkin (north Vietnam) mandarin and escorts.
ABOVE: Hang Bo Street, Hanoi, in the late 1930s.

Around the same time, Ho's principal collaborator, Vo Nguyen Giap, set up guerrilla units in several regions of northern Vietnam and created an intelligence network. Communist cells were organised throughout the country under the supervision of Truong Chinh, the young secretary-general of the Indochinese Communist Party. These later became of inestimable value to Ho after Japan's sudden surrender in 1945. Here was the *thoi co* – the opportune moment – in which to launch the general insurrection.

Ho's resolute certainty of victory is reflected in the conclusion of one of his poems: "In

Party and the Viet Minh as intermediaries, Ho Chi Minh endeavoured to become the dominant political force by occupying as much territory as possible.

Start of revolution

The so-called August Revolution began on 16 August 1945, when the Viet Minh announced the formation of a National Committee of Liberation for Vietnam. Three days later, Ho's guerrilla forces took Hanoi. Hue's turn came four days later when Bao Dai's government was besieged and "asked" to hand over the royal seal. Bao Dai abdicated, believing that the Viet

1945, the work will be accomplished". But, of course, in 1945, the work had really just begun.

At the end of World War II, Vietnam faced a political void, as Bao Dai's government existed in name only. Apart from a handful of French civil servants and troops, whom the Japanese had imprisoned prior to France's removal, Bao Dai had no supporting troops – his own or those of outsiders – in Indochina.

Chinese Nationalist forces entered Vietnam as far as the 16th parallel, at Da Nang, to accept the Japanese surrender. The British assumed control of the south. By the middle of August, chaos and uncertainty reigned once again. Using the clandestine Indochinese Communist

THE LAST EMPEROR

Nguyen Vinh Thuy ascended the throne in 1926, taking the title Bao Dai, or Keeper of Greatness. The French kept tight reins on Bao Dai until the Japanese forced France from Vietnam in 1945. The Japanese retained Bao Dai as a figurehead, and when the Viet Minh took power in August 1945, they asked Bao Dai to resign but to link himself to the Viet Minh movement as "Citizen Prince Nguyen Vinh Thuy". Disillusioned, Bao Dai fled to Hong Kong in 1946, where he led a sybarite's life until 1949, when he returned as sovereign. Known as a playboy emperor, Bao Dai took little interest in affairs of state. He retired in 1955 and moved to France.

Minh was a national front supported by the former European allies. Ho's forces now controlled Saigon and practically all the surrounding rural areas. Ho announced the formation of a provisional government in Hanoi, and in early September he proclaimed himself president of the new Democratic Republic of Vietnam.

However, Ho found himself in a strategically vulnerable position when the allied forces arrived. He camouflaged the existence of the communist elements within the

CATALYST

After a skirmish between French and Vietnamese troops, a French cruiser shelled Hai Phong in 1946, killing nearly 6,000 Vietnamese and igniting hostilities.

only 291 members, including 37 from the opposition, turned up. When asked to explain the poor turnout, one Viet Minh minister announced that the absentees had been arrested for criminal offences. The country's first national constitution was approved by 240 votes to one.

France finally recognised the Democratic Republic of Vietnam as a free state, within the French union. However, relations rapidly deteriorated. Hostilities mounted and reached a peak with the French bombing of Hai Phong

Viet Minh and sought support from both the Chinese and the French. In an unprecedented move, the Indochinese Communist Party announced its dissolution in November, although, in reality, it continued to function.

Ho then prepared to negotiate Vietnam's future status with France. In the general elections, organised in early 1946, the Viet Minh won the majority of seats in the first National Assembly. Ho's government was approved at the assembly's first session in March, but at the second session in October,

port, east of Hanoi. In December 1946, Ho ordered a general offensive against the French in Hanoi and at French garrisons in northern and central Vietnam. The decade long war for independence had begun.

War of resistance

The war for national independence that began after the Japanese occupation constitutes a confused period of contemporary Vietnamese history. Thousands of Vietnamese took up arms against the French, yet few know the identity and allegiance of their new leader and his party. The population did not entirely understand the historical events happening in their country, nor

LEFT: Vietnamese, Cambodian, and Laotians in China plot against France. **ABOVE:** Giap planning the war.

could they imagine the consequences that were to follow. At face value, Ho Chi Minh's new party appeared to consist of nationalists fighting for the common cause of national independence against the known enemy. And indeed, today, as the country increasingly adopts what it calls a market-oriented economy and dumps some of its communist system, the wars of resistance are stressed to have been fought by nationalists.

On Ho's orders, Vo Nguyen Giap launched a general offensive against the French forces,

HO'S IMPORTANCE

Amongst all the 20th-century revolutionaries, Ho Chi Minh's importance is that he waged the longest – and most devastating – battle against Western powers.

aggressor nation that had threatened Vietnam's independence, was now an ally and supplied the young republic with military equipment, substantial provisions, and further aid to develop the Viet Minh army.

On his side, Ho attempted to increase his government's base of nationalist support. At the beginning of 1951, he merged the Viet Minh with the Lien Viet, or Patriotic Front, into a new league for the National Union of Vietnam, and he announced the formation of the Workers Party

but in the face of superior fire power, Ho's troops were forced to retreat to the countryside. They adopted Mao Zedong's guerrilla strategy of a "people's war and people's army" by attacking and sabotaging isolated French units, rather than becoming embroiled in large-scale battles. It was a tactic reminiscent of Le Loi's against Chinese forces in the 15th century and one that would be used against the Americans.

The emergence of Communist China towards the end of 1949 favoured the communist-dominated struggle. After Ho's guerrillas had wiped out several French posts on the Chinese border, China and Vietnam established direct contact for the first time. China, the old

(Lao Dong), a disguise for the Communist Party that officially had disbanded but in reality was still active. The nationalists and non-communists were forced to choose between the new regime or the French colonialists. Giap's forces progressively extended their territory.

By the spring of 1953, several divisions were training in Laos and had joined forces with the pro-communist Pathet Lao.

In May of 1954, the French base at Dien Bien Phu *(see Northern Vietnam chapter, page 195)* suffered a humiliating defeat after a heavy artillery attack from Giap's forces, who used bicycles to carry supplies. The French forces in northern Vietnam evacuated to below the

16th parallel, at Da Nang. The war officially ended on 20 July, after long negotiations in Geneva. In finally gaining full national independence, Vietnam lost its unity. The Geneva Agreement signed in August divided the country at the 17th parallel, pending general elections scheduled for the middle of 1956.

The northern part of the country became the Democratic Republic of Vietnam – North Vietnam – under the leadership of the Lao Dong party; the southern part became the Republic of South Vietnam.

The last French troops left Victnam and Indochina in April 1956. Bao Dai made a last

appeal on behalf of the royalists. He asked Ngo Dinh Diem to become prime minister of what would become South Vietnam. Diem was a curious choice, a Catholic in a predominately Buddhist country who had been away from Vietnam for two decades and returning in the midst of a nationalist uprising.

In fraudulent elections, Bao Dai was deposed by Diem, marking the end of the Nguyen dynasty and the beginning of the Republic of South Vietnam. But rather than stability, things

LEFT: Gen. Giap's Vietnamese forces take Dien Bien Phu from the French army. **ABOVE:** Ho Chi Minh in the field during the early 1950s.

THE LEGACIES OF WAR

Of course, Vietnam is a country and not a war. For the past quarter century the country has sought to move beyond the decades of conflict that defined its history and outlook. And while the war against first the French and then the Americans is history, its importance is considerable as a turning point not only in Vietnam's history but in those of the world's superpowers, especially the United States.

Militarily, the Vietnam War solidly redefined the nature of war, especially in regards to conflict between a technologically endowed army and a low-technology adversary. The guerrilla war of the Viet Cong, drawing from history (Vietnamese resistance against occupying China in the 15th century and American resistance against the British in the 18th century), redefined the nature and history of warfare.

From 1965 onwards, the United States not only brought more than half a million troops to Vietnam, but it undertook an immense construction program that built deep-water ports, air bases, roads, bridges, and pipelines. Helicopters not only introduced a new type of warfare but they tripled the survival rate (on the American side) of the wounded over World War II. By the end of the war, there were 4 to 5 support personnel for every American soldier in combat.

On the North Vietnamese side, a resilience based on a village-centred agricultural system and minimal industrial strength (North Vietnam produced just 20 percent of the electrical power of a single American generating plant) permitted it to carry on a war despite concentrated bombing and a technologically superior opponent. The United States brought in supplies via deep-water ports and 3,000-metre-long (10,000-ft) airfields while the North Vietnamese used the so-called Ho Chi Minh Trail through Laos and Cambodia. Supplies brought south along the dirt-road route took from three to six months via vehicle, bicycle, and foot. In 1968, non food requirements of all communist forces in South Vietnam totalled 120 tons daily, just five times the amount required by a single division of American troops.

The end of the war in 1975 brought peace and reunification to Vietnam. In the United States, it redefined politics, military strategy and theory, and social agendas. America became more introspective.

The aggregate cost of the war is estimated at US$200 billion. Around 900,000 North Vietnamese and Viet Cong troops were killed; South Vietnamese Army deaths were 200,000, and 50,000 Americans were killed. It is estimated that more than 1,000,000 Vietnamese civilians died on both sides.

would only get worse, setting the stage for Vietnam's next conflict.

The North-South divide

The elections stipulated by the Geneva Agreement never occurred. From 1954 to 1974, the two Vietnams had no diplomatic, cultural, or commercial relations with each other. Immediately after the Geneva Agreement, a virtual state of war existed between the two divided parts of the country. North Vietnam's intensified armed and revolutionary activities made the prospect of reunification through free elections increasingly unlikely.

himself on a street corner in Saigon (now called Ho Chi Minh). As his image blazed across the world's television screens and newspapers, the flames that consumed him were burned into the consciousness of Vietnamese, Americans, and the international community.

This signaled the beginning of the end for Diem's regime. Diem and his brother were murdered five months later in Saigon's Cho Lon district by Diem's own officers following a coup d'état, which was supported by the American government.

The following years witnessed a succession of coups d'état. Several generals and civilians

Meanwhile, the United States had reinforced Diem's troops, in effect turning South Vietnam into an American military protectorate.

In December 1960, the National Liberation Front of South Vietnam (NLF) was formed and began launching revolutionary activities against the unstable regime in the south. This southern communist movement, christened the Viet Cong, grew stronger in the early 1960s.

Facing mounting pressures, Diem ordered repressive measures against the Buddhist establishment. This move provoked a wave of suicides by Buddhist monks, who set fire to themselves in protest. In June 1963, Thich Quang Duc, a 66-year-old monk, immolated

took turns presiding over the unstable and corrupt Saigon regime.

The beginning of 1965 marked the escalation of direct American involvement in Vietnam, when US President Lyndon Johnson decided to send large numbers of troops to Vietnam. By the end of 1967, there were more than 500,000 American and 100,000 allied troops (mostly coming from Korea, Australia, and New Zealand) in Vietnam.

What many consider the war's turning point came in 1968, when the Viet Cong launched surprise attacks on Saigon and other cities throughout the south during the Lunar New Year, Tet. This Tet Offensive included a raid on the American embassy in Saigon that stunned and embarrassed the United States, who began to see the war as futile. Domestic opposition in the United States increasingly took on political and social legitimacy. Eventually, Johnson announced he would not run for re-election.

His successor, Richard Nixon, had promised a secret plan to end the war during the election campaign, but this turned out to be nothing more than turning the bulk of fighting over to the South Vietnamese.

In 1969, Ho Chi Minh died without seeing his work completed, and peace negotiations dragged on in Paris between 1968 and 1973.

On 30 April 1975, the northern army entered Saigon as the last American troops and diplomats fled by helicopter from the American embassy. The Communist Party's long struggle for power under the banner of national liberation and reunification finally ended in their complete victory.

Vietnam was now independent of foreign troops and control, and it could set its sights on unification. But there would not be peace, nor freedom from foreign influence, for years to come. Vietnam became militarily involved by occupying neighbouring Cambodia and in military battles with China itself. ❏

The 1973 Paris Peace Agreement aimed to put an end to hostilities. The Americans pulled out their troops, but the two warring Vietnamese sides lost no time in violating the agreement. In 1975, as the Communist forces steadily moved south and the Saigon regime finally crumbled, the US Congress refused to offer additional military aid, in effect ending South Vietnam's ability to continue the war. The North's leadership launched its final offensive against South Vietnam.

LEFT: North Vietnamese MiG-17 in American sights in 1967; US pilot captured by North Vietnamese militia.
ABOVE: communists enter Presidential Palace, 1975.

AGREEMENT AND PRIZES

Two episodes encouraged serious peace talks: the US had found détente with both Moscow and Beijing, and North Vietnam had failed in a spring 1972 offensive. Secret 1972 talks in Paris between US Secretary of State Henry Kissinger and North Vietnam's Le Duc Tho (who later oversaw the offensive that took Saigon in 1975 and Cambodia in 1978) led to a ceasefire, the release of prisoners, the withdrawal of US forces, and political negotiations amongst the Vietnamese. The war continued, however, even after the Americans left in May 1973. Both Kissinger and Le Duc Tho received the 1973 Nobel Prize for Peace, which Le Duc Tho declined.

MARCHING INTO A NEW CENTURY

*An innate pragmatism and a zest for the new challenge of economic prosperity
have allowed the Vietnamese to move ahead despite government bureaucracy*

Abright future seemed to stretch before socialist Vietnam after 1975, with the communist leadership making great plans for the rehabilitation of the country and the long years of war finally at an end. But a series of strategic blunders made – and later admitted – by the Hanoi leaders shattered all hope for a new era in Vietnam's history.

The party leadership, under the pressure of the northern conservative factions, dissolved the Revolutionary Provisional Government of South Vietnam and the National Liberation Front of South Vietnam.

In July 1976, Vietnam was officially reunified, thus breaking the fragile dual balance between the two parts of the country. A radical programme of socialist construction was put forward at the Communist Party congress. It called for the rapid socialisation of the southern economy, with the forced collectivisation of agriculture, small industry and commerce. This rapidly led to an unprecedented economic disaster, provoking new waves of refugees trying to flee the country. Further sapping the nation's resources was the internment of the south's intellectual and governmental leaders, along with other highly skilled and educated people, in so-called re-education camps.

Just a couple of years after the reunification of Vietnam, the country found itself in open conflict with neighbouring Cambodia (then known as Kampuchea) and on a collision course with China – once again – less than two years later.

In 1978, Vietnam signed a friendship treaty – in fact, a security pact – with the Soviet Union at the same time as its relations with China went into decline. Once again, Vietnam was entangled in the bloc politics of the communist powers and their proxies. The invasion of Cambodia by Vietnamese troops at the end of 1978 and the subsequent so-called "Chinese lesson" *(see box below)* were to augur a new cycle of war that was to absorb most of Vietnam's post-war energies and delay its long-overdue recovery.

Vietnam's all-out alliance with the Soviet Union did nothing, in the long run, to help

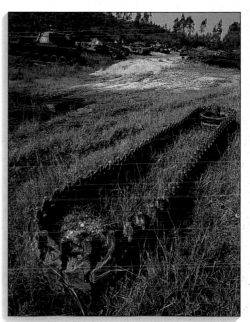

LEFT: a war veteran of the 1954 Dien Bien Phu battle, which ended France's presence in Vietnam.
RIGHT: the residue of war peppers the countryside in both the north and south.

boost Vietnam's position internationally. And for the next decade, the presence of Vietnamese troops in Cambodia remained a central issue in the international arena, around which a coalition of nations – China, the United States, and the members of ASEAN (Association of South East Asian Nations) – managed to enrol international support to isolate Vietnam.

Meanwhile, the Khmer resistance rendered Vietnam's control over Cambodia into a no-win dilemma. A coalition government in Cambodia, established in 1982 with Prince Norodom Sihanouk as president and with Khmer Rouge participation, received growing

Economic shifts and *doi moi*

New economic policies introduced earlier in 1979 had managed to bring some respite on the domestic front without improving the chronic weaknesses of Vietnam's economy. The 1980s, however, saw the domestic economy worsen. People were starving, and there wasn't enough rice to go around. Meat was rationed, and people stood in line for monthly and weekly allotments of food. It was only in 1986, following the Soviet example of *glasnost* and *perestroika,* that the party decided to launch the country on an ambitious programme of socio-economic renovation called *doi moi*.

support from the international community. The coalition occupied Cambodia's seat at the United Nations while at the same time Vietnam lost most of its hard-earned international sympathy from the wars with France and the United States.

The Cambodian war was a costly stalemate. At the Fifth Party Congress in 1982, the old guard, under the guidance of party secretary general Le Duan, obstinately maintained Vietnam's course, hoping that, against all odds, it could consolidate its political and military edge in Cambodia and at the same time stabilise Vietnam's own internal economic and social situation.

Under the new leadership of Nguyen Van Linh, the motto of the party was then "to change or to die". A new contract-system was implemented in 1988 to encourage Vietnamese farmers to cultivate their land, and as a result rice production witnessed an immediate upsurge in 1989. Progress was also recorded in the sector of manufactured goods and commodities exports.

Until the end of 1988, socialist Vietnam followed the path of Soviet *perestroika*, but the Vietnamese leaders were soon to discover the bold and unchartered nature of Soviet leader Mikhail Gorbachev's "new thinking" and its social and political consequences. A surge of domestic turmoil in China and the collapse of communism in Europe in the late 1980s was a severe shock for Vietnam's leaders, who feared the impact of these events upon their regime. While reaffirming the Communist Party's commitment to reform, Nguyen Van Linh repeatedly rejected any idea of political pluralism for Vietnam.

Withdrawal of Vietnamese troops from Cambodia in September 1989 cleared the way for the political settlement of the Cambodian conflict. The peace process was

socialism in the Soviet Union and Eastern Europe contributed to the worsening economic crisis in Vietnam, as former members of the now-defunct Soviet bloc, besieged with domestic crises, were no longer in any position to continue their economic help to Vietnam and other client states such as Cuba. It was in this uncertain context that, in mid-1990, Vietnam adopted a new course in foreign affairs. Vietnam's top leaders secretly visited China in order to mend fences with Beijing. With Vietnamese forces

> ### STUNNING NEWS
>
> The Tiananmen Square massacre in China and the collapse of the Warsaw Pact in Europe in the late 1980s no doubt stunned Hanoi's communist leaders.

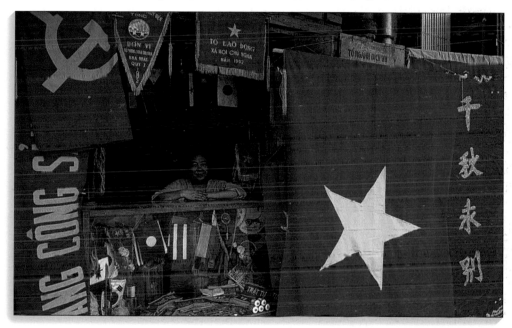

a difficult one involving the efforts of all the parties directly and indirectly involved: the former Soviet Union, China, ASEAN countries, the United States, Japan, France, and Australia. In September 1990, a UN plan was finally endorsed calling for the setting up of a Supreme National Council, a ceasefire, and the cessation of foreign military assistance to the Khmer factions under a UN-control mechanism contingent upon the organisation of free general elections in Cambodia.

Meanwhile, the continuing demise of

LEFT: contemporary soldiers in their reading room.
ABOVE: patriotism in the old quarter of Hanoi.

withdrawn from Cambodia, it seemed that the three-decade-old American embargo against Vietnam would finally be lifted. However, political pressure from the US Senate hinged the end of the embargo on the full accounting of all missing American servicemen from the Vietnam War.

The foreigners return

Meanwhile, European and Asian companies flooded into Vietnam seeking investment opportunities in what many proclaimed as the last economic frontier. Hanoi and Ho Chi Minh (the former Saigon) became boom towns – hotels were renovated and new ones built, international airline service increased, and telecoms and other infrastructures upgraded.

In late 1992, Americans working on the search for US servicemen listed as missing in action from the war were convinced that Vietnamese authorities were cooperating sufficiently in the search. American businesses lobbied the administration of US President George Bush to lift the trade embargo. The United States then permitted American companies to open representative offices in Vietnam.

economy and opening the door to foreigners; some who want to limit foreign investment to Asian countries; and some who want to slow down reform, fearing the party is losing control. The country's leaders are ageing, yet there are no clear indications that anybody is ready – or being groomed – to replace them. For now, the leadership appears to have little to fear in the way of political or social opposition. This is primarily because the country's economy has been steadily moving up, and people throughout the

In 1993, the new American administration of Bill Clinton allowed the release of International Monetary Fund loans to Hanoi. Foreign investment in Vietnam increased. In early 1994, the United States lifted its trade embargo, and in the following year Clinton restored diplomatic ties and an embassy was opened in Hanoi. In 1995, Vietnam became a full member of ASEAN, putting behind it the international ostracism of the 1980s.

Elusive consensus

Within the government and the Communist Party today there are divisions of thinking: some who want to continue liberalising the

country feel as if their lives are improving, however gradually. The country's growth increased at a pace of about 8 percent a year throughout much of the 1990s. Income levels are still low – the average per capita income is about US$500 a year – yet there are pockets of wealth developing in the urban centres. And because costs for basic needs – food, housing, and schooling – are still relatively low, people in the cities have begun to enjoy a better lifestyle. Inflation, which had been spiralling out of control in the 1980s, is now under 10 percent a

ABOVE: disco scene in hip Ho Chi Minh.
RIGHT: foreign businessmen on the slow road in Hanoi.

year. Vietnam is now one of the world's largest exporters of rice, and the country is pinning hopes of future economic revival on a fledgling offshore oil-and-gas industry, though the oil glut that greeted the 21st century pushed oil development to the background.

This is not to say there aren't problems. Much of the country – particularly rural areas – is still mired in poverty. Nearly 75 percent of the population lives outside the urban areas, and many live without running water or electricity; private telephones are uncommon. While Ho Chi Minh City and Hanoi appear to be humming with modern motorcycles and cars, in fact, a motorcycle is still a luxury for most rural people.

Ahead is a widening gap between rich and poor as a wealthy class emerges. People from the countryside are flooding the cities looking for jobs; they find few places to live and little support from the government. Average salaries in Ho Chi Minh City are very low, and it is difficult to see how the man in the street manages to scrape a living. As Vietnam begins to adopt a market economy, the socialist safety net is unravelling, meaning the elderly, veterans and the uneducated are losing benefits to which they have grown accustomed.

THE FUTURE OF *DOI MOI*

In the early 1990s, opportunities for a "new" Vietnam seemed unlimited as the government declared a stance of *doi moi*, ostensibly intended to invigorate and move the country's economy forward. Unfortunately, by the end of the 1990s, the programme was a big, resounding dud.

The inability of the government to allow market forces to define the economy, along with an institutionalised and prenicious corruption, led many foreign companies to abandon the country as the 21st centure began. In 1998 alone, 19 foreign banks closed their doors in Vietnam, while in the same year, more than 120 foreign companies – excluding banks and law firms – left Vietnam, up from 70

in 1997. While the professed excuse for foreigners' exit was the region's economy, it was well known that the real reasons were corruption, diaphanous "special" fees, opaque regulations, and high operating costs.

Fortunately, the 21st century is seeing a change for the better. The latest phase of *doi moi* involves more sweeping steps being taken to liberalise the economy and attract more foreign investment. In addition, Vietnam is working towards being recognised as a mature trading nation – a trade pact was signed with the USA in 2001, and its current goal is to gain acceptance into the World Trade Organisation (WTO) by the end of 2005.

State agencies and state-owned companies – notoriously bloated and inefficient – are having to cull their workforces to compete in the market economy, adding to an increasing problem of unemployment. The population, too, is young – more than two-thirds of Vietnamese are under the age of 30. Many college graduates are unable to find jobs.

The government still tightly controls the press, although newspapers and magazines have become livelier, and include a broader range of socio-political issues. In 2001, a large part of the government subsidy of state-controlled publications ended, forcing newspapers and

magazines to fund their projects with advertisements as well as to boost readership with articles that are of higher quality. However, stories involving the government or its leaders are still strictly censored.

Up to recently, corruption was rampant in business – foreigners and Vietnamese alike complain that they are nickel-and-dimed to death, with bureaucrats at all levels demanding "tokens" in order to get paperwork completed, licenses approved and offices opened. By the end of the 1990s, many Western companies had become so fed up with the corruption and constantly changing regulations that they pulled out of the country. Recently, however, following a number of high-profile trials, the government is finally being perceived as willing to confront this spectre of corruption.

The new century

Vietnam still feels threatened from the north. In the late 1990s, it pushed Laos, its neighbour, to improve air strips as possible emergency bases for the Vietnamese air force should China and Vietnam once again clash. At the same time, Vietnam sweetened its relationship with Moscow. In exchange for a 50-percent interest in a new oil refinery, Russia wrote off Vietnam's $15 billion decades-old debt.

In 1999, daring dissent came from within the Communist Party's ranks. Retired Gen. Tran Do, a Party member, called for political reform – considered a blatant criticism of government policies – to ensure economic development in Vietnam. The general was expelled from the Party. Shortly afterwards, a second general, Pham Hong Son, criticised the Communist Party and government officials who live expensive lifestyles in one of the world's poorest nations.

More recently, social pressures led to open unrest in the Central Highlands. Poverty and corruption remain endemic. In 2001, a bilateral trade pact was signed with the US and investors are now making a tentative return. The situation is set to improve further if Vietnam is accepted into the WTO at the end of 2005, although some of this optimism is tempered by the knowledge that the economic environment is often subject to haphazard reversal of policies by the Vietnamese leaders. ❑

SIGNIFICANT ISLES

A possible flashpoint of conflict in Southeast Asia is the Spratly Islands – coral reefs, really – peppering the South China Sea midway between Vietnam and the Philippines. Barely breaking the ocean's surface, the largest of the Spratly's 12 main isles is Itu Aba at 36 hectares (90 acres). Spratly Island itself is but 275 metres (900 ft) by 450 metres (1,500 ft) in size. France held the islands until World War II, when Japan used them as a submarine base. Since then, China, Taiwan, the Philippines, Malaysia, and Vietnam have all claimed these islands by stationing small garrisons on one or more islet, all of which sit atop a potentially rich oil field.

LEFT: foreign companies invade.
RIGHT: mausoleum of Ho Chi Minh in Hanoi.

THE LAND AND ITS NATURE

While its contours and coast rival that of Thailand, Vietnam's bewitchments also include exceedingly rare fauna, a challenging climate, and universally dismal roads

Shaped like an immense and elongated letter S, Vietnam stretches the length of the Indochinese peninsula, bordering the Bien Dong, or the South China Sea, to the east. Its 3,730-km (2,320-mile) frontier shares a 1,150-km (715-mile) border with China in the north, and to the west, a border of 1,650 km (1,000 miles) with Laos and 930 km (600 miles) with Cambodia. Mountains and forests make up more than three-quarters of Vietnam's total land area. With an area of 327,500 sq. km (126,500 sq. miles), Vietnam's territory also encompasses a vast sea area, including a large continental shelf and a string of thousands of islands stretching from Vinh Bac Bo, or the Tonkin Gulf, to the Gulf of Thailand. These include the disputed Spratly (Truong Sa) and Paracel (Hoang Sa) islands, which China and other Southeast Asian nations also claim, mostly because of rich oil reserves deep underground. The isles themselves are hardly islands *(see box on page 54)*.

As the crow flies, Vietnam stretches 1,650 km (1,000 miles) from Mong Cai in the north to Ha Tien in the south. At its widest point in the north, Vietnam is just 600 km (370 miles) across; at its narrowest part, in the centre, it is 50 km (30 miles) wide. The 2,500-km (1,500-mile) coastline is dotted with beautiful beaches.

On the same latitude as Bombay, Hawaii, and Mexico City, Vietnam is a land endowed with great physical beauty and diversity. The fertile imaginations of some geographers have likened the country, with its three regions – Bac Bo (north), Trung Bo (centre) and Nam Bo (south) – to a set of scales, the north and south constituting two balancing baskets of rice supplied by rich deltas of the north's Song Hong (Red River) and the south's Mekong.

Chains of mountains and profoundly carved valleys separate Vietnam from China to the north, geography that has not impeded China's

numerous invasions of Vietnamese territory. The country's highest summit, Fan Si Pan, rises to 3,160 metres (10,370 ft) over the Hoang Lien Son mountain range, in the province of Lao Cai near the Chinese border.

The plains of Cao Bang, Lang Son, and Vinh Yen and the valleys watered by the Lo, Chay,

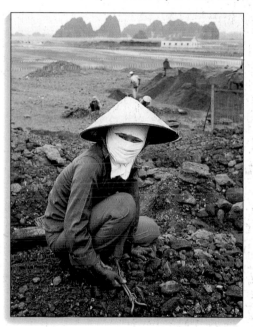

Cau, Luc, Nam, and Cung rivers occupy the northern part of the country, extending over the immense delta of the Song Hong, or Red River, home to 90 percent of northern Vietnam's population. The Song Hong flows from its source in the Yunnan region of China across the north of Vietnam and then southeast to its coastal mouth near Hai Phong.

Central Vietnam forms a long convex curve, within which are small plains wedged between the South China Sea and the high plateaus of the Truong Son mountains. This terrain is characterised by dunes and lagoons in the east towards the coast and terraces of ancient alluvial deposits towards the mountains. The lime-

---

PRECEDING PAGES: boat crossing the Mekong; the pass at Hai Van, central Vietnam. **LEFT:** Ha Long Bay. **RIGHT:** extracting coal near Ha Long Bay.

stone peaks of Pu Sam Sao stretch along the border with Laos. The Central Highlands between Da Nang and Da Lat are rich in volcanic basalt soil and constitute one of Vietnam's most important forest areas, in addition to tea- and coffee-growing regions.

The Mekong River, known as Cuu Long Giang, or the River of Nine Dragons, is one of the longest rivers in Asia at 4,180 km (2,600 miles). The Mekong flows from its source in the mountains of Tibet across China, through Burma (Myanmar) into Laos and northern Thailand, and then across Cambodia before flowing through southern Vietnam into the

the Equator, gives rise to a complex and humid climate that varies from region to region. The average temperature of 22°C (72°F) varies slightly from one season to another, but like anywhere, it is prone to sudden changes. A persistent dampness tends to make the temperature feel cooler.

Northern Vietnam's climate is influenced by the winds of central Asia, which gives rise to a climate similar to that of China. Generally, two distinct seasons prevail in Vietnam. From November to April, the northern part of Vietnam experiences a relatively cold and humid winter. This is precipitated by invading polar

South China Sea. Over many centuries, the Mekong's deposits collected on a shallow, undersea shelf forming an immense, low-lying alluvial plain – the Mekong Delta – which now extends over 75,000 sq. km (29,000 sq. miles). These alluvial deposits do not accumulate on the natural delta but rather at the mouth of the Mekong and around the Ca Mau Peninsula in Vietnam's extreme south, where the deposits contribute to enlarging Vietnam by dozens of square metres annually.

Climate

Vietnam's location in the Southeast Asian monsoon zone, between the Tropic of Cancer and

SOUTHEAST ASIA'S RIVER

More than 810,000 sq. km (310,000 sq. miles) of Southeast Asia are drained by the Mekong River. Geographers divide the river into two parts: the upper Mekong in China and the lower Mekong, beginning at the border of Burma and Laos before reaching the ocean nearly 2,400 km (1,500 miles) later. Among Asian rivers, only the Chang Jiang (Yangze) in China and the Ganges in India have larger flows. The management and development of the river's lower extents is under the auspices of the Committee for Coordination of Investigations of the Lower Mekong Basin, which consists of Laos, Cambodia, Thailand, and Vietnam.

air currents that sweep into Vietnam from Siberia and China, often bringing temperatures down to 0°C (32°F) in the mountainous regions lying north and east of Hanoi, and with a fine, chilly drizzle throughout most of the winter months. Summer, from May to October, is characterised by higher temperatures and heavy rain, and often typhoons.

The northern and central regions of the country experience their hottest months during June, July, and August.

The climate varies from north to south in the

> **WOODY LIMITS**
>
> Rainforests are few in Vietnam, and forests of a single species of tree are rare, limited mostly to pine trees found in the highlands and coastal mangrove forests.

rainy season from May to October. There is a relatively dry season from November to February and a dry season from February to April before the rains.

The south experiences its hottest months from March to May, when temperatures may reach 35°C (95°F).

The rains, affected by the monsoon winds arriving across the ocean and the geographical position and relief of the various regions, are often abundant. Between May and December, the warm and humid summer monsoon brings

central part of the country. The area near the northern provinces has a climate that is almost identical to that of the Red River Delta, whereas towards the south the central provinces have more in common climatically with the Mekong Delta area. In Hue, in the centre of the country, the cold season lasts from November to March, with almost continual drizzle falling for periods of up to a week.

Southern Vietnam's climate is characterised by a relatively constant temperature, sudden changes during the monsoon, and a punctual

higher temperatures, a humidity of between 80 and 100 percent, and heavy rain to most of the country. During this season, violent typhoons often ravage the southern coastline between Nha Trang and Ca Mau, causing considerable damage. High plateau regions are usually much cooler than the coastal areas, with a marked drop in nightly temperatures year-round.

Flora and fauna

The country's topographical diversity is matched only by the diverse species of flora and fauna in its mountains, forests, plains, and plateaus. In prehistoric times, much of Vietnam was covered by dense forest. Tropical forests

LEFT: monsoon flooding on the Mekong; lightning near Hue. **ABOVE:** water buffalo are essential.

still cover around 40 percent of the country and contain more than 1,200 identified plant species, constituting a rich source of oils, resins, some precious woods, timber, and medicinal plants. Over several centuries, exploitation of the environment has greatly reduced Vietnam's forested regions, which have virtually been halved since 1945 alone.

War, chemical defoliation during the Vietnam War, and an ever-increasing population growth have greatly accelerated this deforestation. Precious hardwoods are being felled in massive quantities for export. However, this wholesale depletion of forest could cost the country far more as flooding and erosion take their environmental toll, much as happened in the 1980s in Thailand with devastating effects.

Despite efforts to reverse this alarming trend, the government's reforestation programme, which replants some 1,600 sq. km (620 sq. miles) annually, is not enough to cover the annual forest losses of 2,000 sq. km (770 sq. miles).

Vietnam's wildlife is, in general, identical to that of Bengal and the Malaysian peninsula. It includes species extinct in other parts of Asia amongst its 273 species of mammals, 180 species of reptiles, 273 species of birds, and hundreds of species of fish and invertebrates. Among these are elephant, wild buffalo, rhinoceros, antelope, tapir, monkey, wild boar, tortoise, crocodiles, and hornbills. In the 1990s, a previously unknown species of mammal was found in Vietnam: an antelope living in Nghe An Province, near Laos. Moreover, the horns of a bovine previously thought to be extinct were found near the Cambodian border, in Dak Lak Province.

Environment

The country's development is putting new pressures on an already fragile environment. A growing population – now estimated to be 83.5 million – means that there are more demands on Vietnam's land.

Since the 1980s, the government has wrestled with how much rice-growing land to convert into industrial use. The forests continue to be threatened by the slash-and-burn farming techniques of the highlands regions often practised by hill tribes, which in turn creates more erosion and flooding.

Much of the country was sprayed with chemical defoliants – such as Agent Orange – during the years of the American involvement in the war in an attempt to deprive the Viet Cong of ground protection and cover. The resulting contamination to the food chain was devastating. In the 30 years since the end of the war, however, the contamination of land has continued as farmers have doused their crops with noxious chemicals. Along with rural decline, the cities are overcrowded also, with water sources polluted by industrialisation, and with factories dirtying the air. ❑

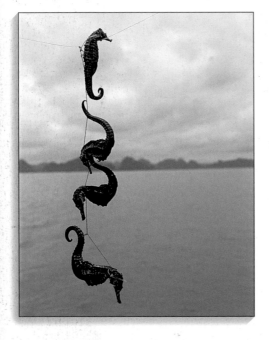

LOST WORLD DISCOVERIES

Despite war and industrialisation, Vietnam harbours some unique sanctuaries. In 1992, biologists studying the Vu Quang rainforest along the Laos border northwest of Vinh uncovered the skull of a previously unknown species of antelope, *Pseudoryx nghetinhensis*, which looks more like an onyx and is called *saola* in Vietnamese. In 1994, two live specimens of the 100-kg (220-lb) animal were captured. Since then, other previously unknown species of animals have been discovered in the remote rainforest, including the giant muntjac, a deer-like animal with large canine teeth. The government has expanded the area protected by the reserve and halted logging.

LEFT: drying sea horses for use as medicine.
RIGHT: chartering a boat among Ha Long's islands.

THE VIETNAMESE

Settled at the crossroads between China to the north and Southeast Asia,

Vietnam's population reflects an eclectic swirl of races awash in many cultures

Although 90 percent of Vietnam's population lists its ethnicity as *kinh* – the commonly accepted term for the indigenous race – in reality most Vietnamese have evolved from a mixture of races and ethnicities over thousands of years.

That mixture is quite naturally the result of repeated invasions from outside Vietnam, particularly from China, along with continual migrations within Vietnam, most commonly from north to south. So in Vietnam today there are the predominant kinh but also dozens of distinct minority groups, including the Cham and Khmer of the south, two groups whose own kingdoms were long ago vanquished by invading Vietnamese armies from the north.

Minority groups have been among the last to share in the prosperity under Vietnam's recent economic renovation – with one exception. Ethnic Chinese, who as recently as the late 1970s were ostracised if not run out of the country because of tensions arising during a brief northern border clash with China, have not only benefited from Vietnam's recent economic progress but, in many ways, have fuelled an economic revival, particularly in Ho Chi Minh, Vietnam's entrepreneurial centre.

Other minority groups have not been so fortunate. Usually living in remote, undeveloped, mountainous regions with little fertile ground for agriculture, their existence is worlds removed from the hustle of Vietnam's urban centres.

Viet origins

Studies of folk songs from the hill regions of northern Vietnam, and from the coastal area in the northern part of central Vietnam, affirm that the Vietnamese originated in the north's delta of the Song Hong (Red River). These agricultural, fishing, and hunting people were probably animistic. Their dress, although unique in Indochina, is also found in certain Pacific island

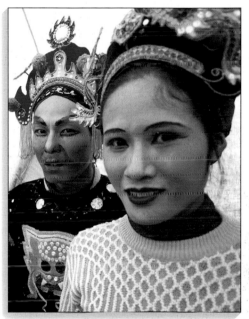

cultures. The scenes – mostly of nautical, dance and war themes – depicted on ancient bronze drums reveal a notable similarity to the mystical traditions of the Dayaks of Borneo and the Batak of Sumatra. In fact, artefacts of five races have been uncovered in Vietnam: the Melanesians, Indonesians, Negritos, Australoids, and Mongoloids. The most predominant of these were the Indonesians and Mongoloids.

Throughout monsoon Asia, which includes northern Vietnam, a shared culture existed from a very early era as evidenced by its tools, vocabulary, and certain essential rites and traditions such as the blackening of teeth, water festivals, bronze drums, kites, tattooing, betel nut and cajeput, pole houses, cockfighting, and mulberry cultivation.

The times of the prehistoric Vietnam are retained in the collective memory of the Vietnamese people through numerous tales, legends, and popular songs that recount at length the traditions, customs, and manners of this people,

PRECEDING PAGES: students at flight attendant school.
LEFT: young violin student in Hanoi.
RIGHT: theatre performers in traditional costume.

including the making of large and elaborately ornamented bronze kettle drums, which have been discovered as far south as Bali (*see photograph on page 26*).

Continuing studies on the origins of the Vietnamese people show that the people who settled on the Indochinese peninsula and its bordering regions most likely came from southern and eastern China, the high plateaus of Central Asia, islands in the South Pacific, and perhaps other parts of the world. Thus, Vietnam can be considered a proverbial melting pot into which major Asiatic and Oceanic migrations converged.

Ancient migrations

It is most likely that the first inhabitants of Vietnam originated from several ethnic groups. The most important of these were the Hung, or Lac, specialists in wet-rice cultivation and inventors of the bronze drums, and who inhabited the Song Hong Delta and central regions of Vietnam, and the Muong, who came from the high, wooded plateaus and mountainous regions.

Two major Viet emigrations from the coastal and southern provinces of the Chinese empire added to this population. The first occurred during the 5th century BC at the fall of the Viet kingdom of the low Yangze valley, and the second during the 3rd century BC, when the Au, or Au Tay, from Quangxi invaded the northern part of Vietnam.

They progressively established themselves in the coastal regions, gradually making their way inland via rivers until they eventually reached the high regions, which were inhabited by the native Lac people in the delta and the Muong at Hoa Binh and Thanh Hoa, just south of present-day Hanoi.

The Vietnamese population's southward expansion from northern Vietnam brought an important native Malayo-Indonesian element to the fair-skinned contingent from the valleys

into central Vietnam in 982, reaching Hue in 1306, Quang Ngai in 1402, Binh Dinh in 1470, Phu Yen in 1611, Ba Ria in 1623, Nha Trang in 1653, Bien Hoa in 1658, Saigon in 1674, Phan Rang in 1693, Phan Thiet in 1697, and finally Ha Tien in the southernmost province of the Mekong Delta in 1714.

In this southward expansion, they overran the kingdoms of Champa and part of Cambodia. By 1714, the Viet empire extended from the Chinese frontier to the Gulf of Thailand.

Several thousands of years ago, the Viet tribes moved from China in the southern (*nam*) direction towards the Song Hong (Red River)

of the Yangze when they merged with the first native occupants of the Red River Delta around the third century BC to found the Kingdom of Au Lac.

The numerous centuries of intermingling between these races has produced the Vietnamese people of today.

In their search for vital living space, this vigorous, tenacious, and courageous people crossed the mountain ranges of central Indochina and more than 3,000 km (1,800 miles) in their move to the south. They crossed

LEFT: the universal piano lesson.
ABOVE: relaxing in the cool of the evening.

CONTRADICTION

The country's standard of living ranks amongst the lowest in the world. Despite a protracted effort to revive the rural economy, disastrous economic polices coupled with the drain of more than 50 percent of the country's budget on its occupation forces in Cambodia for so many years have had devastating effects on Vietnam's economy. In an effort to revive the ailing economy, the country has opened its doors to encourage foreign investment and tourism, but the effort has been shackled by bureaucratic bungles, corruption, and suspicions. Still, one will find the average Vietnamese open to new ideas and entrepreneurial zest.

Delta. They settled in a beautiful land surrounded by high mountains, deep waters, thick forests, and narrow plains. Inspired by the wonders of nature, the Viet soon realised that only with blood, sweat, tears, and sharp eyes could they preserve their newly acquired *dat* (earth) and *nuoc* (water).

To succeed, for centuries the Vietnamese have had to be conscious of the forces around them – the seen and the unseen, the favourable and the hostile – and to understand their nature and intentions and to resist them if necessary and co-exist with them if possible but never to provoke their anger.

namese culture, are actually borrowed from the Chinese, who colonised Vietnam 2,000 years ago. Among the colonialists were the usual tyrants and exploiters, but, along with these, there were compassionate administrators and dedicated teachers who brought with them religions, philosophies, organisational skills, and especially their written characters, the *chu han*.

This influence from the Chinese created the possibility of losing a Viet identity and independence but also the opportunity of assimilating and adapting the best of Chinese civilisation and culture. (In some ways, it is a process that continues today, as the proud

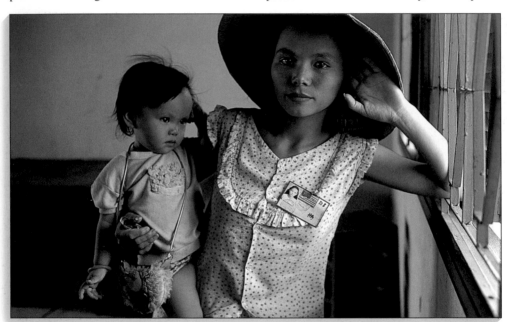

To make sense of this immense web of influences and the matrix of powers ruling existence, the Vietnamese have looked to what is in heaven, on earth, and amongst the people themselves. To penetrate the mysteries of heaven, to understand the workings and movements of the earth, and to establish relationships with other people, Vietnamese traditionally have sought to know the way in which things emerge, exist, progress, disappear, and re-emerge. They seek the religions. In Vietnamese, they are *ton giao*, the highest and most elevated knowledge, or *dao giao*, the knowledge of the Way, or simply, Dao.

These words and concepts, like much in Viet-

BRIBES TO MAKE ENDS MEET

Low wages in government and the civil service still account for a nagging problem of corruption, as bureaucrats at all levels look to supplement their meagre incomes. Doctors sometimes insist on separate payments to treat patients or insist that patients buy medicine from them. Teachers sometimes tutor students in examination preparatory classes, covering the necessary material in exchange for a small payment. At government ministries, licences and permissions often require a "special payment". The government criticises these practices and has prosecuted high-profile cases, but they persist.

Vietnamese now open the doors to foreigners, attempting to learn the best from other cultures and societies while maintaining their hard-fought independence.)

The early attempts at making the best of Chinese domination were honed within the village, the *cha* (later called *xa*) that is the foundation of Vietnamese life. The village's economic and commercial activities, in which all inhabitants participate, are concentrated on growing food, especially rice, which requires constant observation of nature, the

CHAM PRESERVATION

Today, the Cham people preserve their customs, language, and script with a religion that is a modified form of Hinduism.

identified ethnic groups.) Vietnam's 1.7 million Chinese constitute another important minority group. Only about 3,000 have kept their Chinese nationality, however, while the rest, referred to in Vietnam as *hoa*, have adopted Vietnamese nationality.

On the whole, whether naturalised or not, many Chinese remain loyal to the costumes and traditions of their country of origin. Mostly shopkeepers and traders, they settled in Ho Chi Minh City's Cho Lon district, which has long flourished as the Chinese

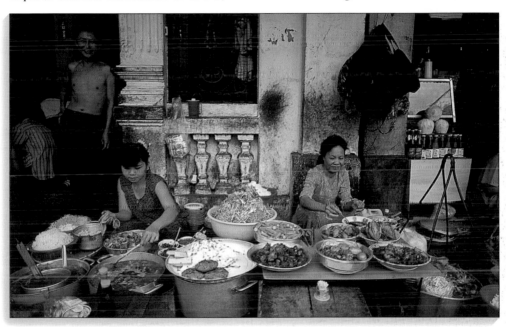

precise coordination of cultivation, and a bonding communal effort.

The Chinese

The Viet, or Kinh, form the majority of Vietnam's people, representing about 87 percent of the population. Numerous ethnic minorities inhabit the mountainous regions that cover almost two-thirds of Vietnam. (At the end of the 20th century, a small tribe of fewer than 100 members was found in a northern province, a tribe distinct from previously

LEFT: Amerasians are offspring of American fathers and Vietnamese mothers. ABOVE: Cho Lon food stall.

community's primary commercial centre in southern Vietnam.

Hill-tribe minorities

The ethnic minorities living in the mountainous regions in central and southern Vietnam form another important group. Called Montagnards by the French, these tribes include the Muong, Ra De, Jarai, Banhar, and Sedang living in the high plateaus of the west. Totalling around 1.5 million people, they have always opposed foreign influence and only recently have begun to integrate more into the national life.

The Cham and Khmer number around

1.2 million. The Chams inhabit the Phan Rang and Phan Thiet regions in southern Vietnam, east of Ho Chi Minh City, while Khmer are found in the Mekong Delta. Chams once possessed a brilliant culture that lasted for several centuries. Its vestiges can still be seen in Nha Trang's Po Nagar ruins and the shrines and monasteries at Dong Duong, and also in the temples, towers, and large-scale irrigation systems found in central Vietnam. Most of the architectural and sculptural traces relate to their religious beliefs,

ANCESTRAL WORSHIP

An ancestral altar has the central position in a Giai home. Each vase of incense represents a divinity such as the sky, the earth, the ancestors, or the god of the home.

Son, Bac Thai, Quang Ninh, Ha Giang, and Tuyen Quang, and in the Dien Bien Phu region. Their villages, or *ban,* are located in valleys near flowing water, where they build their traditional houses, usually on stilts. They cultivate rice, soybeans, cinnamon, tea, tobacco, cotton, indigo, fruit trees, and bamboo on the mountainsides above the village. The influence of Viet culture is evident in their dialect and customs, which distinguish them from the other Tay-Tai speaking groups.

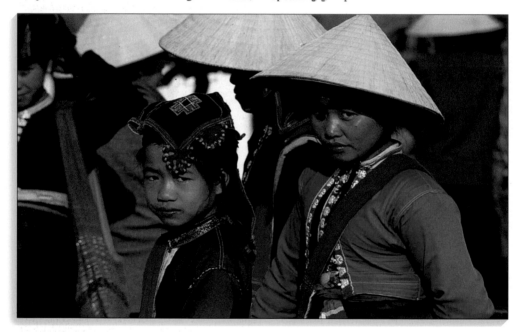

linked with ancient legend and polytheist in nature. Its prevailing image was that of a woman regarded as the mother of the country who gave birth to the dynastic rulers. Large blocks of vertical-standing stones symbolising the God of the Earth represented another Cham cult. Later, Hinduism and Indian culture would influence the Chams, as can be seen in *lingga* images; Mahayana Buddhism, too, also became an important influence.

The highlands and midland regions of northern Vietnam are home to many ethnic minorities and diverse tribes, including the Tay, who number over 1.5 million and are found in village groups in the provinces of Cao Bang, Lang

The Nung, in many aspects similar to the Tay, share the same language, culture, and customs, often living together in the same villages where they are referred to as Tay Nung. Numbering about 875,000, they live in Cao Bang and Lang Son provinces.

There are more than 1.3 million Tai living along the Song Hong, in the northwest of Vietnam, often together with other ethnic minorities. Their bamboo or wooden stilt houses are constructed in two distinct styles. The Black Tai build homes shaped like tortoise shells, while the White Tai construct rectangular dwellings. The women wear long, black sarongs and short tops with silver buttons. They are very skilled weavers and produce beautiful embroidery using motifs of flowers, birds, animals, and dragons.

The San Chi, numbering more than 150,000, live in village groups mainly in Ha Giang, Tuyen Quang, and Bac Thai provinces, but they are also found in certain regions of Lao Cai, Yen Bai, Vinh Phu, Ha Bac, and Quang Ninh provinces. They are of the Tay-Tai language group and arrived from China at the beginning of the 19th century. San Chi ritual dances reflect the life of the community. Groups of boys and young girls perform traditional love songs in festivities that can last all night.

The Giai, also of the Tay-Tai language group, number about 51,000 and emigrated from China about 200 years ago. Their villages are often built very close to those of the Tay, Nung, and Tai. The Giai believe the universe has three levels, with humans in the middle between the highest level of heaven and the lowest level, a vile place inhabited by sinners. The Giai have numerous proverbs and maxims that constitute a kind of moral code.

The Lao number about 12,000 and belong to the Tay-Tai language group. They are actually

LEFT: glances from Black Tai girls in north Vietnam.
ABOVE: Muong woman's attire.

NAMES: LAST COMES FIRST

There are only approximately 140 Vietnamese family names in use today. The most common are Nguyen, Pham, Phan, Tran, and Le. Children take the father's family name, though people with the same family name need not have the same origin. In fact, most Vietnamese surnames are the same as one of the 16 imperial families, or dynasties, that have ruled in Vietnam: Thuc, Trung, Trieu, Mai, Khuc, Ly, Phung, Kieu, Ngo, Dinh, Le, Tran, Ho, Mac, Trinh, and Nguyen (listed in chronological order). While a person today with one of these family names may be a descendent, the name was probably acquired otherwise: a voluntary change of name to show loyalty to the current monarch; an imposed name change when a new dynasty rose to power, especially if the old family name was the same as the former – and now disgraced – royal family; or as a reward or honour bestowed upon a person or family by the reigning ruler.

Only around 30 of the 140 or so family names used in Vietnam are actually of Vietnamese origin. For the most part, family names are of Chinese (Khong, Luu, Truong, Lu, Lam), Cambodian (Thach, Kim, Danh, Son), or ethnic minority origins (Linh, Giap, Ma, Deo).

Vietnamese names follow the structure of family name–middle name–given name. Most of the time, Vietnamese address each other by their given names.

Traditionally, the most common middle names are Van (meaning an educated person or scholar) for men and Thi (meaning a woman) for women. Some language experts suggest that these middle names derive from Malay influences, in which traditionally *van* means "son of" and *thi*, "daughter of". In recent times, however, Vietnamese have taken more meaningful middle names. A middle name may also indicate the order of a child within the family (Ba for first son of first wife, Manh for the first son of second wife, Trong for a second son, etc.) or the children of a particular brother (Thuc indicates a son of a younger brother).

Today, most given names are chosen for their meaning, often derived from objects or themes of nature such as geographical features (rivers, mountains), flora, fauna, precious gems, or the seasons. Sometimes children within the same family will have given names from the same category, for example, the seasons or flowers. Contrary to Western traditions, the Vietnamese usually will avoid the given names of ancestors or relatives out of respect.

Another tradition that runs contrary to Western ways is the order of learning a stranger's name. Nicknames or given names are usually learned first; only when trust is established is the family name shared with another.

closer to the Tai minority than their Laotian namesakes across the border. They are found along the Vietnam-Laos border in the Song Ma district of Son La Province and around Dien Bien Phu and Phong Tho in Lai Chau Province. Their homes are built on stilts in the form of a tortoise shell, like those of the Black Tai. Their traditional costume also resembles that of the Tai, and their elaborate rice-growing techniques are similar to those of the Tai. They are also skilled craftspeople, particularly in ceramics, weaving, and embroidery.

The Lu also belong to the Tay-Tai language group. They number around 5,000 and are found in the Phong Tho and Sin Ho districts of Lai Chau Province in well-arranged villages of 40 to 60 dwellings. They arrived from China and occupied the Dien Bien Phu area as part of the Bach Y migrations in the first century AD. The Lu's famous Tam Van Citadel, dedicated to Buddha, was noted by the Black Tai on their arrival in the 11th and 12th centuries.

The Hmong, who number about 900,000, are found in villages known as *giao* throughout the highlands of 11 provinces: Cao Bang, Lang Son, Bac Thai, Ha Giang, Tuyen Quang, Lao Cai, Yen Bai, Son La, Lai Chau, Hoa Binh, and Thanh Hoa. Due to their wars with the feudal

ROLL CALL

Over 2,000 years ago, imperial edicts in Vietnam required that local administrators establish family registries in which they recorded all names, marriages, births, and deaths within a family. Known as *gia pha* (family history), such registries have their origin in ancient China and are found elsewhere in Asia, including Japan. The oldest recovered *gia pha* in Vietnam is dated AD 1026. Family registries are more common in the northern and central parts of the country. Vietnamese names typically follow the structure of family name, middle name, and given name last *(see box on previous page)*. Vietnamese usually call one another by their given names.

Chinese in the north, Hmong emigrated to Vietnam from the southern Chinese kingdom of Bach Viet at the end of the 18th and beginning of the 19th century. Once in Vietnam, they settled in northwestern provinces. Maize is their main staple, but rice is often grown on terraces watered with the aid of an irrigation system. Hemp is grown as the main textile material, and cotton is also cultivated in some villages. Poppy and Job's tears are among the plants cultivated for medicinal purposes. Fruit such as plums, peaches, and apples produced by the Hmong is highly valued throughout the country, although transportation problems make selling the produce difficult. They collect gentian, cardamom, honey, fungi, bamboo, and many medicinal herbs from the forests, all of which constitute an important source of income.

As skilled artisans, the Hmong produce a variety of items, including handwoven indigo-dyed cloth, paper, silver jewellery, leather goods, baskets, baby carriers, kitchen utensils, and embroidery. Many of these are increasingly sold to tourists.

The Hmong have no written language. Their legends, songs, folklore, and proverbs have been passed down from one generation to the next through the spoken word. They have

to women. Catholic missionaries attempted to convert the Hmong at the beginning of the 20th century, and although some churches were built at Sa Pa and Nghia Lo, the evangelical efforts didn't succeed.

The Dao first arrived from China in the 18th century. Part of the Hmong-Dao language group, the Dao number about 630,000 and are found in the mid- and lower-regions of Thanh Hoa Province, living in large villages or small isolated hamlets, cultivating rice using the slash-and-burn method. The Dao are very skilled artisans. They make their own paper, used primarily for writing family genealogies,

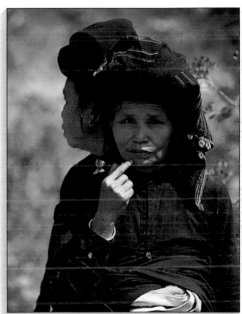

developed a varied culture, rich in popular knowledge concerning the nature of society – extolling liberty, justice, charity, the work ethic, and virtue, and condemning laziness, meanness, hypocrisy, and lying.

Totemism – the veneration of symbolic objects – is still evident in Hmong culture in which spirit worship, animist rites, and even exorcism are still practised. Buddhism, Dao-ism, and Confucianism have left their mark on some Hmong societies, introducing beliefs in reincarnation and the idea that men are superior

official documents, and religious books. For centuries, the Dao have used Chinese characters to record their genealogies, rhymes, folk tales, humourous tales, fables, and popular songs. The women plant cotton, which they weave then dye with indigo. Their embroidery is worked directly onto the cloth from memory, the traditional designs fixed in their minds.

Central Highlands

The Jarai, or Gia Rai, are located in the provinces of Gia Lai, Kon Tum, and Dak Lak, and in the north of Phu Khanh. They belong to the Malay-Polynesian language group and arrived in the Tay Nguyen highlands from the

LEFT: Hmong at a village's sacrificial pledge to central government, 1960s. **ABOVE:** Dao and Meo women.

coast a little less than 2,000 years ago. They live a sedentary lifestyle in villages known as *ploi,* or sometimes *bon.* Jarai villages, with at least 50 homes, are built around a central *nga rong,* a communal house.

The community is composed of small matriarchal families, with each family an economically independent unit within the village. A council of elders, with a chief, directs village matters. The chief is responsible for all the village's communal activities.

Jarai cultivate fruit trees, rice, beans, and other cereals and raise buffalo, goats, chickens, and pigs, primarily to offer as sacrifices to their

various gods and spirits. Oxen, horses, and elephants are raised as working animals, and horses are also used to hunt wild boar.

Young girls take the incentive in choosing a marriage partner, making their approach through an intermediary. The promise of marriage is sealed with the exchange of bronze bracelets, with the ceremony proceeding in three steps. First, the bracelet-exchanging rite is performed in front of the two families and the intermediary. Then the young couple's nightly dreams are interpreted, a ritual that predicts their future prospects. Finally, the actually wedding ceremony is held at the home of the man's parents.

Jarai funerals are extremely complex affairs with endless rites, particularly in connection with the careful construction of the burial house. Carved wooden sculptures representing men, women, and birds are placed inside it. Jarai believe the deceased is transformed into a spirit and joins ancestors in another world.

The Ra De, or E De, found mainly in Dak Lak Province, number more than 200,000. Like the Jarai, they belong to the Malay-Polynesian language group. They live in wooden longhouses, built on stilts, in villages known as *buon,* with as few as 20 and as many as 70 dwellings. Each longhouse shelters a large matriarchal family under the authority of a *koa sang,* the most senior and respected woman. She directs community affairs, settles internal conflicts, and is also responsible for the safe-keeping of all the communal heirlooms, bronze gongs, ancient jars used for preparing rice beer, a large seat carved from a single tree trunk reserved for the *khoa sang*, and special stools reserved for hosts and musicians. The village's autonomous organisation is run by the *po pin ea,* the chief who is elected to take care of communal affairs.

The Ra De employ the slash-and-burn techniques to clear the land for agriculture. Rice, the main crop, is cultivated along with sugar cane, melons, cotton, and tobacco.

Nearly every village has its own forge to produce and repair metal farming implements. Basketry, somewhat rudimentary pottery, and indigo cloth are produced by the Ra De for their own use. ❏

LEFT: 19th-century Meo tribeswomen.
RIGHT: court mandarin in his imperial finery.

RELIGION

Predominantly Buddhist, Vietnam's spiritual foundations are rich and deep,
also embracing Confucianism, Daoism, animism, and Catholicism

Foremost in the Vietnamese religious hierarchy – regardless of the dogmatic undergirding – is a heaven above, which the Vietnamese (who have a tendency to humanise everything, in order to better deal with it) called *Ong Troi*, the honourable Heaven with a masculine cast. They approach him with food offerings, requests, complaints, and prayers. In principle, Ong Troi is the keeper of human fate and in charge of all the unseen powers and vague mysteries of the universe.

Together, the gods of the earth, water, and mountains define and transform the geomantic structures and rules that determine – in the same way that the Chinese use *feng shui* – the orientation of houses, businesses, cities, graves, and temples and configure the good and bad luck of families, communities, and nations.

Between heaven and earth, but never separate from them, is the human being, both male and female, the dead and the living, the ancestors and the descendants.

Each of the realms – heaven, earth, and human – has its own rules, regulations, modes of transformations, elements of good, bad, ugly, and beautiful, and above all, its own deities. These deities are everywhere – in stones, trees, lakes, and animals – and they are praised, fed, housed, and revered with ritual offerings and appropriate behaviour. The richness and variety of these worlds and their manifestations has preoccupied, confused, and even dazzled the traditional Vietnamese, often leaving them little sense of space or privacy to eat, sleep and make love – the basic human needs.

This perception results from the Vietnamese sense of awe for the visible and invisible forces of nature, their observation and interpretation of these forces, and the ways and means they have found to compromise and co-exist with them, or resist them. Above all, the belief is grounded in their intimate relationship with the land on which they live, procreate, and bury their dead, in their deep faith in the continuity of the Viet nation, and in their sacred mission to defend and build their land and water (*dat* and *nuoc*). The secret wish of all Vietnamese is to attain *nhan* – a word borrowed from the Chinese meaning "contemplating the moon through a

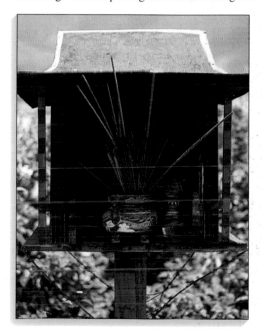

SACRED PLACES

In addition to the traditional pagodas *(chua)* and communal houses *(dinh)* found in common villages, there are smaller places of worship where both the benevolent and malevolent divinities and spirits are worshipped. These temples include the *den*, which is typically used to commemorate a deified emperor who offered particular help or safety to the village, or perhaps to a national hero; the *mieu*, which is usually situated on an elevated piece of land and is reserved for the cult of both benevolent and malevolent gods and spirits; and finally the *ban*, where all divinities of nature and life not worshipped elsewhere are worshipped.

PRECEDING PAGES: monk at Giac Vien Pagoda, Ho Chi Minh City. **LEFT:** Buddha image. **RIGHT:** small roadside shrine with incense sticks.

window" – laughing off the glory and the burden of the day and instead immersing one's self in the serenity of a moonlit night.

When the Chinese imposed their rule on Vietnam, they brought along their agricultural know-how and their books on religion, philosophy, and other ideas, written in one of the most complicated scripts of all time. While today a roman script is used, having replaced the adopted Chinese script, the Vietnamese once loved these Chinese characters, which visually and stylistically

HINDU BELIEFS

Hinduism was brought to Vietnam by Indian merchants about 1,000 years ago. The Champa empire in central Vietnam worshipped Shiva, later converting to Islam.

generations, including Hinduism and Islam brought from India, and Christianity imported from Europe and America.

As in other societies, religion and politics have never been far removed from one another in Vietnamese society. Under Communist rule, the religious faithful have sometimes faced persecution, and churches and pagodas were shuttered. In recent years, however, the government has loosened its restrictions and there has been a resurgence of religious interest within the coun-

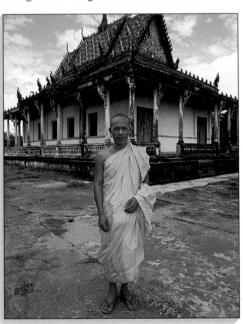

represented the meaning and feeling attached to each word.

Although the Vietnamese fought against Chinese political domination and economic exploitation, they selectively screened and assimilated what they considered the best of Chinese culture.

The Chinese teachers, some of whom were administrators, were usually accompanied by Confucian scholars, Buddhist masters, Daoist wanderers and even I-Ching diviners. The Vietnamese absorbed much of what they had to offer, melding them into their lives. All of these religious influences persist in Vietnam today, as do the religions introduced in later

try. Pagodas are crowded with the faithful and curious on holidays and on important dates of the lunar calendar; schools for training Buddhist monks have been allowed to open; and Catholic churches are filled.

Yet, there are still signs of restraint. An example is the government preference of particular Buddhist organisations or sects over others. For example, some Buddhist monks are loyal to a rival sect that existed in South Vietnam before the end of the Vietnam War in 1975, but which was then outlawed by the Communists when they installed their own state church. Some monks and lay people associated with that particular outlawed sect were arrested and imprisoned, not for religious reasons, authorities say, but because they ostensibly tried to organise anti-government movements under the guise of helping flood victims. There is little evidence that today the outlawed Buddhist organisation has much of a following in Vietnam.

Any government restraints are low-key. Like the emperor Minh Mang's anti-Catholic policies and South Vietnam's President Ngo Dinh Diem's jailing of Buddhists in earlier years, any crackdowns today on dissident Buddhists would only call attention to them and turn them into symbols of repression.

teacher. Confucius was more of a moral and ethical guide than a spiritual leader. He refused to discuss life after death, as well as the unseen or the mystical, and he was primarily interested in a social order based upon compassion, etiquette, loyalty, knowledge, and trust.

Confucianism reached Vietnam through the Chinese over 2,000 years ago. It became the official doctrine of the imperial government examinations, the first of which was held in 1706 and the last in 1919.

The Vietnamese monarchy recruited its high officials according to the results of these competitive examinations, which were in theory

Confucianism

As an ideology, Confucianism has endured longer than any other belief system, in both the East and West, and its influence, sometimes as just a remnant, has crossed many national borders into all parts of the world. It is based on the teachings of Confucius, born around 550 BC and who lived at a time of great political turmoil. As a teacher and unsolicited adviser to kings, he compiled rules and ideas to define the relationships between ruler and subject, parents and children, husband and wife, student and

open to anyone except actors and women. Many, however, learned Confucianism at home from their parents. The examinations, which also required knowledge of Buddhism, Daoism, and Tan Giao, were extremely competitive. From 1075 to 1919 – more than 800 years – just slightly over 2,000 doctorate degrees were granted.

Those who earned their degrees received a hat and tunic from the emperor and were welcomed home as wise scholars with great pomp and ceremony by the entire population. Those who failed the examinations went quietly home to their villages and earned their redemption, and living, as teachers. In this

LEFT: Tay An Pagoda, Chau Doc; Khmer monk in the south. **ABOVE:** retreat near Hue; Hoi An temple.

way, villagers were indirectly introduced to the teachings of Confucianism.

For over 2,000 years, Confucianism has remained a pillar of the Vietnamese moral and spiritual establishment. By the time Vietnam regained its independence from China, it possessed a large number of Vietnamese scholars with almost a millennium of institutional Confucian studies behind them. Officially and pragmatically, the Vietnamese imperial dynasties adopted Confucianism because of its ability to sustain a system of social order, but without much repression, and for its code of social mobility based on merit.

Buddhism

Vietnamese Buddhism is a fascinating blend of several branches of Buddhism. Introduced across the sea from India and overland from China, Buddhism extended the question of knowledge from the social order and rules of Confucianism to the general human condition. In this Buddhism, existence is unhappiness; unhappiness is caused by selfish cravings. Unhappiness ends when the selfish cravings – which can be destroyed – end. Attaining this last of the truths could be done by following the steps of the so-called eight-fold path: right understanding, right purpose (aspiration), right

CAO DAI DIVINITY

The Cao Dai sect began when an obscure Vietnamese official in the French colonial government received a message from a "superior spirit" – Cao Dai, meaning High Terrace or Supreme Being – in the early 1920s. Cao Daism attempts to bring all faiths, including Buddhism, Daoism, Confucianism, Islam, and Christianity, under one supreme deity. Many figures are revered by the Cao Dai sect, extending to a diverse collection such as Sun Yat-sen, Napoleon Bonaparte, and Winston Churchill. Appealing primarily to peasants, Cao Daism gained political influence following World War II. Estimates are that there are several million members of the sect.

speech, right conduct, right vocation, right effort, right alertness, and right concentration. "Right" means conforming to the Four Noble Truths. Central to Buddhism is the concept of Brahman, the Absolute origin, the equivalent of the Chinese *taiqi (tai chi)*.

Vietnamese have embraced Buddhism for more than 2,000 years; today, it is the predominant spiritual belief in Vietnam. To Vietnamese Buddhists, Brahman represents the unknown and unknowable, the source and embodiment of reality, knowledge, and bliss.

More than 1,000 years ago, a Vietnamese Buddhist master was sent to the Japanese court to teach Buddhist music. From the 2nd century

AD to the 10th century, two popular sects – the Ā Hàm (Āgama) and the Thiền (Dhyāna in Sanskrit and Zen in Japanese) – competed peacefully for Vietnamese followers and believers. Gradually, Thiền prevailed, despite its exacting practice that requires continual training in self-discipline and in mastering the focused "techniques" of breathing, meditation, and right concentration.

Thiền is one of the many sects of Mahayana Buddhism widely observed in China, Japan, Korea, and Vietnam. Less dogmatic than others, it is receptive to the diverse cultural and social conditions of different countries and of differ-

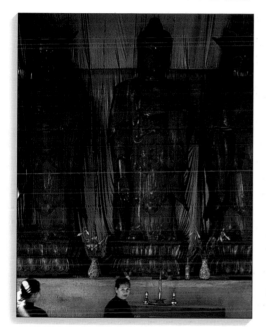

ent eras. The other branch of Buddhism, the Hinayana or Theravada (found in Sri Lanka, Burma, Thailand, Laos, Cambodia, and parts of southern Vietnam), is more orthodox yet coexists with Mahayana.

In practically every Vietnamese village, from north to south, one finds a *chua* (pagoda) and a *dinh* (communal house). The villagers worship Buddha in the chua, which is cared for by resident monks. On the first and 15th days of the lunar months, villagers visit the chua, bringing flowers, joss sticks, and fruit for the Buddha.

LEFT: Cao Dai temple in Tay Ninh, southern Vietnam.
ABOVE: images in a Buddhist temple.

TET NEW YEAR

Tet Nguyen Dan (Festival of the First Morning of the Year) is Vietnam's most important festival and is the beginning of the lunar year. Embodied in Tet is the whole spectrum of Vietnamese mythology and of one's place within family, with one's ancestors, and with the universe. It is a mixture of Buddhism, Daoism, and Confucianism.

Tet rites begin a week before the lunar New Year. This is the time for the gods to return to the Kingdom of Heaven and present their annual report on the state of earthly matters to the Jade Emperor before returning to earth on New Year's Eve. During the gods' week-long journey to Heaven, the Vietnamese guard themselves against bad spirits. In the countryside, they erect a *cay neu* (signal tree), a high bamboo pole with a sonorous clay tablet with a piece of yellow cloth attached to the top, in front of the home.

With malevolent spirits now deflected, the Vietnamese prepare the *banh chung*, or glutinous rice cakes stuffed with pork, fat, beans, and dried onion. Another indispensable feature, even for the poorest families, is a tree branch of peach blossom, the *cahn dao*. During Tet, branches of peach blossom can cost more than a day's average wages. In southern and central Vietnam, the peach blossom is replaced by *canh mai*, a branch of yellow apricot blossom.

For maximum security against any possible intrusion by demons and bad spirits, the Vietnamese traditionally lit firecrackers to thwart the notorious devils Na A and his terrible wife, who cannot bear noise and light. However, firecrackers had turned the cities and countryside into a battle zone; in 1995, firecrackers were outlawed. Ingenious Vietnamese turned to tape recordings of firecracker noise.

After all these precautions have been taken, the Vietnamese calmly await the arrival of spring. The first day of Tet is for the worship of ancestors, who are ceremoniously welcomed back from heaven on New Year's Eve during the Giao Thua, the transition between the old and new year.

Elaborately prepared food offerings, together with the perfume of burning sandalwood, incense, and *thai tien*, a type of fragrant white narcissus that blooms during Tet, await the ancestors at the altar. At midnight on the last day of the old year, all human problems, war, political intrigue, and commercial transactions are left behind. A temporary general truce is declared between human beings and spirits.

All events – whether favourable or unfavourable – that take place on the first day of Tet are believed to affect the course of one's life for the year ahead.

They also attend services at the pagoda on the evenings of the 14th and 30th days of the month to repent for wrongs committed and vow to act in the right, proper way. Buddhist practices at the village level are not exactly those of Zen, which requires guidance by a well-trained master, but rather are a mixture of Zen and Amitabha, commonly called Pure Land and a devotional faith. It is believed that Amitabha achieved Buddhahood on the express condition that he receive all who sincerely call upon his name at

good deeds will ensure a happy and joyful present life and a safe delivery to the land of absolute bliss, the Pure Land, after death.

THE BODHISATTVA

The compassionate *bodhisattva (bo tat)*, who postpones entrance to Nirvana through loving concern for the salvation of others, is at the heart of Amitabha Buddhism.

Daoism

Dao Te Ching, the *Book of the Way and its Power,* begins: "The Dao that can be told is not the eternal Dao".

Dao is the highest and most active level of an otherwise static consciousness, the general law of the motion of the universe and of all things. It is both energy and matter, and the moment when the

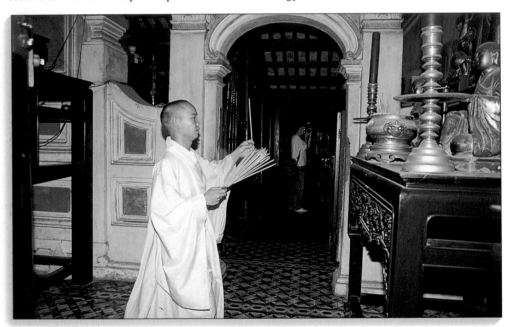

death and so carry them to the Western Paradise, where they may seek the ultimate perfection (Nirvana) under happier auspices than found on earth.

The practice of Amitabha Buddhism consists essentially of concentrating the mind through a self-absorption and chanting the name of Buddha. Those who practise Pure Land Buddhism must abstain from killing, stealing, banditry, lying, adultery, wrong speech and intoxicants. Its adherents are expected to recite the name of Amitabha Buddha, the Amitabha Sutra, and perform good deeds to gain merit for self and family. They believe that merits accumulated through

contradictory forces of *yin* and *yang* fuse in temporary harmony to provide people and things with a sense of direction. In Chinese writing, it is represented by a character meaning 'way' or 'path'.

An important book of reference for Daoists and Buddhists alike is the *I Ching,* or *The Book of Changes,* which uses symbols – simplified and stylised in signs and codes – to integrate a number of separate systems into a seemingly "mysterious" whole. It contains 64 triangles and hexagons arranged in broken and unbroken lines that, along with its basic text, represent "the process of vast and never-ending cosmic change. These endless chains of actions

and interaction assemble and divide the myriad objects proceeding from and flowing into
taiqi, the Still Reality underlying the worlds of
form, desire and formlessness". In the Chinese
characters for I Ching, the word "I" represents
a lizard, perhaps a chameleon.

In villages where Buddhism, Confucianism,
animism, and other forms and places of worship co-existed, Daoist priests were also welcome. In these villages, special places of
worship known as *dien,* or *tinh,* are found.
Introduced to Vietnam at about the same time
as Confucianism, Vietnamese Daoism does not
have the hierarchy of schools and systems as

ancestors. Although many traditional beliefs
and superstitions have waned, ancestor worship remains of high moral and social significance within Vietnamese society.

On anniversaries of deaths and on traditional
festival days, the relatives of the deceased
gather together. The eldest son of the deceased
presides over the ceremonial offerings of food
and incense, then the entire family visits the
grave of the deceased. The ceremony ends with
family members prostrating themselves before
the altar and burning paper "money", which
provides the dead with funds to make their life
happier in the other world.

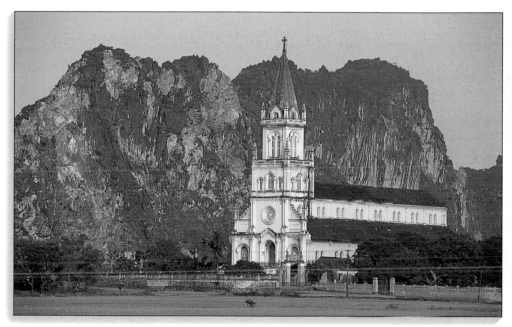

in China. On the philosophical level, it is
expressed in the thoughts and poetry of both
Confucian and Buddhist intellectuals. However,
Daoist priests and their places of worship are
found in villages among the common people.
At this level, Daoist practices become a maze
of superstitions, magic manifestations, and
mystic healings.

Ancestor worship

Within many Vietnamese homes and inside all
pagodas, one can find an altar dedicated to

Failing to worship one's ancestors is considered an act of grave filial impiety that con-
demns the ancestors to a life of hellish
wandering and subsisting on charity.

Christianity

To this universe with its rainbow of institutionalised religions, philosophies, and animistic beliefs came Catholicism. The first
Western missionaries set foot in Tonkin, in
northern Vietnam, in 1533, followed later in
central Vietnam in 1596.

But theirs was only a brief stay. It was not
until 1615 that the first permanent Christian
missions were founded – in Hoi An, Da Nang,

LEFT: Giac Lam Pagoda, Ho Chi Minh City.
ABOVE: Catholic church south of Hanoi.

and Hanoi – by the Portuguese Jesuits. The introduction of this highly organised and culturally alien religion generated, unavoidably, misunderstanding and conflict. Yet Catholicism contributed two major transformations to Vietnamese culture: the romanisation of the written language and the introduction of Western scientific methods and logic.

Many Vietnamese from all classes of society converted to Catholicism. This development worried the mandarins and ruling classes, who saw the new religion as a threat to the traditional order of society and its rites, particularly the belief of heaven *(nam giao)*

and ancestor worship. Between 1712 and 1720, a decree forbidding Christianity was enforced in the north. In the south, foreign missionaries were sent packing in 1750 when Christianity was forbidden.

Levels of tolerance towards Christianity varied among leaders. Under Emperor Minh Mang, who viewed Christianity as "the perverse religion of Europeans" that "corrupts the heart of men", a decree was enforced forbidding the entry of Christian missionaries to Vietnam. Thieu Tri, who reigned for a time afterwards, was more tolerant, but his successor, Tu Duc, reinforced the prohibition of Christianity. This period of persecution lasted until

the mid-1860s, when a treaty ceded territory and commercial rights to the French and granted freedom for Christians to practise their faith. Between 1882 and 1884, another wave of persecution hit the Catholic church, and many followers paid with their lives. The persecution ended in 1885 with the French conquest of the entire country.

After the signing of the Geneva Agreement in 1954 and the division of the country, over half a million Catholics fled North Vietnam for the tolerance of the former South Vietnam.

Since the reunification of Vietnam in 1975, the Catholic Church has lived under the written law of the Socialist Republic of Vietnam, which guarantees the freedom of religion or non-religion under an official Marxist–Leninist ideology. All Catholic schools in the country have been nationalised. Churches are crowded on Sundays and on religious holidays.

The Hanoi government has loosened its restrictions on the Catholic Church in the past decade. Seminarians have been allowed to be ordained, and parishes have been allowed to teach children the faith. In heavily Catholic areas, such as Dong Nai Province, just north of Ho Chi Minh City, the countryside is dotted with churches in the midst of a rebuilding frenzy. However, the government can still veto who the Vatican names as a cardinal in Vietnam, in part because the Vatican had once attempted to nominate a relative of the former South Vietnam leader Ngo Dinh Diem.

Islam

Vietnam's small Muslim community consists mainly of ethnic Chams and South Asians. A 10th-century stele inscribed in Arabic, found near the central coastal town of Phan Rang, provides the earliest record of Islam's presence in Vietnam. Although the Chams consider themselves as Muslim, their religious practices are not fully orthodox.

They don't make the pilgrimage to Mecca, and although they don't eat pork, Vietnamese Muslims drink alcohol; they pray only on Fridays, observe Ramadan for only three days instead of the normal full month, and their rituals co-exist with other animistic and Hindu-based worship. ❏

LEFT: Muslim men in southern Vietnam.
RIGHT: interior of the cathedral in Hue.

COLOURFUL FESTIVALS FOR ALL SEASONS

Festivals in Vietnam are a time of fun and plenty. The main festival of Tet is especially vibrant as the whole country joins together in celebration

Festivals are held throughout the year, but the most interesting take place in spring and autumn. Visitors wishing to join in should acquaint themselves with the lunar calendar. The most important festival for Vietnamese people is Tet, the lunar new year.

In the weeks before Tet, the streets are a frenzy as people buy food, presents, and the peach blossom and *kumquat* trees – without which no family Tet would be complete. On New Year's Eve, ceremonies are held to "close the year". Offerings to the ancestors are placed on the family altar and then burnt, the smoke carrying their respects to heaven. The weeks after Tet are a popular time for ceremonies outside the home and people gather at local temples or make a pilgrimage to places like the Perfume Pagoda. They have their fortunes told and present wishes for the coming year. These are written in Chinese on pink paper, which are displayed while joss sticks are burned.

The autumn equinox *(trung thu)* festival is for children. On the 15th day of the eighth lunar month, children are taken to water by day and to watch the moon at night. They carry simple toys and lanterns, making this a particularly charming festival.

◁ **DRAGON DANCING**
The colourful rong mua lan, or dancing dragon, is a centrepiece of Tet festivals in villages throughout the country. The dance scares away evil spirits.

△ **BURNT OFFERINGS**
On lunar New Year's Eve, families burn paper offerings to their ancestors. They often do so right on the pavement outside their house, so watch your feet!

◁ AUTUMN FESTIVAL
Beautifully crafted toys and candle lit lanterns are the main feature of the children's festival, celebrated at the autumn equinox in mid-September.

△ NEW YEAR WISHES
Monks literate in Chinese characters write people's New Year wishes onto pink paper slips. These are then displayed in the pagoda or burned.

VILLAGE FESTIVALS

The best time to visit village festivals is just after Tet, a word which itself means "festival". During the first two lunar months (February and March), most villages organise a fete. Families visit the village pagoda and light incense to local deities and their ancestors. Young people play games, swinging on giant bamboo swings or playing "human chess" with people or metre-high models moving between squares marked on a courtyard. Villages near the Red River send boats to collect ceremonial water to offer to the water god, Ha Ba. Most spectacular of all, young men put on the elaborate costumes of the dancing dragon and dance among the revellers to the sound of beating drums. One of the most popular of these occasions is the *quan ho* festival at Lim village, near Hanoi. Here young couples sing love songs to each other in a fertility rite to welcome the spring.

▷ INCENSE
Incense offerings are made in the form of joss sticks. They are an essential part of all worship, both in the home and, as here, in temples and pagodas.

▽ ANCESTORS' ALTARS
Tet offerings to the ancestors include rice, betel nuts, false money, and pink "New Year's wish" papers. After incense is offered, paper items are burned.

▽ PAGODA EFFIGIES
Ancestor worship is the main religion of the Vietnamese, co-existing with Buddhist, Confucian, and Daoist practices. The ancestor cult is a homely affair but it is also celebrated publicly with effigies on pagoda altars.

PERFORMING ARTS

*Vietnam's eclectic performing arts, while having roots in China,
tell great tales of Vietnamese gods and heroes in time-honoured adventures*

According to the wise teacher Confucius, "personal cultivation begins with poetry, is made firm by the rule of decorum, and is perfected by music". Before Western influences penetrated into Asia, music had long played an integral part in religious ceremonies but was not used for public entertainment.

The Dong Son bronze drums, which depict dancers performing to the accompaniment of musical instruments, and the lithophone of Ndut Lien Krat, in the southern highlands of Vietnam, testify to the importance of musical and dance traditions in Vietnam for over 2,500 years. Along with the other arts, music received its share of Chinese influence over the years. It was also influenced by the music of the Hindu kingdom of Champa, in the southern part of present-day Vietnam, which the Viet dynasties gradually absorbed during their long southward march.

Court music had its beginnings during the Le dynasty (1428–1788), when a Vietnamese mandarin was asked to establish a system of court music, following that of the Ming dynasty in China. He organised the following categories of music, each to be played at different religious and social occasions: *giao nhac,* played as an offering at the Esplanade of Heaven during the emperor's triennial celebration of the Cult of Heaven; *mieu nhac,* played during ceremonies at the Court of Literature in honour of Confucius, and at anniversary commemorations for deceased emperors; *ngu tu nhac,* music of the Five Sacrifices; *cuu nhat giao trung nhac,* music for helping the sun and moon during an eclipse; *dai trieu nhac,* music for ordinary audiences; *dai yen cuu tau nhac,* music for large banquets; and *cung trung chi nhac,* or palace music.

Throughout the 15th to 18th centuries, Vietnamese leaders took great interest in unifying the diverse orchestrations.

PRECEDING PAGES: backstage at a *cai luong* performance, Ho Chi Minh. **LEFT:** performer in Ho Chi Minh. **RIGHT:** traditional dancer.

Ceremonial and religious music

In the coastal provinces of central Vietnam, songs known as *hat ba trao* – songs for worshipping the ocean spirits – are a popular tradition. One, called the *hat chau van,* is an incantation used in hypnotising a person through musical tunes, rhythms, and lyrics.

Buddhist music falls into two styles: the *tan* or melismatic chant, and the *tung* or sutra prayers. The tan is accompanied by a string and percussion orchestra in syncopated rhythm, while the tung is a chant on knowledge and enlightenment and is recited by a monk and punctuated by strokes on a wooden slit-drum.

Chamber music, performed by small instrumental ensembles for selected audiences of intellectuals, was confined to major cities. The most popular, known as *a dao,* takes its name from a historical story from the 15th century, at the time of the Ming invasion from China. During the military struggle, all manner of weapons were used, including on one occasion a combination of female beauty and music. A country girl from a Dao village in Hai Hung province, in northern Vietnam, used her charm – together with dance, song, and music – to distract the Ming soldiers and so gain time to allow her countrymen to organise a guerrilla attack. *Hat A Dao*, the Song of the Lady from the Dao village, was composed by a group of mandarin scholars to commemorate the heroine's beauty, talent, and patriotism.

Each region of Vietnam has its own musical tradition, as do the country's 50-plus ethnic minorities. But, generally, Vietnamese music falls into two basic groups: the *dieu kach,* or northern tune, with its Chinese influence, and the *dieu nam,* or southern tune, with the slower tempo and sentimentality of the Cham culture.

Folk music takes the form of tunes sung and composed by villagers illustrating their life in the countryside. This music falls into several broad categories: lullabies, known as *hat run* in the north, *ru em* in the centre, and *au o* in the south; work songs, or *ho;* and the eternal love songs, *ly.*

There are ho and ly songs for each region, and for each season, every type of work, and every leisure activity. Ho refers to calling people to work in a rising and prolonged voice. A

SUNG POETRY

Essentially, Hat A Dao is sung poetry performed at the home of a songstress. The audience takes famous poems and composes verses themselves, all sung to the rhythmic accompaniment of the *phach*, a bamboo instrument beaten with two wooden sticks, and the *dan day*, a long-necked lute with three strings. The audience registers approval by beating a drum. By the beginning of the 20th century, the Hat A Dao had gradually become a refuge for pleasure rather than a centre for song and poetry. Its counterparts, though lacking the same significance, include the *ca hue*, music-song of Hue, and the *dan tai tu*, music of the amateurs in southern Vietnam.

lead singer begins the chant, which is then taken up by others in the working party. The most cherished of the ho is one called Ho Mia Nhi, usually sung by young boatwomen on the Perfume River, in Hue. Structured like a poem, this ho's four lines express deep thoughts and feelings, suitable for a river's transient moods.

Theatre

The oldest recorded form of performance is the *tro he,* a farce created by Lieu Thu Tam under the Tien Le dynasty. During the Tran dynasty, two new types of theatre emerged: the *hat giau mat,* or masked performances, and the *hat coi tran,* or coat-less performances.

Today's theatre, a blend of court theatre, folk performances, and foreign influence, includes three types of performances: *cheo, hat tuong,* and *cai luong.* Cheo is as old as the Vietnamese nation itself. The word "cheo" is a distortion of *tieu,* the Chinese word for laughter. Cheo's origins can be found in the religious and social activities that are depicted on the engravings of Bronze Age drums and urns.

Developed from animistic customs, mime, dance, song, prayers, and poetry, cheo reached

CIVIC CHEO

Anti-establishment *hat cheo* educates peasants on how to expose the injustices of those in power. Under some rulers, cheo was forbidden and its performers prosecuted.

a flute. These are not the only sounds to be heard. To start the play, someone from the audience beats a large drum. When a performer sings well, this drum will be beaten by a member of the audience to register approval; when the performance is poor, however, then the drum's wooden barrel is struck.

The length of a performance is determined by how much the audience has paid, and this is represented by a burning incense stick. When approval is marked by the drum, incense tapers are laid in

its present form of technique by the 1100s. Performances usually are staged in front of a village community house or Buddhist pagoda. The troupe's equipment is carried from village to village in a single box, which also serves as a unique part of the stage setting, representing whatever is required of it. Cheo plays provide a framework within which the players improvise. The troupe is judged according to its ability to vary and renew a familiar theme. The musicians sit to the right of the stage area with drums, gongs, rattles, stringed instruments, and

LEFT: ancient image of Cham dancers, Da Nang.
ABOVE: dragon-dance troupe members on a break.

a pile in honour of the player, lengthening, in turn, the performance – and the fee.

The audience knows every detail of cheo, whose strict rules were set as early as 1500. Throughout a performance, the players explain events, stop to question the audience, and take replies. Melodies familiar to everyone symbolise certain life-cycle events: marriage, birth, death. And all gestures, including movements of the eyes and mouth, have a specific meaning. A chorus and a clown express emotional high points. The clown, wearing black makeup, interrupts the players to comment on their lies and tricks, make fun of them, and praise their good deeds. The audience often stops a player to demand a replay of an interesting or intriguing detail.

Unlike hat cheo, which is clearly and uniquely Vietnamese, hat tuong arrived from China in the 13th century under the Tran dynasty after the defeat of Mongol invaders. Among the war prisoners was a master of Chinese theatre, Ly Nguyen Cat, who later became a Vietnamese citizen and taught Chinese drama to the Vietnamese court. From China came face makeup, ceremonial costumes, masks, stylised gestures, percussion and wind-instrument music, and emphasis on the heroic and noble.

Hat tuong begins with a song introducing the the Cham culture. Today, the hat tuong orchestra includes cymbals, gongs, drums, tambourines, flutes, and an arsenal of stringed instruments: the *dan nguyet,* a moon-shaped lute; the *dan nhi,* a violin with a high register played by drawing two strings tight over a drum skin; the *thap luc,* a zither-like instrument with 16 strings plucked with the fingers; and the *dan bau,* whose single string, stretched over a long lacquered sound box, is both bowed and plucked to produce a variety of vibrato effects and long resonances of great subtlety. The result is truly exquisite.

Hat tuong originated as a theatre for the

drama's story line. Each player describes his character and role. The stage is nearly empty, except for special props representing the landscape: a branch for a forest, a painted wheel for a cart. The action, always dramatic, is guided by Confucian moral virtues and concepts – for example, loyalty to kings or devotion to parents. The orchestra sits on the stage's side, accompanying not only the singing but also details of the activity and movement on stage. In typical Vietnamese fashion, the hat tuong, although a copy of Chinese drama, was adapted to the Vietnamese character. Women replaced men in the female roles, and the orchestra was enlarged, incorporating Indian influences from elite. It allows criticism and flexibility, but in the end it is still a theatre for the moral and social status quo.

Cai luong, or renovated theatre, made its first appearance in the southern part of Vietnam in 1920. It interprets classical Chinese stories in a more accessible style. Influenced by the European stage, cai luong has evolved into its present spoken-drama form, abandoning the cumbersome epic style in favour of shorter acts, emotional and psychological play, and free dialogue. *(See photo on pages 94–95.)* ❏

ABOVE: bamboo instrument at Hanoi conservatory.
RIGHT: water-puppet performance in Hanoi.

Fluid Movements

The delta of the Song Hong, or Red River, of northern Vietnam is a low-lying plain that would be submerged in water during the rainy season every year if not for a vast series of dikes, the 7,000 km (4,500 miles) of levees that criss-cross the rice paddies and villages. The dikes were first built out of soil 1,000 years ago. Prior to that time, during the Ly dynasty of the 11th century, the Red River would swell each year like clockwork, spill over its banks, and flood much of the region.

communal house. Their techniques were closely guarded secrets. Even now, some elderly water-puppet masters are reluctant to pass on their secrets to younger generations. But the fear that the art will die out completely has persuaded some of the masters to teach apprentices.

Today, there are just a few troupes in Vietnam, with two in Hanoi. Many of the northern provinces have a touring troupe.

A performance usually consists of about 12 acts, each of them telling a mythological story about Vietnam and its history, while traditional musicians provide background music. One story, for example, tells the story of the tortoise that

The annual flooding of the lowlands inspired a form of entertainment to be found only in Vietnam, the water puppets. "The farmers did not know what to do during the flood season, so they created this form of art", explained the artistic director of Hanoi's leading puppetry troupe, which travels the globe exporting this bit of Vietnamese culture.

Water puppetry combines the Vietnamese love for mythology with the fierce nationalistic pride that is encouraged in the country.

The puppeteers stand behind a screen in water up to their waists, controlling the puppets' movements with long bamboo poles. Centuries ago, every village would have a troupe that would perform in a pond in front of the *dinh*, or

lived in Hanoi's Hoan Kiem Lake and supposedly emerged from the depths to provide the good King Ly Thai Tho with the sword he needed to fight off Chinese invaders. Other stories detail village life: the planting and harvesting of the rice crop, fishing, boat races.

Some have suggested that the puppets be mechanised. For one thing, some have argued, they are heavy, at times weighing 20 kg (45 lbs) and requiring up to four people to manoeuvre. For another, the puppets usually can perform just one movement at a time, limiting their repertoire. Directors have toyed with the idea of adding contemporary stories to the repertoire, but of course traditionalists resist changes. ❏

LITERATURE AND ART

The Vietnamese are among the world's most literate and poetic people,
and now their contemporary art is seducing collectors around the world

rt in Vietnamese is *my thuat,* which literally translated means "beauty skill". Vietnam's artists use traditional art to communicate their ideas through the mediums of music, literature, poetry, dance, theatre, painting, sculpture, and even architecture. Although Vietnam is a civilisation some 4,000 years old, the country has no great monument like Cambodia's Angkor Wat.

Many of Vietnam's ancient monuments have fallen prey to the ravages of war and the climate, as well as to neglect. However, despite the destructive forces of both nature and war, nothing has succeeded in destroying the vast legacy of art, crafts, architecture, theatre, music, and the written word.

Literature and poetry

Writers and poets have always occupied a place of high esteem in Vietnamese society. Well acquainted with struggle and hardship over the centuries, Vietnamese find their rich literary heritage a source of comfort, hope and inspiration. A seemingly endless wealth of oral story-telling traditions – consisting of myths, songs, legends, folk and fairy tales – constitutes Vietnam's most ancient literature. Later, as the society developed, scholars, Buddhist monks, kings, and court ministers (many of whom were talented writers and poets) wrote down their thoughts and epics using adopted Chinese characters *(chu nho).* This literature was greatly influenced by Confucian and Buddhist thought.

Even more poems and literary works were undertaken with the advent of *chu nom,* a complicated script based on chu nho. However, the Vietnamese found the romanised alphabet, introduced by foreign missionaries, to be a more accessible means of communicating, rather than the foreboding need to use the thousands of different ideograms in Chinese writing. Vietnamese literature was soon enriched

---

PRECEDING PAGES: "Lucky or Not", by Le Thiet Cuong.
LEFT: "Girl with Banana Leaf," by Nguyen Quan.
RIGHT: calligrapher working on Chinese characters.

with new ideas of Western thought and culture. Indeed, Vietnamese literary prose and poetry was influenced by European literature, which introduced new ways of expressing ideas in novel ways – and, too, reflected the rising sentiment of nationalism.

During the 20th-century wars for Vietnamese

independence from outside powers, northern writers limited themselves mostly to stories meant to unify the people and to inspire the population during difficult times. Communist Party cadres strictly controlled publishing after the end of the Vietnam War in 1975 as well, and even today government censors must approve writings before publication.

However, in recent years control has been loosened somewhat. The publication in the early 1990s of *The Sorrow of War,* by a Vietnamese War veteran from the north under the pseudonym of Bao Ninh *(see photo on next page)*, was the first war novel to confront the gruesome realities of war and the psychological effects upon surviving soldiers. Another writer, Duong Thu Huong, has had her works translated, which include thinly veiled criticism of government and Communist Party officials. For a time, she was expelled from the Communist Party and put under house arrest for crimes against the socialist state.

Today, scribes with reputations for writing critically are presumed to be under close surveillance. Despite the appearance of a new period of openness, Party leaders have warned writers that they must focus on ideas that are of benefit to the nation. As one literary standard-bearer says, "We can write about problems,

development in the long run. "We get rid of a lot of bad writers. Only the good ones can survive", he says. "Now people have other ways to use their creativity. Maybe instead of trying to write, they become good traders or businessmen. That is better for them and better for the country".

Above all else, poetry dominates the Vietnamese arts. The language of Vietnam is a natural tool for poetry, as each of its syllables can be pronounced in six tones to convey six meanings. By simply combining these tones and modulating certain words, a sentence turns into a verse; and plain speech becomes a song.

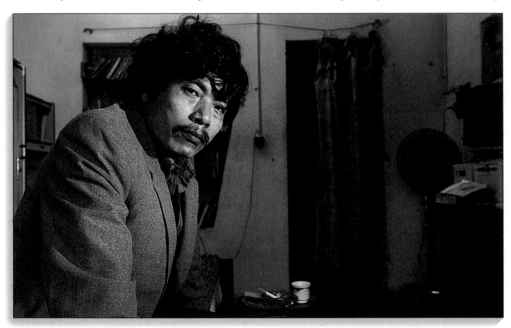

about negative things in society. But we must also finish with optimism". An improved economy and increased contact with the outside world has meant that Vietnamese interest in Vietnamese literature, always intense, has declined somewhat. Today, there is television, translations of foreign works (American writer Sydney Sheldon is popular), and for children, comic books. (Kids are addicted to Japanese *anime*.) Still, it is not unusual to find people reading in their spare time, whether it be a cyclo driver waiting for a customer, a labourer from the country taking a tea break, or students at a cafe.

There are fewer writers nowadays, but a professor of literature thinks this is a positive

Another group of Vietnamese words made up of repeated syllables can cast a discreet shade on the meaning of words, conjuring up a particular colour, movement, attitude, or mood.

Vietnamese poetry falls into two major categories: *ca dao,* a popular folk song, oral in origin but collected and transcribed in written form; and *tho van,* the literary poetry written by kings, scholars, Buddhist monks, mandarins of the court, Daoist recluses, feminists, revolutionaries – even Marxists.

Poetry has become such an important medium of communication in Vietnam that even present-day political slogans must be written in verse to be effective.

The Tale of Kieu

Nearly every Vietnamese reads and remembers a few chapters of a 3,254-verse story published 200 years ago called *The Tale of Kieu*. Pupils begin studying it in the sixth grade. *Kieu* was written by one of Vietnam's most esteemed and respected forefathers, Nguyen Du, and is now considered the cultural window to the soul of the Vietnamese people. One may wonder how *Kieu* came to occupy its special position in Vietnamese literature. Why is the complex tale

Xuan, in northern Vietnam's Ha Tinh Province, Nguyen Du came from an old aristocratic family of mandarins and scholars. His father was prime minister in the royal court of Emperor Le. Nguyen Du grew up in a country, under the nominal rule of the Le dynasty, torn by civil war. When he was 24, the Le dynasty, which his family had faithfully served for generations, was overthrown by the peasant-based Tay Son revolution. After Gia Long, a descendant of the southern Nguyen warlords, defeated the Tay

of a woman's personal misfortunes regarded by a whole people as the perfect expression of their essential nature, of their national soul? After all, the protagonist Kieu, although beautiful and talented, is forced by unfortunate circumstances into selling herself.

Regardless of age, gender, geography, or ideology, all Vietnamese perceive the epic as the heart and mind of their nation. To them, its author, Nguyen Du, is the faithful interpreter of their hopes, and, too, the discreet confidant of their misfortunes. Born in the village of Nghi

Son brothers and was declared emperor, Nguyen Du became an official of several northern provinces, distinguishing himself as an honest and able administrator. In 1806, at the age of 41, he was summoned to the capital of Hue to serve as high chancellor.

Having reunited Vietnam, Gia Long faced the problem of national security, foremost of which meant establishing diplomatic relations with China. All Vietnamese envoys to China were chosen from the cream of Vietnamese *literati,* as it was by intellectual, rather than military, might that Vietnam sought to impress China. So Nguyen Du, already recognised as a great poet, was a natural choice to be emissary.

LEFT: Bao Ninh, author of *The Sorrow of War.*
ABOVE: Temple of Literature gate, Hanoi.

THE TALE OF KIEU

The *Tale of Kieu*, considered by Vietnamese to be reflective of their national character, was adapted from a Chinese Ming-period novel.

Where bamboo covers case
Old manuscripts of countless price
Preserved in fragrant spice,
Sit by a lamp and study well
The story that they tell
How in the dynasty of Ming
When Jia-ching was the king
And all his empire was at rest,
Among those who were blessed
With learning was a man named Vuong.
He had a son, the young
Vuong-Quan, to carry on his name
And literary fame;
And two girls, Thuy-Van and Thuy-Kieu,
Who were as slim as two
Young poplar-trees, as pure as snow.

❖

But Kieu was yet more fair,
The elder's merits took the prize.
Like autumn seas her eyes,
Eyebrows like spring hills far away.
Flowers wished they were as gay;
The aspen shook with envying her.
One glance of Kieu's could stir
Cities or empires to revolt!
Her beauty had no fault,
Nor in her mind was any flaw
She'd write in verse, or draw,
Excel at playing on the lute,
And, choosing tunes to suit,
Compose songs for herself to sing.
One such, so sad a thing
The listeners wept, she called "Cruel Fate".

❖

It's always been the same:
Good fortune seldom came the way
Of those endowed, they say,
With genius and a dainty face,
What tragedies take place
Within each circling space of years!
"Rich in good looks" appears
to mean poor luck and tears of woe;
which may sound strange, I know,
but is not really so, I swear,
since Heaven everywhere
seems jealous of the fair of face.

After five years in China, he returned and devoted most of his time to literary pursuits until his 1820 death at the age of 53. A literary school founded in 1979 to train writers was named after Nguyen Du over the objections of government officials, who preferred to name the school after a war hero.

What makes *Kieu* as relevant today as it was two centuries ago is Nguyen Du's ability and courage to lay bare the whole spectrum of society. Vices and virtues, ugliness and beauty, nobility and trickery – all are entangled in a seemingly hopeless tragic comedy reflecting the true face of Vietnam. *Kieu* also personifies the inherent contradiction faced by the Vietnamese.

"Within the span of a hundred years of human existence, what a bitter struggle is waged between talent and fate", lament the opening lines. And, in the conclusion, Nguyen Du writes, "When one is endowed with talent, do not rely upon it".

Deep in their hearts and behind their gracious modesty, the Vietnamese know they are not lacking in talent, *tai.* At the same time, they do not understand why this tai, which has helped them win independence from formidable foreign invasions and enabled them to develop a respectable culture and civilisation, has failed to bring them lasting peace and enduring prosperity. Unable to solve this paradox, most believe they are *oan,* a word meaning wronged and which appears throughout *Kieu.* Indeed, the epic explores the Buddhist notion of karmic fate and retribution.

The Vietnamese, like Kieu, see themselves as victims who are punished for crimes they are not aware that they have committed. (One might speculate that when the United States bombed Vietnam under the guise of stopping the spread of communism, peasants probably wondered why they, and not Moscow, received the brunt of the firepower.)

Even Vietnamese who fled their country after the war ended in the 1970s turn to the woes of Kieu for comfort, especially in the cultural isolation of a new land and language. Huynh Sanh Thong, a Vietnamese scholar at Yale University who translated *Kieu* into English, wrote in his introduction that immigrants "know most of its lines by heart, and when they recite them out loud, they speak their mother tongue at its finest. To the extent that the poem implies something at the core of the Vietnamese experience, it addresses [Vietnamese people] intimately as victims, as refu-gees, as survivors".

Art

After being the subject of countless war movies, Vietnam has found a certain peace in the pleasures of a different kind of artistic expression: painting. Upon arriving in Vietnam one of the first things a traveller may be surprised to discover is the country's vigorous contemporary art scene.

Much of the work creating this international acclaim shares a gentle, lyrical quality – rarely is any self-indulgent anger expressed – while styles explored range from figurative to abstract and surrealist, at other times expressionist or realist. The abundance of this impressionist and figurative art in Vietnam is testament to the tenacious influence a foreign cultural heritage has on a country. While China, Japan, and Korea share long painting histories, Vietnam's painting tradition emerged entirely from the French colonial

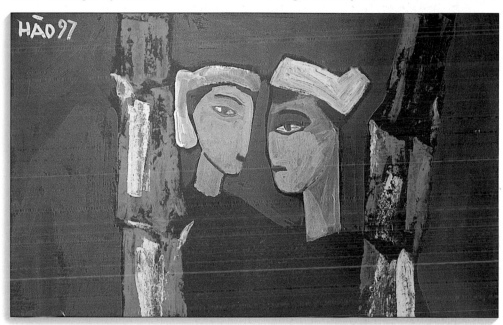

Away from well-trodden tourist streets, a dozen galleries are beginning to showcase the works of a small legion of talented artists who dedicate their life to the single-minded pursuit of artistic excellence. After decades of obscurity and isolation, these artists are making inroads into the international arena, with well-attended – and well-received – exhibitions in Australia, Denmark, France, Germany, Great Britain, the Netherlands, Sweden, the US, Hong Kong, Japan, and Singapore. The most acclaimed artists' works fetch prices up to US$50,000.

imposition dating from the 19th century. Prior to this time, Vietnam's artistic achievements had been restricted to decorative arts for religious and communal purposes, with only a limited output of paintings, coloured embossments, and portraits on silk.

In spite of the largely destructive arrival of the French, new opportunities for creative achievement arose during the colonial period, with painting becoming the most developed artistic expression. Through this Western influx a unique French-Vietnamese amalgamation of cultures emerged, identifiable by four distinct periods: the first extending until 1925; the second from 1925 to 1945; the third

ABOVE: "Bamboo", by northern Vietnamese artist Truong Dinh Hao.

from 1945 to 1980; and the last from 1980 until the present. The first period was notable for producing a small handful of Confucian scholars who would become the first European-educated painters.

In 1925, under the initiative of the French painter Victor Tardieu, the Ecole des Beaux-Arts de l'Indochine (EBAI) was founded in Hanoi. Through its 18 courses of study offered over just 20 years, 128 painters and sculptors were taught in the European tradition.

MIXED COLOURS

Early works had a blend of culture and education in their European compositions completed in oil, while simultaneously retaining the quiet Vietnamese spirituality.

locally styled impressionism that is injected with nationalist sentiments.

While the influence of these first graduates was felt in the 1930s, the artistic influence of the last group of notable graduates – Bui Xuan Phai, Nguyen Sang, and Nguyen Tu Nghiem – was not felt until the 1960s and 1970s.

Sang set about elevating the stature of the ordinary people through his skilful European-styled oil and lacquer portraits, which featured elements of folk paintings. On the other hand, Phai,

The school was responsible for creating the "first generation" of Vietnamese masters, most notable of whom were Nguyen Gia Tri, Nguyen Phan Chanh, To Ngoc Van, Bui Xuan Phai, Nguyen Sang, and Nguyen Tu Nghiem. While Nguyen Gia Tri's works continue to generate acclaim for transforming the traditional decorative art form of lacquer to an Art Nouveau style depicting Vietnamese subjects and atmosphere, Nguyen Phan Chanh became renowned for his silk paintings of women, which are expressed using his own form of Asian expression. To Ngoc Van, on the other hand, is attributed with using French impressionism, realism, and romanticism to create a

Vietnam's most internationally renowned artist, left an enormous legacy of beautiful and sentimental works depicting Hanoi street scenes and humble subject matter. Nghiem has gained great credit for de-academising the painting language and for generating a return to a national art by integrating old traditions into modern painting.

While not all of the above artists shared the same vision or produced the same style of painting, each shared a desire to champion a European modernism while remaining true to their Vietnamese spirit and heritage. Through their innovative use of traditional materials and their depiction of domestic themes in warm colours, all of these artists can be accredited with freeing Vietnamese painting from its colonial academism.

These philosophies were then passed onto their students at the Hanoi College of Fine Arts – the EBAI's successor – and the College of Applied Arts in Hanoi. The result today? Every Vietnamese painter has roots, in some way, instilled in the traditional European school of painting. Through this method of art education, somewhere between the French school and Asian aesthetic idea, Vietnamese art has emerged as something very unusual and absolutely unique in Asia.

munity. Nearly everything from nudes to abstraction, even impressionism, was banned.

Meanwhile, in the north, artists influenced by the increasingly close relationship with Socialist Realist art of the Soviet Union, Eastern Europe, and China (prior to the 1970s) found themselves confined and bound to recording the solidarity of the large social movement. As such, this style of painting of politics, soldiers, and labourers has gained its own level of importance as a valuable witness to this complicated period of Vietnam's history. Creatively, however, it was fiercely criticised after 1975.

While artists from the first two periods used their European technique to give shape and expression to their Vietnamese soul, after 1945 artists from the cities of Hanoi, Saigon, and Hue developed their own particular styles. Isolated through partition and continual war, artists in the south had few opportunities to witness directly the artistic heritage of the north and instead were increasingly exposed to the artistic trends of Europe and America. Despite always being more open to foreign and artistic influence, the war tore apart the artistic com-

It was not until 1986, when *đổi mới* (the policy of economic "renovation") began, that the artistic climate throughout the country began to flourish once again. With openness in economic and cultural intercourse and with the overall renovation in the political, economic, and social fields, Vietnamese art began to undergo dramatic changes with exhibitions and paintings being sold. Nowhere was this rebirth better captured than in the 1991 exhibition *Uncorked Soul,* organised by Plum Blossoms Gallery in Hong Kong in the first full-scale, post-war show of Vietnamese contemporary art outside of Vietnam. The exhibition not only introduced a span of

LEFT: Tran Van Thao, and Buu Chi's "The Testament".
ABOVE: hill-tribe women, watercolour on silk.

Vietnamese art to the rest of Asia but highlighted the difficulties faced by artists during Ho Chi Minh's repression of the Aesthetic Humanism movement from the mid-1950s until the mid-1980s. (The Aesthetic Humanism movement was short-lived, from 1955–57, and sought cultural democratisation and political reform, led by intellectuals.)

Since then, the Vietnamese art scene has not looked back. While an indisputable wave of crass, commercialised art has infested the tourist market, over a dozen exciting young artists have emerged who are showcasing Vietnamese art to the international art world.

Subtle experience

Looking back at the fertile soil of their traditions and realities, and with wounds still raw from their suffering and solitude, Vietnamese artists have much to discuss and share with an increasingly receptive audience.

Surprisingly, however, despite its decades of destructive influence on the country, war is rarely portrayed directly in Vietnamese art. Instead, there are reflections on the pain and sorrow caused by armed conflict.

Similarly, the bitterness, anger, angst, and inhumanity of war are not depicted. Instead, Vietnamese canvases are predominantly filled

With an increased individuality of artistic expression and greater contact and receptivity to international art currents – from the Paris school to native art, surrealism, abstraction, and the latest artistic currents in Asia, Europe, and America – the world is seeing an increasing spectrum of images, motifs, and methods being used.

This fourth and fifth generation of artists, who were educated after 1975, are now free from the constraints of a social or political agenda and enjoying artistic freedom. They are interested in portraying something more interesting, and so are representing more personal freedom.

with soulful characters in a variety of warm, soft shades depicted in smooth, sensuous, expressive lines, hinting at the more recent influence of Buddhism across the country. Portraying the beautiful is very important to the artists, who respect this attribute and as such don't like to portray the violent, the strange, or the suffering.

Receiving international notoriety are the "Gang of Five" and "Five New Faces". These two groups of five artists are products of the same Hanoi College of Fine Arts class, 1987–90. The haunting yet sensuous and soulful works of Tran Quoc Tuan, Dinh Quan, Pham Ngoc Minh, Tran Quang Huy, and

Nguyen Quoc Hoi have gained recognition not only for their fresh style but also the international quality of their contemporary works.

The Gang of Five's first exhibition in 1990 brought Dang Xuan Hoa, Hong Viet Dung, Ha Tri Hieu, Tran Luong, and Pham Quang Vinh acclaim for their affinity at portraying everyday life by striving to wed tradition with modernity. Bold, fresh, and full of vitality and self-expression, each work is distinctive for the artist's idiosyncrasies. Despite the fact they don't exhibit together anymore, they have garnered enormous attention all over the region and are regarded as the most promising of the

against the French and in the first years after partition in the mid-1950s. The third generation graduated from art schools or were self taught during the "American" 1960s and 1970s. It consists of dynamic artists such as Trinh Cung, abstract artist Nguyen Trung, metaphorical surrealist Nguyen Quan, and the achingly melancholic works of Buu Chi, one of the country's most haunted artists.

Such sensibilities may be the reason Vietnamese art is attracting the eyes of international buyers, who now pay prices that were unthinkable 10 years ago. Prices have shot up very quickly, with a gouache painting on paper by

new generation of artists. Other exciting artists to have emerged in recent years include Truong Dinh Hao, Van Ngoc, Hoang Hong Cam, abstract artist Tran Van Thao, Nguyen Thanh Chuong, Le Thiet Cuong, Do Quang Em and Le Quang Ha, each of whom bears his or her own unique style.

Already highly regarded and well established in the history books are the second-generation artists such as Tran Luu Hau, Le Cong Than, and Viet Hai, who trained at the Hanoi College of Fine Arts during the war

LEFT: "Bathing", a gouache by Van Ngoc.
ABOVE: gallery staff in Ho Chi Minh City.

GUARDED AESTHETICS

With Vietnamese artists now in the international art market, authorities are ever careful to oversee foreigners' perceptions of the country. Paintings with political overtones and opinions opposing the government's ideals are potential firecrackers, such as the works of Truong Tan. Blatantly depicting his own individual sexuality by confronting traditional family values and traditional hierarchy, his graphic works of irony are often hidden from public viewing. Eighteen of Truong's paintings were confiscated by the Ministry of Interior during an exhibition in 1995, an intervention not seen for 10 years. Generally, however, Vietnamese artists simply avoid such subjects.

one of the "old masters" now selling in Vietnam for US$4,000, as opposed to US$200 a decade or so ago. While this phenomenon comes as no surprise to those in the industry, particularly the artists who have long been patiently waiting for recognition, to buy Vietnamese art solely for investment purposes is a risky speculative game, especially with faultless imitations of the older masters quite common on the open market.

This growing internationalisation can be credited with providing an international influence that is helping produce better quality, more mature works – not to mention the financial rewards that enable better working conditions, more motivation, and larger budgets to experiment with styles and techniques – the globalisation of the Vietnamese art market has created many negative changes as well.

With the influence of so many foreign cultures in Vietnam, it is not easy for the younger artists to remain true to their vision and their traditional style. As a result, the strong works they were producing some years ago are now coming under constant threat from being commercially "produced". Choosing which path to follow and developing their own style is an increasingly difficult challenge.

CONTEMPORARY GALLERIES

The best way to ensure your purchase is a genuine original painting by the artist being proposed is to purchase from reputable galleries. Hanoi boasts Red River Gallery (or Galerie Fleuve Rouge), a modern, well-lit gallery with large contemporary paintings. Tran Phuong Mai, the daughter of influential Hanoi poet, translator, and art critic/patron Duong Tuong Duong, opened Mai Gallery in 1993 in her parents' home using contacts she'd made through her father and her artist friends. They promote artists who have already achieved recognition as well as promising young painters who are still subject to controversy. Also in Hanoi is the tiny hole-in-the-wall gallery-atelier Salon Natasha. The workplace of self-trained Vietnamese artist Vu Dau Tau, the bohemian gallery is a popular meeting place with artists, who chat with the artist and his Russian wife.

Down in Ho Chi Minh City, Gallery Saigon gained notoriety as the first modern, Western gallery in the city and for being the first custom-built art gallery in Vietnam when it opened in 1995. It represents about 30 new and established artists from Hanoi and Ho Chi Minh, many of whom meet daily at the gallery, located within the grounds of the Museum of Ton Duc Thang. Others are Gallery Vietnam, on Dong Khoi, and Blue Space Contemporary Art Centre within the Fine Art Museum on Le Thi Hong Gam.

However, with 200 exhibitions a year, 300 art galleries nationwide, and over 1,500 arts association members, the best artists are also working even harder to pull themselves above the market's glut. In doing so, it is hoped the flooded market will correct itself and price inflation will go down. The best artists, though they use Western language and technique, still have their Asian soul and work full-time as professional artists, living proudly and with respect from society for their art.

> **COMPLEX AESTHETICS**
>
> The works of Vietnam's artists are becoming less homogeneous and more complex and experimental, ensuring their future in Asia's vibrant art scene.

examples of woodcuts are the Tranh Long Ho Dong paintings. This art form – which is known as Ho village painting – existed from as early as the 11th century during the Ly dynasty. At first it was limited to black-and-white prints of the woodcuts, but after the 15th century, colour was introduced.

In accordance with the craft tradition, whole villages were given solely over to block printing. Many families in Dong Ho village, located in Bach Ninh Province north of Hanoi, are collectively

Despite the financial temptations, the dedicated artists are constantly searching and injecting new styles and forms into Vietnam's contemporary art.

Crafts

Vietnamese folk art and crafts had gone into decline with the onset of French colonisation at the end of the 19th century. By the end of the 20th century, however, efforts were thriving to revive both. Two successful examples are woodcuts and lacquerware. The best

LEFT: studio producing fakes of famous paintings.
ABOVE: fine detail of inlaid lacquer work.

engaged in producing coloured prints of traditional themes.

The village craftsmen make their own paper and natural colours, and they prepare the blocks in variations of classic models depicting good luck signs, historical figures and battles, spirits, popular allegories, and social commentary.

Good fortune is symbolised by a corpulent pig decorated with garlands, often accompanied by a litter of suckling piglets. A hen surrounded by chicks symbolises prosperity. The cockerel, herald of the dawn, is the symbol of peace and courage. Social criticism is expressed by caricatures of mandarins, represented by croaking frogs and rats marching with drums and trumpets. Warriors are shown together with apes, tigers, and other animal spirits, all in splendid colours, with humour and optimism ridiculing the corrupt and powerful.

Objects made of lacquered wood have been found in tombs dating from the 3rd and 4th centuries. Today, lacquer *(son mai)* work – including paintings, screens, boxes, vases, trays, and chessboards – are fast becoming a main export item. Their quality is a result of the meticulous attention given to the preparation of the lacquer and to the designs of a thousand-year-old tradition.

Two types of lacquer are used. Varnish lac-

quer is obtained by mixing lacquer resin with *mu* oil, while pumice lacquer, a higher-quality and more durable lacquer, is produced by mixing lacquer resin with pine resin. Unlike varnish lacquer, pumice lacquer is rubbed and smoothed in water after painting to bring out a gloss finish.

Lacquer is prepared from the resin of the *cay son,* or lacquer tree, which is collected in the same way as latex. After being stored for a while, the resin is diluted with water and then the dark-brown surface layer known as *oil lac* is skimmed off. With the addition of various ingredients, this is used for the upper layer of lacquer paintings.

This high-quality lacquer is poured into a bamboo or wooden vessel and stirred vigorously with a wooden pestle for eight to ten hours. (If stirred in a plastic or iron vessel, the lacquer turns black.) A small amount of colophony, a resin, is added to render it more elastic and suitable for polishing. Normal paint added to lacquer will also produce a black or grey colour.

Special paints are needed for lacquer pictures: cinnabar for various hues of red; pure gold or silver applied as thin sheets or strips; blue gouache; several kinds of aniline dyes that produce carmine red or green; and the yellow dye obtained from the seeds of hydrangeas. Eggshell fragments yield the purest white colour, while fragments of mother-of-pearl, mollusc, and snail shell produce blue or violet.

Lacquer artists painstakingly select and prepare the boards for their pictures. These must be smooth, dry, and free of the smallest crack, scratch, or imperfection before they are coated with several layers of lacquer. This is followed by a thin layer of cotton fabric or silk, followed by another layer of lacquer.

The board is then left in a damp place for two or three days until dry, then coated with another layer of lacquer, a layer of lacquer putty, sawdust, and kaolin, which render the board uniformly smooth.

The dried surface is rubbed with wet pumice before another two to four layers of lacquer are applied and left to dry for several days between coats, then painstakingly rubbed for hours. Only after all this preparation is the board ready for painting.

If the artist uses egg or mollusc shells, he cuts the image in the upper layers of lacquer covering the fabric, smears the depression with black lacquer, which acts as a glue, and then taps the shell into position with a tiny hammer. More lacquer is applied, then tinted with the desired dye.

When this is quite dry, the picture is rubbed down thoroughly to bring out the texture of the shell with its numerous tiny cracks. The craftsman will continue rubbing the picture with the palm of his hand until the contours become outlined and the lacquer acquires transparency and sheen. ❑

LEFT: detail of temple's carving in wood.
RIGHT: page from Latin-Annamese religious text.

Language

In the Vietnamese language, the word for natural disaster is *thien tai,* from Chinese. The word for cheese is *pho mat,* from the French *fromage.* There are sounds and words from English and Russian too. Thousands of words in contemporary Vietnamese – as much as 70 percent of the language – come from Chinese, a reflection of the centuries of non-too-harmonious relations between Vietnam and its massive neighbour to the north, including the influence of Chinese literature.

There is the touch of French with words that entered the lexicon first during the colonial period of the 18th and 19th centuries, and later well into the 20th century. A dab of English was left by the Americans during the Vietnam War, and subsequent years of fraternisation with the former Soviet Union introduced Russian. In fact, expressions and nomenclature indicating 20th-century technology and ideas are often expressed with French, English, and Russian words. The newest foreign linguistic invasion – that of consumer marketers – is represented by Japanese. The word most commonly used to refer to a two-wheeled motorised vehicle, for example, is *honda.*

Variations: Distinct dialects within Vietnam reveal strong regional identities. Often northerners and southerners confess they cannot understand each other. Foreigners might need two translators, one to translate the foreign language into Vietnamese, another to translate the Vietnamese into another dialect. Some letters of the alphabet are pronounced differently, and the vocabularies of northerners and southerners contain distinct words. Even the syntax is different. In addition to Vietnamese, the country's many ethnic minorities speak their own distinct languages and dialects. In the Mekong Delta, for example, so many people speak the Khmer of Cambodia that local television has a Khmer-language broadcast.

Yet the country does share one language, a blend of several languages – ancient and modern – that has evolved through Vietnam's contact with other cultures. Its roots, while still debated, come from a mixture of the Austro-Asiatic, the Austronesian and Sino-Tibetan language families.

Written Vietnamese: Chinese influence during the first centuries of Vietnam's history led to the extensive use of Chinese characters, *chu nho,* which replaced an ancient written script of Indian origin, preserved and used today only by the Muong minority.

After independence in the 10th century, scholars realised the necessity and advantages of developing a separate written Vietnamese language. Several tentative attempts were made to modify the characters of Chinese, but it was a 13th-century poet, Nguyen Thuyen, who first wrote extensively in *chu nom.* The golden age of literature during the 18th century was the age of *truyen* or long narrative poems as well as satirical stories, feminist poems, encyclopedias and historical works.

Although standardised for popular literature, *chu nom* never received recognition, and most writers continued using the more complicated Chinese calligraphy. Today, however, Vietnam has a romanised

alphabet, thanks to a French Jesuit missionary, Alexandre de Rhodes, who developed a script, *quoc ngu,* in 1651. Quoc ngu was, at first, used only by the Catholic Church and the colonial administration, gaining widespread popularity only in the early part of the 20th century. The study of quoc ngu became compulsory in secondary schools in 1906, and two years later, the royal court in Hue ordered a new curriculum entirely in quoc ngu. It became the national written language in 1919.

Now, only scholars use the traditional calligraphic chu nom to decipher ancient carvings and writings. And during holidays, such as the lunar new year (*Tet*), people buy scrolls written in Chinese characters for their homes. ❑

VIETNAMESE TEMPLES AND PAGODAS

Pagodas and temples reflect the cultural diversity of religious practice in Vietnam and are a focus of social, political and religious life

Each Vietnamese village has its own complex of temple buildings, including the *dinh* (communal house), where the village founder is venerated and the village council, an assembly of male leaders, traditionally met to debate local affairs.

The *chua* or pagoda is regarded as an important social centre for women, while the *den* and *mieu* are shrines to the ancestors of individual families. Vietnamese religious practice is eclectic, and this is reflected in the layout of the temple buildings. Large temple complexes may also include a *phuong dinh* (front hall); *ngoai cung* (central hall); a *noi cung* or main altar hall; and a *cay tien huong*, which acts as a gate to the main temple complex. The choice of temple gods also varies from one village to the next. In some temples, statues of Confucius sit alongside Daoist or Buddhist images. In the north, it is common to find Vietnam war heroes joining the statue line up. More than one dinh offers the chance to burn joss sticks before a life-size statue of Ho Chi Minh.

After 1945, religious activity was discouraged but since the 1980s there has been a revival and many Vietnamese have donated money towards temple renovations in their villages.

△ **LILY PONDS**
Water is an important design element of pagodas and lily flowers, symbolic of peace, enhance reflection.

▷ **SWASTIKAS**
The reversed swastika is an ancient Buddhist icon symbolising harmony.

▷ **CEREMONIAL BELLS**
Bronze bells bear Chinese inscriptions paying homage to the donor and describing village and temple history.

◁ **CHUA MOT COT**
First built in wood in 1049, Ha Noi's Chua Mot Cot (One Pillar Pagoda) was destroyed in 1954 and has since been rebuilt in sturdy concrete.

△ **GUARDIAN SOLDIERS**
Every temple gate has its *quan bao ve* or guardian soldiers, one malevolent and one benevolent, as pictured here at the Thien Mu pagoda in Hue.

▷ **BUDDHIST PRAYERS**
Worshippers attend services at the pagoda on the evenings of the 14th and 30th days of the lunar month to repent for wrongs and vow to act in the right way.

▽ **CHINESE ARCHITECTURE**
Chinese influence on Vietnam's culture is reflected in temple architecture and Chinese characters are common features of religious buildings

▷ **MONASTIC WELCOME**
Monks and nuns, dressed in simple white or brown tunics, welcome visiting worshippers and are happy to sit over a cup of green tea, explaining in detail the history and the imagery of their pagoda.

THE IMPORTANCE OF INCENSE

Worship in pagodas is informal, as people come and go, chat to the monks, drink tea, and present offerings. But no one visits a pagoda without burning incense. On festival days, packets of joss sticks can be bought outside the pagoda building. One may burn the whole packet or a small number of sticks, depending on the occasion. But the number burned must be an odd number – it is taboo to burn an even number of sticks.

After lighting the incense, worshippers stand in contemplation before the altar for a few moments. They then make respectful bowing movements before placing the burning sticks in a small urn filled with fragrant ash. The rising smoke symbolises communication with the other world. It allows people to maintain contact with ancestors or present wishes to one of the many gods in the Vietnamese religious pantheon.

A FLAVOURFUL CUISINE

Much as the country has been divided by politics and culture, so too is Vietnam's uncommonly healthy cuisine distinctive in its latitudinal differences

For the sociable Vietnamese, a well-stocked dining table is an important symbol of one's hospitality, and visitors to any home, from Can Tho in the Mekong Delta to Hanoi in the north, will be overwhelmed with generosity from the kitchen pantry. Even in the poorest villages where people subsist mainly on rice, people will scrape together whatever they have to give to their guests.

The cuisine itself varies greatly by region. Even dishes that are staples throughout Vietnam are prepared differently in the north, centre, and south. Vietnam's cuisine is like much of its culture in reflecting its many contacts with other cultures over the centuries – Chinese, Khmer, and French the most notable.

Rice (*com* in Vietnamese) is the staple of the diet and the basis of the country's agriculture. In fact, the changing fortunes in rice production reflect quite a bit about Vietnam's economy. In the early 1980s, Vietnam relied on imports to feed its people, as a result, entire provinces of people were starving.

Today, rid of its collectivised farms, Vietnam is now the third-largest rice exporter in the world – despite persistent fears that the country will run out of rice, which frequently causes the government to halt exports and impose quotas. Any Vietnamese over the age of 25 well remembers standing in long queues for rations of meat, and then stretching a monthly rice allotment to its limit.

The years of Chinese influence and occupation are evident in the use of chopsticks and the tendency to eat plain white rice separately with other foods rather than mixing them together.

On every table

Ubiquitous in Vietnamese cooking is the use of a fish sauce called *nuoc mam*. Set on every table like salt in Western countries or soy sauce in China, nuoc mam is used as an ingredient in many dishes, but it is also combined with other ingredients as a condiment called *nuoc cham*. Every cook has his or her own formula, but usually this dipping sauce consists of chilli, lime juice, garlic, sugar, and pepper and is used for a variety of snack-type foods. The fish sauce has something of a pungent

aroma and flavour that can take some getting used to, but it is nonetheless a complement to the subtle flavours of the food. Manufactured in coastal cities such as Phan Thiet and Phu Quoc, the fish sauce is made by fermenting anchovies and salt in large wooden barrels for about six months.

Vietnamese cooks use many fresh herbs – lemon grass, basil, coriander, mint, parsley, laksa leaf – as well as garlic, lime, and ginger. These ingredients lend the cuisine a subtlety of flavour that sets it apart from its neighbours.

French influence brought with it the *pâté* and baguettes sold in the markets and roadside stalls, and an appreciation of French food

PRECEDING PAGES: shrimp spring rolls, or *goi cuon*.
LEFT: fresh, local seafood in Ha Long, east of Hanoi.
RIGHT: Vietnamese food is focused on fresh foods.

shared by visitors and locals alike in the Vietnamese-run French restaurants.

The 3,000 km (1,800 miles) of Vietnam's coastline, innumerable rivers and waterways provide an ample and varied supply of fresh fish and seafood year-round. Fresh- and saltwater fish, shellfish, and crustaceans are eaten as the main source of protein in delicious dishes such as *cha ca*, a barbecued fish made in Hanoi, and in minced fish-meat cakes.

The Vietnamese have created very innovative dishes with pork, chicken, and beef, sometimes combining meat together with fish and seafood. Whether boiled, barbecued, grilled, stewed, or fried, the dishes are a delicious blend of flavours, textures, and influences.

A culinary primer

Here is a primer on some of the Vietnamese specialities visitors will likely encounter.

Cha gio (called *nem Saigon* in the north): small rolls of minced pork, prawn, crab meat, fragrant mushrooms, and vegetables wrapped in thin rice paper and deep fried until crisp. Cha gio is rolled in a lettuce leaf with fresh herbs and dipped in nuoc cham. It makes a thoroughly satisfying meal.

Cha lua: Wrapped in banana leaves before

CULINARY DIVIDES

Variations of taste and spice in Vietnamese food are quite distinctive, even if dishes are the same. Food in the north tends to be more bland, using fewer spices, herbs, and heaps of MSG. In the central part of the country, the food is quite hot but also boasts creative vegetarian cooking, particularly in Hue, where there are many Buddhists who follow a meatless diet. Southern cooking, familiar to Westerners who have eaten in Vietnamese restaurants in the West, tends to be more flavourful and creative than that of the north.

Many northerners complain they cannot eat southern food, claiming that the southern cooks dump sugar into everything. Sugar is used in dishes such as *pho*, but not in great amounts. In general, southern food isn't sweeter – though coconut milk is often used – just more flavourful.

Southerners, too, don't care for northern food. The south has one essential advantage that diners cannot help but notice: better access to fresh fruits and vegetables – a wider variety of food is grown in the south and the growing seasons are longer. Tropical fruits and vegetables can be hard to find in the north and are often of poor quality. Many southern delicacies are served with raw, leafy vegetables, bean sprouts, and herbs, wrapped up in a do-it-yourself manner probably indigenous to the area.

cooking, this pork pate is served as a snack and on French bread for lunch.

Chao tom: A Hanoi speciality, this unusual appetiser is ground shrimp baked on sugar cane. The shrimp is removed from the sugar cane and rolled in rice paper with lettuce, cucumber, coriander (cilantro) and mint, and then everything is dipped in the obligatory fish sauce.

Cuon diep: Shrimp, noodles, mint, coriander and pork wrapped in lettuce leaves.

Goi ga: Similar to a chicken salad, goi ga is

NOODLE TEMPTRESS

If there is a dish that defines Vietnam, it is a simple broth of rice noodles called *pho*, sometimes referred to as the mistress of Vietnamese cuisine.

Mien ga: Another type of noodle dish, most popular in the south, mien ga is a soup of chicken, coriander, fish sauce, and scallions.

Banh cuon: A steamed rice pancake that is rolled around minced pork.

Canh chua: A sour soup by which Vietnamese cooks are judged. Often served with shrimp or fish head, the soup is a fragrant blend of sweet and tangy flavours, using tomato, pineapple, star fruit, bean sprouts, fried onion, bamboo shoots, coriander, cinnamon, and, of course, fish sauce.

shredded chicken marinated in onion, vinegar, mint, and, sometimes, peanuts.

Ga xao sa ot: Sauteed chicken cooked with lemon grass, fish sauce, garlic, onion, and chillis. Sometimes peanuts are added.

Bun bo: A Hue speciality, bun bo is fried beef, served over noodles with coriander, onion, garlic, cucumber, chillis and tomato paste.

Hu tieu: Also called Saigon soup, hu tieu is chicken, beef, pork, and shrimp served with a broth over rice noodles, with crab meat, peanuts, onion and garlic.

Banh khoai: Called the Hue pancake, banh khoai is a speciality of that area and is something of an omelette. A batter of rice- and corn-flour is fried with egg to make a pancake that is wrapped around pork or shrimp, onion, bean sprouts and mushrooms.

Pho, the noodle mistress

Vietnamese usually eat rice with their meals at home, three times a day. But when they go out, they often eat pho. Vietnamese use foods as a euphemism for their relationships. When you tire of rice (your wife or husband), you take pho (a lover). This analogy suggests a racy — if not spicy — connotation to what is really a

LEFT: central cuisine representative of Hoi An.
ABOVE: *pho*, a traditional and popular noodle soup.

simple food. Pronounced *foh,* the soup typically is eaten for breakfast or for a late-night snack, although many people take pho for lunch and dinner, as well.

While the number and variety of restaurants in Vietnam have grown dramatically in recent years, the ubiquitous pho stall is still one of the most popular kinds of eateries. On nearly every street, someone is selling pho – a broth of rice noodles topped with chicken or beef, fresh herbs, and onion. Sometimes, a raw egg yolk is added, and some pho aficionados like to add lime juice, hot peppers, or vinegar. It is usually served with *quay* – a fried piece of flour dough.

There are indoor pho shops with tables and wooden benches, stalls with tiny stools on the sidewalk, and vendors who carry pho in pots strapped to bamboo poles. None of them have menus or tablecloths or serve anything but pho. The floors are often dirty, the walls streaked with mildew. But the pho is always steaming hot and filling.

Pho is most popular in Hanoi, although it is widely eaten in Ho Chi Minh City and the other major cities as well. It is not consumed as much in the countryside, however, for it is somewhat of a luxury.

In fact, before the country began reforming its economy in the mid-1980s, food distribu-tion was controlled by the government. Private enterprise was frowned upon and independent pho stalls were illegal, as pho was considered contraband. Often vendors would hide their shops in the backs of their houses and sell pho only to knowing customers. Police often raided the joints and confiscated the pho pots, chop-ping blocks and soup bowls.

Today, the shops are everywhere, and the best places have customers queuing up in long lines for their morning pho.

Typically, a pho shop sells either chicken or beef – not both. Pho is one of several kinds of noodles Vietnamese eat. *Bun,* usually served with beef, is not a soup but dry noodles. *My,* more common in the south, is a wheat noodle eaten like pho. *Mien* is similar to pho but eaten dry. Pho, however, is the most common. The recipe is fairly standard, although cooks do add their own variations. One pho chef in Hanoi, a woman in her sixties who has a prosperous business selling 1,000 bowls of beef pho every-day, said she cooks the ingredients "until I feel they are ready".

The chef oversees every aspect of the busi-ness, which means she has little time to sleep. She cooks from midnight into the early morn-ing, serves pho until early afternoon, and then heads to the market to purchase ingredients for the next day's pho.

She begins her day at midnight, putting on a large pot of water to boil with beef bones and pork bones. She adds fish sauce (used in almost all Vietnamese cooking), ginger, onion and star anise, and then lets the pot simmer for about five hours. "The secret", she says, "is boiling lots of beef and bones".

To serve pho, she takes a bowl, drops in some rice noodles, tops them with beef – raw or cooked, depending on the customer's taste – and pours broth over it. Then she adds some chopped onions, mint, basil, and pepper. Pho – like much of Vietnamese food, especially in the north – uses MSG, though customers wary of eating the additive can ask to have it left out. Often cooks ladle on a large amount of fat. To have that omitted from a serving, customers request *khong beo.* Pho is best, the cook con-fesses, in the late afternoon or evening, after the broth has simmered the longest. ❑

LEFT: busy roadside stalls are popular.
RIGHT: drying Chinese vermicelli in the Mekong Delta.

PLACES

A detailed guide to the entire country, with principal sites clearly cross-referenced by number to the maps

Travel in Vietnam is anything but easy. After decades of war and with an economy that was subsequently throttled, the country's infrastructure – or lack of it – and pesky vendors at popular sights can test the most hardened traveller's patience. But Vietnam is truly one of those destinations where the inconveniences pale beside the remarkable, and where the beauty of its culture seduces all.

One expects to find the remnants of a war-shattered country, even after nearly three decades of peace, and indeed, one sometimes does. But the residue of war, in an odd irony, is now part of the country's tourism pull, whether for the Cu Chi tunnels outside of the former Saigon or the rusting heaps at a Hanoi war museum. But the war is history, and beyond the memories of war the bright tropical sun illuminates a coastline of serene, white-sand beaches and clear, blue waters, and mists veil forested mountains alive with exotic animals.

Northern Vietnam is anchored by Hanoi, an ancient city established nearly 1,000 years ago. This political capital clings to the rhetoric of a socialist system while at the same time embracing a government-controlled capitalism. The old villas and facades of the French colonial era give the city an ambience not found anywhere else in Asia.

Beyond Hanoi, the provinces of the vast Song Hong, or Red River, delta reflect the traditional agricultural culture upon which the economy is based. And beyond the delta's plains, the cooler mountain regions, populated by hill tribes, ascend towards the west and Laos and northward towards China.

Southwards, following the historical movement of the Viet people, the traveller finds a chain of coastal provinces washed by the South China Sea. In the old imperial city of Hue, an overwhelming sense of the past pervades the older streets. The antiquities don't end here. In the lands of the ancient kingdom of Champa further south are decaying sanctuaries, temples, and towers that testify to the conquest by the Viet people from the north.

Then there is the city of Ho Chi Minh. Often still called Saigon, it is reviving its long-time image as the clichéd hustling-and-bustling city of people on the make and on the go. Where Hanoi is quiet, Ho Chi Minh is frenetic. Where Hue has a subtle and refined beauty, Ho Chi Minh grabs by the lapels and shakes. If Hanoi is a city of earth tones, Ho Chi Minh is neon, all lit up in gaudy lights.

The country has moved far beyond a century of foreign domination and war, and the traveller will find that Vietnam is a land of the ascending dragon and a place finally at peace. ❑

PRECEDING PAGES: early morning voyage in Vinh Ha Long, east of Hanoi; Khai Ninh's tomb, one of many in Hue; activity outside Ho Chi Minh City's colonial General Post Office. **LEFT:** tomb of Emperor Tu Duc, in Hue.

Vietnam

(*SOUTH CHINA SEA*)

NORTHERN VIETNAM

The northern provinces of Vietnam are fed by the Song Hong,
anchored by the city of Hanoi, and inhabited by hill tribes

A journey through northern Vietnam begins in today's political and administrative capital of Hanoi, once the ancient capital of Thang Long. Visitors to Hanoi will encounter the cultures of both East and West, with the changing fortunes of history reflected in the architecture of its many traditional temples and pagodas, in the lingering presence of a French colonial past, and in the whir of construction as the city's blossoming modern towers rise above it all.

Beyond Hanoi and its populous suburbs are the picturesque provincial regions, with their chequerboard paddy fields of rice, the nation's agricultural staple and export earner and nourished by the delta of the Song Hong, or Red River. Green belts of trees and bamboo enclose the villages, where traditional communal houses, pagodas, and temples remain hidden from view.

Men, women, children, and buffalo toil together in the fields, seven days a week, and in all weather. The scene is one of tranquil beauty, but the hardship and toll of this life is obvious.

On the coast to the east, touching Vinh Bac Bo, or the Gulf of Tonkin, is the busy port of Hai Phong, the country's third-largest city and boasting Vietnam's first casino. Nearby, junks sail among the stunning scenery of Vinh Ha Long, an exquisite bay with its grottoes and caves and jutting rocks often shrouded in a mysterious, bewitching fog.

The northern territory, near the Chinese border, is home to ethnic tribes living in mountainous areas, and there is a booming border trade amidst isolated forest retreats.

Throughout the north, the pagodas come alive with festivals – both religious and nationalistic – that have honoured spirits, gods, and war heroes for centuries. This is a seductive countryside, the kind that leaves one with the desire of never leaving. There are waterfalls, rainforests, mountain trails, and village craftspeople making woodcarvings, pottery, embroidery, and lacquered wood.

Here in the north, contemporary Vietnam has the volume turned down a bit as the traditional love of literature, art, and music maintains a toehold against the modern diversions of television, karaoke, and cellular phones. ❏

Hanoi

0 ——— 500 m
0 ——— 500 yds

N

H o n g   (R e d)

㉙ Chua Phu Tay Ho

Au Co

Yen Phu

Nghi Tam

Chua Kim Lien

An Thanh I

An Thanh II

An Duong

H o   T a y

㉖

(W e s t   L a k e)

Thanh Nien

㉗ Chua Tran Quoc (Pagoda)

Chua Ngu Xa

Ho Truc Bach (White Silk Lake)

Ngu Xa

Yen Phu

Tan Ap

Nghia Dung

Duc Chinh

Cua Bac

Pham Hong Thai

Nguyen Truong To

Hang Than

Hang Nhai

Chua Hoe Nhai

Cau Long Bien

Hai Phong

Bao Tang Dan Toc Hoc Vietnam (Vietnam Museum of Ethnology)

㉘ Den Quan Thanh (Temple)

Quan Thanh

Thuy Khue

Hoang Hoa Thiem

Phan Dinh Phung

Ng. Bieu

Cua Dong

Hang Dau

Tran

Gam Cau

36 PHO PHUONG

CONG VIEN Phu Chu Tich (Presidential Palace)

㉕ BACH THAO

Nha San Bac Ho (Ho Chi Minh House)

㉔ Lang Chu Tich Ho Chi Minh (Ho Chi Minh Mausoleum)

Hoang Van Thu

Tri Phuong

Ba Dinh Square

OLD CITY

CITADEL

Di Tich Hau Lau (Ladies Pagoda)

Di Tich Dien Kinh Thien (Heavenly Palace)

BA DINH

Ngo Ngoc Ha

Ngoc Ha

Bac Son

Cua Dong

Cha Ca La Vong

H. Cot

㉗ Cho Dong Xuan (Market) (OLD QUARTER)

Hang Dau

H. Ga

Hang Giay

Nguyen Thiep

Hang Duong

Den Bach Ma

Hang Buom

㉖ Independence Museum

㉕ Nha Hat Chuong Vang

Lang Hoa Ngoc Ha (Flower Village)

★

㉒ Chua Mot Cot (One Pillar Pagoda)

㉓ Bao Tang Ho Chi Minh (Ho Chi Minh Museum)

Hanoi Ancient Capital

Chua Mot Cot

Hung

Le Hong ng

Ong Ich Khiem

Vuong

Doi Can

Son Tay

Cot Co (Flag Tower)

㉑ Bao Tang Lich Su Quan Su (Military History Museum)

㉒⓪ ㉑

Dien

HOAN KIEM

Roi Nuoc Thang Long (Water Puppet Theatre)

Lo Su

Ham Tu Quan

Tran Quang Khai

Bach Dang

Kim Ma

G.V. Mau

Vo Phuc

Giang Vo

Ngo Hao Nam

Cat Linh

Lenin

Tran Phu

Chu Van An

Khuc Hao

Bien Phu

㉘ Bao Tang My Thuat (Fine Arts Museum)

Nguyen

Trinh Hoai Duc

Van Mieu (Temple of Literature)

㉙

P. Van Mieu

Quoc Tu Giam

N. Thong ng

D. Thi Diem

Thai Hoc

P. Nguyen Khuyen

Nha Tho Lon (St Joseph's Cathedral)

⑨ ⑩ Chua Ba Da (Pagoda)

Ly Thai To

Den Ngoc Son

Hang Bac

Cau Go

⑭

① Ho Hoan Kiem

②

Dinh Tien Hoang

Nha Hat Kim Dong

Le Lai

Le Thach

Bao Tang Cach Mang (Revolutionary Museum) ⑧

Bao Tang Lich Su (History Museum) ⑦

Buu Dien ③ Metropole Hotel

H. Khay Trang Tien ④

⑤ Nha Hat Lon (Municipal Theatre)

Hang Bot

Hang Bai

Ton Duc Thang

Ga Ha Noi (Station)

Le Duan

Thien Huong

Ngo Thinh Hao 1

Ngo Van Chuong

Ngo Quan Tho

Hai Ba Trung ⑪ Hoa Lo (Prison)

Thu Vien Quoc Gia

Trang Thi

Chua Quan Su (Ambassadors' Pagoda) ⑫

Cung Van Hoa Huu Nghi (Cultural Palace)

Ly Thuong Kiet

Tran Hung Dao

Quang Trung

Ba Trieu

Phan Boi Chau

Tho Nhuom

Ham Long

Le Van Huu

Ba Trieu

Nguyen Du

Phan Chu Trinh

Ngo Quyen

Trang Tien

Le Thanh Tong

Dai Hoc Tong Hop Ha Noi (University) ⑥

Pham Ngu Lao

Tran Khan Du

Tran Binh Trong

Yet Kieu

Hang Bai

Hue

Ng. Thuong Hien

⑬ Ho Thien Quang

Tran Quoc Toan

Nguyen Du

Nguyen Thuong Hien

Bun Cha

Nha Hat Dai Nam

Nha Hat Tuoi Tre

Nha Hat Cheo

Tran Nhan Tong

Nguyen Dinh Chieu

Binh Khiem

Tue Tinh

Ham Long

Lo Duc

Nha Hat Rap Xiec (Circus Theatre)

CONG VIEN THONG NHAT (REUNIFICATION PARK)

Tran Xuan Soan

Hoa Ma

Den Hai Ba Trung

Kham Thien

La Thanh

Nguyen Luong Bang

De La Thanh

Ngo Xa Dan

DONG DA

Go Dong Da

HANOI

Few cities anywhere in Asia can wink seductively at a traveller as can Hanoi, with its worn but experienced French charm and a history that extends back to the rise of an ancient dragon

Map on page 142

anoi is written as two words in Vietnamese: Ha Noi – *ha* meaning the river, in reference to **Song Hong**, or the **Red River**, and *noi*, meaning inside. The city's rich and complex history dates back to the Neolithic era, when the ancient Viet people settled in the Bach Hac and Viet Tri regions – in present-day Vinh Phu Province – at the confluence of the Red and Lo rivers. Today, Hanoi is a decidedly cosmopolitan city with an uncanny European embellishment. Indeed, it is ironic that this capital city of fiercely independent people, who have battled for generations against foreign invaders, possesses a decidedly European air. While people in Hanoi love to brag about their beautiful city, they don't often admit that much of what makes it beautiful is the French legacy.

Over the decades, the face of Hanoi increasingly reflected a harmony between progress and tradition, although this harmony did not extend to the relations between the Vietnamese and their French overseers. In the wake of new roads and buildings, tradition suffered. As was the case with many old structures, the Ba Tien Pagoda was knocked down to make way for a cathedral, and the Bao An Pagoda was replaced by a post office; today, all that remains of that pagoda is a small shrine beside Hoan Kiem Lake.

The French architectural legacy, and an abundance of trees and lakes around the city, give Hanoi a romantic air unusual for an Asian city. Still, aside from being spruced up and illuminated in the past decade, the city centre has evolved little since 1955 – there are the same pagodas and temples, colonial architecture, tree-lined streets, and lakes. The soul of the ancient city rests in the Old Quarter, an area of artisans and craftsmen dating from the 15th century.

The construction of luxury hotels and gleaming office towers, which boomed in the mid-1990s when it seemed that Vietnam was jumping into capitalism with both feet, is continuing, albeit at a more sedate pace after the Asian economic crisis of 1997. But smaller, crumbling buildings are getting knocked down or, more commonly, receiving new facades. The new exteriors aren't usually all that charming but are, rather, the standard glass-and-chrome front with large, brightly lit signs.

BELOW: veterans having a trim.

Hanoi's history

In the third century, after a bloody, decade-long war against Chinese invaders, King Thuc Phan descended from the 100 Viet Principalities (a region of 100 separate states encompassing all of southern China) and founded Au Lac. He installed his capital at Ke Chu, the site of the vast spiral citadel of Co Loa (Old Conch). After regaining independence, Vietnam's

Ngo, Dinh, and Le dynasties – of the middle of the 10th to the beginning of the 11th century – installed their capitals at Hoa Lu, 100 km (60 miles) south of Hanoi. There it remained, until Ly Thai To arrived in Dai La – an ancient city along the Song Hong (Red River) – in the early 11th century.

According to legend, Ly Thai To saw an enormous golden dragon emerge from the lake and soar into the sky above the site. On the strength of this omen, he moved the capital from Hoa Lu to Dai La, which he then renamed as Thang Long, or Ascending Dragon.

He found the surrounding countryside at the new site too flat for defensive purposes, so he ordered that dikes and artificial hills be built. Even today, it is still possible to make out the contours of these ancient earthworks in the area.

The royal capital grew from a small lake-side village built on stilts into a town. The area between the West Lake and the citadel became the administrative city *(kinh thanh)*, where the mandarins, officers, soldiers, and general public lived. In the heart of this was the royal city *(hoang thanh)* and behind its high walls was the forbidden city *(cam thanh)*, where the king, queens, and concubines lived in seclusion. In 1010, the centre of the royal city contained eight palaces and three pavilions. Eight new palaces were built during 1029, and further additions were made in 1203. The Temple of Literature, the One Pillar Pagoda, and the Tran Quoc Pagoda were built during this time. In 1400, the capital was transferred to Thanh Hoa by the usurper Ho Qui Ly, who took over from the Tran dynasty. His capital, Tay Kinh (lit. Capital of the West), lasted until the Le dynasty restored the capital to Hanoi in 1428.

From the 16th century onward, few new buildings were constructed in Hanoi. King Gia Long built a smaller Vauban-style citadel, but the French colonialists

BELOW: near the old Opera House on Trang Tien, 1905.

tore down the walls and gates, and all that remains today is the flag tower. The royal city was destroyed twice in less than 30 years: first in 1786, when King Le Chieu Thong ordered the destruction of the Trinh Palace, then in 1820 by Gia Long's son, Minh Mang, in his fury at the Chinese emperor's recognition of Thang Long – and not Hue – as the capital. In 1848, Tu Duc had most of the remaining palace destroyed and its valuable contents moved to Hue, the 19th-century capital of the Nguyen emperors.

The dawn of the 17th century marked the arrival of Dutch, Portuguese, and French traders. Hot on their heels came Christian missionaries. The great influx of newcomers and diverse ideas from Europe brought many changes to the capital of Thang Long. The French presence and influence grew, eventually changing the course of Vietnamese history. When Hanoi fell into the hands of the French in 1882, the city underwent transformation and modernisation.

In the heart of the city

In the very heart of the old town of Hanoi lies **Ho Hoan Kiem ❶**, or Lake of the Restored Sword. Early-rising travellers can catch locals seriously pursuing their morning exercises of *taiqi quan*, calisthenics, badminton, or running before going off to work. In the evening, especially on holidays, the lake is ringed by a carnival atmosphere as vendors sell balloons and toys, with little girls dressed up in frilly dresses and music blaring from loudspeakers. Several outdoor cafes sell ice cream, coffee, and beer while looking out onto the water.

A legend that sounds like a Vietnamese version of Excalibur tells of how King Le Thai To received a magic sword that he used during his 10-year resistance against the Chinese Ming court in the early 1400s. After liberating the

Map on page 142

One of Hanoi's early names, Dong Kinh, or Capital of the East, became Tunquin when Vietnamese became romanised. Tunquin, in turn, begot Tonkin, which is what France called the northern "protectorate" of Vietnam.

BELOW: couple at Ho Hoan Kiem.

*Thap Rua reflected in
Ho Hoan Kiem.*

country, the king took a boat to the centre of the lake to return the magic sword given to him by the Divine Tortoise. The tortoise is said to have snatched the sword from his hand and disappeared into the lake. That, apparently, is how the lake acquired its name.

Near the middle of the lake stands the small, 18th-century tower, **Thap Rua**, or Tortoise Tower. A large tortoise is said to still live in the lake and on certain days of the year – usually when the seasons change – people claim to see the tortoise emerge from the water. Perched on a tiny islet in the lake not far from the tower is the **Den Ngoc Son ❷** (Temple of the Jade Mound). The temple is reached from the shore via the brightly painted red, arched bridge known as The Huc, or Sunbeam Bridge. On the small hillock at the end of the bridge stands a stone column in the form of a brush next to an ink well and inscribed with three Chinese characters, *ta tien qing*, meaning "written on the blue sky". Also on the islet are the remains of a small communal house.

The city's main post office is on Dinh Tien Hoang, on the southeast side of the lake. One block north of the **Buu Dien ❸** (Central Post Office) there is a small park where sweethearts hold late-night trysts and where during the day young men and boys play soccer. Opposite the park's eastern border, on Ly Thai To, is the great Art Deco-style bank. Across from the park's southeastern corner is the arresting **State Guest House**. Yellow-coloured with green trim and protected by a wrought-iron fence, the building began in 1918 as the palace of the French governor of Tonkin.

BELOW: State
Guest House.

Southwards, straddling Ly Thai To and Ngo Quyen, is the white **Sofitel Metropole Hotel ❹**, the only international-class hotel in French days and a rat-ridden firetrap by the 1980s. Thoroughly gutted by new French management in

Map on page 142

the 1990s, it is purportedly the most expensive hotel in town. It's then only a short walk down Ly Thai To to the columned **Nha Hat Lon** ❺ (Municipal Theatre, often called the Opera House). After years of renovation, this renewed beauty has begun hosting performances by foreign and local orchestras, ballet and opera companies, and pop stars. A few days after the Japanese surrender in World War II, Viet Minh cadres rushed into the city. On 19 August 1945, they declared the establishment of an independent democratic republic from the theatre's balcony and unfurled their banners. Tens of thousands of peasants armed with machetes and bamboo spears were joined by tens of thousands of city residents. A few days previously, few of the latter had heard of the Viet Minh, but now they were caught up in patriotic euphoria and obeyed orders to seize important buildings from the Japanese and their Vietnamese collaborators.

Skirting the southern tip of the lake, **Trang Tien**, which terminates in front of the Municipal Theatre, was once the high shopping street of the French Quarter. When communists closed private enterprises, Trang Tien was one of the few areas retaining any commercial air; today it houses upmarket art galleries, bookshops offering translated books by Western authors, and – in the once drab, old government department store – the National Stock Exchange. In the blocks to the south and west, on quiet tree-lined streets, the colonialists' old villas now house many embassies and diplomatic residences.

The road southeast of the theatre, Le Thanh Tong, runs by the **University of Hanoi** ❻ with its colonial-era buildings. Walk into the courtyard, which has a fusion of colonial and Vietnamese architecture. Founded in the 1920s as the University of Indochina, it offered vocational and agricultural courses. In the 1930s, schools of law, medicine, science, and arts were added. The Indochinese

Restored to its colonial-era charm, the Sofitel Metropole Hotel was once the elegant epicentre for Hanoi's colonial society. Past guests have included Noel Coward, Somerset Maugham, Charlie Chaplin (who spent his honeymoon here after his secret wedding to Paulette Goddard), Graham Greene and Jane Fonda.

BELOW:
the Municipal Theatre at night.

*Offerings at a
Hanoi antique shop.*

students that studied here, including the future Gen. Vo Nguyen Giap, truly were an intellectual (and probably financial) elite, given that the French commitment to lower education and literacy was always trifling. In 1937, the student body here numbered 631 and included French students. It was the only genuine university in all of Indochina, which then had a population of about 25 million.

Behind the Municipal Theatre, with a cupola resembling a pagoda, is **Bao Tang Lich Su** ❼ (History Museum; open Tues–Sun 8–11.30am and 1.30–4pm; admission fee). It occupies the old archaeological research institution of the French School of the Far East, which opened in 1910 and was substantially renovated in the 1920s. High on content and low on propaganda, this is perhaps the best museum in town. The excellent archaeological collection includes relics from the Hung era and Neolithic graves, Bronze Age implements, bronze drums from Ngoc Lu and Mieu Mon, Cham relics, stelae, statues, ceramics, and an eerie sculpture of the goddess of mercy, Quan Am, with her 1,000 eyes and arms. An ornate throne, clothes, and artefacts belonging to the 13 Nguyen-dynasty kings are displayed. Nearby, **Bao Tang Cach Mang** ❽ (Revolutionary Museum; open Tues–Sun 8–11.30am and 1.30–4pm; admission fee) at 216 Tran Quang Khai offers a carefully edited version of the struggles of the Vietnamese people from ancient times up until 1975. Displayed are the long, wooden stakes that crippled the Mongol fleet in Ha Long Bay, during one of three invasion attempts in the 13th century, and a bronze drum from 2,400 BC.

South and west of Ho Hoan Kiem

BELOW: streetside
flower vendor.

Where Pho Nha Chung joins Ly Quoc Su is the oldest church in the city, **Nha Tho Lon** ❾ (St Joseph's Cathedral; the Vietnamese call it the "big church").

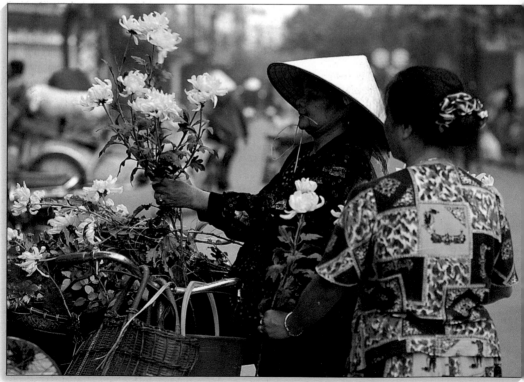

Simplified Gothic in style, it was consecrated on Christmas night in 1886. Some of the stained-glass windows date from then. The cathedral was built on the site of the Bao Thien Pagoda, which was razed to build the cathedral. Celebration of the Mass resumed here only in 1990. After more than 30 years of repression, faith proved to be remarkably resilient after reopening its doors; on Sundays, services are absolutely packed. Several shops in this area sell tribal clothing, handicrafts, water puppets, and painstakingly painted copies of famous Western art.

A narrow passageway next to 5 Nha Tho, the street facing the cathedral, leads to **Chua Ba Da** ⑩, between the cathedral and Ho Hoan Kiem. This charming pagoda was built in the 15th century after the discovery of a stone statue of a woman during the construction of the Thang Long citadel to the west. The statue, which was thought to have magic powers, disappeared and has since been replaced by a wooden replica. The pagoda's modest exterior belies its exquisite interior and atmosphere. An impressive line-up of gilt Buddha statues forms the central altar.

On Ly Quoc Su, to the north of the cathedral, is the small **Chua Ly Trieu Quoc Su**, a pagoda also known as Chua Kong, the Pagoda of Confucius. It was founded under the Ly dynasty in the 11th century and later restored in 1855. The pagoda contains some attractive lacquered wooden statues and carved roof beams.

South about three blocks is the site of the infamous **Hoa Lo Prison** ⑪, known as the Hanoi Hilton to both American prisoners-of-war incarcerated and tortured here and to present-day cyclo and taxi drivers. The prisoners included the US ambassador to Vietnam in the late 1990s, Pete Peterson. It is of importance to Vietnamese for other reasons: the French imprisoned, tortured, and guillotined countless revolutionaries within the walled compound that until recently occupied an entire block. In 1932, 10,000 political prisoners were incarcerated in this and other prisons altogether.

In 1994, the prison was almost totally demolished to make way for an enormous foreign-financed, curtain-glass office tower and hotel complex. Topped with barbed and electric wire, the yellow concrete main gate and a few cells of Hoa Lo have been preserved as a museum, with exhibits of stocks and a guillotine. The vintage government propaganda found here is increasingly out of style elsewhere in Vietnam. Across the street from the prison is the Hanoi People's Court.

One block south and west, the **Chua Quan Su** ⑫ (Ambassadors' Pagoda), located on 73 Pho Quan Su, is perhaps the busiest pagoda in town. On the 1st and 15th days of the lunar month, throngs gather to make offerings. In the 17th century the site was a guesthouse for envoys from other Buddhist countries, hence its name. Rare for a Vietnamese pagoda, one is likely to catch sight of monks here. In the long, low buildings surrounding the temples are schoolrooms for novice monks and a small library of parchment and texts in Vietnamese and Chinese; this is a centre for Buddhist research. Quan Su Street dead ends at a

Map on page 142

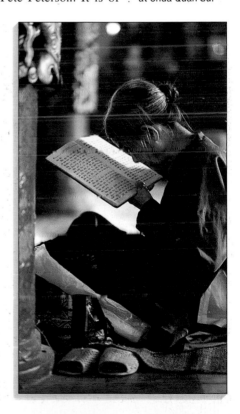

BELOW: studying the life of Buddha at Chua Quan Su.

bare stone plaza to the south and the forbidding Soviet-style **Cung Van Hoa Huu Nghi** (Cultural Palace), sometimes used for pop concerts and trade shows.

To the south of Quan Su pagoda about 500 metres (1,600 ft) is a lovely small lake, **Ho Thien Quang** ⑬, where visitors can rent paddle boats. Just south across the street is an entrance to **Cong Vien Tong Nhat** (Reunification Park) and, to the west, Hanoi's circus. Facing Pho Tran Nhan Tong, the park is said to have been built by local volunteer workers on marshy land once used as a rubbish dump. This attractive, well-maintained park is designed around the large **Ho Bay Mau** (Bay Mau Lake). A small train for children runs through the park.

The Old Quarter

Northward of Ho Hoan Kiem (Hoan Kiem Lake), many streets lead to a favourite haunt of travellers, the area known as **36 Pho Phuong** (36 Streets or the **Old Quarter**). This area was one of the main resistance centres against the French colonialists. The charm of the Old Quarter's narrow lanes lies in a 600-year history as an artisans' district, with crafts and trades concentrated in a single area on 36 lanes. Silverworkers were found on Pho Hang Bac (Silver Merchandise Street), bamboo basketmakers on Hang Bo (Bamboo Basket Merchandise), and so on. The present-day commercial frenzy (not to mention intense motorbike and bicycle traffic) has evolved from virtually nothing in less than a decade. It's all the more amazing considering that, with very few exceptions, the communists prohibited private trade for more than 40 years.

The new tradesmen still tend to concentrate by speciality, but the speciality doesn't necessarily match the street name any longer. Silver jewellery, as well as gravestones, can still be found on Hang Bac, but the future of this street clearly rests on travel agencies and tourist cafes. The street of Hang Gai (Hemp) specialises in silk, clothing, and embroidered articles. Hang Dau (Cooking Oil) is full of shoe shops. However, Hang Chieu (Mat) is still the place to find mats and Hang Ma (Paper Votive Objects) features stationery shops.

Each of the 36 craft guilds once had its own *dinh* (communal house). But like most of the quarter's pagodas and temples, they were shut down during the communist takeover and transformed into schools or housing. Similarly, the narrow storefronts, some less than 3 metres (10 ft) wide, once fronted single-family dwellings; these "tubehouses" still extend far back, punctuated by courtyards, but were re-apportioned among many families.

By examining the roof lines, one can sometimes discern an old temple. For example, at 120 Hang Bong (Cotton), a yellowing pagoda arch crowns a barber stall and a banner shop. A side alley affords entry to a tiny courtyard and a single remaining hall that still draws worshippers and seekers of good luck. The Hoa Loc Dinh, at 90 Hang Dao (Peach), was once a communal house for people from the village of Hai Duong. It is now a shop selling blue jeans. According to records discovered on a stele, these villagers settled here towards the end of the Tang-dynasty era and founded the artisan district of Thai Cuc, which became the street of Hang Dao.

There is a delightful nightly performance of water puppets, accompanied by traditional music, on the northeast corner of the lake at the **Roi Nuoc Thang Long** ⓮ (Thang Long Water Puppet Theatre) on the corner of Dinh Tien Hoang. In a small house on Hang Ngang is the **Independence Museum** ⓯. Here, Ho Chi Minh wrote Vietnam's declaration of independence, which borrows considerably from America's own declaration.

Map on page 142

BELOW: breakfast of *pho* at street stand.

Den Bach Ma (White Horse Temple) on Hang Buom (Sails Street) is dedicated to the deity Bach Ma. Other than the giant wooden horse statue inside, there is a palanquin adorned with carvings of phoenixes, cranes, and turtles. Originally built during the 9th century, the temple was reconstructed in the 18th and 19th centuries. In regular use, it remains in a good state of repair. This street runs into a little street called Ma May, which has a good selection of crumbling colonial facades. At No. 87, you will find a beautifully restored "tube house", which is a good example of the way the people in this part of town used to live.

The area around the **Cho Dong Xuan**, the large market in the northern part of the Old Quarter, is an interesting place to explore. The old colonial-era market, destroyed by fire in 1994, has been replaced with an already grimy four-storey building; its escalator, perhaps the city's first, is permanently frozen. This is the wholesale source for many dry goods. The counterfeit Calvin Klein T-shirts and other low-quality apparel seem intended for the Vietnamese customer, but it's a good place to shop for cooking utensils and kitchenware. In the streets around the market, farmers squat on the pavement selling their produce directly to passers-by. Florists add a welcome splash of colour with their fragrant blooms. On Lang Ong Street, traditional medicine shops sell all manner of cures, including snake wine and lizards preserved in alcohol. Do not be put off by appearances: the gecko elixir is excellent. Other vendors sell live snakes, birds, and monkeys.

Near here, at the end of Hang Chieu and close to Tran Nhat Duat, is the crumbling brick gate of **Quan Chuong**, the last remnant of a wall that once encircled the Old Quarter.

The 1,682-metre-long (5,520-ft) Long Bien Bridge, once known as the Doumer Bridge, dates from 1902. The bridge suffered damage from American bombing but was continually repaired. Until 1983, all northbound road and rail traffic passed over it. These days, it is reserved for cyclists, trains, and pedestrians.

BELOW: Long Bien Bridge.

Western Hanoi

At the **Dao Tang My Thuat** ⓲ (The Arts Museum; Tues, Thurs, Fri and Sun 8.30am–5pm, Wed and Sat 8.30am–9pm; admission fee), at 66 Nguyen Thai Hoc, exhibits include displays on minority folk art and history and Dong Son bronze drums, Dong Noi stone carvings, Cham statues and carvings, communal house decorations dating from the 16th century, and 18th-century wood Buddha statues in some surprisingly undignified poses. There is information, too, on the evolution since the 17th-century Le dynasty of a Vietnamese speciality – lacquer painting on wood. Note the rare examples of lacquer painting on paper. In the 20th century, Vietnamese artists quickly adopted perspective and the use of oil paint and later were inspired by impressionism, post-impressionism, and the modernism of Picasso and Dali – right up until the present day. Some visitors are disappointed that most of the Social Realist and war-time propaganda paintings have been removed, but for content, this and the History Museum are the best in town.

Nearby, across the street just to the south, is the **Van Mieu** ⓳ (Temple of Literature). Built in 1070 under the reign of King Ly Thanh Tong, the temple is dedicated to Confucius. In 1076, the temple was adjoined by the Quoc Tu Giam, School of the Elite of the Nation, Vietnam's first university. Under the Tran dynasty, the school was renamed the Quoc Hoc Vien, or the National College, in 1235. After passing exams at the local levels, scholars aspiring to become senior mandarins came here to study for rigorous triennial examinations. The subjects of study were literature, philosophy, and ancient Chinese and Vietnamese history, which Confucians believed provided the ideal training for government administrators. The Van Mieu became known as the Temple of

Sculpture at the Fine Arts Museum.

BELOW: altar at the Van Mieu Temple.

Literature when the capital was transferred to Hue at the beginning of the 19th century. Above the main entrance gate is an inscription requesting visitors to dismount from horses before entering.

The large temple enclosure is divided into five walled courtyards. After passing through the Van Mieu Mon and the first two courtyards past this gate, one arrives at the Gac Khue Van (Pleiade Constellation Pavilion), where the men of letters used to recite their poems. Through the Dai Thanh Mon (Great Wall Gate), an open courtyard surrounds a large, central pool known as the Thien Quang Tinh (Well of Heavenly Clarity). Now regrouped and sheltered under a roof, the 82 stone stelae, survivors of an original 117, rest on the backs of stone tortoises. Until a few years ago, they were exposed to the elements under the trees on either side of the courtyard. (American Express funded the preservation effort, as they did with Beijing's Imperial Palace.) The stelae are inscribed with the names, works, and academic records of 1,306 scholars who succeeded in the 82 examination sessions held between 1442 and 1779. The French halted examinations here in 1915 (and in Hue in 1918). By then, the importation of Chinese-language materials had been prohibited for seven years; the French set out to shut down all Sino-Vietnamese schools still operating in villages. Dai Thanh (Great Success Gate) leads to the temple itself.

Facing it is the Bai Duong (House of Ceremonies), where sacrifices were offered in honour of Confucius. Today, musicians perform traditional music and charge a small fee to those who choose to sit and listen. Behind are the Eastern Gate and the Great Success Sanctuary, which have been renovated. In the final courtyard was the National Academy, destroyed by French aerial bombing in 1947. These were the academy buildings where the examinations were held. A newly built two-storey building contains a small museum and shrines to great scholars.

BELOW: street-side baguette seller.

To the north on Duong Dien Bien Phu is one of the symbols of Hanoi, the flag tower of **Cot Co** ⓴. Built in 1812 under the Nguyen dynasty as part of the Hanoi citadel, the hexagonal 33-metre (108-ft) tower is more or less all that remains of the citadel, which was destroyed at the end of the 19th century. Next to it, the **Bao Tang Lich Su Quan Su** ㉑ (Military History Museum; Tues–Thurs, Sat–Sun 8–11.30am and 1–4.30pm; admission fee), renovated in the 1990s, chronicles Vietnam's battles for independence and unification against the French and American patrons of South Vietnam. The crumpled wreckage of a B-52 bomber sits in an outside courtyard. Inside are the uniforms of captured American pilots, photographs of Vietnamese war heroes and items belonging to the fallen leaders of what was South Vietnam.

South across the street is a small, triangular-shaped park with a bronze statue of Lenin, depicted striding forth in a business suit and larger than life. It must be one of the world's last extant monuments to the Russian revolutionary. Children play soccer on the plaza in front of the statue and in the pleasant park behind it.

Continuing northwest up Dien Bien Phu, a small road called Chua Mot Cot leads to the unique **Chua Mot Cot** ㉒ (One Pillar Pagoda). Originally built in 1049 under the Ly dynasty, this wooden pagoda rests on a single concrete pillar rising out of a lotus pool. It was most recently reconstructed after departing French soldiers blew it up in 1954. The banyan tree behind the pagoda was planted by Pres. Nehru of India in 1958 during an official visit to the young Vietnamese republic.

Legend has it that in a dream King Ly Thai To saw the goddess Quan Am seated on a lotus leaf offering him a male child in her outstretched arms. Shortly after his dream, he married a young peasant girl who bore him the male heir of which he had dreamed. The king built the pagoda as a sign of his gratitude.

Behind the park with the pagodas rises a massive, angular Soviet-style structure, the **Bao Tang Ho Chi Minh** ㉓ (Ho Chi Minh Museum; daily except Mon and Fri afternoons 8–11.30am and 2–6pm; admission fee). The museum, which is arranged into three sections, celebrates Ho's revolutionary life and the pivotal role he played in Vietnam's history, in the context of international Communist development, and contains many of his personal effects. But the museum is more well-known for its modern and symbolistic – and often abstract – displays, including a gigantic lopsided table with a giant bowl of artificial fruit, a reconstruction of *Guernica*, a Constructivist iron tower, and a red brick volcano.

Ho Chi Minh's house.

Immediately north looms the massive marble-and-granite **Lang Chu Tich Ho Chi Minh** ㉔ (Ho Chi Minh Mausoleum; open Apr–Oct, Tues–Thurs 7.30–10.30am, Sat–Sun 7.30–11am; Nov–Mar, Tues–Thur 8–11am, Sat–Sun 8–11.30am; free), in **Ba Dinh Square** where Ho Chi Minh delivered Vietnam's declaration of independence in 1945. The embalmed corpse lies in a glass casket within this monumental tomb, contrary to Ho's wish to be cremated. In autumn, it is advisable to check beforehand whether he is in residence. Rumour has it that he is packed off to Russia for an embalming refresher. Dressed in his favourite khaki suit, the guarded body lies displayed on a platform in a cold room.

BELOW: queuing at Ho Chi Minh Mausoleum.

Visitors are ushered quickly past either side. No cameras or handbags may be taken inside. Foreigners are whisked to the front of the queues. He died in 1969 on the same date as his independence declaration. (It was officially reported as 3 September for years, so as not to dampen National Day celebrations.)

Behind the mausoleum to the west is the charming **Nha San Bac Ho** ㉕ (Ho Chi Minh House; open daily except Mon and Fri morning, Apr–Oct 7.30–11am, 2–4pm; Nov–Mar 8–11am, 1.30–4pm; admission fee), overlooking a carp pond in a quiet and shaded park. Built on stilts, tribal-style, the modest living quarters consist of two small rooms. Below is an open-air meeting room. Ho lived here from 1958 to 1969, preferring it to the sumptuous colonial mansion on the same grounds, the former **Presidential Palace**.

Closed to the public, the palace was formerly the residence of the French governor-general. Behind the palace, but best reached from Hoang Hoa Tham, is a quiet public park with rolling hills, contemporary sculpture, and trees.

The Ancient City

From Ba Dinh Square, where the National Assembly building is located across from the mausoleum and

New wealth on the shores of Ho Tay.

where there is a war memorial, head north until you come to one of the greatest archaeological finds in Vietnam – a 6th-century **royal city**. Unearthed during excavations for a new government building, the site is not open to the public at the moment, but one can peek through the hoardings to see the immense size of this discovery. Across Hoang Dieu is the western side of the **Citadel**, which served as the centre of administration in pre-colonial times. The area is now a restricted military area. If you walk further along, you will come to **Di Tich Hau Lau** (Ladies Pagoda) and **Di Tich Dien Kinh Thien** (Heavenly Palace).

Around Ho Tay (West Lake)

Otherwise, backtrack and towards vast **Ho Tay** ㉖ (West Lake), formerly known as the Lake of Mists. This lake, the largest in Hanoi, lies in an ancient bed of the Song Hong (Red River). Royal and warlord palaces once graced its banks; these were destroyed in feudal battles. Since the 1990s, the lake has seen considerable building activity – large villas, hotels, and restaurants, mostly of dubious taste, have sprung up. Many foreigners and new Vietnamese millionaires live in this area. Legend says the lake was previously the site of a huge forest, the lair of a wicked fox with nine tails. The creature terrorised the neighbourhood until it was drowned by the Dragon King, who, in the process of unleashing the waters to get rid of the beast, created the lake.

No less fantastic is an alternative legend that tells the story of an 11th-century bonze and a golden buffalo. The bonze, Khong Lo, had an enormous bronze bell made. When its sound first reached the ears of the golden buffalo, the confused creature, believing that he had heard his mother's voice, rushed immediately towards the south and in his stampede transformed the site into a lake.

BELOW: the Presidential Palace.

During an uprising against the occupying Chinese in 545, the national hero Ly Bon built a wooden-and-bamboo citadel at the mouth of the Song To Lich, at the same time building Chua Khai Quoc (Foundation of the Country Pagoda) beside the Red River. In the 17th century, the pagoda was transferred to its present site on the tiny peninsula of the Ho Tay and renamed **Chua Tran Quoc ㉗**. The Tran Quoc is perhaps Vietnam's most ancient pagoda; its stele, dating from 1639, recounts the pagoda's long history.

Separated from the lake by Duong Thanh Nien is **Ho Truc Bach** (White Silk Lake). This was the ancient site of Lord Trinh's summer palace, which later became a harem where he detained his wayward concubines. The lake derives its name from the beautiful white silk these concubines were forced to weave for the princesses. Nearby, the ornate **Den Quan Thanh ㉘** beside the lake was originally built during the Ly dynasty (1010–1225). This temple houses a huge bronze bell and an enormous, four-ton bronze statue of Tran Vu, guardian deity of the north, to whom the temple is dedicated. It was Tran Vu who helped King An Duong dispose of the devils and ghosts that harassed and plagued the building of Vietnam's ancient capital at Co Loa.

Situated at the lake's centre, at the tip of a small peninsula, is **Chua Phu Tay Ho ㉙**, a popular destination for pilgrims and unmarried Vietnamese, particularly on the 15th day of the lunar month. The long lane from Yen Phu is lined with restaurants, shops, and karaoke bars. The hall on the right is especially garish and will appeal to children. The altars are crammed with statuettes of strange beasts, grottoes, and miniature sailing ships. Added daily by worshippers are heaps of fruit and packets of biscuits, amongst other things, brought to the pagoda as offerings.

Map on page 142

West of Hanoi, hills extend up to the 1,200-metre (4,000 ft) summit of Mt Ba, 65 km (40 miles) from the city. In the northwest, the city is bordered by Ho Tay, or West Lake.

BELOW: cyclo drivers at Ho Tay.

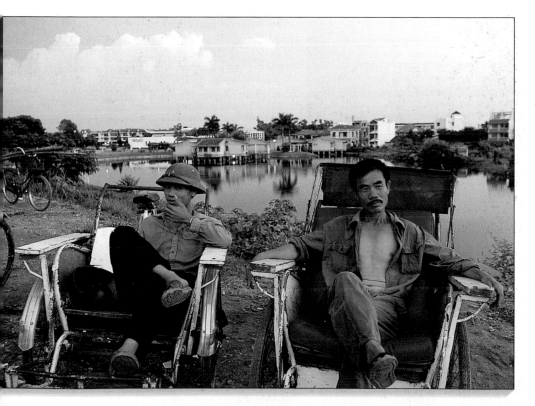

Map on page 142

Outside the city centre

In the south of the city on Pho Tho Lao is **Den Hai Ba Trung** (Temple of the Two Sisters), also known as the Dong Nhan temple, after the village that surrounded the site at the time of its construction in 1142. The temple is dedicated to the two Trung sisters who organised an uprising against the Chinese Han invaders in AD 40. Two unusually formed stone statues recovered from the Red River and said to represent the two sisters are kept in a small room inside the temple. They are brought out annually for a February procession, dressed in new clothes.

A little further south on Bach Mai, **Chua Lien Phai** and the pagoda's Buddhist monastery, Lien Phai Tu, or Lieu Khai, are sheltered in an attractive garden. The temple was built under the Le dynasty and reconstructed by one of the Trinh lords in 1732. It has been restored at least twice since. Three statues, two representing good and evil, occupy the main room.

The Tay Dang *dinh*, or communal house, in Hanoi's Bay Vi suburb is worth visiting for its beautiful architectural structure and carving. The original construction date is unknown, but inscriptions on a beam reveal that the *dinh* was extensively restored in the 16th century and that further repairs were carried out in 1808, 1926, and 1942. Built entirely of hardwood, it comprises five partitions and four roofs – the latter have curling tops that are decorated with *tu linh* – dragons, unicorns, tortoises, and the phoenix – the four animals that according to folklore bring happiness. Many valuable woodcarvings grace the interior of the communal house.

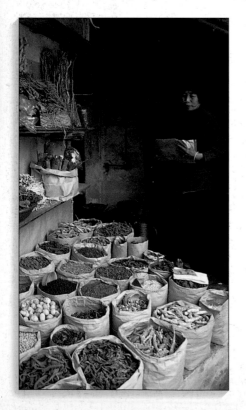

BELOW: offerings at a spice shop.

Behind Thu Le Park in the northwest of the city is the 11th-century **Voi Phuc** (Temple of the Kneeling Elephants), built by King Ly Thai To in honour of his son who distinguished himself during the war against Chinese Song-dynasty invaders by charging the enemy with his squadron of elephants. The simple lakeside temple houses statues of the prince and his generals. In front of the temple are stone statues of kneeling elephants.

Southwest of the city, in Dong Da district, is the **Go Dong Da** (Mound of the Multitudes) on Tay Son, next to number 356. Legend says that Go Dong Da was formed by the bodies of Chinese soldiers killed after Quang Trung's victory. Very little remains of the temple that was constructed on the site, but dozens of steps lead to the top of the mound. Beyond the mound is a large statue of Quang Trung, built in the Social Realist style.

Bao Tang Dan Toc Hoc Viet Nam (Vietnam Museum of Ethnology), on Van Huyen, is Hanoi's newest and most modern museum. As special events, such as artisans' skills demonstrations, traditional games, films and lectures, are often held here, especially on weekends and during the holidays, it is not just tourists but also Vietnamese families who visit. In the garden, there is a water puppet stage. For those heading out to the northwest part of Vietnam, this is a good introduction to tribal clothing and housing. There are audiotapes, videos, full-scale models, crafts, and musical instruments. All of Vietnam's 54 ethnic groups are represented. ❏

Co Loa

I n the Dong Anh district of Hanoi's western suburbs lie the remains of the citadel fortress of Co Loa. Excavations in the area have uncovered ancient arms and many bronze arrowheads. Co Loa dates from 257 BC, when it served as the capital of the Thuc dynasty under King An Duong Vuong. Of the nine ramparts that covered an area of more than 5 sq. km (2 sq. miles), three are still visible. Architectural and sculptural works remain in the citadel's centre.

Within the citadel's gateway, an historical banyan tree shades the shrine dedicated to Princess My Chau. Inside is a rough stone statue of a headless woman thought to be the princess. Further on is the upper temple dedicated to King An Duong Vuong. People gather here on 6 January every year to celebrate the king's efforts against foreign invaders. The Vietnamese, with their irrepressible talent for blending history and legend, will tell you that King An Duong Vuong, of Tay Au, invaded Lac Viet after his request to marry the king of Vietnam's daughter was unceremoniously refused. He managed to annex the country of his coveted princess and amalgamated the territories of Tay Au and Lac Viet to form the kingdom of Au Lac.

Aware that this expansion would antagonise his great northern neighbour, China, An Duong Vuong wasted no time in building the walls of his new capital. But for some mysterious reason his efforts were frustrated and the walls repeatedly collapsed. The mystery was finally revealed when the golden tortoise, Kim Quy, appeared to the king in a dream and disclosed that occult forces were responsible. Aided by the tortoise, the king was able to defeat the evil forces and complete his indestructible fortress. China, however, wanted the fortress destroyed. Gen. Trieu Da was picked for the task. But the repeated attempts of his powerful forces proved futile.

The golden tortoise again appeared to the king and this time provided him with a magic crossbow. The following day the Chinese forces suffered heavy losses from the arrows of the crossbow. Seeing this, Trieu Da realised that all was not as it appeared and

so called for peace. He asked for, and was granted, the hand of the king's daughter, My Chau, for his son Trong Thuy. During the honeymoon, Trong Thuy asked his young wife to show him her father's crossbow. The unsuspecting My Chau obediently did so, but Trong Thuy took the magic crossbow and substituted another in its place. The king was so furious when he discovered this that he beheaded the princess. Her inconsolable husband is said to have drowned himself.

Co Loa was not only Vietnam's first capital but also something of an architectural marvel. Three earthen walls, 4 to 5 metres (13 to 16 ft) high and at certain strategic points 8 to 12 metres (26 to 39 ft) high, enclosed the capital. The 8-km-long (5-mile) outer wall was reinforced with thorny bamboo hedges and surrounded by a deep moat. Watch towers were built at the eight cardinal points of the citadel's ramparts. Guards held vigil throughout the night, kept awake by gongs that resounded every half hour until dawn. The citadel's spiral form amplified sound from within and carried it to nearby villages. ❏

Beyond Hanoi

BEYOND HANOI

Northern Vietnam is defined by the fecundity and moods of the Song Hong, or Red River, whose delta makes the area a lush rice-growing region and cradle of Vietnamese civilisation

Map on page 162

Excursions beyond **Hanoi ❶** add an element to the Vietnam experience that makes the effort well worthwhile. Some of the trips can be booked with tour agencies in Hanoi, others require use of local buses (slow and uncomfortable) or even trains (slow and uncomfortable). The area is agriculturally rich and expansive, nurtured by the **Song Hong**, or **Red River**, which spreads its alluvial deposits over much of northern Vietnam. Beyond the rice paddies, several ancient pagodas are within reach in a day or two, as are some highland escapes. Closer to Hanoi, craftsmen offer their efforts in shops.

The province neighbouring Hanoi to the northwest, Vinh Phu, is the cradle of the pre-Vietnamese Hung Lac people and the ancestral land of the Viet, who first settled here before moving into the Song Hong delta region. Bronze relics 4,000 years old have been discovered in the region. The area still bears the mark of the early settlers' presence in the remains of the Hung temples. These were built by the rulers of the Van Lang kingdom between the 7th and 3rd centuries BC, when a line of 18 Hung kings graced the throne of Vang Lang.

West of Hanoi

Leaving Hanoi by the southwest, Highway 6 traverses a plateau. It takes about an hour to negotiate the sprawl of vehicles and construction around Hanoi, but then traffic thins markedly. The two-lane paved road, flat and in good condition, is well suited for touring by bicycle or motorbike through the rice fields. There are two ways of getting to the Chua Thay and Tay Phuong pagodas. Highway 6 passes through **Van Phuc ❷**, a traditional silk-weaving village in the town of **Ha Dong**, which is sometimes a stop on day-tours from Hanoi to the pagodas. This route snakes some 40 km (25 miles) from Hanoi. A much quicker route is via the new Lang Hoa Lac Highway to Chua Tay, just 25 km 15 miles) from Hanoi.

One of Vietnam's oldest pagodas, **Chua Thay ❸** (Pagoda of the Master) nestles against the hillside in **Sai Son**. (Its official name is Thien Phuc Tu.) Sharing its compound is a smaller pagoda, **Chua Ca**. Founded in 1132 by King Ly Thai To, the pagoda has often been renovated. Its dedication is threefold: to Ly Than Tong, king of the Ly dynasty from 1127 to 1138; to Sakyamuni, the historical Buddha, and his 18 *arhat*, or disciples; and to the venerable bonze Dao Hanh (the Master). All are represented by many statues here, some dating back to the 12th and 13th centuries.

Dao Hanh was a great herbalist who had been a medical man in his native village before entering the pagoda. He was also very fond of the choreographic arts, particularly the traditional water-puppet theatre, which was performed in the artificial lake in front of the

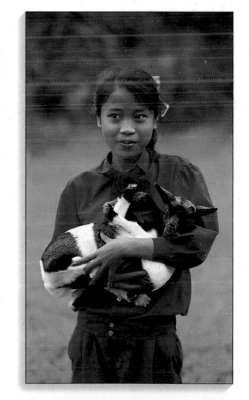

PRECEDING PAGES: terraced rice fields. **BELOW:** a schoolgirl cradles two goats.

Rice is a mainstay of agriculture in the fertile delta of Song Hong, or Red River.

BELOW: a temple just outside of Hanoi for good luck in business.

pagoda. Between the 5th and 7th days of the third lunar month, the districts' premier puppet troupe stages shows in this authentic outdoor setting. Folk theatrical plays, chess games, a recital of Dao Hanh's feats, and a procession of tablets are also features of the festival, which draws participants from four villages. The two arched, covered bridges spanning the lake date from 1602. Within the pagoda is a large, sandalwood statue of Dao Hanh, which can be moved like a puppet using cleverly intertwined strings. A climb up the hillside leads to two more small shrines and a superb view of the pagoda, lake, village, and surrounding countryside. This idyllic place is an excellent spot for a picnic. Several limestone grottoes in the vicinity are worth exploring, notably Hang Cac Co (The Mischievous).

Usually linked with Thay Pagoda on day-tours is **Chua Tay Phuong** ❹ in the picturesque village of **Thac Xa**. It perches on top of the 50-metre (160-ft) Tay Phuong hill. The pagoda dates from the 8th century and is famous for its 62 wooden lacquer statues, which are said to illustrate different stories from the Buddhist scriptures; their facial expressions reflect the varying attitudes and faces of human nature. The pagoda is reached by climbing 238 laterite steps, where incense and fan sellers will be hot on your ascending trail hoping to be rewarded for their efforts, if not on the way up, then while you're catching your breath at the top. Built of ironwood with bare brick walls, the pagoda with its round windows comprises Bai Duong (Prostration Hall), Chinh Dien (Central Hall), and Hau Cung (Back Hall). Together they form the Tam Bao (Three Gems). The overlapping roofing of the halls is richly decorated with carvings and lacquer figures of dragons and animals. Perhaps the best examples of 18th-century sculpture are here, including beautiful wooden statues of the *arhat*, Buddha's disciples. Day-tours to Thay and Tay Phoung also sometimes stop at the village of **So**, where the age-old occupation is the production of noodles from the flour of yams and manioc.

Highway 6 continues on into the outer limits of the Song Hong delta and the culture of irrigated-rice cultivation. The area was once inhabited by the prehistoric Lac Viet people, and many relics from the Hoa Binh culture of the Lac Viet have been recovered in the area. Ethnic groups – including Muong, Hmong, Tai, Tay, and Dao (pronounced *zao*) – make up the local population.

Constructed by the French with forced labour, by the early 1950s the unpaved "Road Number 6" hadn't been repaired in more than a decade and had been bombed by French and Viet Minh alike during the war against the French. There were many French fortifications along this 75-km (45-mile) route between Hanoi and **Hoa Binh ❺**, but the thick roadside underbrush was perfect camouflage for Viet Minh. The guerrillas regularly attacked forts and convoys and then melted back into the distant cliffs and hills.

For the French in the early 1950s, this road became especially treacherous after crossing the Song Day (Day River). Song Da marked the western boundary of the so-called de Lattre line, a defensive perimeter intended to protect French-controlled Hanoi and the Song Hong delta, although throughout the war it always enclosed about 30,000 regular and irregular Viet Minh troops. Beginning in November 1951, a famous set-piece battle – the Hell of Hoa Binh or the Hell of Road Number 6 – raged for two months in this vicinity. In the previous year, the French had lost all their positions north of the Song Hong (Red River) to the Chinese border. On 14 November French paratroops easily recaptured the Viet Minh-held town of Hoa Binh. The rationale was that Hoa Binh would underpin the communication routes to Hanoi via Road No. 6. Hoa Binh was also

Map on page 162

BELOW: soldiers at a military academy outside of Hanoi.

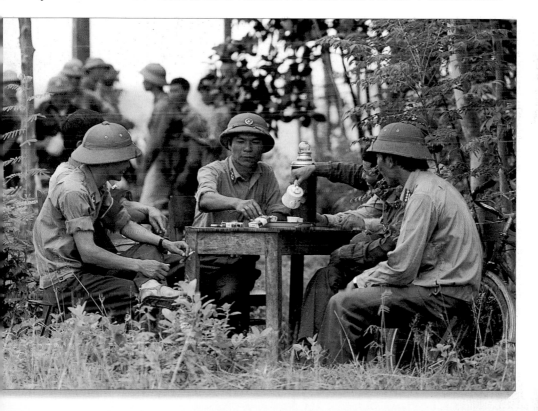

the de facto capital of the Muong people, who were allied with the French; two Muong battalions were among the French-led troops. A victory here would be a psychological boost for the Muong and for the Tai armies loyal to the French in the northwestern mountains. In the beginning, the Western press hailed the operation as "a pistol pointed at the heart of the enemy".

The Viet Minh infantry employed human-wave attacks that left barbed wire entanglements covered with carpets of their bodies. The French troops – which included Muong, Vietnamese, Moroccan, and Algerian units, in addition to Foreign Legionnaires – fought the Viet Minh hand-to-hand. Some of the bloodiest battles were on the Song Da (Black River) around the so-called Notre Dame Rock. No longer a ragtag collection of guerrillas, by now the Viet Minh were armed with tanks, mortars, automatic weapons, and howitzers of both Chinese and American make. The latter were captured by the communist Chinese in Korea and transferred to the Viet Minh. At the end of February, the French painfully evacuated via the Song Da and Road 6. The war lasted two more years, but for the Viet Minh, Hoa Binh was a dress rehearsal for the showdown at Dien Bien Phu. Hoa Binh means "peace".

Today, Hoa Binh, the provincial capital, is a substantial industrial town. Five km (3 miles) away sits Southeast Asia's biggest hydroelectric project. Built with technical assistance and money from the former Soviet Union, construction of the dam took 10 years and displaced approximately 50,000 ethnic minority people from the Song Da (Black River) valley, which is now under a reservoir. However, running the facility now employs around 35,000 people. Electricity generated is the main source for a transmission line running north to south and supplying places as far away as the Mekong Delta.

BELOW: ferrying a load of shrimp nets.

It's not obvious that minority people are the majority in this area because few wear traditional clothing, but from Hoa Binh town, one can arrange tours and overnight stays to tribal villages. The town's markets and shops are good sources of tribal souvenirs. On the whole, though, foreign tourists have shunned Hoa Binh, stopping only briefly before heading for the more rural ambience of Mai Chau, a valley, 60 km (40 miles) further down the road.

Map on page 162

North of Hanoi

From 1945 on, the wooded Tam Dao mountains were Viet Minh sanctuary. But the road leading here from Hanoi, now Highway 2, was within the French domain. Visitors today will notice that the road up to the Tam Dao resort branches north off Highway 2, about 16 km (10 miles) from Hanoi, at the industrial town of **Vinh Yen** ❻. In 1951, it was reduced to rubble and, for a short time, Vinh Yen seemed to augur the French path to victory.

Gathering 81 battalions, Gen. Vo Nguyen Giap believed the Viet Minh were ready to switch to counter-offensive battlefield warfare and push into Hanoi by the Tet New Year holiday. His well-armed troops began on 13 January by destroying small hill posts around the town. With the most intensive aerial bombardment of the entire French war, the French (including battalions of Senegalese, Moroccans, Algerians, and Vietnamese) emerged the victors as the Viet Minh retreated back into the mountains four days later. Six thousand Viet Minh were killed in three days and perhaps 8,000 were wounded. Several thousand were roasted to death by napalm.

To escape the heat and humidity prevalent through much of the year in the capital city, Hanoi residents flock to the mountain retreats and cooler tempera-

A Viet Minh officer described the terror in his diary: "Hell comes in the form of large, egg-shaped containers... sheets of flames, extending over hundreds of metres... napalm, the fire which falls from the skies".

BELOW: boys with good hands, and a music teacher.

Established by the French as a cool retreat from Hanoi, the hills of Tam Dao were once peppered with French-style homes and buildings. After the French defeat of 1954 at Dien Bien Phu, most of the homes were destroyed by the French before the Viet Minh arrived.

tures at the **Tam Dao** ❼, established by the French in 1902 as a hill station. At an altitude of 880 metres (2,850 ft), Tam Dao sits on a large plateau within a valley about 90 km (50 miles) northwest of Hanoi in the Tam Dao mountain range. These mountains stretch from the northwest to the southeast, separating Vinh Phu Province from Bac Thai Province in the north.

Tam Dao means "three islands". The name derives from three mountains – Thien Thi, Thach Ban, and Phu Nghia, all at about 1,400 metres (4,500 ft) and which dominate the landscape – appearing from a distance like three islands jutting above a sea of clouds. Rare trees and plants cover the mountain slopes, while the forests harbour many species of animals, butterflies, birds, and flowers. It's chilly and very damp during most of the year, but it's a refreshing escape from Hanoi in the depths of summer, although facilities and accommodation are, for the most part, rundown and tired. Suoi Bac (Silvery Stream) meanders its way past the foot of Thien Thi, creating languid pools perfect for swimming. A waterfall cascades in three stages to form a lake; nearby are several pagodas.

For Vietnamese, Tam Dao also has melancholy revolutionary significance. After the disastrous Thai Nguyen mutiny and uprising in August 1917, 100 or so remnant survivors fled here to make a doomed 3-month last stand against the French army. Close to the end, one legendary leader, Sgt. Trinh Van Can, committed suicide. The French made a meticulous effort to track down and kill every rebel soldier and escaped political prisoner; in the end, the French claimed that only five eluded them.

There are three Hung temples on the slopes of Nghia Linh, 80 km (50 miles) northwest of Hanoi. The lowest temple, **Den Ha** ❽, is reached by climbing up

BELOW: Black Tai girls in the far northwest.

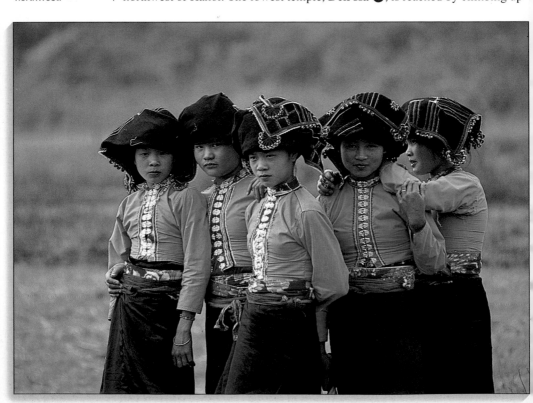

225 steps. Below the temple at the foot of the hill is an arched portal flanked by two huge stone columns engraved with two parallel sentences glorifying the origins of the Vietnamese people.

A further 168 steps lead up to the middle temple, **Den Hung**. Only 102 steps remain to reach the superior temple, **Den Thuong**. This temple is dedicated to the deities of heaven, earth and rice and to Than Giong, the infant hero who in the 3rd century BC is said to have chased out the Chinese Han invaders, assisted by a genie in the form of an iron horse. It was here that the last of the Hung kings transferred his power to the Thuc king at the end of the 3rd century. Vinh Phu's diverse scenic beauty is enhanced by a range of flora, extensive green-tea plantations, and, in winter, the beautiful white blooms of sasanca.

In Lap Thach district in the northwest, the **Binh Son Tower** of the **Chua Vinh Khanh** ❾ rises 16 metres (50 ft) into the sky. Built under the Tran dynasty in the 13th century, the 11-tiered, baked-clay tower of this pagoda is adorned with a wide variety of sculpture. Nearby is the Vinh Son snake farm, in Vinh Lac district. Established over a decade ago, it breeds snakes and produces snake wine and an ointment containing snake venom that is used to relieve muscle and joint inflammation.

In 1945, with the Japanese defeat by the Allies on the horizon, Ho Chi Minh came south and settled in **Tan Trao** ❿. This village is located high in the mountains east of Tuyen Quang, north of Vinh Phu. Here, Ho Chi Minh set up the Communist Party headquarters. A few days after the Japanese surrender on 10 August 1945, Ho organised the Viet Minh march into Hanoi and seized governmental power from the disordered Japanese rulers. Ho himself followed the Viet Minh on 26 August.

Map on page 162

BELOW: boats for the journey to Chua Huong, and fishing in flooded fields.

BELOW: boats to
Chua Huong.

South of Hanoi

One makes a pilgrimage to the mountain cave of the **Chua Huong** ⓫ (Perfume Pagoda) for the journey as much as the sacred site itself. Almost 60 km (40 miles) southwest of Hanoi, it is best approached by rowboat on the wide, swiftly flowing Song Yen. Looming over the strangely quiet countryside are the jagged karst Hoang Son mountains.

This dreamy landscape has been compared to Guilin in China. Each of the flat-bottomed boats is propelled by a powerful oarswoman, who rows in an unusual and demanding fashion: facing the bow, she pushes the oars forward. Many women are even adept at rowing in this way with their feet. If a Vietnamese interpreter is along for the ride, the boatwoman can identify the shapes that identify such peaks as the Crouching Elephant, Nun, and Rice Tray.

After 4 km (2½ miles), the boats pull up to the riverside near a cluster of pavilions and market stalls. The most important pagoda is the 17th-century **Thien Tru** (Heaven's Kitchen). In front of it stands a 3-tiered bell tower. Pilgrims shouldn't dawdle, though. The winding, often slippery route up the crags of **Huong Tich** (Ancient Vestiges of Perfume Mountain) to Chua Huong is less than 4 km (2½ miles) long, but the hike is arduous even when there aren't hordes of tourists pressing ahead. The pagoda itself is inside a big cave. During festival time, the "perfume" from the incense offerings is so thick that it obscures the view of the Buddha images. Visiting during the annual 7-week festival, in March and April, is an incredible experience. From the racing boats, the passengers cry greetings of "A di da phat!" ("Praise to Amitabha Buddha!"). Yet it may be best to avoid this time because the crowds can be frustrating and even frightening, and the aggressive souvenir sellers turn out in greater intensity than usual.

Chua Dau ⓬, 30 km (20 miles) from Hanoi, dates from the 13th century. The pagoda is a bit off the beaten track but the trip is well worth it, for the route passes through picturesque countryside and affords glimpses of traditional village life. The pagoda houses two lacquered statues that contain the mummified remains of two bonzes – brothers Vu Khac Minh and Vu Khach Truong – who lived here three centuries ago. Not far away and also in Tien Son district, the village of **Lim** is the site of a popular festival held every year shortly after Tet. For 3 days, from the 13th to the 15th of the first lunar month, people from all over the region converge on the village for the competitions of popular *quan ho* folk songs, sung alternately by young men and women.

Map on page 162

East of Hanoi

In the village of **Bat Trang** ⓭ potters carry on a 500-year-old tradition. Rather incongruously, shiny showrooms with large glass windows dominate the main street, only 10 km (6 miles) southeast of Hanoi. The oldest part of town, near the river, is threaded with walled alleys. What look like cowpats stuck on the brick walls are blobs of coal, drying out for use as fuel. A new ceramics market has been built for tour groups, but the most interesting areas are hidden in the alleys behind the modern shop fronts. Inside are brick kilns and great vats of white, liquid clay fed by a network of troughs. Bat Trang artisans used to make bricks, but now they concentrate on glazed ceramics, which include teapots, dinnerware, and 3-metre-tall (12-ft) blue-and-white urns destined for temples and pagodas. Along the riverside is the village's communal house, dedicated to Bach Ma (White Horse), King Le Thanh Tong's guardian spirit, as well as five village heroes, including Hua Chi Cao, who introduced ceramics here. A wall plaque, villagers

Quality ceramics of Bat Trang.

BELOW: master potter in Bat Trang.

say, was a gift from Emperor Gia Long and honours Bat Trang for bricks used to construct the imperial city of Hue in the early 19th century.

The once infamous craft village of **Dong Ky**, 15 km (9 miles) from Hanoi, was the country's firecracker hub until 1995, when firecrackers were banned. The highlight of the year was once the January firecracker festival, when elderly competitors with pillar-sized firecrackers vied to produce the loudest bang. The festival no doubt evolved from ancient religious rites of begging for thunder, lightning, and rain. Firecrackers have now been banned throughout Vietnam and Dong Ky villagers are alternatively engrossed in making carved hardwood furniture in both private and state workshops. In these dark brick buildings with corrugated metal roofs, barefoot men and women labour away with chisels and hammers, earning US$50 a month, a decent wage by Vietnamese standards.

The final products and plenty of carved knick-knacks are for sale in show-rooms along the dusty main street. The evidence here is that rich Vietnamese have abandoned all pretensions to austerity. Heavy, black-wood settees with matching chairs seem constructed for giants and are riotously adorned with rococo carvings of dragons and snarling lions. With complementary armoires, side tables, and 10 or so other pieces, the entire set can be had for a mere US$30,000. Salespeople say buyers are overseas Vietnamese and newly wealthy domestic "millionaires". Fortunately, there are a few simpler designs and lighter finishes, with and without mother-of-pearl inlay. Pieces can also be made-to-order and sent abroad. *Caveat emptor.*

The return to Hanoi can be timed for a delicious snake dinner at **Le Mat**, only 7 km (4 miles) from Hanoi. Le Mat is in the business of hunting snakes, raising snakes, and serving snake cuisine. The cobra and buffalo snakes are

TIP

A word of warning: restaurant staff are very tourist-friendly, but visitors should ascertain the price before tasting even a crumb of fried snake-skin. Bargaining is advised. The less adventurous can partake of samples at street stalls.

BELOW: harvesting salt from ponds.

cooked in many ways and served as soups, entrees, and appetisers. They all taste like chicken. One can observe the snake being captured from a cage, gutted, and its blood squeezed into a glass of rice alcohol. Bottles of this snake "elixir" with a cobra draped attractively inside make challenging souvenirs.

Le Mat is a legendary village apart from snakes. A daughter of the 11th-century king Ly Thai Tong was cruising on the Song Duong when a devil overturned the boat. A young Le Mat man dived in, killed the snake, and rescued the princess. The king offered a reward, but the young man instead requested that he and many poor people be allowed to reclaim land west of Hanoi. They were successful, established 13 settlements, and returned to Le Mat every year to express their thanks at festival time. At this annual festival in March, a big pot is carried on a palanquin to a pond and solemnly filled with clean, filtered water. A carp from the pond is added to the palanquin and escorted into the communal house, where a ceremony of gratitude ensues. Of much more recent origin is a snake dance related to martial arts and performed by village youth.

A visit to **Chua But Thap** ⓮, near Dinh To village in Ha Bac Province, makes a pleasant day-trip. The style of this pagoda, originally built in the 13th century, is very Chinese. In this quiet site by a canal there is also an unusual 4-storey stone stupa, Bao Nghiem. Among the many wood statues is one that depicts the goddess of mercy, Quan Yin, the Buddhist manifestation of ancient India's *bodhisattva* Avalokitesvara, with her thousand eyes and arms. Those who worship her believe that her many eyes and arms have supernatural power, the eyes to see and the hands to help those in need. Martial arts and other competitions that mark But Thap's annual festival, falling on the 23rd and 24th day of the third lunar month, are of very ancient origin.

Map on page 162

BELOW: ploughing a field with hand-plough and buffalo.

Map on page 162

The traditional theatre at the communal house in Dinh Bang is something of an architectural marvel on stilts. Built of ironwood in 1736, the building is one of the largest of its kind in Vietnam.

BELOW: a durable truck carries the load.
RIGHT: tending to the rice.

Heading towards the east, on the way to Hai Phong and the coast, the road passes through the relatively flat province of Hai Hung, famous for its beautiful orchards. Fruit from Hai Hung, especially longan and lychee, is reputedly the best in northern Vietnam, supplying the Vietnamese royal court in earlier centuries. Today, Hai Hung is known for its porcelain; the largest factory of porcelain in northern Vietnam, built with the assistance of China, is located here. A food known as *banh cuon*, which is a rice pancake wrapped around minced pork, originates from Hai Hung.

In Hung Dao commune, **Den Kiep Bac** ⓯, 60 km (40 miles) from Hanoi, dates from the 13th century. It is a temple dedicated to the national hero Tran Hung Dao, who vanquished the Mongols in the 13th century and was made a saint by the people. His army encamped here in the Kiep Bac Valley. His statue – plus those of Gen. Pham Ngu Lao and the genies of the Northern Star and Southern Cross, not to mention his two daughters – are venerated in this temple. The temple festival falls on the 20th day of the eighth lunar month. This site is shared by an old garden of medicinal plants, formerly used in the army's medical service.

Nearby, the pagoda of **Chua Con Son** ⓰ is the home of another national hero, Nguyen Trai (1380–1442), who helped King Le Loi chase out the Ming invaders from China and free the country from Chinese domination at the beginning of the 15th century. At the foot of the hill, the well-maintained Hung pagoda contains statues of Nguyen Trai, his maternal grandfather, and the three superior bonzes who founded the Truc Lam Buddhist sect. Some 600 stone steps lead up to the summit, where the energetic will find a superb view of the surrounding mountain ranges.

North to China

The northern circuit from Hanoi to the Chinese border begins in Ha Bac Province and its key region of Bac Ninh, then crosses the rice paddies of the Hong Song (Red River) delta before entering the mountainous regions near the Chinese border, the site of several skirmishes between the Chinese and Vietnamese armies in 1979.

Ha Bac Province is full of historical, cultural, and religious vestiges, and the area around **Bac Ninh**, the largest city, is home to more cultural and religious festivals than any other area in Vietnam. Among the architectural remains are the ancient Luy Lau citadel, and the temple and mausoleum of Si Nhiep, the governor of ancient Giao Chi. The pagoda of **Phat Tich** (Relic of Buddha), on a hill in Phuong Hoang village, was built in the 11th century under the Ly dynasty. It has been badly damaged by the ravages of time and war, but a 40-metre (120-ft) stone statue of Amitabha Buddha dating from the 11th century remains intact.

Dong Ho, in Bach Ninh, is a village famous for its communal production of woodcut prints. The prints depict traditional themes and their preparation is as historic in nature as the prints themselves. The various stages of production – carving the wood block, preparing the paper, obtaining natural colours from plants and minerals – are tasks shared by the family. ❑

HAI PHONG AND HA LONG

Northern Vietnam's most important port, Hai Phong, gladly yields to what's beyond: Vinh Ha Long, the most wondrous of bays sculpted when an ancient dragon swished its immense tail

Map on page 178

Heading east from Hanoi eventually leads to white-sand beaches washed by **Bien Dong**, or the **South China Sea** (which remains a constant source of contention between Vietnam and China, as both claim rights to the sea and to the archipelago offshore, possibly rich in oil reserves). Even more enticing to travellers are the limestone islands of Vinh Ha Long, or Ha Long Bay. Before reaching the coast, the road passes through the relatively flat province of Hai Hung, which is famous for its beautiful orchards and delicious fruit.

The 120-km (75-mile) road from Hanoi to **Hai Phong** ❶ winds ever deeper into the densely populated **Song Hong** (Red River) valley. In the late 1940s and early 1950s, this road, Highway 5, was lined with garrisons, watchtowers, and "Beau Geste" forts surrounded by barbed wire fences, trenches, and mine-fields. The larger ones had airfields. At the small end of the scale were hundreds of isolated, 10-man, reinforced-concrete bunkers (by the end of the French period, there were 2,200 such bunkers throughout the delta). Vehicles ventured along this road only in convoys and during daylight hours. At night, the road was officially closed – though not to the elusive Viet Minh guerrillas.

Today the road is jammed with trucks carrying goods to and from the port and bicycles and motorbikes laden with chickens, bags of rice, and pigs on their way to market. The city's industrial area sprang up after the French departure. Today, many industrial plants, engineering factories, glass, brick and cement works, and lime kilns are evident from the main road into Hai Phong. More recently, local industry has grown to meet the demands of construction in the area. In the early 1990s the government had hoped to build an industrial zone along this route, but the withdrawal of foreign investments towards the end of the 20th century brought many plans to a standstill. Only recently has development been revitalised.

Hai Phong, the country's third-largest city and the north's most important port, is in the northeast of the Bac Bo delta. It occupies the right bank of the busy Cua Cam, 20 km (13 miles) and many sand banks from the open sea. A small port town at the time of the French conquest of Tonkin in 1883, Hai Phong quickly became a city as the colonialists drained swamps and threw up monumental buildings. Since the city is crossed by 16 rivers, setting the foundations in the soggy soil was no simple task.

The most famous of these rivers is the Bach Dang, where in 938 the national hero Ngo Quyen defeated the large southern Chinese fleet. The Song invaders suffered a bitter defeat here in 981 and the Mongols suffered the same fate in 1288. The first of the French warships arrived in Hai Phong in 1872. The lure was access, via the Song Hong, to China's Yunnan region.

LEFT: unloading rice in Hai Phong from the Mekong region. **BELOW:** keeping cool in the heat.

Some 35 km (21¾ miles) south of Hai Phong is Dong Minh village (Vinh Bao District), known for its high-quality woodcarving since its founding by a master craftsman in the late 1600s. The fragrant jackwood is preferred by the craftsmen, who value its beauty, lightness, and softness. This is also a good place to buy water puppets.

The last units of the French expeditionary forces also exited the same way in 1955.

Hai Phong was also where, in late 1946, a skirmish between French and Viet Minh militia – occupying different zones of the city – erupted following a dispute over which had the authority to collect customs duties. Anxious to forestall similar incidents throughout the country, the French fleet shelled the city and aircraft bombers demolished residential neighbourhoods. French and Viet Minh soldiers fought house to house. With the help of artillery, the French quelled the uprising in a few days. The much-disputed death toll was perhaps 6,000. During the war with the United States, Hai Phong was sporadically bombed from air and sea between 1965 and 1972. In 1972, the US President, Richard Nixon, ordered the mining of the harbour to stem the influx of Soviet military supplies.

Hai Phong's troubles didn't end with peace in 1975. For more than a decade, the harbour was the most popular departure point for northern "boat people" fleeing economic and political hardship. Hai Phong's fishing fleet was decimated. Persecuted during the 1979 war with China and always suspected as "commercial opportunists", most members of the city's large ethnic Chinese community joined the exodus, if they hadn't already fled to China.

Rambling through Hai Phong

Hai Phong doesn't attract many tourists. Even by Vietnamese standards, Hai Phong is notorious for official corruption, individual avarice, and quick tempers. Most of the tourism trade for Ha Long has therefore shifted to Bai Chay *(see page 182).* This is perhaps unfortunate because Hai Phong is, for Vietnam, an attractive city. There are wide shady streets, well-tended spots of greenery, and a surprising number of colonial-era administrative buildings.

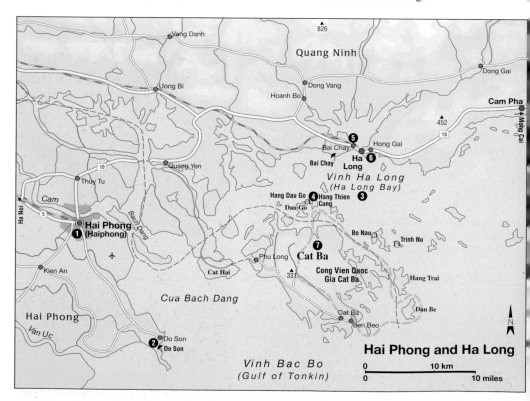

Hai Phong and Ha Long

0   10 km
0   10 miles

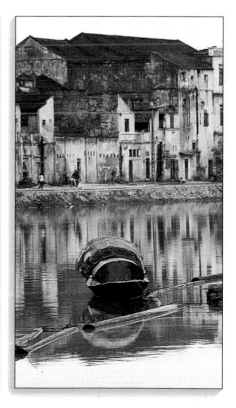

The city centre curves around the Song Tam Bac. In the city centre are several impressive colonial era hotels, administrative buildings, and the red city museum. Beyond the Catholic cathedral is a square overlooked by the yellow, neo-colonial municipal theatre, also known as the Opera House. During the first days of the 1946 French attack, actors with antique muskets held off French troops here.

Like every city in Vietnam, Hai Phong has its temples. The pagoda of **Du Hang** in the south of the city was built three centuries ago, but it has been restored often since. It is dedicated to Le Chan, the valiant woman warrior who aided the Trung sisters in the uprising against the Chinese in AD 39. The long, low wooden building with a swooping roof is reached by passing through a triple-tiered bell tower and an open courtyard. Behind the carved offering table is a baby Buddha protected by nine dragons. Visitors are warned not to confuse – as many locals and even cyclo drivers do – the pagoda of Du Hang with the nearby **Hang Kenh** *dinh*, or communal house. The communal house – well worth a visit – is off Nguyen Cong Tru and fronted by a neglected lotus pond. Beyond the spacious courtyard is the long and low wooden building with a curling, tiled roof. Within the dim interior, 32 ironwood pillars support the roof, and there is an enormous palanquin decorated with carvings of dragons. The beams of the ceiling are adorned with hundreds of relief sculptures of contorted dragons. Once upon a time, every village had a dinh. Where they still exist, dinh are often shut up and many of the centuries-old decorations have been destroyed.

About 20 km (12 miles) southeast of Hai Phong, at the tip of a peninsula, is **Do Son ❷**, home of a legitimate gambling casino.

BELOW: placid canal of Hai Phong.

GAMBLE IN ISOLATION

At the very end of the peninsula southeast of Hai Phong and housed in a renovated 1930s hotel is Do Son Casino, Vietnam's first legal gambling den. With little islets sprouting off the peninsula, it would have the best view in town if it had any windows. In the heady days of 1994, Stanley Ho, Macao's casino impresario, made a very risky bet that a casino could succeed here. It was the country's first since South Vietnamese Pres. Ngo Dinh Diem closed the last legal one in the 1950s. Vietnamese love gambling. Before the communist takeover in the 1950s, people of all ages and classes were chronic gamblers.

However, under the terms of Ho's joint casino venture with the Vietnamese government, Vietnamese are forbidden to enter it. Instead, the casino hosts gambling tours from China. Of course, well-connected Vietnamese do sneak in occasionally. It's nowhere near as seedy as any of the Macao joints. Slot machines, roulette and card games are on offer.

Although gambling is declared one of the "social evils", along with prostitution and drug abuse, casinos are now opening throughout the country, drawing foreigners and "overseas Vietnamese".

Ha Long vegetation.

Vinh Ha Long

No trip to northern Vietnam could be complete without visiting Quang Ninh Province. This province shares a common border with China in the north and harbours one of the wonders of the world, **Vinh Ha Long ❸** (Ha Long Bay), with probably the most stunning scenery in Vietnam. The bay's tranquil beauty encompasses 1,500 sq. km (580 sq. miles) and is dotted with well over 3,000 limestone islands and islets, many of them without names. Bizarre rock sculptures jutting dramatically from the sea and numerous grottoes have created an enchanted, timeless world. The sails of the junks and sampans gliding on the bay add further to the beauty of the scene. Not surprisingly, the bay was twice declared a UNESCO World Heritage Site: first in 1994 for its natural scenic beauty, and again in 2000 for its great biological interest.

Ha Long means "dragon descending" and the name originates in local legend. A celestial dragon and her offspring were ordered by the Jade Emperor to halt an invasion from the sea. The creative dragons spewed out bits of jade that turned into wondrous islands and karst formations, thereby scuppering the enemy ships. According to other versions, the jewels were pearls and the bay was created when the dragon flung herself into the sea; on the way, her swishing tail dug deep valleys and crevices in the mainland, which were subsequently filled by the sea. Regardless, the dragon was so pleased with her creations that she settled amongst them. She is said to live under the bay to this day. All of the well-known caves have their own legends. Even humble limestone piles are known to local fishermen by fanciful nicknames: limestone outcrops like the Dog, Turtle and Toad are derived from the dolomite rocks' uncanny resemblance to the respective animal's shape.

BELOW: fishing junks, Ha Long Bay.

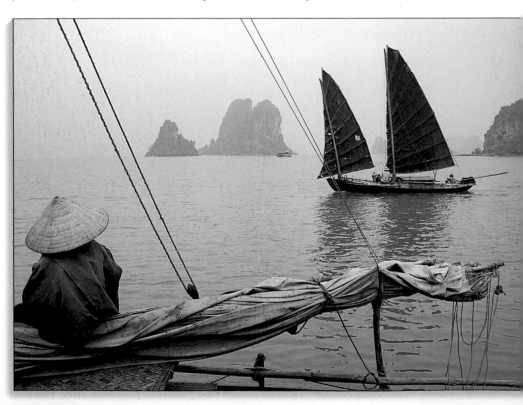

No typical one-day tour can take in more than a few caves. Those with enough time and specific sites to visit in mind could spend days cruising. Boat tickets are available at the pier in Bai Chay *(see page 182)*. A much better option is to book a package from a Hanoi-based tour operator *(see text box on page 183)*.

An alternative is to base oneself on Cat Ba *(see page 184)*, the bay's largest island and a national park. Not only is it more rustic, clean, and quiet, it's closer to many of the most dramatic grottos. Whichever you choose, bring along a swimsuit so the boatman can drop you within swimming distance of an uninhabited island with a pristine beach.

Folklore claims that **Trinh Nu** (Virgin) cave was named after a young girl whose parents were poor and could not afford to own a boat. They had to rent one from a rich man, but when they could not pay what they owed him, the rich man demanded their beautiful daughter in lieu of their debt, and so forced her to marry him. The poor girl refused all his advances. He had her beaten but still she would not submit to him; he finally exiled her to a grotto, where she starved to death. She was immortalised in stone by a rock resembling her figure that emerged from her burial site.

The most spectacular of the bay's grottoes is the beautiful cave of **Hang Dau Go ❹**, with its stalactites and stalagmites resembling beasts, birds, and human forms. It was christened the Grotte des Merveilles (Wonder Grotto) by the first French tourists who visited it in the late 19th century. On the same island, **Hang Thien Cung** encloses a chamber that is worthy of royalty – or so its name claims – or giants and is adorned with stalagmites and stalactites.

Ha Long has been the setting of many historic battles against invasions from

Map on page 178

TIP

The best time to visit Ha Long is in warmer weather from April to October as you can swim off the boat and relax on sundecks. Between January and March, the weather can be cool and drizzly, but even then it can be enchanting with the limestone outcrops peeking in between the swirling mists.
BELOW: luxury Chinese-style junk at Ha Long Bay.

Altar detail of a fisherman's temple in a grotto of Ha Long.

the north. It is believed that the sharp bamboo stakes that Gen. Tran Hung Dao planted in the Song Bach Dang to destroy Kublai Khan's invasion fleet were stored in caves here. **Hang Hanh** is a tunnel cave that extends for 2 km (1¼ miles). Access by sampan is strictly regulated by the tides. A visit to the lagoon on Dau Bo also must be carefully timed, since it can only be reached from the sea by navigating through three low tunnels at low tide.

Its decaying villas now sinking back into the forest, the island of **Tuan Chau** once served as a most exclusive retreat for the colonial elite. Ho Chi Minh used to summer here and his house, of course, has been preserved as a memorial. In such a place it comes as no surprise to hear that some people claim to have seen the Vietnamese equivalent of the Loch Ness monster. It is said to be a black creature resembling a snake about 30 metres (100 ft) long, which supposedly inhabits the bay. (Maybe it's the ancient dragon?)

Created only in 1994, the town of **Ha Long** actually comprises two towns, Bai Chay and Hon Gai, as well as surrounding districts. Locals, as well as transport companies, still treat them as distinct entities. **Bai Chay ❺** is the quintessential tourist trap, devoid of character or attraction. Shops specialise in key chains and other bric-a-brac fashioned from precious coral and limestone formations. There are dozens of new or renovated luxury hotels, filled with Chinese gamblers on a junket, and scores of new but rickety mini-hotels. On summer weekends, the latter are filled with Vietnamese tourists and their overseas relatives, apparently drawn by the karaoke facilities. Outside the summer months, Bai Chay is nearly deserted, save for the persistent postcard hawkers.

BELOW: fisherman at a grotto altar praying for a good catch.

At least there is plenty of fresh, well-prepared seafood. Most popular are the umbrella-draped, open-air restaurants lining the main avenue, which runs along the waterfront. A short walk further along this avenue reveals two swimming beaches that are packed in the summer. Tons of sand were dumped on the mud beach and, although less than appealing to overseas visitors, the view over the bay at sunset is stunning.

Hon Gai ❻ is nevertheless more interesting than Bai Chay. The ferry from Bai Chay only takes a few minutes. Hon Gai appropriately enough means "coal mine" in Vietnamese. When the French colonisers launched their final successful onslaught of the north, they seized Hon Gai in 1883 to safeguard the coal mines. Today, although open pit-mining continues in the surrounding hills and sooty warehouses hunker near the docks, Hon Gai is bustling with the construction of new shophouses, hotels and homes.

Visitors are advised to soldier on to the knobby hill called Nui Bai Tho. At its base, close to the long-distance (Hai Phong and Cat Ba) ferry pier, are a market, food stalls, and fishing village.

The gaudy pagoda of Long Tien, guarded by statues of fierce armoured soldiers, is reputed to be 500 years old and dedicated to the ever-popular general Tran Hung Dao, who beat back Mongol invaders in 1284. Along the path around the hill and through the fishing village are inscriptions carved into the rock face. These are poems in praise of Ha Long's loveliness and date back hundreds of years. At 102 Le Thanh Tong, a small lane climbs to the summit – about one hour's hike – for a view of Halong Bay. At 165 Nguyen Van Cu is **Bao Tang Quang Ninh** (open Tues, Wed, Fri and Sat 8–11.30am and 1.30–4.30pm; admission fee), a small museum that contains archaeological artefacts and fishing implements, and displays explaining Vietnamese ethnic groups and the historic struggles of coal miner unions in Vietnam.

Map on page 178

BELOW: cuisine of Vinh Ha Long.

SAILING ON HA LONG BAY

The best way to appreciate Ha Long Bay is by boat. Every Hanoi tour operator arranges one- to four-day tours of the bay, with transfers, meals and accommodation on a boat. Valiant efforts have been made to regulate the boats and ticketing systems. Complaints of being held hostage by boat captains are no longer heard of, but booking a tour with an agency in Hanoi is still more convenient and recommended. Boats depart from Bai Chay, some 165km (102 miles) east of Hanoi by road. For those with limited time, there are one-day tours with roughly four hours of cruising, but this is not worthwhile given the three-hour road journey to Bai Chay.

Most tour operators use standard engine-powered wooden boats with dormitory-style cabins. Luxury junk boats, with top-notch dining, large sundecks and en-suite cabins, are also available. Handspan (tel: 04-933 2377, www.handspan.com) operates the most economical trips on board its *Dragon's Pearl* junk with 18 cabins. Buffalo Tours (tel: 04-828 0702; www.buffalotours.com) operates the mid-priced *Jewel of the Bay* luxury junk with five cabins. Emeraude Classic Cruises (tel: 04-934 0888, www.emeraude-cruises.com) runs the most expensive luxury cruises on a replica paddle steamer.

Map on page 178

Deer antlers are harvested in the Cat Ba archipelago for their medicinal qualities.

BELOW: hotel in Ha Long Bay.
RIGHT: cleaning rice in Halong Bay.

Cat Ba archipelago

The Cat Ba archipelago consists of 366 islets and islands that cover some 20,000 hectares (50,000 acres), peppered with beautiful beaches and grottoes. Twenty km (12 miles) from Hai Phong, with the Gulf of Tonkin to the west and Vinh Ha Long to the east, the island of **Cat Ba** ❼ covers 190 sq. km (75 sq. miles). Its beautiful landscape features forested hills, coastal mangrove and freshwater swamps, lakes, and waterfalls.

Much of the island is covered in forest. Half of the island and 90 sq. km (35 sq. miles) of surrounding waters are part of the **Cat Ba National Park** (open daily, dawn to dusk; admission fee). The park's rich diversity of flora and fauna includes 69 species of birds – among these the hornbill – reptiles, and 32 species of mammals, including wild cats, boar, porcupines, monkeys, deer, and gibbons. Wherever you hike, don't count on glimpsing any of the fabled wildlife, though a lucky few report butterfly sightings. Poaching is declining with effective education programmes, an increased number of park rangers and greater affluence brought about by tourism. Human remains and stone tools from the Neolithic era have been discovered in some of the island's caves. Submerged vegetation, hot springs, and limestone lakes add to the attractions.

The island's population is less than 15,000, perhaps not even half the number of 20 years ago. With its remote harbours, Cat Ba's fishing fleet was ideally situated to serve the needs of fleeing "boat people" throughout the north in the late 1970s. Endemic poverty combined with communist economic policies might have been sufficient incentives to set out for the high seas and new homelands, but there was yet another incentive: the majority of islanders were also ethnic Chinese. When Vietnam launched persecutions of its Chinese minority shortly before its war with China in 1979, Cat Ba islanders joined the flood in earnest. As a consequence, many of those left behind now have relatives in the United States, Canada, and Australia.

Gifts and loans from overseas relatives helped to build the line-up of narrow mini-hotels in the village of Cat Ba. Overlooking the Gulf of Tonkin, it is the island's main settlement and port. There are three scraps of clean beaches within walking distance.

For those who want to explore the interior, a bus regularly travels from the waterfront, passing though lychee orchards and abandoned farms before reaching the park entrance about 18 km (11 miles) later. The easiest hike is only a 2½ km (1½ miles). As long as it's not muddy, the walk isn't difficult, but it's a good idea to engage the services of the guide, who will be more adept at spotting forest life. Alternatively, you may wish to buy a trail map from the ticket counter. You will find the forest path clearly marked with numbered signs, and these correspond to the informative descriptions on the map. Camping is allowed in the park, but you'll need to bring your own gear.

For the more adventurous, a much more challenging 18-km (11¼-mile) hike through the park and to the top of one of the mountains can also be arranged. Ask at your hotel or book a group tour. Lasting about 5 or 6 hours, the walk requires proper hiking shoes and a generous supply of water. ❑

Northern Vietnam

0   50 km
0   50 miles

THE FAR NORTH

Map on pages 186–7

Dismal roads embedded with memories of the French and Viet Minh at war lead to Sa Pa's ethnic minorities in the northern reaches along the Lao and Chinese frontiers

To the north and northwest of Hanoi, the flat rice-growing delta of the **Song Hong** (Red River) quickly gives way to craggy mountain peaks inhabited by ethnic minority tribes and draped by winter's cold. This region has long and often violent borders with Laos and China, where today minority tribal people farm in the shadow of modern hydroelectric dams supplying power for much of the country. Ancient kings, warriors, and rebellions are honoured throughout the northern mountains. The Vietnamese defeat of the French colonial rule happened in a remote and mountainous valley known as Dien Bien Phu. For all the allure of its tribal peoples and historical footnotes, travel in most of the far north is anything but convenient and predictable. Roads have improved dramatically but this is still for the traveller with time, patience, and an appreciation of adventure and roughing it.

PRECEDING PAGES: Black Tai girls. **LEFT:** Hmong farmer. **BELOW:** Black Tai villagers.

West of Hanoi

The Moc Chau district west of Hanoi and **Hoa Binh** ❶ is a stunningly beautiful highland valley surrounded by low mountains. The valley is sprinkled with the prosperous villages of Muong and White Tai and is laced with a vast irrigation network. The canals extend not only through the fields of wet-rice and manioc but throughout the villages of high-stilted houses; many houses have their own fish ponds. Yet Moc Chau's wealth probably stems from gold. The valley's dirt roads are ideal for strollers (and water buffalo); one may stumble on villagers in a shallow stream using a primitive pump to suck the mud and then sifting for grains of gold.

The Muong people are among Vietnam's oldest inhabitants, perhaps even predating the Viets. Relative newcomers, the Tai peoples began migrating from southern China over 2,000 years ago. It's possible, though, that the ancestors of the White Tai in Moc Chau arrived much more recently from China or Laos; the Lao province of Sam Neua (famed for its government re-education camps) is less than 30 km (20 miles) south of the valley, over mountainous terrain. Despite the long distance, travellers speaking Lao or Thai will recognise many words of the White Tai dialect (there are actually several local Tai sub-dialects; this is Tai Khao). As examples, *ban* is still village and *muang* is district.

Muong and White Tai are first languages, but there is some intermarriage and much intermingling of cultures. Both peoples, for example, live in wooden houses perched on high, thick stilts, with springy bamboo floors, wooden shutters, and overhanging thatched or tiled roofs that are often compared to a turtle's shell. Indoors is a single and enormous, high-ceiling room. An ancestral altar near the front is a hint that this is a Muong household. This room is where foreign visitors sleep on mats – sheltered in individual mosquito nets – if they wish to stay overnight. Both Muong and White Tai women embroider, but the White Tai, like Black Tai, are the master weavers. Beneath each of their stilt houses is a loom or two, and sometimes a display of fine shawls and scarves for the tourist trade.

Moc Chau is the gateway to the valley of Mai Chau, dotted with villages of minority groups, especially White and Black Tai.

Neither people ordinarily wear traditional dress in Moc Chau, but performers do when they provide visitors with an evening of traditional songs and dance. Women of both groups wear tight blouses held together in front by a row of silver clasps; their sarong-type skirts are usually dark-coloured with thin plain or warp *ikat* horizontal stripes and sometimes embroidered hems. The supplementary warp waistbands are peculiar to Moc Chau. The musicians play reed pipes, clappers, drums and cymbals, and the less traditional accordion. The evening is topped off with a tasting of manioc alcohol, sipped through reed straws from a communal bowl.

About 130 km (78 miles), or three hours' driving time from Hanoi, the village of **Ban Lat** in the valley of **Mai Chau** ❷ makes an ideal overnight outing. It's also a base for treks to highland villages. The people of Ban Lat are willing guides. Mai Chau is also the first (or last) stop for those on the way to Dien Bien Phu and other points on the northwest loop. You will know you are approaching the sprawling 1,500-metre (5,000-ft) market town of **Moc Chau** by the black-and-white cows wandering across the road – much of the area is devoted to dairy farming, thanks to Australian – and later UN – aid. Traffic is very thin in the northwest. During the coldest months, January and February, the temperature can fall to –3°C (27°F). Central heating is unknown anywhere here.

BELOW: dusk over flooded rice fields.

Map on pages 186–7

As Highway 6 from Moc Chau climbs to the west, the hills are cultivated with tea, cotton, and fruit trees, including mulberry, whose leaves feed silkworms. Highway 6 winds through the mountainous far-western province of Son La, which borders Laos on the south. The region is home to many ethnic minorities, including Hmong, M'nong, Muong, Mun, Kho Mu, Dao, Tay, White and Black Tai, Xinh Mun, and Chinese.

From Moc Chau to **Son La ❸**, 100 km (60 miles) to the northwest, and indeed further northwest, the scenery is much the same. Where the mountains aren't barren, the bushes and trees are young enough to indicate recent deforestation. Some of the devastation is due to logging, which continues apace despite being outlawed. Much has also been caused by the inhabitants of this hostile terrain. Mostly tribal people, they have plundered the forests for firewood and house construction and, at least traditionally, the Hmong and other highlanders practised slash-and-burn cultivation. From here on as well, one will often see Black Tai people plodding along the roadside. The women are identified by the colourful and elaborately embroidered folded cloths that they balance precariously on their heads.

Son La, which is also the capital of Son La Province, sits on the southern bank of the Song Nam La. It is the familiar, faceless provincial town of dusty roads and tall and narrow houses. In early morning, however, many traditionally garbed Hmong, Muong, Xinh Mun, and Black and White Tai come to trade in the town market. On **Khau Ca**, overlooking the town, are the brick ruins of **Bao Tang Son La** (Son La Prison; open daily 7.30–11am and 1.30–5pm; admission fee), built in 1908 and once the residence of many a political prisoner. Most of the compound was blasted away during the war against the French.

BELOW: tobacco plants, and grave of a Meo girl.

In French times, Son La was so remote, inaccessible, and disease-ridden that being sent there was akin to a labour-camp sentence in Siberia or Qinghai. As the prison superintendent promised a superior in a 1932 letter, "If they stay in Son La for six months, malaria will weaken and subdue them."

In the old warden's building is a small ethnographic museum that displays crafts, jewellery, and clothing of tribal people. A few watchtowers and cells have been reconstructed and there are displays of shackles, weapons, possessions of well-known political inmates, and contemporary black-and-white photos. Among the prison guests were future Communist Party secretary-generals, including Le Duan and Truong Chinh. Communist prisoners here were renowned for teaching fellow inmates to read and write *quoc ngu,* and for circulating clandestine newspapers. Today at the site there is also a rare mention of a Tai chieftain, Bac Cam Chau, who was beheaded at Son La after leading a major Black Tai insurrection from 1915 to 1916.

After the bleakness of the town, Son La's environs are refreshingly verdant and lush, laced with rice fields and fruit orchards. **Ban Mong**, a Black Tai village outside of Son La and about 6 km (4 miles) south of the prison, has hot springs. The caves of **Tham Tat Toong**, northwest of town, aren't worth the effort nor the admission prices.

End of a colonial era: Dien Bien Phu

Continuing west from Son La for two hours (75 km/50 miles) brings you to the small town of **Tuan Giao**. The road intersecting to the west is Highway 42, the route to **Dien Bien Phu ❹** (Chief Frontier Post), which is 80 km (50 miles) and at least another two hours away.

BELOW: mother and daughter.

Called Muong Thanh by its Tai rice farmers, the heart-shaped, pancake-flat valley of Dien Bien Phu is 29 km (11 miles) from north to south and 8 km (5 miles) wide. The valley was the site of a 57-day siege – the battle of Dien Bien Phu – and the ignominious end to French colonialism in Asia. It is encircled by steep, green hills from which tens of thousands of Viet Minh troops launched their assault on the French. To the south and west, it is less than 20 km (12 miles) to the Lao border.

The town of Dien Bien Phu sits on the east bank of the Song Nam Rom near the northern half of the valley. It was just another blocky concrete provincial town until the first half of 2004, when the celebration of the 50th anniversary of the French defeat brought about a tourism surge and building boom; the latter continues to this day. The planned inundation by a reservoir of former provincial capital Lai Chau, to the north, also contributed to the improvements. Dien Bien Phu was made the capital of Lai Chau Province in 1993 and provincial buildings have been constructed. There are now three flights daily from Hanoi or Ho Chi Minh City.

For the moment, tribal people slightly outnumber Vietnamese. For the French, subduing the wild northwest was a 40-year process. To occupy the Dien Bien Phu Valley in 1889 they evicted Siamese soldiers. Long before, the area had been the domain of Tai kingdoms, Vietnamese, and Chinese warlords.

In 1953, Gen. Vo Nguyen Giap launched excursions into northern Laos, reaching the outskirts of the royal city of Luang Prabang before withdrawing with the onset of summer rains. The French therefore believed Dien Bien Phu was key to preventing a Communist takeover of Laos, and French paratroopers easily recaptured it from the Viet Minh in late 1953. Dien Bien Phu was an old

TIP

Although Dien Bien Phu is known for its history, it's not known for its choice of accommodation, which is minimal and often noisy. The fact that it's a somewhat arduous land journey to the area might account for this.

BELOW: Gen. Giap in Dien Bien Phu on the 40th anniversary of the French defeat.

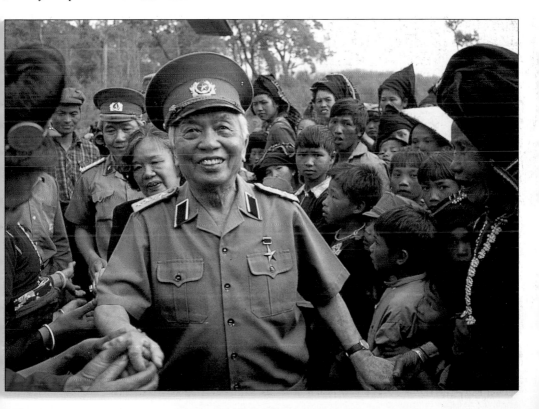

but ramshackle trading village where Hmong came down from hills to sell their opium to Tai brokers. The valley had strategic significance as the intersection of three supply routes. The road north to Lai Chau linked to China. The road northeast to Tuan Giao was the gateway east to central Vietnam. And just across the hills was the Lao province of Phong Saly.

French politicians were already resigned to the loss of Vietnam; more than 90,000 troops under the French flag had been killed or wounded. For the major powers, the recent armistice in Korea foreordained a settlement in Indochina. The momentum towards talks was accelerating as additional French troops were airlifted into the basin and Giap's army grouped in the surrounding hills. French forces numbered about 16,500 and the Viet Minh regulars at least 50,000, with well-maintained supply lines.

Apparently both sides believed that any victory on the battlefield would strengthen positions at the conference table. The French built fortified bases and two airstrips.

Beginning on 13 March, human-wave assaults quickly toppled three French bases. The French vastly underestimated Viet Minh strength and were astonished by the anti-aircraft guns and heavy artillery supplied by the Chinese and laboriously pulled over mountainous roads. The Viet Minh then spent weeks digging tunnels and trenches that encircled the valley. The final Viet Minh assaults were launched on 1 May. One by one the French outposts were overrun or abandoned when the French ran out of ammunition. On 7 May, Viet Minh troops planted a Viet Minh flag on the command bunker. Today, travellers can visit a reconstruction of the French command bunker, set amid a litter of rusty tanks and artillery. On the edge of modern-day downtown Dien Bien Phu, the

Viet Minh dead and wounded totalled about 23,000. On the French side, about 11,000 survived to walk into captivity; not even half of these survived the 800-km (500-mile) death march and the appalling conditions of the northern prisoner-of-war camps.

BELOW: war veterans at Dien Bien Phu.

site of the **Army Museum** (open 8am–4pm; admission fee) was once a battleground. On display are black-and-white battle photos, a model of the battle, and a selection of weapons. Across the street is a Viet Minh cemetery.

Map on pages 186–7

North from Dien Bien Phu

Running straight north of Dien Bien Phu, Highway 12 connects with the historic Tai town of old **Lai Chau** ❺, 100 km (60 miles) away. This small town is a good place to stop for lunch, or for an overnight stay for visitors who are on their way to Sapa. The road is now in good condition but during the rainy season between May to August, landslides can cause your journey to come to an abrupt halt. Fortunately, for the moment, road repair crew who are improving the roads are usually nearby with their heavy equipment to help clear the debris.

The **Song Da**, or Black River, cuts through a deep mountain valley around which Lai Chau, once the provincial capital, is situated.

The market, a few stalls and small shops with corrugated roofs, occupies a lonely strip on the floodplain. If the shops look new and temporary, they are. In 1991 and 1996, the Da overflowed, causing fatal floods. Most housing is now far up on the grassy hillsides.

The plan is to construct a dam and permanently flood the entire valley. Since Lai Chau will disappear under the water, the provincial capital has already been transferred to a new Lai Chau; this was formerly known as Tam Duong. Besides visiting the market, which is frequented by tribal buyers and sellers, travellers may climb up the hillside near the People's Committee Guesthouse. Here there are vestiges of the French garrison – a cluster of dilapidated buildings in peeling ochre plaster.

BELOW: young men near Lai Chau.

VIETNAMESE ZODIAC

The Vietnamese calendar, like elsewhere in Asia, is based on the lunar cycle. Referenced to the solar calendar, the lunar new year changes annually. Each year in the 12-year lunar cycle is represent by an animal: rat, ox, tiger, cat, dragon, snake, horse, ram, monkey, rooster, dog, and pig. The dragon, for example, rules every 12 years – in 2000 and then in 2012. Rats are charming, active, and fussy; oxen are patient and industrious. Tigers are flexible but indecisive and volatile, while cats are ambitious and with supple mind. The dragon is strong and sincere. Snakes are wise, quiet, and determined, while the horse is generous and popular, but stubborn. The ram is calm, unassertive, and helpful. Monkeys are erratic and inventive, and the rooster is busy, smart, and a thinker. Dogs are vigilant, pigs honest, impulsive, and gallant.

The Vietnamese calendar has a repeating cycle of 60 years, similar in importance to the Western century of 100 years. In addition to the 12 zodiac signs, there are 10 celestial signs called "stems". The 60-year cycle starts when the first of 12 signs is matched with the first of the 10 celestial stems. When each of the 10 stems is attached to a zodiacal animal, 60 different sets result. Each stem has a modifying influence on the zodiacal animal.

Wandering in benighted Lai Chau today, it's a struggle to conjure up the fate of the last Lai Chau chieftain. After the Geneva Conference, Deo Van Long was eventually allowed to retire to a villa in France, where he lived comfortably on his opium profits.

With the disappearance of Lai Chau, so will go a symbol of an illustrious history. A Tai people, the Lu, first immigrated from southern China in the 3rd or 4th century BC and settled in the Dien Bien Phu Valley, from which a Lu kingdom reigned for three centuries. Black and White Tai came later, perhaps in the 11th century. Today there are few Lu in Vietnam (though many in Laos).

During France's last war in Vietnam, the town of Lai Chau was one of the few French strongholds in the entire northwest. From a Lai Chau airstrip, long since erased, French planes dropped French-tribal guerrilla bands into remoter pockets of the northwest. After the July 1954 ceasefire, hundreds were stranded behind Viet Minh lines. The last were not captured or killed until the end of the 1950s.

Lai Chau Province shares a border with China in the north and Laos in the west. Among the ethnic groups here are Tai (or Thai), Hmong, Xa, and Ha Nhi. Much of the land – about 75 percent – is covered in forest containing valuable timber and animals, some of them rare, including tigers, bears, bison, and pheasants. Vietnam's most sparsely populated province, Lai Chau probably numbers around 30 people per square km. Yet it is 15 percent larger than the entire Song Hong (Red River) Delta, where average population density exceeds 1,000 people per square km.

The 200-km (125-mile) stretch from old Lai Chau to Sa Pa – Highway 32 – runs north and then east. The mountains become higher and craggier and are more thickly forested. This is the Hoang Lien range. Along the way, the nondescript towns are little more than fuel stops, but the Monday market day at **Phong Tho** attracts a panoply of tribes. The road carved into the steep mountainsides, which disappears above you into fog and mist, was once subject to fierce landslides because the mixture of dirt, laterite and gravel perpetually

BELOW: harvesting near Sa Pa.

underwent back-breaking repair by men wielding sledgehammers, while women workers hauled big wooden baskets filled with gravel, patching up holes and depressions. Nowadays, this work is performed by heavy machinery.

Map on pages 186–7

Sa Pa and hill tribes

Travellers will know they are approaching **Sa Pa** ❻, the northwest's tourism capital, from a few Dao shacks by the roadside shortly before the village of Binh Lu. For the first time, tribal people are neither shy nor indifferent to tourists or their cameras. On the contrary, they take off their metal jewellery and headpieces and proffer them for sale. Unlike the Dao villages closer to Sa Pa, these women have very close-cropped hair, usually hidden under a black turban, which holds the headpiece, a sort of metal cap with a small box-like crown.

Sa Pa was founded by the French as a hill station, and it's obvious why Sa Pa was rediscovered by backpackers in the mid-1990s and is now thriving on a burgeoning tourist trade *(see text box on page 203)*. The blue peaks in the distance are a study in shifting mists and clouds. The lower hillsides are ripples of terraced rice fields. It's the Swiss Alps crossed with Nepal. Best of all, it doesn't take more than 10 minutes to stroll outside the still-small frontier town and be traipsing on a path through the countryside.

And for the truly adventurous or foolhardy, there is **Fan Si Pan** ❼, Vietnam's highest peak at 3,143 metres (10,311 ft) and directly west of Sa Pa. A guide is mandatory, although there is a trail blazed by migrant workers from China. Sa Pa's guesthouses provide guides, porters, tents, and camping equipment. Located in the nature reserve of **Hoang Lien Son**, Fan Si Pan is good territory for sighting birds and rhododendrons. While it is not technically demanding, the

BELOW: northern waterfalls abound.

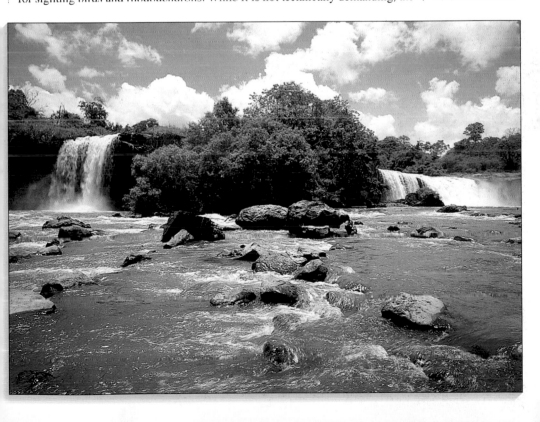

excursion takes at least four days and often more if rain or mist is thick. March is perhaps the best time to visit as it is the dry season.

With temperatures dropping below freezing, along with frequent winds and even snow once a decade, Sa Pa itself can be very uncomfortable in the winter, especially in January and February. The heaviest tourist season is summer, when both Vietnamese and Chinese flee here to escape the heat, yet rain can be quite common then.

Year-round, Sa Pa experiences a tourist surge from Fridays to Sundays. Apparently travel agencies in Hanoi have ridiculously hyped the weekend as a "love market" to visitors from the big city. No doubt local youth come to town in the hope of meeting the opposite sex from other villages, but they are wise enough to avoid the gawking tourists and their cameras. What foreigners will see is the weekly rendezvous when villagers come to town to buy, sell, and socialise. It's all the more picturesque, since Sa Pa's market spans several levels connected by stairways.

Both Hmong men and women in this area wear dark-blue, almost black clothing. It's been dyed with indigo and there are always indigo fields near Hmong villages. The women and girls wear indigo turbans, skirts, vests, leggings, and many big silver hoop earrings. Men wear baggy shirts and trousers and a long vest, as well as silver and bronze necklaces. Although their embroidered decorations are minimal, the motifs are unmistakably those that the Hmong use in Thailand and Laos. Hmong babies here too wear colourful little tasselled caps. Dao dress, like Dao culture and architecture, varies a lot in Vietnam. Here Dao men's attire is similar to the Hmong, but the little patches of embroidered decoration instantly identify them. Like that of their counterparts

TIP

Guesthouses run tours with English-speaking guides for day treks to nearby Hmong, Dao (pronounced *zao*), and Giay (pronounced *zay*) villages. Also on offer are two- to five-day treks to more remote villages.

BELOW: in the town of Sa Pa.

in Laos and Thailand, Dao embroidery is incredibly dense and colourful. Like their relatives in Thailand and Laos too, Dao women wear loose trousers that stop below the knee. Unlike them, however, Dao women here wear a jacket with a very long back panel. Some of these back panels are works of art, almost completely covered with dense embroidered designs. Both Dao men and women carry tasselled shoulder bags.

All of these items, some quite old, are sold – after fierce bargaining – by tribal vendors in Sa Pa. There is no need to worry about missing market day. In addition to the main Saturday market, there is a smaller market held every day. Also, throughout the week, Hmong and Dao women wander about town aggressively touting their clothing and jewellery. If tourists have even once glanced at her wares, the vendor will pursue them for days, even ambushing them in guesthouses and restaurants. Perhaps the best course for visitors is not to contemplate shopping until their last day in Sa Pa.

In various stages of decay, a few villas, with balconies and cupolas, linger from Sa Pa's days as a hill station, but the future holds more karaoke bars, more nouveau and Chinese claptrap architecture. Many of the old buildings were destroyed during the Chinese occupation of 1979 when the Catholic Church was shelled. It was repaired in 1994. A priest comes from Lao Cai twice a week to a full church; in the early mornings and early evenings, the congregation gathers to recite Mass from memory.

On the border

The town of **Lao Cai** on the Chinese border should be rushed through as quickly as possible. The 35-km (22-mile) descent from Sa Pa, however, has

Homestays are becoming increasingly popular. Service fees remain in the villages and the ambience is less "touristy" than in Sapa town.

BELOW: White Tai woman.

Warm northern Vietnamese dish.

spectacular views, and the road, finally, is sealed. In the French days, the colonial elite were carried up and down this route on sedan chairs. Unless tensions crank up again between China and Vietnam, it's perfectly legal to enter and exit China by walking across Lao Cai's new bridge during daylight hours. Beyond is the Chinese border town of Hekou and the train to Kunming. Travellers must have a Chinese visa in hand if they wish to go across the border.

Lao Cai is partly such an ugly, sterile city because it was flattened when China invaded in 1979. It was not the first time the city had been occupied by Chinese. Ironically, the Vietnamese rebuilt it to resemble just another communist Chinese city, with lots of grim, oversized cement boxes, wide streets, and very little in the way of attractive greenery. But the Chinese aren't solely to blame. In early 1951, still testing out his new heavy artillery and the practise of offensive warfare, Giap pinpointed Lao Cai. With Viet Minh troops outnumbering French 5 to 1, he took the city within a few days. These days, however, the scene feels a little livelier as a casino plays host to busloads of Chinese tourists and a bustling market is filled with crates of goods destined for Hanoi or Beijing.

Twenty-seven km (17 miles) to the east of Lao Cai, little **Bac Ha** ➒ may give Sa Pa a run for the tourist money. It's smaller, usually warmer, and has more of a frontier feel, probably due to the pony traffic. The appeal stems from the sheer variety of minorities represented, especially at the weekend markets. Most people in this area belong to one of the Hmong groups, but there are also Dao, Giay, Laichi, Lolo, Nhang, Nung, Phulao, Tai, Thulao, Chinese, and Vietnamese. There are several villages within walking distance of Bac Ha. Further afield are two photogenic markets, in addition to Bac Ha's on Sunday.

BELOW: moving goods near the Chinese border.

The Can Cau market, in a village 18 km (11 miles) north of Bac Ha, runs on Saturday and features livestock sales. As for the unusual two-storey house on the edge of town, now sheltering several families, townsfolk say it was the residence of their last "king", or chieftain, who now lives in France.

Back towards Hanoi

The 340-km (210-mile) road journey from Lao Cai to Hanoi is slow and tedious. The train is definitely preferable. Most likely only history buffs would bother stopping two-thirds of the way at the substantial concrete provincial town of **Yen Bai** , which also has a railway stop and is famous for its rubies. Yen Bai was the scene of several battles during the First Indochina War, but it is most famous for the "Yen Bai Uprising" of 1930.

Although communist annals would have it differently, it was actually the plan of another nationalist group, the Vietnamese National Party (better known by its Vietnamese acronym, VNQDD) to oust the French by military uprising. Only the Vietnamese troops at the Yen Bai garrison, however, proceeded with mutiny by killing their French officers. French troops quelled the mutiny within a day. It was the first time that aerial bombardment and napalm had been employed in Vietnam. Hundreds of Vietnamese soldiers and 12 VNQDD leaders were summarily guillotined. It was perhaps coincidental and simply a response to hunger and heavy taxes, but following the Yen Bai uprising, the country was racked for a year with anti-colonialist strikes, riots, and even the creation of two "soviets" at Nghe-Tinh in Annam. Repression was so harsh that for the next 10 years, at least in the north, both the VNQDD and the Communist Party were broken.

Map on pages 186–7

TIP

The best time to visit is September to November and March to May. The rainy summer months, particularly July and August, are Sapa's busiest months (with the most expensive hotel rates), when Hanoians flock here to escape the heat.

BELOW: cycling canines en route.

GETTING TO SAPA

Every Hanoi tour operator organises Sapa tours – from one to several nights – with guide, transport and accommodation, and a wide choice of tours. Sapa is one of the relatively few easy destinations for independent travellers, but book your return train ticket (and hotel) in advance. Trains can get very booked up, especially at weekends. Night trains (soft-sleeper four-berths with fan or air-conditioning cost US$12–16 one way; for more comfort, book the Tulico berths, tel: 04-828 7806; www.tulico-sapa.com) which depart daily from Tran Quy Cap station (behind the main station on Le Duan Street) at 10pm, arriving at Lao Cai station the following morning at 6–7am.

Sapa hotels can organise transfers but there also tourist minibuses (tickets cost 25,000 dong) which await incoming trains for the 35-km (22-mile) drive to Sapa. If money is no object, book a package with the Victoria Sapa Hotel (tel: 020-871 522; www.victoriahotels-asia.com), which also transfers guests on board its luxurious Victoria Express Train, departing four times a week. The Victoria is Sapa's first international standard hotel. Package deals from US$217 include train, hotel, tours, meals and transfers.

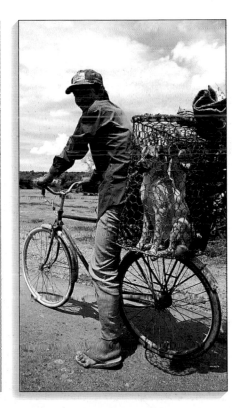

Northward from Hanoi

Due north of Hanoi, **Thai Nguyen** ⓫ is a grimy industrial city and home of Southeast Asia's first steel mill, built with Chinese aid in the 1950s. It's worth a brief stop for Thai Nguyen's excellent museum of ethnic minorities, which has many handsome ethnographic displays. Although they can't be recognised by their dress, many of the factory workers in this area are in fact tribal people. Eighty km (50 miles) from Hanoi, Thai Nguyen claims a landmark in revolutionary history. In 1917, Luong Ngoc Quyen, a nationalist student, was imprisoned here after the French had him arrested in Hong Kong by the authorities there. His torture triggered the indigenous garrison to mutiny and seize the town.

The soldiers were supported by peasants and miners under the banner of the League for the Restoration of Vietnam. French troops from Hanoi suppressed the rebellion within a few days and Luong Ngoc Quyen was killed. Remnants of the group who fled westward were ultimately slaughtered in Tam Dao in 1918. During the First Indochina War, Thai Nguyen, like Yen Bai, had considerable strategic importance as the key Viet Minh depot for supplies from China in the fight against the French.

Potentially, Cao Bang Province's greatest attraction for visitors is **Cong Vien Quoc Gia Ba Be** ⓬ (Ba Be National Park, open daily; admission fee), due north of Thai Nguyen and Hanoi. The national park covers an area of more than 7,000 hectares (17,297 acres), and is home to high mountains and deep valleys, as well as waterfalls, rivers, lakes and caves. It is also inhabited by many animals, including bears, macaques, and pheasants – supposedly well over 200 animal species. A few colonies of the indigenous Tonkin snub-nosed

BELOW: coal-field workers in Quang Ninh Province.

monkey, recently suspected of being extinct, have also been found here.

Located on a modest mountain top in the southwest, **Ho Ba Be** (Ba Be Lake, or Three Seas Lake) is one of three lakes – which are linked – and also the largest natural lake in the country. Over a kilometre wide and 9 km (5 miles) long, it reaches a depth of 30 metres (100 ft) and offers an opportunity for a spot of boating. The lake is surrounded by limestone cliffs and lush forests. In the summer, the height of the Vietnamese tourist season, there are many tour boats for hire for visits to surrounding caves and minority villages.

Previously, rapacious civil servants were a big obstacle to enjoyment of the region. Up to the mid-1990s, foreigners were allowed to travel in the Cao Bang area only if they gained special permits. Even after the ban was lifted, park or provincial officers demanded sizeable visitors' fees, and insisted that foreigners stay in the park guesthouse or in Cho Ra, a village 18km (11 miles) from the lake. Only recently have park officials set up policies to regulate fees, accommodation, and ferries, and to ensure visitor safety.

For visitors wishing to spend the night, there are two options. The Tay minority, who live in the park and the surrounding areas, have cottages or rooms for rent. Outside the park area, slightly more expensive lodging in the form of guesthouses or air-conditioned villas are also available. For more information, enquire at the park headquarters (tel: 0281-894 014).

The park's southern border straddles Bac Thai Province, a region intimately linked with anti-colonial resistance, particularly useful as its mountainous terrain rendered the region virtually inaccessible to French troops. The climate here is both tropical and subtropical, with an average temperature of 28°C (82°F) during the hottest month and 14°C (56°F) during the coldest. Lush and tall

Map on pages 186–7

BELOW: country road in Bac Thai.

palms brandishing wonderful, fan-shaped leaves and numerous varieties of bamboo abound throughout most of the province.

Beautiful Cao Bang Province is to the northeast and has only opened its borders to foreigners in the past decade. Highway 4 runs through ravines and mountain passes almost parallel to the Chinese border from the coast to the west. It was the site of numerous clashes in the late 1940s between French colonial troops and the Viet Minh guerrillas. Protected by a thin string of French forts, which were constantly under attack, Highway 4 was dubbed "Street Without Joy" by French-speaking soldiers, but the name soon came to apply to a wider geographical area.

With the 1949 communist victory in China, the Viet Minh not only benefited from a good supply of heavy weapons and Chinese advisors but also from training camps in China. In 1950, Giap switched from guerrilla attacks on isolated forts to full-scale attacks on the sizeable garrisons of Dong Khe and Cao Bang. As the Cao Bang defenders fled south to Lang Son on Highway 4, Giap ambushed them. Panicked, the French forces, which included many Vietnamese and North African soldiers, withdrew from Lang Son shortly after. The colonial side had lost almost the entire critical Chinese frontier. And the border town of Lao Cai to the west was soon to follow. Thus the Viet Minh had an assured line of supplies and support. And some would say that the French had already lost the war.

The province's capital and principal town is also called **Cao Bang** ⓭, which has a very pleasant climate by virtue of its location high above sea level. Shelled by the Chinese in 1979, Cao Bang town itself has little tourist appeal, but it is the customary launching point for visits to the glorious mountainous

TIP

One only needs to watch other tourists around hill-tribe people to recognise the truth: foreign tourists can be insensitive and intrusive – and often obnoxious – with their cameras.

BELOW: fake money at a temple for bringing good luck.

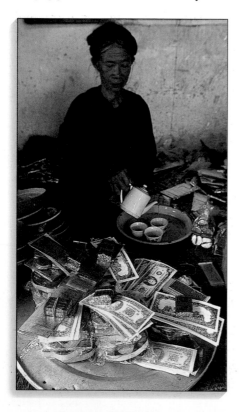

ALLURE OF THE AO DAI

The national dress of Vietnamese women is the *ao dai*, alluring, beautiful, and provocative yet discreet *(see photo on pages 66–67)*. Before the 18th century, women wore long skirts (still found in northern villages) but never the trousers of the *ao dai* (lit. long gown). In 1744, the Nguyen dynasty, ruling central and southern Vietnam, dictated a change in dress towards the lines of the Chinese style. Buttoned coats and trousers replaced skirts and split coats tied in front. Emperor Minh Mang imposed the wearing of trousers on all women. Colour and design were dictated and regulated by ceremonial requirements, social class, and professional hierarchy.

In the 1930s, an artist from a liberal reform group attempted to modernise the Vietnamese woman's dress through diversity in colour and designs. His new creation of a longer coat used different materials and could even be bare-shouldered. His innovations, gradually tempered with modifications, evolved to become today's *ao dai*. After the end of the Vietnam War in 1975 and the subsequent reunification of north and south, a period of severe austerity forced the *ao dai* into temporary retirement. In the late 1980s, however, the *ao dai* began to return to daily life, especially in the south.

surroundings and the Chinese border. The hill leading up to the war memorial has spectacular views from its summit: a pleasant way to begin the day.

The early morning markets in the surrounding villages are visited by throngs of tribal people, including the Tay, Hmong, Nung, Dao and Lolo. Enquire at your hotel for the participating towns and respective days, and be prepared to make an early start.

Cao Bang Province shares a long border with China. Forest covers 90 percent of the province, and the climate is cool, particularly in winter. The multicultural province has a population of about 800,000, covering an area of 8,450 sq. km (5,400 sq. miles), but the harsh terrain makes it a hard scrabble to survive from farming. The province's economic value lies in its rivers, which have been harnessed by hydroelectric stations.

Along with Lang Son, Cao Bang Province is the home for almost all of the Nung minority, which totals about 875,000. They farm at both valley floors and high altitudes, such as the 1,000-metre-high (3,300-ft) Dong May plateau. They are fine weavers and makers of bamboo furniture and baskets. The women traditionally wear long indigo dresses and headscarves. Linguistically and culturally, the Nung share much with their neighbours, the Tay (or Tho), who number over 1.5 million. Their shared language is clearly Tai, but because both the Nung and Tay have been in Vietnam for nearly 2,000 years and have been isolated from most other Tai, their cultural practices seem closer to the Vietnamese than to the Tai of Vietnam or anywhere else. Notable, for example, are their ancestral worship practices, which appear to have Confucian origins. They also have many Buddhist practices.

In 1941, when Vietnam was occupied by the Japanese but still administered by the Vichy French, Vo Nguyen Giap and other party cadres began from here to build an organisation of scattered agents and guerrilla units, omitting the usual messages of propaganda about class struggle and emphasising instead resistance to foreign aggression and "national salvation".

Encouraged by Ho Chi Minh, the Viet Minh made assiduous efforts to recruit members of various ethnic minorities, most of whom were hardly predisposed to fight for a sovereign Vietnamese state. The Vietnamese *(kinh)*, after all, were a distinct minority and a historical enemy in the northern provinces, but now they shared a hatred of the French. And the *kinh* promised an autonomous tribal state after victory.

Tay and Nung cadres rose to high positions in the Communist Party hierarchy. One of the original Tay leaders of the aforementioned Bac Son units, Chu Van Tan, was defence minister in Ho Chi Minh's August 1945 cabinet. After the final defeat of the French, a Tay-Nung autonomous region was created in the late 1950s. Schools were allowed to teach native languages and the region did have some self-governing functions, but this and a Tai region in the northwest were abolished in 1980.

From 1943, the Viet Minh received weapons and funds from US intelligence groups. In return they provided intelligence on the Japanese and rescued downed Allied pilots. By early 1945 the Viet Minh

Map on pages 186–7

BELOW: tribal woman and smile.

Hmong children outside of Sa Pa.

controlled large parts of four northern provinces but it wasn't until then that Giap organised here the first regular troops.

A good 2-hour drive north of Cao Bang, the cave at **Pac Bo** is yet another stop on the Ho Chi Minh pilgrimage trail. Just a kilometre from the Chinese border, this is near the spot where the man then known as Nguyen Ai Quoc crossed into his homeland for the first time in 30 years, in 1941. Later taking the name Ho Chi Minh, he only lived in the cave near the Nung village of Pac Bo for a few months, in early 1941, leaving the area in August 1942 and returning to China for two years. Nonetheless, there's a museum, Ho artefacts, a replica of his simple bed, and tourist trinkets. Ho named the stream flowing in front of the cave "Lenin Stream".

Also very close to the Chinese border, the waterfall at **Ban Gioc** – perhaps the country's largest – is very popular with Vietnamese and Chinese tourists. Nearby is Nguom Ngao Cave. The picturesque falls of **An Giac**, in Trung Khanh district, are formed by a stretch of the Song Quy Xuan falling from a height of 30 metres (100 ft). Many wild orchids grow in the region. Limestone mountains and forests surround another of the province's beauty spots, Thang Hen, one of seven lakes in the area.

To the northeast

Ho Cam Son ⑭ (Cam Son Lake), in the district of Luc Ngan, is surrounded by limestone mountains. This tranquil, picturesque setting offers accommodation, with rest houses on some of the small islands in the lake.

The road north begins to climb into the higher elevations as it leaves Ha Bac Province and enters Lang Son Province. The ascent into the mountains presents

BELOW: northern minority women.

stunning scenery. Lang Son Province shares a common border with China's Guangxi Province. Mountains and forests cover 80 percent of the province's land area, and tigers, panthers, bears, deer, pangolin, chamois, and monitor lizards are among the animals found here.

Provincial specialities include forest products such as fragrant mushrooms, anise, and a fine-flavoured tobacco. Tay, Nung, Hmong, Dao, Nghia, and Chinese are among the ethnic minorities living in the province. The Song Ky Cung that flows through the province is unique in that it flows northward to China. The other rivers in the region all flow south.

The narrow gorge at **Chi Lang**, a series of passes connected by tortuous tracks forged between high mountains south of the Chinese-Vietnamese border, is a battleground where the Vietnamese have fought many major battles against Chinese invaders throughout history. In 1076, the Vietnamese defeated 300,000 Chinese Song-dynasty troops here, and in 1427, nearly 100,000 Ming-dynasty troops received the same treatment. The gorge's northern entrance is known as **Quy Quan Mon** (Barbarian Invaders Gate) and the southern exit is called **Ngo The** (Swearing Path). The almost incessant fighting on this northern border has forged the temperament and galvanised the resilient character of the northern Vietnamese people.

Highway 1 runs right through the provincial capital of **Lang Son ⑮**, about 150 km (100 miles) northeast of Hanoi. Unsightly new buildings are fast replacing the bombed-out old ones. When 85,000 Chinese troops invaded Vietnam in February 1979, Lang Son was a prime target. By the time the Chinese occupied the Vietnamese city 16 days later, 80 percent of the buildings were rubble. Almost immediately, they began to withdraw. The town was

Map on pages 186–7

Long a smuggling post, Lang Son is now a legitimate trade centre. It is just 18 km (11 miles) from the Chinese border. With proper visas, foreign travellers may cross into China from here.

BELOW: Black Tai.

Map on pages 186–7

TIP

The train between Vietnam and China crosses the border near Dong Dang. But it's not possible to board the train here for the trip into China. Foreigners must board it in Hanoi for the border crossing.

BELOW: festival crowd at temple.
RIGHT: market talk in Sa Pa.

reviving on smuggled Chinese goods even before trade was legalised in 1993. Today all manner of capitalism – legal and illegal – flourishes.

The town of **Ky Lua** is the transit point for trains from Hanoi. In early 1996, the line reopened to cross the Vietnam-China border. Only a few kilometres west of town is **Nhi Tam Thanh**, an area that includes numerous caves and grottoes, many of which are used for worship of spirits.

Overlooking the site is Waiting Woman Mountain. Legend says an outcrop of rock is a woman who waited so long for her husband that she turned into stone. In the area are also ruins of forts and walls built to keep the Chinese at bay.

In the mountains just west of Lang Son is a highland valley called **Bac Son**, inhabited by Tay (Tho) people. Briefly allied and supplied by the newly arrived Japanese, Tay guerrilla bands attacked isolated French military posts and retreating French soldiers in 1940. While the Japanese soon reconciled with the Vichy French, the guerrilla insurgency already had momentum. Communist Party cadres took over coordination and near the end of 1940 staged a general uprising in Bac Son and eight southern provinces – collectively known as the Bac Son Uprisings. The French quickly stamped out the rebellion and executed 100 cadres. The repercussions were especially devastating and long term for the Communist Party in the south. But it meant that Bac Son in particular and the far north in general became the base from which the Party would rebuild from virtually nothing.

A half hour's drive northwest is **Dong Dang 16**, a town right on the fortified border. Flattened during the 1979 invasion, the town has arisen anew on cross-border trade. The crossing here is known as the **Friendship Gate**, optimistically named given the sporadic exchanges of gunfire between Vietnam and China until 1992. For foreigners, this is probably the most popular exit to China. Once called Porte de Chine, it was through here that Japanese troops entered Vietnam in 1940 before attacking Lang Son.

Along the northeastern coast

Southeast from Lang Son along Highway 4 is **Mong Cai 17**, situated along the coastline on Vietnam's northeastern border with China and a busy town growing fat on trade in low-quality Chinese consumer goods, and tourism. The town was destroyed by retreating Chinese troops in 1979 and reconstruction began only when the border was reopened in 1991. This is one of three land-border gates to China open to foreigners.

A few kilometres to the east, on an island separated from the mainland by a narrow sea channel, is **Tra Co**, which many say is the north's most attractive beach, with beautiful beaches and shallow water. It probably is its longest as well, at 17km (10½ miles), and its numerous guesthouses do attract many foreigners in the summer months.

However, the foreigners are mostly Vietnamese and Chinese, because many Westerners object to the black sand and mud flats. At the southern end of the island is Mui Ngoc, a haven for local smugglers. Southwest (240 km/150 miles) are Hai Phong and Vinh Ha Long (*see Hai Phong/Ha Long chapter, page 177*). ❑

ETHNIC MINORITY CULTURE AND CLOTHING

Vietnam's ethnic minorities live mostly in isolated upland areas but in recent years outside contact has changed their traditional culture

There are two types of ethnic minority in Vietnam, each with its own distinct origins, cultural practices, and reactions to change.

In the northern highlands, groups of Tai, Dao, Hmong, Tay, and Nung people are "recent" settlers, having migrated from southern China over the past 500 years. The landscape here is rugged and isolated, and most of these groups have maintained their traditional way of life. They live in houses on stilts, wear decorative home-spun costumes on a daily basis, and sustain some of the best-preserved traditional upland cultures in Southeast Asia.

In the central highlands, by contrast, the Bahnar, Ra De (E De), Jarai and Sedang are indigenous to the region. But the rolling hills are suitable for coffee and have recently been settled by large numbers of Vietnamese who make money from cash crops.

Many minorities have adapted, building houses on the ground and abandoning their loincloth for clothes. Traditional costumes are used only on festival days and for ceremonies. Some of them, wishing to maintain their traditional lifestyle, move deep into the remaining forest to live in isolation and sustain themselves through slash-and-burn agriculture. They can be seen in urban centres on occasional market days trading their produce.

▷ **TAI HEADSCARVES**
Tai women in the northwest still wear the *khan pieu*, or headscarf. Men traditionally give young women a khan pieu in declaration of their love.

△ **THRESHING RICE**
Many agricultural tasks are done by women. This Tai woman in the Son La province typically wears her khan pieu even while threshing rice.

△ **HMONG TEXTILES**
Hmong people wear their home-spun clothes on their way to sell produce in Sa Pa market, Lao Cai Province.

▷ **EMBROIDERY**
Embroidery is thriving as minorities find a market among visitors and in Hanoi.

▷ **SILVER NECKLACES**
Apart from its decorative value, Hmong and Dao women believe silver jewellery has the ability to heal and prevent disease.

HILL-TRIBE TEXTILES

All the hill tribes of the northern highlands have retained their own textile industries, and these are enjoying a revival as the number of overseas tourists and Vietnamese visitors increases.

Tai people in Mai Chau valley (Hoa Binh Province) use home looms to weave long cotton scarves, which are then dyed in brightly coloured stripes using traditional vegetable dyes and tied at the ends into elaborate tassels. In the Sa Pa region, Hmong women (above) carry their embroidery with them to the terraced rice fields. Pausing from agricultural work, they make use of the rest time to decorate bags and hats, which they sell at Sa Pa market to supplement their income.

Unfortunately, large numbers of imitation embroidered items, mass produced in the plains and transported up to Sa Pa, are now sold at the market. Visitors are urged to make their purchases with caution if they are after the genuine article.

▷ **SA PA MARKET**
Hmong people use home-grown linen and indigo to make clothes and exchange these goods for modern conveniences such as umbrellas and radios.

∨ **HILL-TRIBE CHILDREN**
Children in this central highland village traditionally went semi-naked. It's more common now to see them in imported shirts and dresses.

▷ **INNOVATIONS**
This E De woman illustrates the response of many central highlands people to change. Her clothes look traditional but are in fact an innovation.

THE TONKIN COAST

*Northern Vietnam was called Tonkin by the French,
and the French colonial charm is often encountered
along the coast of the Gulf of Tonkin*

Map
on pages
186–7

ighway 1 stretches the length of the eastern coast for more than 2,000 km (1,200 miles), from Dong Dang at the Chinese border to Nam Can in the Mekong Delta. Recent development projects have improved the condition of the roads – previously in poor repair – and the new Ho Chi Minh Highway (Duong Ho Chi Min) is beginning to relieve the congestion of the coastal road. On arterial roads, traffic still moves slowly as buffalo and bicycles vie for space and it doesn't help that produce is placed to dry on the dusty edges of the road – rice, straw, corn, chilli peppers, peanuts and tea. Heading south out of Hanoi, Highway 1 passes through the varied landscape of several provinces that contain every terrain imaginable – mountains, limestone hills, low-lying plains, inland waterways, rice paddies, and long stretches of sand along the **Vinh Bac Bo**, or **Gulf of Tonkin**.

The area surrounding **Nam Dinh** ⓮, on Highway 21 about 30 km (20 miles) from Highway 1 and the capital of Nam Ha Province, remains a Catholic stronghold, although many from here were among the 500,000 Vietnamese that fled south after the Communist takeover. Their ancestors were converted to Catholicism by Portuguese, Spanish and French missionaries in the 16th or 17th century, long before the French conquest. According to Vietnamese records, one of the first friars preached in this province in 1533.

This large industrial city lies 90 km (60 miles) from Hanoi on the southwest bank of the Song Nam Dinh (Nam Dinh River). Under the French, Nam Dinh became a centre for the domestic textile industry, which still flourishes today as the largest in the country. In the early 19th century, Nam Dinh was surrounded by a large citadel. The French dismantled it after occupying the area in 1882, but a single look-out tower still survives. The city was also heavily damaged during a 1947 Viet Minh siege and by US aerial bombing in the 1960s. The most interesting part of the city is by the riverside, where artisans and merchants still concentrate in the manner of Hanoi's Old Quarter.

Just to the north of Nam Dinh is the village of **Tuc Mac** and the ancient Tran ruins of **Thang Vang** (Golden City). These ruins are all that remain of the palaces built by the kings of the Tran dynasty, who defeated the Mongol Yuan-dynasty invaders from China three times in the 13th century. Tran Bich San, founder of the Tran dynasty, was born nearby. Among the ruins are the Thien Truong temples, which were dedicated to the 14 Tran kings, and the temple of Co Trach, which was dedicated to Tran Hung Dao. The only buildings left intact are the beautiful **Pho Minh** pagoda and a 13-storey tower, built in 1305 and which contains the remains of King Tran Nhan Tong.

PRECEDING PAGES:
train between Hanoi
and Ho Chi Minh.
LEFT: making
baskets.
BELOW: Catholic
church, Nam Dinh.

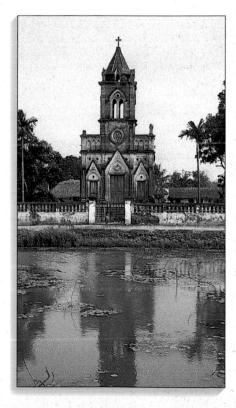

East of Nam Dinh, on the road to Thai Binh and Hai Phong, is the site of 11th-century **Chua Keo** 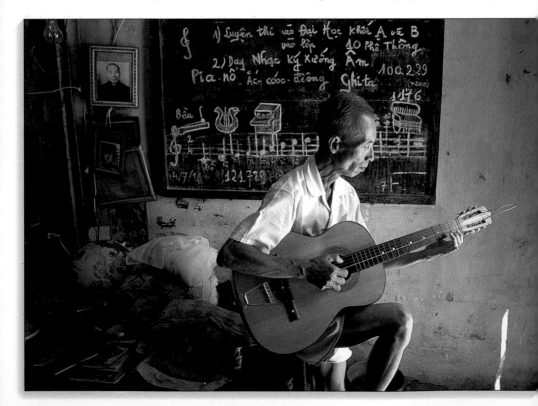. Since the 17th century it has undergone much reconstruction, but it retains the spirit of the original design. It is considered one of the finer examples of traditional Vietnamese architecture in the northern delta, dedicated to Buddha, his disciples, and the bonze superior, the 11th-century Minh Khong. No metal nails were used in the construction of this impressive wooden pagoda and its three-storey bell tower, which contains bronze bells cast in the 17th and 18th centuries. Many traditional rituals and diverse forms of entertainment are performed here – some of them centuries old – particularly during the Tet holidays.

Ancient New Year wrestling festivals are justly famed in Nam Ha's Thanh Lien district. At **Cua**, folk games as well as contests in martial arts and wrestling honour a village son who helped 10th-century King Dinh Tien Hoang quell a rebellion of 12 vassals. This festival falls every year on the fourth day of the first lunar month. The more spectacular, 5-day Lieu Doi wrestling festival starts the next day in nearby **Liem Tuc**. The tale giving rise to the festival lacks not a single element of a Vietnamese legend...

A young village man of extraordinary strength, skilled in the martial arts and swordsmanship, volunteered to fight the foreign invaders. Prior to a glorious battlefield death, he had fallen in love with a female soldier. When she came to visit his hometown grave – after the victory, naturally – she was so distraught that she dropped dead.

The village subsequently built two temples honouring the star-crossed couple, now metamorphosed into a Thanh Ong (Male God) and a Tien Ba (Female God). The festival is launched with a procession carrying the Thanh Ong statue

The famous Magnum Agency photographer Robert Capa was killed on a road near Nam Dinh when he stepped on a land mine in 1954, shortly after the fall of Dien Bien Phu.

BELOW: guitar teacher.

on a palanquin from temple to wrestling place. The matches include face-offs between new male infants (whose fathers actually wrestle on their behalf), native villagers, and wrestlers representing surrounding villages.

To the east of Nam Dinh, small Thai Binh Province has the highest population density in the Song Hong (Red River) Delta and in the country as a whole – well over 1,200 people per square kilometre. Salt fields cover extensive areas on the coastal shores. Under the French, all the salt had to be produced under the aegis of the government's salt monopoly. With the monopoly also on opium sales, the government reaped great revenues but at tremendous cost to peasants and fishermen, who were crippled (and sometimes inspired to revolt) by prices that continued to rise regardless of demand. Private production of salt was severely punished. In addition to rice, today jute, rushes, mulberry, sugar cane, and ground nut are also cultivated. Among the crafts found in Thai Binh, carpet making, silk weaving, wickerwork, and embroidery are common.

Back on Highway 1, about 30 km (20 miles) from Nam Dinh and 100 km (60 miles) south of Hanoi, the dusty town of **Ninh Binh** ⓴ has few redeeming features. However, situated only 1½ hours from Hanoi, it is a good base for explorations of the eminently redeeming features of Hoa Lu, Tam Coc, Kenh Ga, Cuc Phuong, and Phat Diem.

Ninh Binh is dusty mainly because of a nearby rock quarry. Most inhabitants of the town seem employed in carting around large rocks or repairing motors. Down by the riverside is a covered wet market.

Across the river rises up a very large, bare crag. In French days, a fort perched on top. In 1951 Viet Minh – temporarily – overran the French positions in and around Ninh Binh. Eighty French soldiers holed up in the local Catholic church;

Map on pages 186–7

TIP

Ninh Binh is full of mean dogs kept by families to protect their homes from robbers. These dogs know their territory, though, so unless you step over the boundary, they will only watch you.

BELOW: fisherman and stilt house.

TIP

Behind and to the left of Phat Diem Cathedral is a pure, white, marble reproduction of Michelangelo's *Pieta*, respectfully enshrined in a tiny man-made grotto covered with ferns and moss.

19 survived. In the eastern part of town, in front of the train station, stands a new church with a decidedly Asian spire; the eave and window treatments echo the curved lines of a temple.

It's obvious why Ninh Binh was an anchor in the so-called de Lattre line, the triangular cordon established in 1950 to protect Hanoi, Hai Phong, and the great rice-growing, coal-mining Song Hong (Red River) Delta from Viet Minh incursions. Ninh Binh straddles both Highway 1 and the Song Day (Day River). Immediately to the north of Ninh Binh, the Song Day runs parallel and just to the west of Highway 1, which in the early 1950s was lined with French fortifications. To the west of the river was solid Viet Minh territory.

Across Highway 1 and only 13 km (8 miles) northwest of Ninh Binh is **Hoa Lu**, the beguiling site of the 10th-century capital of a Vietnamese kingdom known as Dai Co Viet. It was a rather small feudal kingdom, covering an area of 300 hectares (740 acres) and reigned over by the Dinh and Le dynasties of the 10th century and by the early phases of the Ly dynasty in the 11th century. The kingdom was enclosed by a citadel, bordering the Song Hoang Long and running along the Yen Ngua limestone hills. It's instantly evident why this defensible site was selected. The enemy were the Chinese, who had been expelled in 939.

An inner citadel enclosed the royal court. There are some remains of the earthen citadels and of the valley's palaces, shrines, and temples, but they are in a state that only archaeologists would appreciate. An enormous stone column engraved with Buddhist sutras, dating from 988, was found here. What do survive are two 17th-century temples modelled on 11th-century originals.

After the capital was transferred from Hoa Lu to Thang Long (now Hanoi),

BELOW: kids at Hoa Lu, the ancient city.

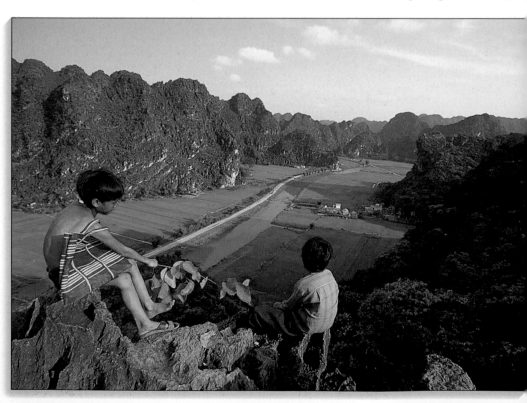

the two temples were built, one dedicated to the founder of the 12-year Dinh dynasty, Dinh Tien Hoang, who reigned in the late 10th century, and the other to his successor, Le Hoan. **Den Dinh Tien Hoang** was reconstructed in 1696. The temple now faces east, although the original faced north. It is entered by passing through two brick arches, the so-called Outer Triumphant Arch and the Inner Triumphant Arch. The 17th-century Dragon Bed, in an area once used for sacrifices, lies in the centre of the courtyard in front of the main building. It was carved out of a single rock. Lightly carved on the surface is a very strange dragon floating in a mass of clouds: it has a long beard, the head and ears of a buffalo, paws resembling human hands, and fish-like scaly skin. Surrounding carvings depict a carp, shrimp, and mouse. Gifts and food offerings are placed on the slab during festivals.

Statues of mythical animals – part dog, part lion – guard the doorway of the small temple. A huge drum in the forecourt was used by peasants to get the attention of mandarins. Inside the temple, King Dinh Tien Hoang, also known as Dinh Bo Linh, is worshipped at a central altar. The large characters written in ancient Chinese script translate as, "From this day onwards we have our independence". On one pillar is written "Dai Co Viet", the name Dinh Tien Hoang gave Vietnam. On the other, the script reads "Hoa Lu is prosperous as the capital". Behind the altar, passing by heavy carved beams, is a windowless back room with a 19th-century wooden statue of a paunchy Dinh Tien Hoang, framed by statues of his three sons. The single statue next to the king, on the viewer's right, depicts his eldest son, Dinh Quoc Lien. While Dinh Quoc Lien was the eldest, he was not chosen as heir apparent by his father, so he masterminded the assassination of the anointed brother, Dinh Hang Lan, in

Map on pages 186–7

BELOW: Hoa Lu.

979. The next year, a palace official assassinated both the king and Dinh Quoc Lien. The six-year-old youngest son (whose statue does not appear childlike), Dinh Toan, became king but only ruled for six months. Gen. Le Hoan somehow eliminated him and founded the 29-year-long Le, or "Earlier Le", dynasty and defeated the Chinese at the gate.

A narrow road, site of an annual 3-day festival, connects to the **Den Le Hoan** or **Le Dai Hang**, a miniature of the Dinh Hoang temple and close to the present-day village of Truong Yen Ha. The 17th-century carvings around the entrance door and on roof beams portray dragons holding a pearl in their mouth, surrounded by clouds. The temple has a series of three chambers: Hall of Worship, Hall of Heavenly Fragrance, and the Inner Shrine. In this last, a dim back room, are statues of Le Hoan, his queen, Duong Van Nga (supposedly the widow of Dinh Tien Hoang), and his sons, Le Long Dinh and Le Long Viet. These sons also quarrelled over succession after Le Hoan's death in 1005. The dynasty was finished in 1010, only 30 years after it began.

Near the entrance to Den Dinh Tien Hoang temple is a steep hill. Those who can climb 200 stone steps (and withstand aggressive hawkers flogging souvenirs and waving fans in the hope of tips) will be rewarded with a shrine to Confucius and a panoramic view of the ancient kingdom. The atmosphere within the temple grounds is blessedly peaceful because souvenir-selling pests are barred from them. However, it's a gauntlet to pass between the two temples.

Another scenic pagoda worth visiting in Hoa Lu district is **Chua Bich**, in the mountains. Built in 1428, the pagoda is renowned for its beautiful bronze and marble statues and for its huge bronze bell.

The enchanting inland waterworld of **Tam Coc** (Three Caves) can be entered from the Van Lam village docks, only 9 km (6 miles) southwest of Ninh Binh. Here, travellers hire a flat-bottomed boat and a pair of helmspersons (rower and poler). In the initial segment of the 2- to 3-hour journey, the lazy Ngo Dong River blends with flooded rice fields. But soon the waterway is wending through three tunnel caves *(tam coc)* that have bored through the limestone hills. Through the lowest, passengers must duck to avoid scraping the roof. The largest has stalactites and stalagmites. In between are clear, shallow, glass-smooth lagoons encircled by green-furred limestone cliffs, where butterflies flutter and women in small boats claw through the vegetation for edible morsels. Birdwatchers might catch sight of herons and kingfishers.

Tam Coc has been called an inland Ha Long Bay, but the utter quiet and tranquillity are nothing like being near the sea. In the final lagoon, a lonely goatherd mills around a ruined pagoda on a small spit of land. An initial tributary reaches Den Thai Vi, a temple where a 13th-century king, Tran Nhan Tong, retired after his abdication.

The tourist police have issued strict rules to the villagers after numerous complaints from visitors of being harassed by the oarswomen and village shopkeepers to *buy – buy – buy!* embroidered T-shirts by the dozen. Still, be warned that a purchase to stop the sales pitch only stimulates more intensive

BELOW: eating *pho.*

Map on pages 186–7

pestering, and the best strategy would be not to even glance at the articles.

Close to the boat dock and the stalls of T-shirt sellers is **Van Lam**, a village where shirts and table linen are embroidered. This is where most of the items sold in Hanoi's Old Quarter originate. At least one member of every family is engaged in this art, and tourists are welcome to browse. Tam Coc is usually linked with Hoa Lu on day tours from Hanoi.

There is another charming alternative. The fishing village of **Kenh Ga** clings to karst cliffs – that is, the portion of the village that doesn't live on boats and return to the cove after a day of fishing. Kenh Ga can only be reached by boat, preferably a silent rowboat, though groups might like the larger, chugging ones. The journey begins by canal but then enters the Song Hoang Long, which is plied by loaded and slow barges.

The simple houses are constructed of stone, cement, and plaster; all the materials must have been hauled in. While the ground space is restricted, kids do learn from an early age to scoot around by boat. The villagers are pleased but puzzled when foreigners come to Kenh Ga.

Their pride and joy is the rustic Catholic church with ancient wooden shutters. Inside there are heavy wooden beams and pillars with interesting carvings. Donations are much appreciated and could conceivably prevent the entire population from becoming rapacious T-shirt hawkers. Lucky visitors will be at Kenh Ga at Saturday sunset as a fleet of small boats converge on the church, conveying ladies in their best sarongs.

To reach Kenh Ga, take the road jutting west off Highway 1 about 11 km (7 miles) north of Ninh Binh. A similar distance brings the desolate boat dock, but a caretaker can rustle up transportation to Kenh Ga.

karst (kärst): a lime-stone region marked by sinks, abrupt ridges, irregular protuberant rocks, caverns, and under-ground streams.

– MERRIAM WEBSTER
DICTIONARY

BELOW: babysitting the water buffalo.

Quiet walking trail in Cuc Phuong.

Cuc Phuong National Park

By continuing west 24 km (15 miles) along on the same semi-paved road that runs by the Kenh Ga boat pier, one arrives at the entrance to the 25,000-hectare (61,000-acre) **Cong Vien Quoc Gia Cuc Phuong** ㉑ (Cuc Phuong National Park). If visitors can only visit one national park in northern Vietnam, this should be it because the biodiversity here is the most compelling. The park shelters 250 bird and 64 mammal species, including tigers, leopards, bats, boars, civet cats, flying squirrels, and the endangered Delacour langur primate. As is true with other Vietnamese national parks, there is little likelihood of glimpsing an animal, least of all a dangerous one, because poaching is so extensive. But unlike other parks, the staff here genuinely do seem to have an interest in wildlife and environmental protection, as indicated by their spotted deer research centre near the park's entrance.

And visitors can get a sense of the great diversity of insects and flora within the park. Some large trees *(Parashorea stellata and Terminalia myriocarpa),* which reach about 50 metres (165 ft) in height, are estimated to be over 1,000 years old. Close to 500 medicinal plants and herbs, of both native and foreign origin, have been discovered growing in the park. Some of the park's many caves and grottoes are also easily accessible within two mountain ranges that enclose a valley, with a micro-climate quite different from that of the surrounding region. Three tombs, excavated in one of the grottoes in 1966, contained shells, animal teeth, rudimentary stone tools, and prehistoric human remains. For a therapeutic warm dip, try the park's thermal springs. These remain at a constant temperature of 37°C (99°F) and contain more than 20 chemical elements believed to have assorted healing properties.

BELOW: wilderness hikers.

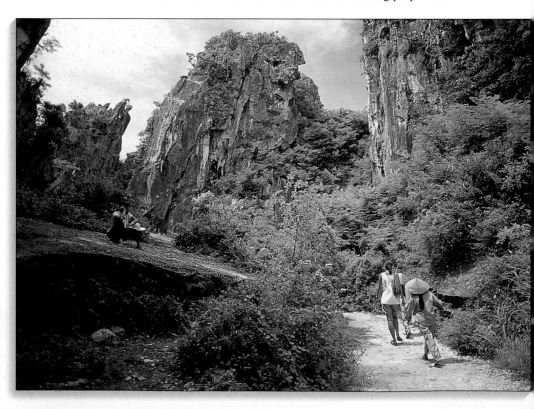

Since the entrance is located 45 km (30 miles) from Ninh Binh and 140 km (80 miles) from Hanoi, Cuc Phuong can be visited on a day trip, but that may not leave time for more than the 7-km (4-mile) tourist trail. Visitors can take longer hikes, for which they must hire a park guide, if they stay overnight in one of the Muong villages within the park.

The bishopric of Phat Diem is eventually reached by a sealed road that runs southeast from Ninh Binh for 30 straight and flat kilometres (20 miles) to the small town of Kim Son. While the road is a bit bumpy, traffic is thin, making it well suited for motorbikes or bicycles. Unquestionably, this is Catholic country. Alexandre de Rhodes, the indefatigable Jesuit, won converts here in the early 17th century. The road is lined with Catholic cemeteries, their white coffin-shaped tombs sinking in the marshy land, and at least 10 well-maintained churches. More spires can be seen in the distance. Most are granite, in simplified gothic style with Vietnamese touches.

Notable is the one at **Phu Nhia**, set behind a pond about 20 km (12 miles) from Ninh Binh. Four-storey towers flank the Gothic doors. Behind is a bell tower with a pagoda roof and, behind it, a rare Buddhist pagoda, Thanh Anton. On the sides of the main church are two more chapels. Behind the northwestern wall is a Catholic school.

Once thinly lined with French forts (there are no obvious remnants), the western side of the road was Viet Minh territory, the eastern held by the French. Catholics here were in a bind. Few were pro-French; after all, most were poor peasants. In fact, throughout the 20th century many Catholics had been active in anti-colonialist movements. But by the late 1940s, the communists had killed off or out-organised rival nationalist groups and Catholics (like other Christians

Map on pages 186–7

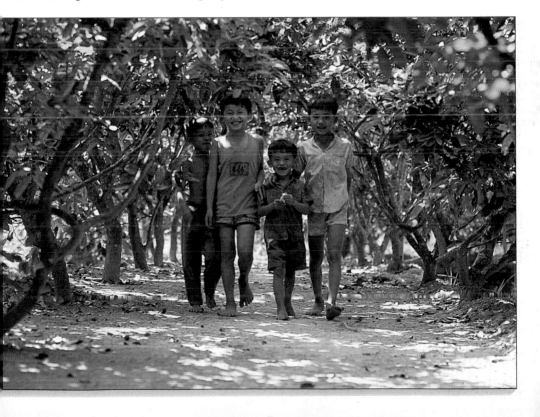

BELOW: strolling in a fruit orchard.

and the Buddhist clergy) were anti-communist. During the battles around this road in the early 1950s, locally organised militias, supplied by the French, successfully fought off the Viet Minh attacks.

The towering **Phat Diem Cathedral** is located in the friendly little town of **Kim Son ㉒**. Built in 1891, the Sino-Vietnamese-style cathedral has stone walls and towers, extends for 74 metres (240 ft), and is fringed with boxy cupolas with upturned tiled roofs. It was designed by a Vietnamese priest, Father Six (Tran Luc), who demanded that stone be towed from hundreds of kilometres away. Not counting the bishop's quarters behind a rear wall, there are a half-dozen other structures in the complex, including a cool, tomb-like stone chapel; a two-storey church with Romanesque arches, gargoyles, and a vaulted apse; and an 1890 stone bell tower.

Mounting the internal staircases of the bell tower, visitors eventually reach the enormous bronze bell protected by a Vietnamese-style tiled roof. The bell itself, capable of sheltering several good-sized people, represents an engineering feat as it was hauled up here on a ramp of earth.

The top of the bell tower offers a sweeping view of the cathedral complex and the town. The complex is fronted by an island in the middle of a large pond. On the island a white stone statue of Jesus triumphant in resplendent attire rises above the tree-tops. Although Mass is celebrated at least once daily (at 5am), during most of the day all the buildings are locked. Phat Diem is a popular destination for Vietnamese tourists, however, and tour group leaders are likely to have a key for at least the bell tower.

As for Kim Son itself, on the road back to Ninh Binh there is a 19th-century wooden covered bridge, arching across the Song Day.

TIP

Kim Son has a simple hotel quite near the Phat Diem Cathedral, but whether foreigners are allowed to stay depends upon the political temperature of the moment.

BELOW: riding the train from Ho Chi Minh to Hanoi.

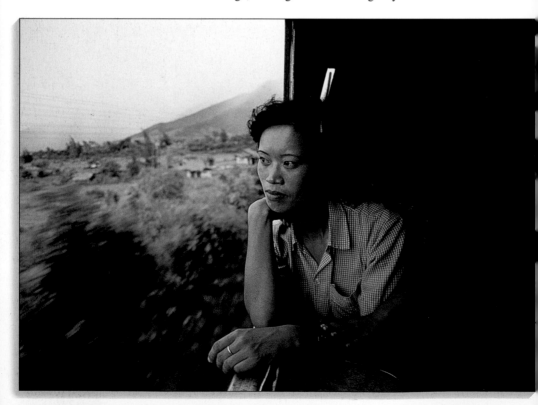

Annam and Thanh Hoa

Leaving behind Ninh Binh Province, one enters Annam, the central region, and the beautiful but impoverished province of Thanh Hoa. It is the first in an almost unbroken succession of seven coastal provinces hemmed between the South China Sea and the Indochinese mountain range.

From Thanh Hoa down to the former Demilitarised Zone (DMZ) – that is, through Thanh Hoa, Nghe An, Ha Tinh and Quanh Binh provinces – Highway 1 is narrow and filled with bicycles, buffalo carts and pedestrians. Think of the train as an option. Provincial governments are charged with road maintenance, so the state of the road reflects a province's poverty. The sandy soil has never made for good harvests. Only able to grow one rice crop a year, peasant families scrape by on manioc and peanuts. But with seed money from Britain, many farmers in Thanh Hoa since the 1980s have become successful apiarists and honey producers.

Thanh Hoa, the cradle of the Dong Son culture, harbours a great many historical sites and is an important settlement area for the Muong minority. At the beginning of the 20th century, archaeologists discovered many relics of the Dong Son civilisation dispersed along the length of the Song Ma (Ma River) valley: bronze drums, musical instruments, statues, jewellery, various tools, and domestic objects. Some of these are now displayed at the Fine Arts Museum in Hanoi. The Muong still adhere to their ancient language, similar to Vietnamese, and use the bronze drums inherent to their unique culture and festivals. Although there has been much intermarriage and cultural melding over the centuries, the Muong probably predated the Viets in Vietnam.

As the Vietnamese grew in strength, however, they pushed the Muong further

Map on pages 186–7

BELOW: the north-south train.

and further from the Song Hong (Red River) valley. Trieu's invasion in 208 BC was responsible for the Viet southward migration, and these first emigrants settled in the Phu Ly and Dong Son regions.

Before reaching Thanh Hoa, in Nam Ha Province, Phu Ly is where the first bronze drum was discovered in 1902. Other similar drums were acquired from the Long Doi Son Monastery and the village of Ngoc Lu. The figurative and stylised designs on the drums depict birds, animals, and scenes from everyday life. The Ngoc Lu bronze drum, 80 centimetres (30 in) in diameter, is decorated with an image of the sun. Its many rays are surrounded by 16 concentric circles of various designs depicting deer, aquatic birds, people, and vignettes of daily life. The drum's surface is engraved with pairs of animals and birds heading east towards the sun. In 1924, a member of the Ecole Francaise d'Extreme Orient unearthed several bronze drums and other bronze objects at Dong Son.

Mieu Than Dong Co (Temple of the Spirit of the Drum) is found in the village of Dan Ne, on the hill of Tam Diep. The temple contains a bronze drum 2 metres (6 ft) in diameter, which, according to popular belief, is said to have belonged to one of the Hung kings. The drum's face is decorated with nine concentric circles engraved with ancient characters.

The megalithic-style Ho Citadel in **Tay Giai** ㉓ was built in 1397 under the orders of the usurper king, Ho Qui Li. He named the new citadel Tay Kinh (Capital of the West). It was more or less a replica of the citadel of Dong Kinh (Capital of the East). But unlike the other citadels of Hoa Lu and Co Loa, whose walls were built of earth, the Ho citadel's huge walls, 5 metres (16 ft) high and 3 metres (10 ft) thick, were made of stone. Some blocks weigh an estimated 16 tons and show a high degree of quarrying and stone-carving skill.

BELOW: vendors of fowl at market.

Map on pages 186–7

The Muong minority village of **Lam Son** ㉔, in the Thanh Hoa highlands, was the native village of Vietnam's national hero, Le Loi, who became King Le Thai To. It was from here that Le Loi launched a decade-long uprising against the Chinese Ming-dynasty occupiers of Vietnam. The struggle, waged from 1418 to 1428 in this mountainous region, finally ended in complete victory for Le Loi and his troops.

The temple here is dedicated to Le Loi and contains his bronze likeness, cast in 1532. Nguyen Trai, Le Loi's advisor, penned the epitaph on the large Vinh Lang stele dedicated to the life and works of Le Loi, in 1433.

Other memorials document the 12 reigns of the Le family. Remains of the royal palace's ancient citadel of **Lam Kinh** are still visible. A mausoleum at the foot of Tung Son in Phu Dien is the final resting place of the national heroine Trieu Thi Trinh, who led an uprising against the Chinese in 247, aided by her elder brother Trieu Quoc Dat. The attempt failed and Trieu, rather than have her fate decided by the victorious Ngo rulers, committed suicide. A temple was built in her memory, and today a festival is celebrated here in her honour on the 24th day of the second lunar month every year.

Sixteen km (10 miles) southeast from the provincial capital of Thanh Hoa, the white sands of **Sam Son** ㉕ stretch for 3 km (2 miles) along the coast, from the Song Lac Hoi to the heights of Truong Le. Superb scenery surrounds the clear waters of Sam Son, named after the coastal mountains. Accommodation is of the mini-hotel variety. The resort is packed in the summer months, deserted the rest of the year.

The temple of **The Doc Cuoc**, half-way up the slopes of Truong Le, is dedicated to a one-legged deity said to have divided himself in two and who is

In 1964, attacks by North Vietnamese patrol boats on the USS Maddox (and a disputed attack two days later on another US ship) in the Gulf of Tonkin led to a US Congressional resolution that authorised American military escalation in Vietnam.

BELOW: moving the harvest by boat.

Map on pages 186–7

"Rich in good looks"
appears to mean
* poor luck and tears*
* of woe,*
Which may sound
* strange, I know,*
But is not really so, I
* swear,*
Since Heaven every-
* where seems*
* jealous of the fair*
* of face.*
* — THE TALE OF KIEU*

BELOW: holding up a successful catch. **RIGHT:** ancient tree at Cuc Phuong.

believed to have supernatural powers that protect and save swimmers and navigators in distress. It is also said to guarantee the fishermen a good catch, although the local fishermen may have a different story. At the end of the range is another temple, Co Tien, or Fairy Temple.

Numerous Muong villages lie scattered throughout the highlands of Thanh Hoa. Although the lowland Vietnamese, the Kinh, lost their original written script after 1,000 years of Chinese domination, the Muong have nonetheless retained theirs. Known as *khoa dau van*, it is similar to Thai and Lao, which have Sanskrit origins. Muong has an alphabet of 30 basic consonant signs.

Nghe An

South of Thanh Hoa Province lies Nghe An Province. With a long history of peasant uprisings, it is also the birthplace of several revolutionaries, including Phan Boi Chau and Nguyen Ai Quoc (more famously known as Ho Chi Minh), along with the national poet Nguyen Du (1765–1820), author of *The Tale of Kieu,* Vietnam's poetic epic *(see page 108).* The findings of archaeologists revealed the existence of both a stone-age and a bronze-age culture in the province.

In Nghe An Province and its neighbour to the south, Ha Tinh, mountains and midlands give way to coastal plains along a 230-km (140-mile) coastline, and forests cover three-quarters of the land. The harsh climate often causes rain storms and flash flooding. More than 100 rivers and streams, the longest of which is the Song Lam Dong, feed the two provinces. The Lam Dong is a busy waterway plied by numerous boats, sampans, and rafts carrying bamboo and timber. Deer, raised for their antlers that are used for medicinal purposes, are a common sight grazing amongst the orange orchards.

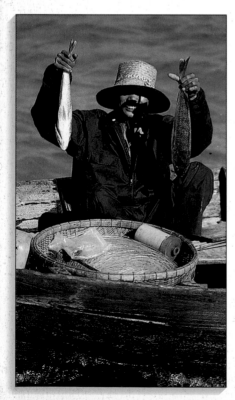

In 1959, the inhabitants of **Hoang Tru** ❷⓺, 11 km (7 miles) northwest of **Vinh**, recreated the humble three-room house, with bamboo walls and a palm-leaf roof, where Ho Chi Minh was born as Nguyen Sinh Cung in 1890. Ho's family moved from here to Hue when he was five.

His father, a mandarin and minor official in the Hue court, became disillusioned by the French rulers and was eventually dismissed and returned to this area in 1901. He settled close to Hoang Tru, in **Kim Lien** (sometimes called Lang Sen), where he and Ho Chi Minh's grandfather taught. Young Ho Chi Minh spent a few years here before he and his father returned to Hue.

Kim Lien villagers constructed a replica of the second house, also in 1959, and turned it into yet another Ho Chi Minh shrine. It is very similar to the one in Hoang Tru. Nearby is Ho's three-room museum displaying memorabilia, old photographs, Ho's poems, and some actual shirts he wore.

It's easy to confuse these two Ho Chi Minh houses. Since there is very little in the way of English explanation at either, it is also not obvious that these are in fact replicas of the original homes or that Ho spent little of his life in either place. During his 30-year odyssey, Ho rarely contacted his family in the area, and he returned to his childhood homes just once in his life, in 1961. ❏

Central Vietnam

N

| 0 | 50 km |
| 0 | 50 miles |

BIEN DONG

(SOUTH CHINA SEA)

H a i n a n

CHINA

LAOS

CAMBODIA

CENTRAL VIETNAM

The central, slender stretch of Vietnam offers some of the country's more arresting sites, including Hue and Hoi An

Along string of coastal provinces, linking the vast rice-growing regions of the Song Hong (Red River) Delta in the north and the delta of the Mekong in the south, forms the narrow neck of central Vietnam. At the heart of Vietnam's centre lies Hue, the imperial city of the Nguyen kings. It is a magnificent city despite the damage of war, with a majestic citadel, fortifications, and imperial mausoleums. Threading through its centre is the River of Perfume – Song Huong – a name that teases with its promise. Centuries ago, after the Champa kingdoms fell to the invading Viets from the north, Hue was called Thuan Hoa: *thuan*, meaning allegiance or submission, and *hoa,* meaning transformation. The name Hue is believed to have come about through the common mispronunciation of hoa.

Outside of Hue to the north, the narrow, central coastal provinces of Quang Tri and Dong Ha suffered mightily during the Vietnam War, as they were directly south of the DMZ, or demilitarised zone.

South of Hue, Deo Hai Van funnels into Da Nang, an active port city and Vietnam's fourth-largest urban centre, with energetic commerce within and lovely beaches nearby. Da Nang is the gateway to Quang Nam Province and the ancient kingdom of Champa. The distinctive red-brick Cham towers and sacred sites, built between the 8th and 12th centuries, stand as silent testimony to the kingdom that flourished here before its absorption by the Vietnamese descending from the north.

Nearby is the charming, though increasingly touristic, 15th-century town of Hoi An, which was the biggest seaport and most important centre of trade in the country during the 17th and 18th centuries, when it was known to Europeans as Faifo. Its beautifully preserved communal houses, pagodas, and other places of worship reflect the presence and influences of the Chinese, Japanese, and Westerners who later settled in the region. ❏

HUE

A dynastic citadel stands in Hue, despite destruction inflicted by the Viet Cong and the Americans. Nearby, along the seductively named Perfume River, are the ancient tombs of the Nguyen emperors

The ancient imperial city of the Nguyen kings, **Hue ❶** is located 12 km (7 miles) from the coast on a narrow stretch of land in Thua Thien Hue Province, which borders Laos in the west. It is approximately midway between Hanoi to the north and Ho Chi Minh to the south. Always an important cultural, intellectual, and historical city, Hue remains one of Vietnam's main attractions. The charm of this timeless old city lies not only in its historical and architectural value, but also in the natural beauty of its location along the banks of **Song Huong**, or the fabled Perfume River. On the river's north bank is the ancient citadel and mostly residential areas, while on the south bank are the city's commercial area and the old French quarter. Further south are the Nguyen tombs. There is a quiet grace to the city.

The first noble to reach Hue was Nguyen Hoang, in the spring of 1601. He found a particularly good location to build a capital and erected the citadel of Phu Xuan. The Nguyen lords administered the whole region with the agreement of the often-rival Trinh lords. This arrangement operated smoothly at first, but the rivalry flared up as the territory was extended southwards. Bloody battles broke out between the two rival families. Each side was fiercely determined to consolidate and assert its own sovereignty, but eventually the Nguyen lords gained the upper hand. As a result, Hue became a new kingdom under the reign of Vu Vuong in the mid-1700s, independent of the north. Nguyen Hoang was the first in an uninterrupted succession of 10 feudal lords to rule over the area of Hue until 1802. That year, after quelling the Tay Son uprising, the 10th Nguyen lord proclaimed himself Emperor Gia Long and founded the Nguyen dynasty, which would last for 143 years, until 1945. But just 33 years into the dynasty's reign, the French invaded Hue.

A quick succession of emperors graced the throne. The anti-French demonstrations and strikes of the colonial era were followed by the Japanese occupation in 1945 and the abdication of Bao Dai, the last of the Nguyen emperors, in the same year.

The relative peace that reigned after 1954, when Hue became part of South Vietnam following the country's division into two parts by the United Nations, was shattered under Ngo Dinh Diem's regime. Repressive anti-Buddhist propaganda sparked off a series of demonstrations and protest suicides by Buddhist monks in 1963. Hue's imperial city suffered extensive damage during the Tet Offensive of 1968, in which the Viet Cong held out in the fortified ancient citadel against American attack for nearly two months. Although many priceless historical monuments and relics were destroyed in the battle, amazingly many survived.

LEFT: the pagoda of Thien Mu.
BELOW: Thien Mu.

Girl in costume for traditional festival.

BELOW: Hue girls in traditional dress at the Imperial City.

Dai Noi: The Imperial City

Three walled enclosures make up Hue's **Dai Noi** ⓐ (Great Palace or Imperial City; open daily 7am–5.30pm; admission fee): Hoang Thanh (Yellow Enclosure) and Tu Cam Thanh (Forbidden Purple City) are enclosed within the all-encompassing Kinh Thanh (the exterior enclosure). Stone, bricks and earth were used for the exterior wall, which measured 8 metres (26 ft) high and 20 metres (65 ft) thick and was built during the reign of Gia Long. Later, 10 large and fortified gates, each topped with watch-towers, were built at points along the wall. Most of what visitors see today is found within the Hoang Thanh, or Yellow Enclosure; other areas were destroyed during the Tet Offensive of 1968. In the first enclosure of the royal city, towards the Chuong Duc gate, are **Sung Than Cong**, or the Nine Deities' Cannons. The five cannons on one side represent the five elements – metal, water, wood, fire, earth – while the other four represent the four seasons. Each cannon weighs about 10 tonnes.

Hoang Thanh (Yellow Enclosure) is the middle wall enclosing the imperial city and its palaces, temples and flower gardens. Four richly decorated gates provided access: Ngo Mon (the southern gate, or Noon Gate), Hoa Binh (northern gate), Hien Nhan (eastern gate), and Chuong Duc (western gate). Ngo Mon, first built of granite in 1834 during the reign of Minh Mang, was repaired in 1921. The gate is topped by the Lau Ngu Phung, the Five Phoenix Watch Tower, with its roofs brightly tiled in yellow over the middle section and green on either side. From here, the emperor used to preside over formal ceremonies and rites. Through the Ngo Mon, walk across the Golden Water Bridge, which at one time was reserved for the emperor. It leads to **Dien Thai Hoa** (Thai Hoa Palace, or Palace of Supreme Harmony), the most important

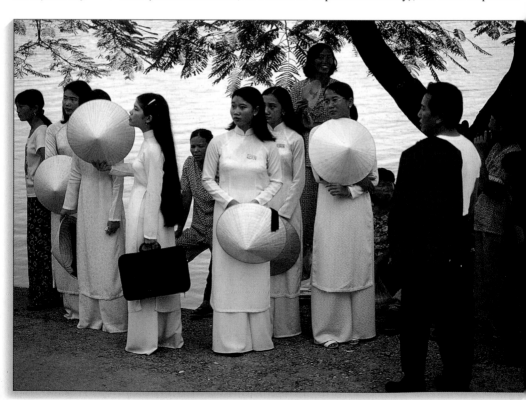

place in the imperial city. Here, the emperor received the high dignitaries of the land and foreign diplomats. The royal court organised important ceremonies here, as well. Built in 1805 during Gia Long's reign, the palace was renovated first by Minh Mang in 1834 and later by Khai Dinh in 1924. Today, it stands in excellent condition, its ceilings and beams decorated in red lacquer and gold inlay. The emperor used to rest in Truong Sanh (Palace of Longevity) and read the classics in the palace or the garden.

Map on page 241

The temples within the enclosure are dedicated to various lords: the temple of Trieu Mieu to Nguyen Kim, the Thai Mieu to Nguyen Hoang and his successors, the Phung Tien temple to the emperors of the reigning dynasty, and the Hung Mieu to Nguyen Phuc Luan, emperor Gia Long's father. The well-preserved The Mieu, dedicated to the sovereigns of the Nguyen dynasty, houses the shrines of seven Nguyen emperors plus monuments to the revolutionary emperors Ham Nghi, Thanh Thai, and Duy Tan, which were added in 1959.

In front of The Mieu temple, completely restored, stands the magnificent **Hien Lam Cac** (Pavilion of Splendour), with the nine dynastic urns known as **Cuu Dinh** lined up before it. The urns, cast between 1835 and 1837 during Minh Mang's reign, are decorated with motifs of the sun, moon, clouds, birds, animals, dragons, mountains, rivers, historic events, and scenes from everyday life. Hundreds of artisans from all over the country were involved in their casting. Each urn represents an emperor of the Nguyen dynasty and weighs up to 2,500 kg (5,600 lbs). **Dien Tho**, a palace built by Gia Long in 1804, served as the Queen Mother's residence.

Beyond Dien Thai Hoa, **Tu Cam Thanh** (Forbidden Purple City) was reserved solely for the emperor and the royal family, who resided here behind

BELOW: Cuu Dinh, the dynastic urns.

Flower vendor at Hue's market.

a brick wall 4 metres (13 ft) thick. Each of seven gates set into the wall had a special function and name glorifying the ancestral virtues. This area was extensively damaged during the Tet Offensive of 1968 – the Viet Cong used the citadel as a bunker – but it is undergoing continuing renovation.

The main building in the enclosure was **Can Thanh**, or Palace of Celestial Perfection. The other once-grand palace, Can Chanh, sadly in ruins, was used by the emperor to receive dignitaries and settle the affairs of the kingdom. Its remaining walls, riddled with shell and bullet holes, stand as a crumbling reminder of the weapons that wrought such destruction to this once-splendid complex. Beyond lies an empty stretch of ground where the royal apartments once stood. Near the Hien Nhan (Eastern Gate) stands a stately library, decorated with ornate tiles and carvings, as well as the Duyet Thi Duong Theatre, where performances of traditional songs are held daily.

Beyond the citadel walls

Another world lies beyond the walls of the citadel, which is surrounded in the south and east by Hue's commercial area. This is confined mainly to the area around the arched **Cau Trang Tien ❸** (Trang Tien Bridge), which spans the Song Huong (Perfume River), and **Cau Gia Hoi**. Both bridges lend their names to the areas surrounding them.

Near the east gate of the citadel, the **Museum of Royal Fine Arts ❻** (open Tues–Sat 7am–5pm; admission fee), built in 1845 under Thieu Tri, houses treasures bequeathed by the royal family and nobility. Sadly, many objects have disappeared without a trace since 1946 during revolution and war.

Across the street, the **Bao Tang Tong Hop** (Hue Provincial Museum; open

BELOW: moat of the old imperial city.

daily, 7am–5pm; admission fee) was opened in 1975 and renovated in 2005. The central building, built in the style of a traditional *dinh* (communal house), contains archaeological discoveries from the Thuan Thien province. To the left, in a colonial pavilion, the history of the First Indochina War is presented through the use of photos and artefacts. The pavilion on the right is dedicated to the Second Indochina War, and includes a large topographical map showing the movements of foreign troops, the South Vietnamese army and the Viet Cong during the Tet Offensive of 1968. Outside, in the open, pieces of abandoned military hardware are now used by Vietnamese children as "jungle gyms".

Northeast of Trang Tien Bridge in the neighbourhood of Phu Cat – home of the Hoa (Vietnamese-Chinese), who had arrived as "boat people" from China – the lively **Cho Dong Ba D**, a market *(cho)* that has been around since the beginning of the 20th century, offers a great variety of local products and gastronomic delights. Buy one of the famous "poem hats" which, when held up to a light source, reveal the shadow of a scene or a poem. Ten km (6¼ miles) to the east are elaborate tombs built on the white sand dunes, recently constructed by overseas relatives in memory of those who had lost their life at sea.

Some 3 km (2 miles) to the west of the citadel, situated on a hill, is **Chua Thien Mu E** (Celestial Lady Pagoda). Built by Nguyen Hoang in 1601, it remains intact on the north bank of the Song Huong. The seven tiers of the temple's octagonal tower – **Phuoc Duyen** – each represent a different reincarnation of Buddha. Six statues of deities guard the Buddhist pagoda, which contains a gilt statue of the laughing Buddha, happy in prosperity, and three superb, glass-enclosed statues of Buddha. Many generations have heard the tolling of the pagoda's enormous 2,000-kilogram (4,600-lb), 2-metre-high

Map on page 241

TIP

It would be foolish to visit Hue and not take a boat journey on the river to Chua Thien Mu, Hon Chen, and the tombs of Tu Duc, Khai Dinh, and Minh Mang. For extra mobility, ask if you can take a bicycle with you.

BELOW: tower at Thien Mu.

(6-ft) bell since it was cast in 1701. It is such a fine bell that it can be heard nearly 16 km (10 miles) away.

The main temple, Dai Hung, is found in an attractive garden of ornamental shrubs and trees. A statue of Maitraya Buddha presides over the first room. Behind this temple is the Quan Vo (God of War Temple), and behind that another, Quan Am, a temple dedicated to the goddess of mercy, Quan Am.

Tombs of the Nguyen dynasty

Unlike the other dynasties, the Nguyen dynasty did not bury its members in their native village, Gia Mieu, to the north in Thanh Hoa Province. Instead, their imperial tombs lie scattered on the hillsides on either side of the Song Huong, to the west and south of Hue. Although the dynasty had 13 kings, only seven of them reigned until their deaths, and only they are laid to rest in this valley of kings: Gia Long, Minh Mang, Thieu Tri, Tu Duc, Kien Phuc, Dong Khanh, and Kai Dinh.

Emperor Minh Mang.

To reach the tombs from Hue, head south, first stopping at **Nam Giao Dan** ❻ (Terrace of Heavenly Sacrifice), an esplanade surrounded by a park of pines and conifers 2 km (1¼ miles) south of Hue's commercial centre. Built by Gia Long in 1802, in its day it was considered the most sacred and solemn place. Composed of three terraces – two square and one circular – the esplanade represents as a whole the sky and the earth. From here, the emperor paid homage to heaven in his capacity as the privileged mandatory on earth.

BELOW: the Song Huong, or Perfume River, located near Thien Mu.

Every three years the Nam Giao (Festival of Sacrifice) took place at the centre of the circular esplanade. A buffalo would be sacrificed to the god of the sky, who is believed to govern the destiny of the world. A communist war

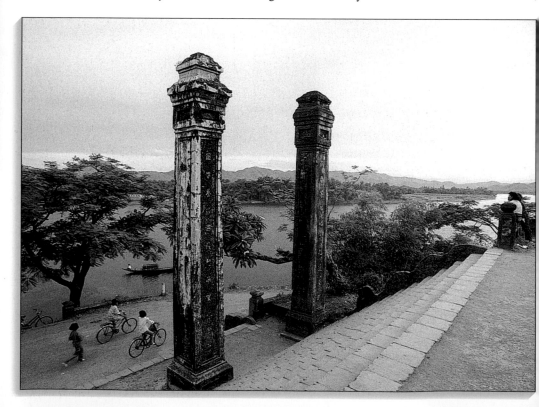

memorial that briefly dominated the Nam Giao has now been removed.

The Nguyen tomb sites themselves are spread out and one could easily budget two full days visiting them. Each has a large brick-paved courtyard *(bia dinh)* containing stone figures of elephants, saddled horses, soldiers, and civil and military mandarins. In front of this stands the stelae pavilion, containing the tall marble or stone stele engraved with the biography of the deceased king written by his successor (except in the case of Tu Duc, who wrote his own). Beyond this is the temple *(tam dien)* where the deceased king and queen are worshipped and their royal belongings displayed. The king's widows would keep incense and aloe wood perpetually burning before the altar until their own deaths. Behind and on either side of the temple are the houses built for the king's concubines, servants, and the soldiers who guarded the royal tomb. The emperor's body is laid in a concealed place *(bao thanh)*, enclosed by high walls behind well-locked metal doors.

When setting foot in any of the tombs, one feels a sense of admiration for the noble grandeur and elegant style of the architecture. This sense of awe is described by one of Vietnam's celebrated writers, Pham Quynh, a former minister of national education: "This tomb is the general blending of all the colours of the firmament and of all the tints of water; it is an amalgamation of high mountains, of thick forests, of wind blowing through foliage. This tomb is a spectacle of nature, a marvel of great beauty, added to another sight, created by the hand of man, of a beauty no less marvellous. It is the patient and inspired work of the artist whose intention was to colour the countryside to awaken the awaiting soul, soaring in the silence of this mournful place or whispering in the top of the lone pine tree. There are not the words to express the bizarre

Map on page 241

BELOW: guardian image at pagoda.

RULE OF THE NGUYEN DYNASTY

The Nguyen dynasty ruled from 1802 until 1945. Three centuries earlier, the Nguyen family had ingratiated itself with the ruling Le dynasty, becoming northern lords for the weak Le rulers. By the mid-1500s, the Trinh family usurped this power, pushing the Nguyens to the south. The rivalry between the Nguyen and Trinh escalated into warfare in 1620, which lasted for half a century before both families agreed to a de facto division of the empire. The Nguyen family ruled over southern Vietnam, extending settlement – mostly by Chinese refugees escaping the collapsing Ming dynasty – into Cham and Cambodian lands. The 1771 Tay Son uprising threatened Nguyen power in southern Vietnam; a young prince, later to become Emperor Gia Long, led the recovery of Nguyen territory. Gia Long would rule over the whole of Vietnam from 1802, the beginning of the Nguyen dynasty.

Nguyen dynasty policy often thwarted foreign interference. In response, the French invaded Vietnam in 1858. The French dominated all of Vietnam after invasions in 1883–85, although they retained the Nguyen dynasty with nominal governance over central Vietnam (called Annam by the French) and northern Vietnam (called Tonkin). In 1945, the last Nguyen emperor, Bao Dai, abdicated.

sensation, both gentle and of tender exhilaration, which grips one with an eagerness for poetry in this scenery charged with depth and mystery".

The **tomb of Tu Duc** ⒢, just a bit southwest of Hue, can be reached by a very pleasant cycle ride through pine forests and lush hills. The mausoleum construction, begun in 1864, took three years to complete. The result resembles a royal palace in miniature and harmonises beautifully with the natural surroundings. A work force of 3,000 men was used in its construction. Tu Duc, the son of Thieu Tri and the Nguyen dynasty's fourth king, reigned for 36 years, the longest reign of any of the Nguyen kings.

He spent his leisure hours in the two pavilions beside the lake, Luu Khiem. Here he wrote poetry, no doubt inspired by the beauty of his surroundings, fished, and enjoyed the fragrance of the lotus. The more popular of the two lakeside pagodas is Xung Khiem, a pavilion that dates from 1865. A staircase leads to the Luong Khiem mausoleum, which contains a collection of furniture, vases, and jewellery boxes. Further on is the terrace leading to the tomb, with its stone elephants, horses, and mandarins. The tomb itself, ritually inaccessible, is covered by dense pine forest. The tombs of Tu Duc's adopted son, Kien Phu and Queen Le Thien An, lie beside the lake.

The tomb of **Thieu Tri** ⒣ is located nearby. Thieu Tri, Minh Mang's son, was the third Nguyen emperor and reigned from 1841 to 1847. His tomb was built between 1847 and 1848, in the same elegant architectural style as his father's but on a much smaller scale.

BELOW: a relative of Bao Dai, the last emperor of Vietnam.

On the western bank of the Song Huong, on the opposite side of the river from the tombs of Thieu Tri and Tu Duc, is the temple known as both **Hon Chen** ⒤ and Ngoc Tran Dien, where the goddess Po Nagar, protector of the

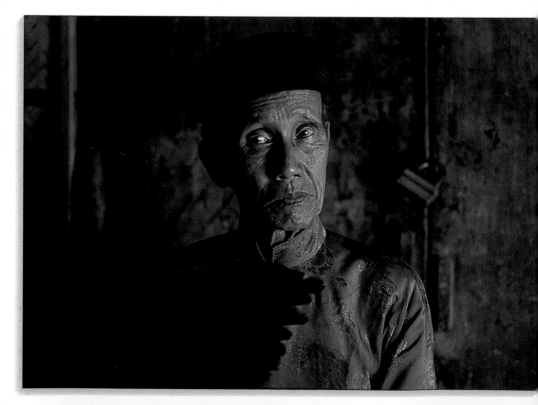

Champa Kingdom, is worshipped. Po Nagar, greatly venerated by the Chams in the past, is also to a lesser extent worshipped today by the Vietnamese, who supplanted them in the narrow stretch of land that was once the Kingdom of Champa. A festival takes place here on the 15th day of the seventh lunar month every year, when worshippers march in a long procession, accompanied by ceremonial music and a heavy cloud of incense.

Map on page 241

Completely different from any of the other Nguyen tombs, the tomb of **Khai Dinh ❶** resembles, if anything, a European castle, its architecture a blend of the oriental and occidental. Made of reinforced concrete, it took 11 years to complete and was finally finished in 1931. Khai Dinh, Bao Dai's adopted father, ruled for nine years during the colonial era. A grandiose dragon staircase leads up to the first courtyard, from where further stairs lead to a courtyard lined with stone statues of elephants, horses, and civil and military mandarins. In the centre of the courtyard stands the stele inscribed with Chinese characters composed by Bao Dai in memory of his father. The exterior lacks the tranquil charm and beauty of Minh Mang's or Tu Duc's mausoleum, and the giant dragons flanking the staircase appear rather menacing.

Tomb guardian.

Once inside, however, the contrast is striking. Coloured tiles pave the floor, a huge "dragon in the clouds" mural, painted by artists using their feet, adorns the ceiling of the middle chamber. Jade green antechambers lead off to the left and right. Bright frescoes composed of many thousands of inlaid ceramic and glass fragments depict various themes. Animals, trees, and flowers provide a visual feast after the less-inspiring blackened exterior of the mausoleum. A life-size bronze statue of Khai Dinh, made in France in 1922, rests on a dais on top of the tomb.

BELOW: tomb of Khai Dinh.

Map on page 241

The tomb of **Minh Mang** ⓚ (open daily; admission fee) can be reached by hiring a small motorboat from any of the kiosks on Tran Phu Street, which is located between the bridges. Alternatively, take a car to the village of Ban Viet and from there, hire a boat to get across the Song Huong. Minh Mang was Gia Long's fourth son and the Nguyen dynasty's second king. He was responsible for the building of the Imperial City and was highly respected for his reforms in the areas of customs, traditions, and agriculture. Minh Mang's mausoleum is located where the Ta Trach and Huu Trach tributaries of the Song Huong meet. Its construction was begun a year before his death, in 1840, and was finished by his successor Thieu Tri in 1843. The setting blends the beauty of nature with the majestic architecture and superb stone sculpture created by its many anonymous craftsmen. The setting is at its best in mid-March, when the Trung Minh and Tan Nguyet lakes bloom with a mass of beautiful lotus flowers.

The tomb of **Gia Long** ⓛ (open daily; admission fee), located 16 km (10 miles) southwards from Hue and on a hillside, is somewhat inaccessible by road; a more pleasant way to reach it is by boat on the river. The tomb, begun in 1814, was completed a year after Gia Long's death in 1820. Unfortunately, the site was in the middle of a guerrilla zone during the Vietnam War and the tomb was considerably damaged by bombs. Reportedly located on a site that was selected by the emperor himself, the tomb has since become rather neglected and is rarely visited, but the wild beauty of the site itself, with its mountainous backdrop, makes the effort to get there well worth the time.

The nearby temple, **Minh Thanh**, also in very bad shape, is dedicated to Gia Long's first wife, Queen Thua Thien Co. On the left is Gia Long's sepulchre, where he and his first wife are buried side by side. ❑

BELOW: tomb of Minh Mang.
RIGHT: royal guardians.

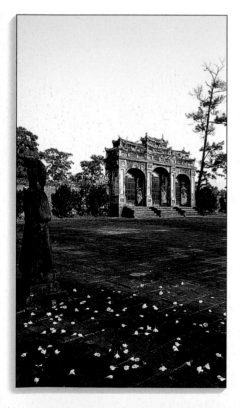

FADING DMZ BLUES

The so-called Demilitarised Zone, or DMZ, is where some of the bloodiest fighting of the Vietnam War took place. The DMZ stretched for 8 km (5 miles) on either side of the Song Ben Hai, 100 km (60 miles) north of Hue. It was the line of demarcation between North Vietnam and South Vietnam, established at the Geneva Conference in 1954 after the end of the war against the French. Following the 17th parallel, the border was supposed to be temporary, until elections could be held in 1956. The elections never were held and Vietnam remained divided along this line until the two countries were officially reunified in 1976, following the collapse of South Vietnam.

Today, there are still desolate stretches of scorched earth. Just south of the Ben Hai, Highway 9, which runs west towards Laos, passes sites of famous Vietnam War battles and old US military bases like Con Thien and Khe Sanh. North of the DMZ, in Vinh Moc, a series of tunnels are where an entire village camped out for several years to escape the constant bombings. Most of the people had evacuated to other parts of the country, but some stayed. For five years, from 1966 to 1971, some 300 people lived in the 2,000-metre-long (6,500-ft) network of tunnels. Seventeen babies were born in the subterranean home.

Rush to Preserve

For a country with a long and rich history, Vietnam boasts relatively few architectural landmarks. Those that have survived the centuries of invasions, war, typhoons, and harsh climate have suffered from human neglect. Historical preservation, after all, is something of a luxury for a country preoccupied with fending off invaders and, later, grappling with poverty.

Today, however, Vietnam has begun to show an interest in saving its historical sites. Some of this has to do with the gradually improving economy, in part due to tourism.

In part, too, this movement to preserve is a facet of the government's emphasis on nationalism – in politics, culture, and entertainment. (Recently, for example, a karaoke contest had one rule: the contestants had to sing a patriotic song.) Restoring architectural ruins is one way to develop national pride.

More importantly, however, restoration is commercially viable. All government officials needed to do was look at tourists climbing about China's Great Wall or Cambodia's Angkor Wat to figure out there is money in a pile of old rocks. If the rocks are well maintained, that is. And until now, Vietnam's architectural gems have lacked historical lustre.

The citadel and tombs of Hue, however, recently grabbed international attention when they were included on a list of endangered sites. "This will make Vietnamese feel they have more responsibility in preserving the site", said one hopeful historian in Hanoi.

The government has pledged to spend at least US$1 million a year on the Hue conservation effort. Foreign organisations, both from Japan and also UNESCO, have also contributed funds. Vietnam does not have many trained restoration workers, but it is attempting to use native crafts people – stone cutters, wood carvers, pottery makers – to learn advanced skills from overseas experts.

Right now, conservationists have their work cut out for them. Many of the stone pillars and statues have crumbled; the wood structures have been badly damaged by termites and water. Damage from the Vietnam War was severe. There are bullet-ridden stone walls visible on the grounds of the Citadel.

Many statues and artefacts were destroyed. There are still standing reminders, however, that look as if the fighting ended just last week, such as a broken mirror in a house behind the Thai Hoa Palace.

Hue is not the only place in Vietnam drawing the interest of historic preservationists. Others include Hoi An, the 18th-century port, with Chinese and Japanese architecture; the Cham towers along the south-central coast, near Nha Trang; pagodas throughout the country; and the monuments of My Son.

Historians also are keen to preserve the cultural traditions that are threatened with extinction because older practitioners have either died or have not passed down their knowledge. So there are efforts to research and preserve traditional music, festivals, handicrafts, and even royal cuisine. Much of this tradition, of course, is linked to Vietnam's old dynasties, a royalist tradition fought against by the Communists. But reviving traditions doesn't seem to faze the government. "This is our history", said one official. "We must not lose it". ❑

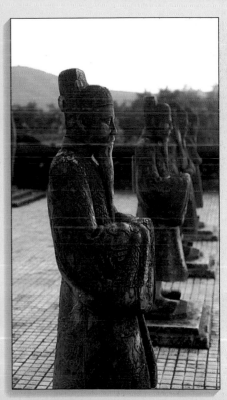

THE IMPERIAL CITADEL AT HUE

The citadel's history reflects that of Vietnam. Built by Confucian kings, it was occupied by the French, damaged in war, and is now under restoration

The imperial citadel was built by the early 19th-century Nguyen kings. It was fortified in the style of the French military engineer Vauban, but its internal arrangement reflects Chinese architectural principles. The interior comprised three concentric walled cities: the Kinh Thanh (Capital), Hoang Thanh (Imperial) and Can Thanh (Forbidden). The entrance to the Imperial City was the Ngo Mon (South Gate, 1833), which gave access to the Thai Hoa (Palace of Supreme Harmony, 1805) and the Can Chanh (Palace of Heavenly Law, 1811), where foreign visitors were received. The structured hierarchy of this Confucian monarchy was thus abundantly expressed in the citadel's architecture. Symbolically, it took a major blow in 1884 with the entry of the first Frenchman into the Forbidden City. After the abdication of the last king, Bao Dai, the citadel suffered the ravages of weather and war. Today, however, some beautifully restored buildings can be visited among the remains of other palaces, pagodas and gardens.

▷ **THE CITADEL**
Construction of the citadel was started by Gia Long (1802–20), the first of the Nguyen dynasty kings, who made Hue the country's capital.

△ **WAR DAMAGE**
The Forbidden City did not escape damage during the 1968 Tet Offensive, although restoration work has been underway for some years.

◁ **THIEN MU PAGODA**
West of the citadel, Thien Mu pagoda's famous Tower of Confucius, erected in 1661, was built with bricks of Cham origin.

▽ **NGO MON**
The central gateway of Ngo Mon, which gives access to the Imperial City, was reserved for the king. Others used the side gates.

The tombs were constructed on the banks of the Perfume River several miles upstream from the citadel. Each tomb reflected in its architecture the monarch's politics and personality. Minh Mang (1820–41), who was fascinated by Confucian administrative methods, had his tomb built in an elaborately Chinese style. Tu Duc (1848–83), whose tomb is the most aesthetically unusual, was renowned for his poetic and artistic temperament – unfortunate qualities, perhaps, at a time of invasion. The tomb of Khai Dinh (1916–25) contains numerous motifs drawn from Western influences, at a time when the king was a mere figurehead in the French colony. The kings were not buried under the granite tablets erected to proclaim their titles and exploits. To prevent exhumation by usurping dynasties, the actual burial places were kept secret and remain unknown to this day.

▷ THE IMPERIAL TEMPLE
Temple paraphernalia, including Confucian altars and ceremonial umbrellas, reflect the strong influence of China on Nguyen dynasty.

▽ KHAI DINH'S TOMB
The tomb of Khai Dinh (1916–25) reflects an eccentric mix of French and Vietnamese architectural styles.

▷ IMPERIAL DRAGONS
The long nhan (imperial dragon) symbolises mastery over land and water, and hence the king himself. It is distinguished from ordinary four-clawed dragons by its possession of five long ngu chim or claws.

DA NANG AND HOI AN

Anchoring Vietnam's centre, Da Nang was a strategic pivot in the wars of the 20th century. Nearby Hoi An, once an important port, retains enough atmosphere to make it a traveller's draw

Map on page 234

Quang Nam Province lies about 800 km (500 miles) between Hanoi and Ho Chi Minh City, separated from Laos by the western Truong Son mountains. Forests of valuable timber – rosewood, ironwood, and ebony – cover more than 60 percent of the land. The drive from Hue to Da Nang is one of the most spectacular in Vietnam, as Highway 1 follows a vertiginous route up, down, and around mountains that hug the coastline.

The climate becomes noticeably warmer and more humid after descending the 1,200-metre (4,000-ft) summit of **Deo Hai Van** ❷ (Hai Van Pass), which adjoins another mountain, Bach Ma (White Horse), and descends to the scenic coastal region. To the north of Da Nang and east of Hai Van Pass on the road to Hue, the palm-shaded peninsula of **Lang Co** ❸ rates as one of the most superb spots in the country. To one side lies a stunningly clear lagoon and on the other, miles of unspoiled beach washed by the South China Sea. The town, dependent on fishing, is heavily Catholic.

The provincial capital, **Da Nang** ❹, located on the west bank of the Song Han (Han River), has grown from a fishing village into an important port and the country's fourth-largest city with 550,000 people. While it is not quite as hectic as the capital, Hanoi, or the southern commercial hub, Ho Chi Minh, Da Nang is rapidly becoming a thriving city. Officials here are banking on tourism to revive the economy, and limited international flights in and out of Da Nang's airport are available. Right now, there is only one resort on the beach. Overseas developers have been planning for years to build resorts along the coastline south of Da Nang, particularly in an area known to American GIs from the Vietnam War as China Beach.

Those plans, however, have faced a myriad of obstacles; actual construction and opening of hotels, golf courses, and condominiums probably won't be completed for years. That may be a good thing for visitors who wish to avoid huge crowds; for now, Da Nang is a rather sleepy destination.

People here are generally quite friendly, and many speak English because of Da Nang's development as an American military town during the Vietnam War. Don't be surprised to meet middle-aged men and women who worked for the Americans as interpreters, mechanics, bartenders, or in the many businesses that sprung up to offer all kinds of services to soldiers – everything from laundries to bars.

Among the specialities produced in the province are cinnamon from Tra, pepper from Tien Phuoc, tobacco from Cam Le, silk from Hoa Vang, saffron from Tam Ky, and sea swallow nests from the islands off the coast. The *nuoc mam* (fish sauce) produced in

PRECEDING PAGES: Hoi An canal. **LEFT:** clam digging near Da Nang. **BELOW:** guard at Deo Hai Van.

Da Nang transport.

the fishing village of Nam O, about 15 km (9 miles) from the city towards Hai Van Pass, is reputedly the best in Vietnam. (But then, too, is the nuoc mam from Phan Thiet and from the island of Phu Quoc.)

Divided and difficult history

Because of its location in the centre of the country, Da Nang found itself a city divided during the Vietnam War. Many people in the area supported the South Vietnamese regime, but others quietly (until after 1975) worked for the Viet Cong. Sometimes families themselves had split allegiances; it's not uncommon that brothers fought against each other. There are a few relics of the war era still standing. North of town, along the shoreline, are the rusted shells of an old air base, now used by the Vietnamese military for training. The Da Nang airport runway is lined with revetments. The old American consulate was on Bach Dang, parallel to the Song Han.

Known as Tourane under the French, Da Nang is perhaps best remembered abroad from the role it played at the beginning and end of the Vietnam War. The first 3,500 US Marines came ashore here in 1965. Ten years later, communist troops rolled into town facing little resistance as South Vietnamese soldiers shed their uniforms along the side of the road and fled. Two American 727 jets evacuated refugees, most of them soldiers, in a scene of panic broadcast around the world. So many people tried to climb onto the planes that, as one of them took off, people clinging to the wheels fell into the South China Sea.

Other foreigners came here long before the Americans, however. In the 17th and 18th centuries, the first Spanish and French landings were made here. Subsequently, Da Nang became the scene of battles between the Vietnamese

BELOW: avoiding the rainy season.

Map on page 234

who fought first the Spanish and later the French. In the course of the 19th century, it had superseded Faifo (present-day Hoi An) as the most important port and commercial centre in the central region.

The ancient kingdom of Champa once stretched all the way from Phong Nha, in northcentral Vietnam, to Vung Tau in the south. The kingdom incorporated the five provinces of Indrapura , Amaravati, Vijaya, Kauthara and Panduranga. The Quang Nam Da Nang area was the centre of the Cham civilisation for many centuries. The most ancient capital, Singhapura (Lion City) at **Tra Kieu**, 40 km (25 miles) southwest of Da Nang, was built during the course of the 4th century. Early in the 8th century, the capital was moved south to Panduranga. In the late 8th century, it was transferred back to Quang Nam Da Nang and renamed Indrapura (City of the God of Thunder). Indrapura lasted until the early 11th century.

The ancient site of Singhapura – with its dozens of monuments, hundreds of statues, and bas reliefs – attests to the rich culture that once flourished here. A stele, erected by the eighth Champa king to the memory of Hindu poet Valmiki, author of the *Ramayana*, stands intact. The sacred Buddhist-inspired site of Indrapura, which is now known as **Dong Duong**, lies 60 km (40 miles) from Da Nang. The site's scattered monuments – some of them Buddhist and others Brahman-inspired – are engraved with texts about a line of nine kings and their deeds. Archaeologists have discovered many artefacts at the site, including the 2nd-century bronze Dong Duong Buddha that now resides in the National Museum, in Ho Chi Minh City. A large Buddhist monastery and many holy shrines also are located here.

The valley of **My Son ❺**, southwest of Da Nang, was chosen as a religious

Cham, Mnong, Hoa, Ka Tu, Sedang and Co are among the ethnic minority groups found in the region.

BELOW: Cham sculpture.

THE RISE AND FALL OF CHAMPA

Champa was a kingdom established by the Cham, of Malayo-Polynesian heritage and Hinduised culture. It extended over the central and southern coastal region of Vietnam. Champa was founded in AD 192 when the Chinese official in charge of central Vietnam (the Han dynasty in China was collapsing) formed his own empire in central Vietnam. Absorbing Indian cultural influence, Champa maintained a powerful coastal fleet used for commerce – and piracy of the Chinese coast.

In 446, the Chinese invaded Champa and brought the area under their control. In the 6th century, Champa shed Chinese control to start a period of independence, prosperity and aesthetic excellence. In the late 8th century Champa was attacked by Java, unsuccessfully. A century later, the Chams were pushing into Cambodia.

In 1145 the Khmers conquered Champa. Two years later a new Cham king pushed out the Khmers; his successor attacked Angkor, the Cambodian capital. In the 13th century the Chams were fighting the Khmers, Vietnamese, and Mongols from China.

By the late 15th century, the Champa kingdom was crumbling, to be completely absorbed by the Vietnamese in the 17th century.

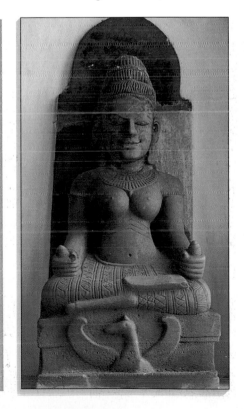

sanctuary by King Bhadravarman I, and from the 4th century on, many temples and towers *(kalan)* were built in the area. Most were dedicated to kings and Brahman divinities, including the god Shiva, who was considered the creator, founder, and defender of the Champa kingdom and the Cham royal dynasties. Some 12th-century stelae discovered here attest to a unified religious belief practised in the sanctuary's first temple, which was erected for the worship of Shiva-Bhadresvara.

The Cham towers were ingeniously constructed of dried bricks and placed together with resin from the *cau day* tree. Once the tower was completed, it was encircled by fires kept well stoked for several days. The intense heat fired the whole structure, completely melding and sealing the bricks and tree resin together to form a structure able to withstand the combined onslaught of time and the elements – but not, unfortunately, 20th-century bombs. Indeed, tourists should not explore off the beaten track, as there are still several unexploded mines in the area. Keep to the main temples and marked paths.

The Chams were divided into two groups: the Dua, who inhabited the provinces of Amarvati and Vijaya, and the Cau, from the provinces of Kauthara and Pandaranga. The two clans differed in their customs and habits, and conflicting interests led to many clashes and even war. But they usually managed to settle disagreements through intermarriage. The influences that shaped the culture and history of the Cham people are revealed through their various sculpture and carvings.

An insight into the Cham people is provided at the excellent **Museum of Cham Sculpture** (open daily 8am–5pm; admission fee), in Da Nang. Established in 1915 by the Ecole Francaise d'Extreme Orient, its extensive

More than 70 architectural sites once stood in My Son. Today, less than 20 remain, as My Son fell in a free-fire zone for B52 bombers during the Vietnam War. There are still unexploded mines in the area.

BELOW: Museum of Cham Sculpture.

Map on page 234

collection is displayed in rooms featuring four different periods according to their origins. My Son, Tra Kieu, Dong Duong, and Thap Mam.

From Da Nang to Hoi An

South of Da Nang, towards the coast, stand five large hills: **Ngu Hanh Son** (Marble Mountains), the Mountains of the Five Elements: Kim Son (metal), Thuy Son (water), Moc Son (wood), Hoa Son (fire), and Tho Son (earth). These mountains were once a group of five offshore islets, but because of silting over the years they became part of the mainland. Mysterious caves within the mountains shelter altars dedicated to Buddha, *bodhisattvas* and the different deities created in stories of the area's inhabitants. The most famous of these is Thuy Son. Used by the Cham for their sacred rituals, these caves today still serve as religious sanctuaries. One can visit several temples, including **Tam Thai**, built in 1852, and **Linh Ung**.

Stay on marked paths at My Son, as there are several unexploded land-mines among the tombs and temples

The paths are well-marked and easy to navigate. The highest cave, Huyen Khong, has a small tunnel that leads to the very top of the hill – a perfect lookout over the sea, the surrounding countryside and the air base.

The mountains are also a valuable source of red, white, and blue-green marble. At the foot of the mountains, skilful marble carvers chisel out a great variety of objets d'art and will proudly tell you that they worked on the construction of Ho Chi Minh's mausoleum. Alongside the mountains is a long stretch of beautiful, quiet beach. To the south is **Bai Bien Non Nuoc ❻**, known to many foreigners as China Beach, near the village of Non Nuoc. China Beach was a place American GIs went for rest and recreation during the war. However, some people contend the real China Beach is to the north, at My Khe.

BELOW: bicycles on China Beach.

Old French print of the harbour of Faifo, or today's Hoi An.

Hoi An

About 25 km (15 miles) southeast of Da Nang and near the coast, the ancient town of **Hoi An** ❼ nestles on the banks of the Song Thu Bon (Thu Bon River), a few kilometres inland from the coast. This charming old town was once a flourishing port and meeting place of East and West, in what was central Dai Viet under the Nguyen lords. Hoi An appeared in western travelogues in the 17th and 18th centuries as Faifo or Hai Po. Originally a sea port in the Champa kingdom and known as Dai Chien, by the 15th century it had become a coastal Vietnamese town under the Tran dynasty.

At the beginning of the 16th century, the Portuguese came to explore the coast of Hoi An. Then came the Chinese, Japanese, Dutch, British and French. With them came the first missionaries – Italian, Portuguese, French, Spanish. Among them was Alexander of Rhodes, who adopted the Roman alphabet for the Vietnamese language.

For several centuries, Hoi An was one of the most important trading ports in Southeast Asia and an important centre of cultural exchange between East and West. By the beginning of the 19th century, Hoi An's social and physical environment had changed drastically. The conflict between the Trinh and Nguyen lords and the Tay Son caused Hoi An considerable damage. Moreover, rivers changed course as the mouth of the Thu Bon silted up and prevented the flow of sea traffic. Another port was built at the mouth of the Song Han – Da Nang, replacing Hoi An as the centre of trade.

Today, Hoi An is a quiet town of about 120,000 people – 12,000 of them living in the old quarter that has been restored and renovated as something of a historical showpiece for tourists. Many of the older homes, built with wood

BELOW: old doors.

beams, carved doors and airy, open rooms, have been turned into souvenir shops fronting as museums.

In the early 1980s, UNESCO and the Polish government took the initiative and funded a restoration programme to classify and safeguard Hoi An's ancient quarters and historic monuments. Unfortunately many of Hoi An's monuments are threatened by yearly floods (mainly between October and November) when water spills over the river banks and submerges some streets in two to three metres of water. Hoi An is today a UNESCO World Heritage Site (www.hoian worldheritage.org). An admission ticket of 75,000 dong gains you entry to all its old streets, one each of the three museums and assembly halls, one of the four old houses, a traditional music concert and a temple. The sites are open daily from 7am to 6pm.

Hoi An has become a popular tourist spot. In fact, older residents worry that the very thing that makes Hoi An attractive – its quiet charm – is being ruined. People will kindly invite visitors into their homes to look at the architecture, but some locals demand a donation. Today, in the old part of town, nearly 80 percent of the people derive their income from tourism. The rest of the residents work primarily as fishermen.

Walkabout

The oldest part of town is in the southern section, bordering the **Song Thu Bon**. Running perpendicular to the river, Le Loi was the first street to be built, four centuries ago. The Japanese quarter, with its covered bridge and Japanese-style shops and houses, followed half a century later on the west side of town, followed by the Cantonese quarter 50 years later. Hoi An's past is superbly

Map on page 234

 TIP

Everywhere you go in Hoi An, you'll see tailor shops. Indeed the best and cheapest tailors in Vietnam are found in Hoi An. A Dong Silk at 40 Le Loi Street (www.adongsilk.com) is one of the more expensive shops but comes highly recommended by many.

BELOW: Phuoc Kien Assembly Hall.

Map
on page
260

TIP

Just 5 km (3 miles) from Hoi An is beautiful Cua Dai beach, lined with several good hotels. Stay here instead for a bit of sand and surf, and use this beach as your base for explorations of Hoi An.

RIGHT: fishing on China Beach.

Hoi An

preserved in its architecture. The old quarter is a fascinating blend of temples, pagodas, community houses, shrines, clan houses, shop houses, and homes.

As in many towns, **Cho Hoi An Ⓐ**, the central market, is a good place to start a proper ramble. Some pagodas and 20 clan houses stand in the centre of the old town. Most of these temples and houses were built by the Chinese migrant community over a span of 40 years, between 1845 and 1885. On Tran Phu at the corner of the market, the **Chua Quan Cong Ⓑ**, built in 1653 and also known as Chua Ong, is dedicated to Quang Cong, a talented general of the chaotic Three Kingdoms period in Chinese history, which lasted from AD 221 until 265. Adjacent is the **Hoi An Historical and Cultural Museum Ⓒ**, which is located in a former pagoda.

The **Fujian Assembly Hall Ⓓ** at 46 Tran Phu was built in 1792 and has been the meeting place of many generations of the same clan, who arrived from Fujian, along the coast in southern China. Here, they remember their origins and worship their ancestors. The assembly hall is dedicated to the cult of Lady Thien Hau and contains many exquisite woodcarvings.

Although many of the old homes and monuments have been restored over the years, they retain their original wooden framework, carved doors and windows and sculpted stuccos, as well as very rare and ancient furniture from Vietnam, China, Japan, and the West. The most characteristic examples of Hoi An's architecture are the old houses at 101 Nguyen Thai Hoc and parallelling the river, particularly the **Tan Ky House Ⓔ**. These elongated houses front onto one street and back onto the street behind. All the houses are built of precious wood in a very refined, two-storey style. The interior is terraced for living, and an inner courtyard is open to the sky with a veranda linking several living quarters.

One of the most remarkable features of these old homes is the diversity in their architectural structure. This varies greatly from one house to another in terms of space distribution, sculptural art, decoration and inner courtyard gardens. Space is creatively utilised. The unique crab-shell roof style extensively used is typical of Hoi An.

Walking in the streets of this lovely and charming town, observe the influence of the architecture, sculpture, and decorative styles of China, Japan and France, along with the skill of the Vietnamese architects who have absorbed these outside influences and created something similar yet somehow different.

Two other 18th-century houses of note are the **Quan Thang House** at 77 Tran Phu – look out for the finely carved wooden doors enclosing the open courtyard – and the **Phung Hung House** at 4 Nguyen Thi Minh Khai, which has both Japanese and Chinese architectural influences.

One of the most remarkable historical architectural examples is **Cau Nhat Ban Ⓖ** (or the **Japanese Covered Bridge**). Built by the Japanese community in the 17th century, it links the districts of Cam Pho and Minh Huong. The bridge's curved shape and undulating green-and-yellow tiled roof give the impression of moving water. In the middle of the bridge is a square pagoda called **Chua Cau**, dedicated to Dac De and Tran Vu, two legendary figures. ❑

SOUTHERN VIETNAM

Entrepreneurial in mind and tropical in ambience, the south is heady and hot and defined by the delta of the Mekong

Far removed from the more traditional north and centre, southern Vietnam has a character all of its own. Saigon, the former capital of South Vietnam until it collapsed in 1975, now bears the name of Thanh Pho Ho Chi Minh, or Ho Chi Minh City, a change that many of its residents (and foreigners) still resist three decades later. Traditions and habits die hard.

But whatever one calls it, this furiously active and commercial city is definitely going somewhere. The streets are filled with new motorbikes and new taxis, and construction is adding a glittering shimmer to the downtown boulevards.

It's always been an entrepreneurial centre, and for decades people from all over the country have flocked here to make their fortunes. This is Vietnam's city of dreams – and sometimes, nightmares. Many become disillusioned and they may be seen on the streets, looking for a job or a place to sleep. But the effort and luck needed to find fortune has done little to deter the flow of hopefuls. Indeed, their spirit gives the city an optimistic edge. Southern Vietnam, especially Ho Chi Minh, has always been noted for its business acumen. Cho Lon, the city's long established and thriving Chinese community, never seems to sleep.

An increasingly important facet of Vietnam's economic growth, however, can be found some 125 km (70 miles) to the east, in Vung Tau, the centre of the country's growing oil industry. One of the country's major ports, Vung Tau bathes in a mild climate and was previously a popular weekend seaside resort.

Although oil may portend a prosperous future for Vietnam, for the moment its export powerhouse is the rice-growing delta of the Mekong River – the River of Nine Dragons, or Cuu Long. The vast delta stretches from the eastern coast to the western border with Cambodia and as far south as Ca Mau, the southernmost tip of the country. An extensive network of waterways, irrigation canals and rivers laces the region, which is plied by ferries and every type of sailing vessel imaginable, linking the various towns and provinces to Ho Chi Minh City.

Rice fields stretch as far as the eye can see, creating a many-hued and textured patchwork. It is a quiet, isolated life, one that apparently makes many a person restless and thus drawn to the bright lights of Ho Chi Minh – or Saigon, if one prefers. ❑

PRECEDING PAGES: overseas Vietnamese buying fowl in Ho Chi Minh.
LEFT: high monsoon waters in the Mekong Delta.

Southern Vietnam

BIEN DONG

(SOUTH CHINA SEA)

NHA TRANG

*If the charm of rustic travel is wearing somewhat thin,
consider Nha Trang's rather fine beaches and unfettered life.
What's more, there are the evocative ruins of old Champa to explore*

Map
on page
266

A long the south-central coast, travellers can glimpse two sides of life in Vietnam: the relaxed beach life of the picturesque Nha Trang and then the hard scrabble existence of the desolate areas around Phan Rang and Phan Thiet. The drive along the Pacific coast, from Da Nang to Nha Trang, provides spectacular vistas of beaches, coves, cliffs and mountains jutting out into the sea, with long stretches of rice paddies bordered on one side by blue-tinted mountain sides and on the other by the sea, even more blue.

Vietnam's most picturesque coastal town and beach resort, **Nha Trang ❶**, is the ideal place to break a journey, relax and soak up the sun. With its population of 500,000, it is now the provincial capital of Khanh Hoa Province, which lies to the east of the Central Highlands. According to popular belief, the town derives its name from the Cham word *yakram* (lit. bamboo river).

Nha Trang is a good place to idle. The beaches are relatively clean and quiet, although the crowds can become frustrating, especially during local school holidays, and vendors are becoming increasingly aggressive – as elsewhere in Vietnam. In recent years, there has been a considerable amount of construction, mainly hotels, along Tran Phu, a street that runs parallel to the shoreline. But the beach itself, especially the southern end, has been left reasonably undisturbed, even though there are now several hotels and resorts lining it.

A small amusement park, with a Ferris wheel and fun house, fronts the shore. There are several good restaurants right on the beach, serving everything from pizza baked in a brick oven to the expected fresh seafood; the large shrimp is especially good.

The attitude here is generally more relaxed and carefree than elsewhere in Vietnam. Visitors will find pick-up soccer games on the beach, the sky filled with colourful kites, and vendors peddling juicy fruit, steamed corn, delicious crabs, tacky T-shirts, relaxing massages, and even manicures on the beach. It's possible to sell and trade books not only in English, but also in French and German. Besides risking a sunburn, reading a book, and napping – in other words, doing not much of anything – there are plenty of things to see in and around Nha Trang.

Just east of the Nha Trang railway station stands the large **Nha Tho Nha Trang ❹** (Nha Trang Cathedral).

PRECEDING PAGES: family on the train. **OPPOSITE:** beach at Nha Trang.

Nha Trang

Pool is popular.

Built in a gothic style, the cathedral is the home of Nha Trang's Catholic bishop. A white, 19-metre-high (62-ft) Buddha statue commands an excellent view from his seat at the top of the hill behind **Chua Long Son B**. The pagoda was built in 1886 and has been reconstructed several times since. Glass and ceramic mosaics depicting dragons adorn the main entrance and roofs.

The Buddha statue was erected in 1963 to commemorate the Buddhist struggle against the repressive South Vietnamese regime of Ngo Dinh Diem, who was overthrown that same year. Images of the Buddhist nuns and monks who laid down their lives as a final protest are at the base of the statue. The most famous of them, Thich Quang Duc, was a bonze from Van Gia, a town a little over 70 km (40 miles) north of Nha Trang. He made headlines when he immolated himself in the centre of Saigon in 1963.

The **Pasteur Institute C** (open Mon–Fri 8–11am and 2–4.30pm; admission fee), on Nha Trang's seafront, was founded in 1895 by Dr Alexandre Yersin, a French microbiologist, military doctor, and overall Renaissance man who had worked as an assistant to Dr Pasteur in Paris. He arrived in Vietnam in 1891 and was among those Europeans who first appreciated Da Lat. Yersin was also responsible for introducing and establishing Brazilian rubber trees and *quinquina* plantations – quinine-producing trees – in the region of Suoi Dau, about 25 km (15 miles) southwest of Nha Trang. He is buried here among his rubber trees.

A new museum has been built at the Institute that displays many of Dr Yersin's personal effects, documents and laboratory equipment. Many of his books are kept in the library opposite the museum, a library he himself designed. Today, the Institute still produces vaccines and carries out research, though with a very limited budget.

BELOW: Nha Trang harbour.

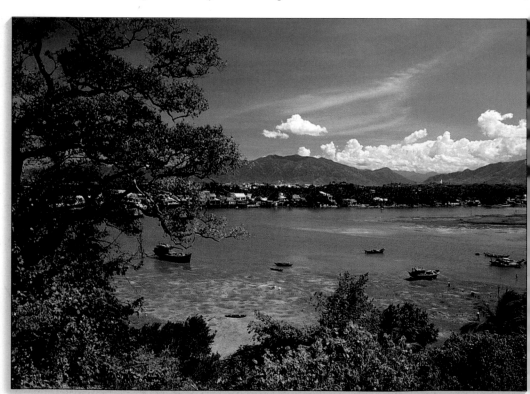

Map on page 271

During the day, one can catch the interesting sights and smells of Nha Trang's main market, **Cho Dam** ⒟, which was built in 1972. Goods include everything from fruit and vegetables to clothing, hardware and electronic goods.

A guaranteed sight is the return of the local fishing fleet to shore in the early morning. One place to watch is from the **Xom Bong** ⒠, a bridge located at the base of the knoll on which the Cham towers rest. The bridge spans the **Song Cai**, which joins several waterways from the western forests and flows to the Song Nha Trang mouth. The province's largest river, the 300-km-long (180-mile) **Song Da Rang**, is also the longest in central Vietnam. Canals branch off, carrying water to the vast fields of rice, maize and beans.

On a hill at the town's northern entrance stand the majestic towers of the famous Cham sanctuary and temple, **Po Nagar** ⒡. The main tower is dedicated to the Cham goddess Po I Nu Nagar, the Lady Mother of the Kingdom and reputedly Shiva's female form. Today, she is still worshipped, adopted by Vietnamese Buddhists who refer to her as Thien Y-A-Na. Her statue resides in the main temple, but it was decapitated during French rule, and the original head now resides in the Guimet Museum, in Paris. Only four of the sanctuary's original eight temples, all of which face east, remain standing. These date from the 7th and 9th centuries. The remaining pillars and steep steps leading up to the towers hint at the majesty of the original temple. At the end of the 1990s, the towers were restored; tourists and vendors continue to flock here.

Along the banks of the Cai near the bridge, the village of **Xom Bong** is known for producing many of the dancers at the Po Nagar festivals. From the top of **Hon Son** (Son Hill), behind the ancient Cham towers, a superb panorama looks out over Nha Trang.

BELOW: Nha Trang fishing boats.

Not far from here, the jagged rocks of **Hon Chong** ⒢ jut out into the clear aquamarine waters of the South China Sea. The beach here is relatively small and quite busy. Northwest of here is **Tien Co** (Fairy Mountain), as its three summits are thought to resemble a fairy lying on her back.

The **Oceanographic Institute** ⒣ (open 6am–6pm; admission fee) is located south of the town in the fishing village of **Cau Da**. The Institute was founded in 1927 on the initiative of a biologist, Armand Krempf. It houses aquatic flora and fauna. Its aquariums – rows of small fish tanks lined up along the walls and a few specimens preserved in jars – and open-air pool are home to many different species of fish and other marine life.

From the Nha Trang harbour located here at Cau Da, visitors can take a 20-minute boat ride to neighbouring **Hon Mieu** (Mieu Island) where the larger **Tri Nguyen Aquarium** is located. Cau Da does a brisk business in shells, coral and tortoise-shell items – necklaces, bracelets, and the like – at reasonable prices. The ever-present Vietnamese condiment, *nuoc mam* or fermented fish sauce, is produced here in large quantities.

Just north of Cau Da, Emperor Bao Dai's five villas are set amongst well-manicured trees and shrubs on three hills. The villas were built in the 1920s, their location obviously chosen for the superb views over the sea, the bay and the port. Three cycles of Vietnamese leadership have used the site for rest and relaxation. Bao Dai and his family came here until the royalty was ousted. From the mid-1950s until 1975, high-ranking officials of the South Vietnamese government enjoyed staying at the villas. After 1975, they were supplanted by Communist leaders from Hanoi. Today, the villas have been restored and given over to the provincial tourism authorities who are using them as a hotel. With

BELOW: beach near Nha Trang.

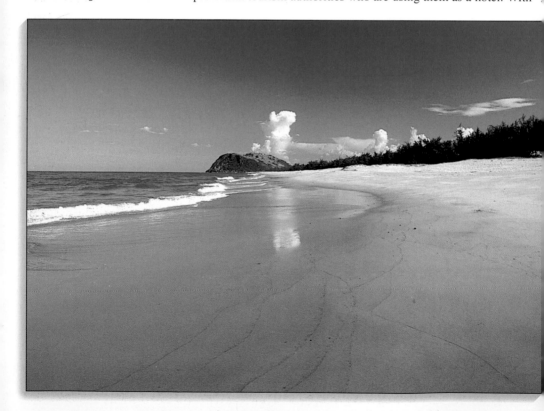

rooms for rent and a restaurant that's open to the public, the *hoi polloi* can now enjoy the site too.

Palm trees line the dazzling sands and clear waters of Nha Trang's gently curving bay. Idyllic islands, easily accessible by boat, lie just off the coast to the west. One of the more popular things to do in Nha Trang is to take a boat excursion to visit the islands and coral reefs, where snorkelling is excellent. Deep-sea fishing is also possible. **Hon Tre** (Bamboo Island) is the largest of the islands, while **Hon Lao** (Monkey Island) to the north is home to more than 300 monkeys.

North of Nha Trang

About 30 km (20 miles) north of Nha Trang, near the village of Phu Huu, is a quiet, isolated park with a stream and waterfalls called **Ba Ho ❷**. The scenery is varied and quite magnificent. Here, amid lush green forests are three pools in ascending height, formed by water cascading over large boulders. Enterprising youngsters will follow you the entire way, offering helping hands and liquid refreshments, all of which become greatly appreciated as the climb grows increasingly steep and slippery. Of course they expect to be rewarded at the end of the trek. Northeast of here on its own peninsula is the lovely and secluded beach at **Doc Let**, which looks out over the South China Sea. In the west, the famous Mother and Child Mountain reaches a height of 2,000 metres (6,600 ft). From a distance its silhouette resembles a woman carrying a child.

Further north, National Highway 1 traverses the plain of Minh Hoa before climbing the sinuous **Deo Ca ❸** (Ca Pass) over the mountain of Dai Lanh. Here, in 1470, King Le Thanh Tong and his troops stopped and erected a stele

Maps
Area 266
City 271

Many islands, such as Hon Yen, are home to sea swallows, whose famous nests, gathered in vast quantities, are a source of nutrition and income. Nests are collected in spring and autumn. Most rare are the orange and red nests, believed to be therapeutic.

BELOW: road traffic outside Nha Trang.

Cham temple detail near Nha Trang.

to mark the boundary between Dai Viet and the Kingdom of Champa. Today, this spot marks the boundary between Phu Yen and Khanh Hoa provinces. Forests in the northern part of the region produce many kinds of wood, including sandalwood, aloe wood, eagle wood, barian kingwood, rosewood, and ebony.

Southward from Nha Trang

Leaving Nha Trang to the south, the coastal road passes **Vinh Cam Ranh** ❹ (Cam Ranh Bay), the deep-water bay used as a naval base, first by the Americans and later by the Soviets. Today the base is occupied by the Vietnamese army and remains off-limits to the public. Absolutely no photography is permitted. The sand from the bay is of a quality much sought-after for manufacturing lenses and high-quality crystal. Before the Vietnam War, enormous quantities of sand were exported to Japan, Europe, and America.

The area of Cam Ranh alone has more than 300 hectares (750 acres) of salt marsh that yield around half a million tons of salt per year. Immense sugar cane plantations cover certain areas of the province.

South of Cam Ranh, the road enters Ninh Thuan Province. The coastal road passes through a rather monotonous, sand-covered landscape. Mountains and forest cover two-thirds of Ninh Thuan and Binh Thuan to the south. They are one of the country's poorest areas, due to the lack of agricultural resources.

The town of **Phan Rang** ❺, capital of Ninh Thuan, is an ancient Cham principality on the **Song Chai**. The town lies in an extremely arid landscape dotted with menacing-looking cacti and poinciana trees. From here, the scenic Highway 20 leads to the central highlands resort of Da Lat *(see chapter on Da*

BELOW: Cham tower near Phan Rang.

CHAM MUSICAL INFLUENCES

Like the music of Korea and Japan, Vietnamese music is derived from Chinese musical tradition. Still, some of its musical elements are local or absorbed from elsewhere in Southeast Asia. Some of it is also derived from Champa, the old Hinduised kingdom of central Vietnam. Most famous, of course, are the kettle drums of Dong Son *(see picture, page 26)*. Archaeological research in Dong Son village uncovered ancient kettle gongs, mouth organs, percussive clappers made of wood, and the conch-shell trumpet or horn. Between the 10th and 15th centuries, both Indian and Chinese influences melded together in Vietnamese music. For example, at least two traditional Chinese musical ensembles and theatrical art were introduced to the Champa repertoire.

By the 1700s, Chinese influence was considerable. Vietnamese court music *(nha nhac)* was performed by two orchestras: one with a 12-stone chime, 12 bells, 25-string and 7-string zithers, flutes, double-headed drum, and mouth organ. The second orchestra offered 16 iron chimes, 20-string harp, lute, double flute, double-headed drum, and mouth organ. The royal ceremonial music, no longer found or heard in Vietnam, was derived from traditional court music.

Lu, page 278). About 7 km (4 miles) down this road, four 13th-century Cham towers known as **Po Klong Garai** stand on an arid hill. These brick towers were built under the reign of the Cham King Jaya Simhavarman III to worship King Po Klong Garai, who had constructed a much-needed local irrigation system. The entrance to the largest tower is graced with a dancing, six-armed Shiva, and inside a statue of a bull known as Nandin is the recipient of offerings brought by farmers to ensure a good harvest. Under a wooden pyramid is a linga painted with a human face. A rock on a nearby hill bears inscriptions commemorating the construction of a linga by a Cham prince in 1050.

Further up the road, 40 km (25 miles) before Da Lat, is **Krong Pha** ❻, with the crumbling remains of two old Cham towers. Even more interesting are the colourful, traditionally clad Cham people who live in the foothills around this extremely poor area. This region is also renowned for its grape production.

About 15 km (10 miles) south of Phan Rang is a Cham tower, **Po Ro Me** ❼, named after the last King of Champa, Po Ro Me, who ruled from 1629 to 1651 and died a prisoner of the Vietnamese. The lovely white-sand beaches and turquoise waters of the beach at **Ca Na**, roughly 30 km (20 miles) south of Phan Rang, is an excellent place to break a journey.

Phan Thiet ❽, the provincial capital of Binh Thuan, has a population of 170,000. Fishing is the mainstay of Phan Thiet and the province as a whole. A great many different varieties of fish are caught in the region. Visit the fishing harbour early in the morning, when the fishermen are unloading their catch, and you'll be treated to an unusual – and quite spectacular – sight. Along the southern coast, another common sight is that of fishermen transporting themselves in large, round baskets known as *thung chai* (pitch baskets). Made of woven bamboo strips and sealed with pitch, these 2-metre-wide boats are paddled standing up. As in many other towns along the coast, the pungent odour of *nuoc mam* hovers over the town. Among the other products of the region are mineral water from a spring called Vinh Hao, cashew nuts, grapes and cuttlefish.

Some 22km (13 miles) east of Phan Thiet along the coast and located on its own peninsula is the small fishing village of **Mui Ne** ❾. With lovely beaches and offshore islands a short boat ride away for the exploring, this is a delightful place to drop out for a while. The stretch of lonely coast leading to Front Beach is bordered on one side by the blue ocean and on the other by the beautiful, stark, salmon-coloured sand dunes for which the village is famous. Visitors can hike, try sand-sledding, and even stay overnight amidst these graceful, sculpted forms. Also of interest is **Suoi Tien** or Fairy Spring, a stream that winds through white and red sand dunes out onto the beach. Be sure to have proper footwear and a hat, as well as plenty of drinking water, for the weather – and the sand – become blazing hot by midday.

Anticipating that this area will be the next hot vacation spot, developers have rushed in to build resort hotels, especially along the road between Phan Thiet and Mui Ne. Mui Ne is turning into one of Vietnam's most popular beach resort destinations as it is within easy reach of Ho Chi Minh City. ❏

Map on page 266

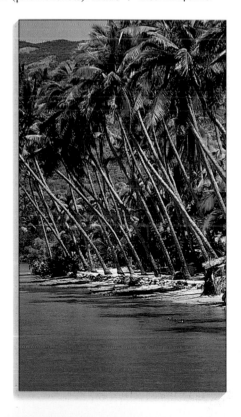

BELOW: beach lined with palms.

Maps on page 266–7

DA LAT AND BEYOND

An old colonial hill retreat, Da Lat is but a few hours from Ho Chi Minh. A favourite of the last emperor, even dour communist cadres have found Da Lat to be a salve for the Party life

A cool, tranquil, and lush retreat from Vietnam's large cities, **Da Lat** ❿ was first developed as a highland getaway by the French. Located in Lam Dong Province, Da Lat, the city of Eternal Spring, is today Vietnam's most popular mountain resort and escape. Although accessible by several inland routes from the coastal provinces of Khanh Hoa and Ninh Thuan, the most used route is the 300 km- (180 mile-) long route via Bien Hoa from Ho Chi Minh, about a 5-hour trip on Highway 1 then northeast on Highway 20. Another route, on Highway 11 from Nha Trang, passes areas with the residue of Cham ruins. Da Lat is nestled among mountains, pine-covered hillsides, lakes and forests on the Lam Viet plateau, beside the **Song Cam Ly** (Cam Ly River). Da Lat's name comes from two words: *da*, meaning river or source, in reference to the Cam Ly, and *lat*, the name of an ethnic minority living here.

With a population of about 150,000, the city's economy is based on agriculture and tourism. The average annual temperature of about 17°C (63°F), fresh mountain air, and tranquil beauty first attracted the French, who developed the resort and built holiday villas on the hillsides.

Da Lat has long been a favourite destination for lovers and honeymooners. Many natural beauty spots await visitors in and around this charming old town,

BELOW: the subtle Da Lat skyline.

COFFEE-CAT COFFEE

One of the world's largest coffee exporters, Vietnam is also home to a rather discriminating connoisseur of the bean: the civet cat, a relative of the mongoose that looks a little like a fox. Said to choose only the best beans from the coffee plant (introduced in the central highlands by the French about a century ago), the cat's discriminating choice of beans usually make it through the complete digestive system of the cat. Later, after the cat has returned to its traditional forest habitat, human connoisseurs of coffee retrieve the undigested beans at the base of forest trees for recycling into what is said to be amongst the world's best cups of coffee: *caphe cut chon*, or fox-dung coffee.

Recipes abound. One is to dry the reclaimed beans in the sun for months. After the outer skin peels off, the beans are mixed with salt, butter, perhaps some sugar, and a glug of French red wine. Then the beans are roasted. However, as the civet cat's habitat of forests is disappearing – often for new coffee plantations – the cats themselves are increasingly scarce. This has led to an industry in counterfeit beans. One restaurateur in Ho Chi Minh claims that Viet Cong soldiers drank caphe cut chon for a caffeine-induced fighting edge in battle.

whose colonial-era villas and buildings are decorated with attractive gardens of roses, poppies, sunflowers and gladioli.

Da Lat was at one time projected to become the capital of the French colonial Indochinese State Federation. In the late 19th century, the French governor of Cochin China sent a delegation to explore the region. On the strength of their findings, the governor established a meteorological and agricultural research centre here. There is still something of a French colonial air about the place. The grand Dalat Palace Hotel commands a prime location in town, above a vast green lawn (perhaps the only such piece of grass anywhere in Vietnam) overlooking the central lake, Xuan Huong. The hotel, built by the French in 1922, was renovated in 1995 and reopened by the French Sofitel chain. Whether staying or not, it is worth a visit for its architecture.

On Tran Hung Dao, more than two dozen villas built by the French in all manner of European styles stand under tall trees, looking out over the valley and the mountains surrounding it. Villas built as summer residences for Vietnam's last emperor, Bao Dai, and one for the French governor-general are nestled among the pine trees. Small houses are cosily perched, side by side, on the town's hilly terrain.

The beauty and serenity have made Da Lat a popular retreat. But its appeal has a downside. All around town, especially at many of the parks, lakes and villas, the tacky side of tourism has sprung up: photographers with hill-tribe costumes for visitors to don while posing for a picture by a lake; young men dressed as American cowboys leading children on pony rides; souvenir stands selling all manner of kitsch. The risk, of course, is that the sideshow of tat will upstage Da Lat's main attraction: its natural landscape, beauty and quiet.

TIP

Nothing is free in Da Lat, including a visit to a hill-tribe village. Once there, travellers are always surrounded by villagers selling their goods and they can be persistent, if not a complete nuisance.

BELOW: vegetable farms near Da Lat.

Central Da Lat

Da Lat's hilly terrain means many of its sights are scattered all over town. The old French quarter, on Tran Hung Dao, has managed to retain much of its old charm. From a distance, this area of town looks like a village plucked from the French Alps.

The colourful **Cho Da Lat ◐** (Central Market) in the heart of Da Lat is an ideal place to encounter some of the ethnic minorities, distinctive in their traditional dress, who come from the surrounding villages to sell their produce. Here also are the great diversity of fruit, flowers and vegetables produced in the region. Da Lat's strawberries – and the jam made from them – are famous throughout the country. Avocados, artichokes, mushrooms, tomatoes, asparagus – just about any fruit, flower and vegetable found in Europe or America can be bought here. Flowers from Da Lat are sent to all parts of Vietnam. A wide range of handicraft items find their way to the market from various parts of the country, including bamboo handbags, rattan boxes, pressed flowers and fur hats. Just to the market's west is Hoa Binh Square.

Ho Xuan Huong ◐ (Xuan Huong Lake), formerly part of the town's golf course during the colonial era, lies in the heart of the town. The surrounding low hills, villas, and pine forests provide a lovely backdrop, although the water itself is muddy with red clay after the rains, even though the surrounding hillsides are anchored by hotels. Drivers offer rides in horse-drawn carts from the edge of the park. On the north side of the lake, a golf course originally built for the last emperor Bao Dai has been renovated and expanded, supplanting what had been a public park. Near the golf course is the small campus of Da Lat University. Not too far away, the well-manicured **Flower Gardens ◐** offer a

Market in Da Lat.

BELOW: garden of Chua Linh Son.

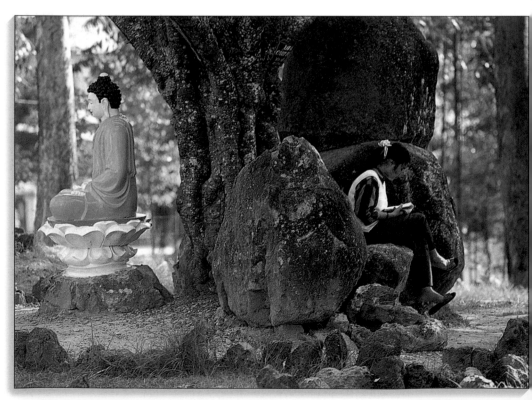

Map on page 281

quiet retreat. Established in 1966, a walkway winds through the gardens and around a small pond.

To the south of the market is a large, pink Catholic cathedral, or **Nha Tho Con Ga D**, built in 1931 and with stained-glass windows made by Louis Balmet, in Grenoble, France. In what is perhaps an ominous sign of things to come, however, in 1997 the government erected a new telecommunications tower resembling the Eiffel Tower across from the cathedral. No doubt built in an attempt to emulate *Le Petit Paris* – what Da Lat was called during its French heyday, this hunk of steel has now become, together with the old villas and churches, an indelible part of the landscape.

North of the central market area is **Chua Linh Son E**, an active pagoda and Da Lat's centre of Buddhism. Not far away is a yellow evangelical church, on Nguyen Van Troi, built in 1940. Since 1975, Vietnam's Protestants have suffered persecution, and even today the government restricts the activities of this church, whose congregation is composed mostly of converted hill-tribe people. The quiet and peaceful Domaine de Marie convent, built between 1940 and 1942, perches on a hilltop on Ngo Quyen. There were 35 nuns in residence before 1975, but only 25 remain today. They operate a school for novices and sell handmade crafts and embroidery.

Da Lat's **Ethnic Minority Museum** at 4 Hung Vuang exhibits traditional costumes, ornaments, jewellery, baskets, hunting implements, and musical instruments. The museum's archaeological display features a statue of the Hindu goddess Uma, 12th- and 14th-century Cham pottery vases, rice-wine jars more than 200 years old, an unusual stone xylophone and tools used in the province more than 1,500 years ago.

Bao Dai, Vietnam's last emperor.

Da Lat environs

Tucked away under pine trees a few kilometres southwest of the centre of town, **Biet Dien Quoc Truong F** (Dinh 3) was the **Summer Palace** of Vietnam's last emperor, Bao Dai. Construction was begun in 1933 and finished five years later. Inside, there is a room with photographs of Bao Dai, his wife and children along with a desk with two telephones, one supposedly used by Bao Dai and the other by a former president of South Vietnam, Nguyen Van Thieu. (South Vietnamese leaders used the villa after Bao Dai left Vietnam; communist government officials have used it since 1975.) Among the items on display are a large map of Vietnam, a grand piano and frayed furniture covered in red velvet. Although guides will say that the furnishings were used by Bao Dai, in fact many of his belongings have been carted away over the years.

Not far from the summer residence, on Thien My to the north and due west of downtown, is **Chua Lam Ty Ni**,

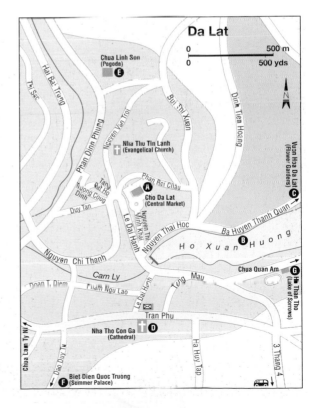

Da Lat

0   500 m
0   500 yds

N

Chua Linh Son (Pagoda) **E**

Nha Tho Tin Lanh (Evangelical Church)

Cho Da Lat (Central Market) **A**

Ho Xuan Huong **B**

Chua Quan Am **G**

Than Tho (Lake of Sorrows)

Vuon Hoa Da Lat (Flower Gardens) **C**

Nha Tho Con Ga (Cathedral) **D**

Biet Dien Quoc Truong (Summer Palace) **F**

founded in 1961. The pagoda's flower beds and garden, and much of its wooden furniture, are the handiwork of the pagoda's founder and sole monk, Vien Thuc, who also has several thousand of his Zen paintings he will happily sell visitors. Vien Thuc is something of a character around Da Lat and not always an endearing one. This hermit monk writes *haiku* poems, speaks several languages, and has been exhibited in Europe, but while many tourists have found him to be rather delightful and profound, a number of locals consider him to be a hypocrite and fraud.

Several waterfalls liberally sprinkle the landscape in and around Da Lat. (Note that most of them charge fees to visitors.) The falls at **Cam Ly**, just to the north of Lam Ty Ni, are best visited during the rainy season, if at all; at other times the dry bed emits a foul odour.

The French governor-general's palace, **Dinh 2**, similar to Bao Dai's Summer Palace, is on Tran Hung Dao, southeast of the centre of town. Local lore has it that there was an escape tunnel built in the basement. Rooms can be rented here for US$25 to $40.

Not far from here down Khe Sanh is **Chua Thien Vuong** or **Chua Dao** (Chinese Pagoda), as it is known to the many domestic visitors who throng the site. Built in 1958, the pagoda houses in its main sanctuary a statue of the Thich Ca Buddha flanked by the goddesses of mercy and power. At 4 metres (13 ft) high and weighing 1,500 kg (3,300 lbs) each, these gilded sandalwood statues were brought from Hong Kong. On a hillside behind the temple is a giant, white statue of Buddha.

That tacky commercialism has infected even a hallowed pagoda is evident in the handful of young people dressed in animal costumes skulking about the

BELOW: produce market, Da Lat.

temple, offering themselves as photo opportunities. (In many ways, the Vietnamese do little to make travelling an authentic cultural experience.)

Much quieter and nicer is the **Thien Vien Truc Lam** (Bamboo Forest Meditation Centre), located 5 km (3 miles) south of the centre of town and accessible by road or cable car. Built in 1993, this Zen Buddhist monastery sits atop a hill overlooking a tranquil Paradise Lake. A large hall contains a statue of Buddha holding a lotus flower. There are 90 monks and 100 nuns in residence here as well as several lay students.

About 6 km (4 miles) north of town is **Thung Lung Tinh Yeu** (Valley of Love), so named for the courting couples from nearby Da Lat University who frequent the park. One can wander in the forest where Bao Dai used to hunt. Sailboats can be rented on the nearby artificial lake, **Ho Da Thien**, formed during flooding in 1972. Visitors must pass through a sometimes tedious gauntlet of souvenir stands, however, which has led locals to dub the place "Valley of Shops".

Ho Than Tho ⑥ (Lake of Sorrows, or Sighs) lies 5 km (3 miles) northeast of Da Lat. It derives its name from the patriotism of a young couple, Hang Tung and Mai Nuong. When Hang joined Quang Trung's resistance forces against the Tsin invaders, Mai, believing Hang would be better able to serve his country unencumbered, drowned herself in the lake. Since then, the lake has been known by its present name, sometimes translated to mean Lake of Sighs – which is what visitors might do when they see the scum-filled lake and tacky gift stands that have sprouted on the lake's edge, not to mention wooden cutouts of a heart where couples can pose for a photo.

Visits can be arranged to hillside minority villages and hamlets, where

Map on page 281

BELOW: bananas are available.

Map on pages 266–7

Ankroet waterfall.

BELOW: mask for Tet.

RIGHT: fast meal in Da Lat.

villagers make a meagre living from the rice, corn, pumpkins, squash, tobacco, and, sometimes, cotton that they grow on hillsides. They also work in tea and coffee plantations. Located about 12 km (7 miles) to the north of Da Lat at the foot of the mountain Lang Bian, the village of **Lat** consists of several hamlets occupied by different ethnic groups. The Maa minority women are excellent weavers and dye their cloth using natural bark extracts. The men use simple traps and spears to hunt and fish. A toxic substance extracted from leaves is sometimes used in fishing. This stuns the fish but is apparently harmless to humans. Other minority groups around Lat are the Lat, Chill and Koho tribes.

Highlands to the north

Far north of Da Lat, the area known as the Central Highlands is often a tempting lure for the adventurous traveller. In the western part of the highlands, the main towns of **Buon Ma Thuot**, **Pleiku** and **Kontum** remain off the beaten path for many travellers, not only because there is comparatively little of interest here, except for visits to different ethnic minority villages and the occasional war-era prison, but much of the road network serving this part of the country is in very poor shape. If you would like something adventurous, though, the "Easy Riders", a group of riders with comfortable Honda 125cc bikes, can take you around Vietnam on "off-the-beaten-track" tours. Ask at your hotel or guesthouse, or email them at wingstours@hotmail.com.

South towards Ho Chi Minh

The area around Da Lat offers a number of fine waterfalls. Be warned, however, that commercialism increasingly threatens what would otherwise be pleasant and refreshing settings. Beyond Da Lat and to the south, the pleasant **Da Tanla** waterfalls cascade into a pool enclosed by high rock walls and surrounded by luxuriant greenery, tree houses and delicate bamboo bridges. Enclosed within the pine-covered hills 9 km (6 miles) south of Da Lat, the falls of **Prenn**, also known as **Thien Sa**, descend 15 metres (50 ft) across the mouth of a cave, entered from behind the falls via a small bridge.

Water from the **Ankroet**, or Golden Stream Falls, drops from a height of 15 metres (50 ft). Some 30 km (20 miles) south of town are the falls of **Lien Khuong**, and 8 km (5 miles) further on, the silvery waters of the **Gougah**, or Pot Hole Falls, drop from a height of 20 metres (60 ft), creating rainbows on sunny days. Most impressive of the waterfalls is **Pongour ⓫**, 55 km (35 miles) south of Da Lat and deep within thick primeval forest. The sound of the waters falling from a height of 30 metres (98 ft) can be heard even from several kilometres away during the rainy season. South of Da Lat, Highway 20 passes through coffee, tea and pineapple plantations. In **Bao Loc ⓬**, 100 km (60 miles) southwest of Da Lat, is a silkworm farm with immense mulberry orchards, one of the largest in the world. New silkworm hybrids, bred to survive the cooler highland climate, are raised year-round. Special permission must be obtained from the authorities before a visit can be arranged. ❑

Ho Chi Minh

QUAN 4

Sai Gon (Saigon)

11 Bao Tang Ho Chi Minh
(Ho Chi Minh Museum)

13 Thao Cam Vien
(Botanical and
Zoological Gardens)

14 Bao Tang Lich Su
(National History Museum)

12 Trung Tam Thuong
Mai Sai Gon
(Saigon Trade Centre)

15 Bao Tang Chien Dich
Ho Chi Minh
(Museum of the
Ho Chi Minh City
Campaign)

7 Nha Hat Thanh Pho
(Municipal Theatre)

Rex Hotel

16 Den Tho Tran
Hung Dao

Phuoc Hai Tu
(Emperor of Jade Pagoda)

2 Nha Tho
Duc Ba
(Notre Dame)

UBND
Thanh Pho
(People's
Committee
Building)

10 Bao Tang My Thuat
(Fine Arts Museum)

An Duong Vuong

Nha Tho
Tan Dinh

Bao Tang Chung
Tich Chien Tranh
(War Remnants
Museum)

1 Dinh Trong Nhat
(Reunification Hall)

Bao Tang Thanh Pho Ho Chi Minh
(Ho Chi Minh City Museum)

8 Tran Nguyen
Hai

9 Cho Ben Thanh

Chua Ba Den
(Mariamman
Hindu Temple)

CONG VIEN VAN
HOA THANH
PHO

Chua
Xa Loi

17 Chua Vinh
Nghiem (Pagoda)

PHU NHUAN

QUAN 3

Ga Sai Gon
(Station)

Thich Quang
Duc

QUAN 1

QUAN 10

Nha Hat
Hoa Binh

Chua Vietnam
Quoc Tu

Lang Truong Vinh Ky
(Lexicographer's
Mausoleum)

Chua
An Quang

Nha Sau

Nha Van Hoa

QUAN 5

Phu Tho
(Race Track)

Chua Ong

Chua Pho Mieu
(Pagoda) 20

Chua Ong
Bon

CHO LON

Nha Tho
Phanxico Xavie
(Cham Tam) 19

Chua Khanh Van
(Nam Vien)

18

QUAN 11

Cho Binh Tay
(Market)

Chua Giac Lam
(Pagoda) 22

Chua
Phung Son

Chua Giac Vien
(Pagoda) 21

Tay Ninh

HO CHI MINH CITY

If coming from relatively sedate and proper Hanoi, prepare yourself for Vietnam's entrepreneurial tempest, where even a Marxist renaming of Saigon failed to quench pursuit of capitalism

Map on page 288

Built on the site of an ancient Khmer city, **Thanh Pho Ho Chi Minh** (Ho Chi Minh City) was a thinly populated area of forests, swamps and lakes until the 17th century. In 1698, Saigon – as Ho Chi Minh City was called before the communists changed the name – was established as a territory of the Gia Dinh Prefecture. By the end of the 18th century, Saigon had been linked with Ben Nghe (present-day Cho Lon), and the area became an important trading centre within the region. In 1998, Saigon celebrated its 300th anniversary.

Different theories expound on the origins of the city's original name of Saigon, still used by many people, even in official capacities: the river coursing through the city remains the **Song Sai Gon (Saigon River)**, for example, and the state-owned tour company is Saigon Tourism.

Some say the name derives from the former name Sai Con, a transcription of the Khmer words *prei kor* (lit. kapok-tree forest) or *prei nokor* (forest of the kingdom), in reference to the Cambodian viceroy's residence that was located in the region of present-day Cho Lon.

In the 19th century, southern Vietnam, particularly Saigon, prospered despite the incessant fighting between the Vietnamese and Cambodians, and between the Vietnamese themselves, who were divided in their support of either the Nguyen lords from Hue, on the central coast to the north, or the Tay Son insurgents from Binh Dinh.

In 1859, French and Spanish ships landed in southern Vietnam. The French unloaded troops and weapons and embarked upon their conquest of the country. Saigon itself was captured later the same year and became the capital of the French colony of Cochin China. Modernisation of Saigon accompanied colonisation, and the French filled in the ancient canals, drained marshlands, built roads, laid out streets and quarters, and planted many trees. The city developed rapidly, acquiring something of the character of a French provincial town and served by two steam-powered trams. After the division of the country in 1954 by the United Nations, Saigon became the capital of the Republic of South Vietnam until the republic fell to the communists in 1975. The revolutionary authorities renamed it Thanh Pho Ho Chi Minh, after the founder of the modern Vietnamese state, who was, of course, anathema to supporters of the southern regime that lost the war. To many of its 6 million inhabitants, the city remains Saigon.

Today, Ho Chi Minh, 80 km (50 miles) inland from the coast and Vietnam's largest city and river port, sprawls across an area of 2,000 sq. km (760 sq. miles) on the banks of the Song Sai Gon. The city is divided into 17 urban and five rural districts.

This is a city on the move, although it is disorderly

PRECEDING PAGES: talk in the slow lane.
BELOW: south along the Saigon River.

TIP

In the Mekong Delta region, including Ho Chi Minh City, the dry season lasts from November to April, while the rainy season usually endures for the rest of the year.

BELOW: Diep Minh Chao, Ho Chi Minh's personal sculptor.

movement bordering on chaos. While the building boom of the late 1990s led to a glut of hotel rooms and empty offices in the city's centre, not to mention the abandonment of several new hotels under construction by international hotel chains, construction nevertheless continues everywhere. The streets and sidewalks overflow with the business of commerce, something that has always come quite naturally to the Saigonese. In the space of a block it is not unusual to see locals slurping *pho* (noodle soup) at Lilliputian sidewalk tables and chairs, a cyclo driver wooing a potential fare, shopkeepers peddling their wares, and young Saigonese transacting business on their mobile phones. After a decade or so of having their entrepreneurial talents suppressed by a socialist system, the business tycoons are out in full force. Much of this comes from the city's large ethnic Chinese community, centred in the Cho Lon district in the western part of the city but branching throughout to other parts of the city.

Called *viet kieu*, Vietnamese who now live in the United States, Australia, France and other countries have had much to do with fuelling the economic boom here, as well, but on a smaller scale than the overseas Chinese. On many streets and in many neighbourhoods, it is easy to pick out the families with relatives overseas – they have newer houses, nicer clothes and more amenities, and often they are the ones who have opened new shops and restaurants. The city is quickly taking on the air of a modern, yet still developing, Asian city as old houses and muddy swamps give way to modern high-rises, shopping complexes and highways. Throughout the city there are new restaurants, bars, cafes and the ubiquitous karaoke lounges catering to the naturally sociable Saigonese, who stay up until late at night socialising, in contrast to early-to-bed Hanoi.

But, in fact, the traditionally darker side of Saigon life – prostitution, drugs,

Map
on page
288

and drinking – has begun to emerge again in Ho Chi Minh. There are massage parlours and drinking clubs with private rooms, and prostitutes advertise themselves on some street corners. Petty crime is up.

Although not to the degree that one finds in Hanoi, the French presence still remains in this southern city, lingering not only in the minds of the older generation but physically in the legacy of colonial architecture and the long, tree-lined avenues and streets they left behind. But the French era is quickly being overwhelmed by today's rush to open a business, make money, get rich. English, not French, has once again become the foreign language to practise on foreigners. Although visitors may encounter disgruntled soldiers who fought on the losing side of the war, in fact, most people long ago stopped living the war years of the 1940s, 1950s, 1960s and early 1970s and are consumed with the task of making a life. Most people are no fans of the communist government, but they nonetheless appreciate recent economic reforms and have learned to simply ignore the government, with the hope that the government will ignore them and that the momentum of capitalism will force the old men at the top to yield. But now, they say, is not the time to talk of politics.

Yet politics still looms within Vietnam's public buildings and museums. While some of the anti-American rhetoric has been toned down, there are still reminders of the war that divided the country for so many years.

Interior of one of the city's renovated colonial-era hotels.

Central Ho Chi Minh City

Prominently located in the city's Quan 1 (District 1) is a building that symbolises, to the communists, the decadence of the Saigon regime. The former Presidential Palace of South Vietnam is today called **Dinh Thong Nhat ❶**

BELOW: Western companies are making inroads.

(Reunification Palace; open daily 7.30–11am and 1–4pm; admission fee). Nowadays, it is occasionally used as a setting for parties and receptions for foreign companies introducing their products to Vietnam. Surrounded by large gardens, this large modern edifice rests on the site of the former French governor's residence, the Norodom Palace, which dated back to 1868. After the Geneva Agreement put an end to French occupation, the new president of South Vietnam, Ngo Dinh Diem, installed himself in the palace.

In 1962, the palace was bombed by a South Vietnamese air force officer, and a new building known as the Independence Palace was erected to replace the damaged structure. The present structure was designed by Ngo Viet Thu, a Paris-trained Vietnamese architect, and completed in 1966. The left wing of the palace was damaged by another renegade pilot in early 1975, and on 30 April 1975 communist tanks crashed through the palace's front wrought-iron gates and overthrew the South Vietnamese government.

Today, the former palace is a museum, with everything left much as it was on that fateful day. The basement houses the combat strategy room, communications room, map room, and the all-important presidential bomb-shelter. The ground floor includes the banquet room; state chamber, from where the South Vietnamese government surrendered; and the cabinet room, which was used for the daily military briefings during the period leading up to the overthrow of the South Vietnamese government.

On the first floor is the president's reception and residential domain, complete with a Catholic chapel, dining room and bedroom. The second floor hosts the reception rooms of the president's wife. A private theatre and a helipad are found on the third floor, which commands an excellent view over Dai Lo Le

BELOW: garden of Reunification Palace, and an interior staircase.

Duan (Le Duan Boulevard), which runs northeast to the zoo and botanical gardens. Behind the palace is **Cong Vien Van Hoa**, a nice and shady green park complete with a small topiary and carnival rides, which attracts flocks of schoolchildren and families, especially on weekends. In front of the palace, Le Duan is bordered by a large park shaded with trees.

Map on page 288

Just northeast of the Reunification Palace, on Duong Dong Khoi (Dong Khoi Street) is Saigon's largest church, **Nha Tho Duc Ba** ❷ (Notre Dame or Cathedral of Our Lady), with two bell towers, which stands in the square next to Buu Dien (Central Post Office), an attractive colonial-style building. Construction of the cathedral began in 1877. A statue of the Virgin Mary stands in front of the cathedral, looking down Duong Dong Khoi.

A busy shopping street that was called Tu Do before 1975 (and rue Catinat before 1954), Dong Khoi has evolved from a seedy strip of hustlers, bars and two-bit souvenir stands into a glitzy parade of art galleries, antique shops and shops selling designer clothes, watches and perfume.

Further up Le Duan about 4 blocks, a new American consulate has been built on the site of the former US embassy, where in 1975 the American ambassador and last US troops escaped from the rooftop by helicopter just as Communist troops were advancing towards Saigon. Earlier, in the Tet Offensive of 1968, an event that marked a turning point of the war, Viet Cong guerrillas attacked southern cities and assaulted the American embassy. Completion of the building is another step in eradicating the physical vestiges of a more turbulent time.

Bao Tang Chung Tich Chien Tranh ❸ (War Remnants Museum; open daily 7.30–noon and 1.30–5pm; admission fee) occupies the former US Information Agency building at 28 Vo Van Tan, immediately west of the

BELOW: the Notre Dame Cathedral, and a store on famous Dong Khoi.

Nearly anything is available in southern Vietnamese markets.

Reunification Palace. Among items on display here are American tanks, infantry weapons, photographs of war atrocities against the Vietnamese and the original French guillotine brought to Vietnam in the early 20th century. Graphic pictures of deformed children show the effects of chemical defoliants like Agent Orange. Although a visit here is likely to be distressing, it is a sobering reminder of the heavy toll of war and is a must-see for many visitors.

The **Bao Tang Thanh Pho Ho Chi Minh** ❹ (Ho Chi Minh City Museum; open daily 8–11.30am and 1–4.30pm; admission fee), one block east from Reunification Palace on 65 Ly Tu Trong, is found in a white neoclassical structure once known as Gia Long Palace. Built in 1866 and renovated as recently as 1998, this grand colonial edifice contains pictures of the wars and displays of the flat-bottomed boats in which Viet Cong soldiers used to hide guns.

A network of reinforced concrete bunkers stretching all the way to the Reunification Palace lies beneath the building. Within this underground network were living areas and a meeting hall. It was here that Pres. Diem and his brother hid just before they fled to a church in Cho Lon, where they were captured and subsequently shot.

Diagonally across from the Revolutionary Museum and next to the Reunification Palace on Duong Nam Ky Khoi Nghia is the **Toa An Nhan Dan** (People's Court). Though not a usual tourist stop, this sprawling yellow building is another example of colonial-style architecture, albeit in need of a renovation.

BELOW: People's Committee building, or City Hall.

If the Reunification Palace is a symbol of the former South Vietnam regime, then UBND **Thanh Pho** ❺ (People's Committee/City Hall) is the symbol of the French colonial era. Formerly the Hotel de Ville, it was decorated by Ruffier and finished in 1908 after almost 16 years of ferment over its style and situation. Its ornate interior, complete with crystal chandeliers and wall size murals, is now the headquarters of the Ho Chi Minh City People's Committee. Unfortunately, visitors are prohibited and must content themselves watching the paint peel off its grand exterior instead. Illuminated at night, the building is a lure for insect-hungry geckos.

In front of City Hall, just to the southeast and at the intersection of Le Loi and Nguyen Hue, there is a plaza with a statue of Ho Chi Minh in his role as favourite uncle to all children. Near the **Rex Hotel** ❻, which sits on the corner in a rather ostentatious fashion and once played host to American servicemen during the war, the plaza is abuzz on many nights, but especially on weekends, with young people, parents with children, and hustlers trying to sell souvenirs or cyclo rides to tourists. Watch out for pickpockets here and for passing motor-cyclists grabbing backpacks, purses and even eyeglasses.

At the corner of Le Loi there is another plaza with a fountain that is crowded with a carnival-like atmosphere late into the night as courting couples and families alike cruise by on their motorbikes. Extending southeast from the plaza, Nguyen Hue is a broad boulevard lined with fancy hotels, upscale restaurants and commercial high rises. This area of town buzzes with energy, especially at night.

At the northeastern end of Le Loi is the **Nha Hat Thanh Pho** ❼ (Municipal Theatre), which faces Dong Khoi between the Delta Caravelle and the Continental hotels. The theatre was originally built in 1899 for opera but was used as the fortress headquarters of the South Vietnam National Assembly. Given a face lift in the late 1990s, this creamy white, colonial-style building now serves its original purpose and presents different programmes, ranging from

Map on page 288

Classic Rex Hotel.

BELOW: popular intersection, with Rex Hotel and the City Hall.

Exterior detail of the Continental Hotel.

traditional Vietnamese theatre to acrobatics, gymnastics and classical music.

At the junction of Ham Nghi, Le Loi and Tran Hung Dao boulevards, a few blocks southeast of Reunification Palace, is the busy **Cho Ben Thanh ❽**. This market covers over 11,000 sq. metres (118,400 sq. ft) and was opened in 1914. Here is an amazing collection of produce, meat, foods, CD players, televisions, cameras, refrigerators, fans, blue jeans, cosmetics, and leather bags, imported or produced pin Vietnam. The smell of spices and dried seafood assails the nostrils, and the colour of the many varieties of fresh fruit and vegetables provides a veritable feast for the eyes. At the back of the market, small food stalls serve a wide variety of local dishes.

The **Mariamman Hindu Temple ❾**, at 45 Truong Dinh and three blocks from the Ben Thanh market, was built at the end of the 19th century and caters to the city's small population of Hindu Tamils, as well as to a number of ethnic Vietnamese. The influence of local customs and practices is apparent in the use of joss sticks in this Hindu temple.

Not far from the Ben Thanh market, down Pho Duc Chinh, is the interesting **Bao Tang My Thuat ❿** (Fine Arts Museum; open Tues–Sun 9am–4.45pm; admission fee), housed in a grand colonial-era building built about a century ago by a wealthy Chinese merchant. Several art galleries occupy the basement. The first floor features changing exhibitions of contemporary Vietnamese art. On the second floor the rooms display what can be described as revolutionary – or war – art, such as a lacquer paintings depicting guerrillas in the jungle and a plaster sculpture of Ho Chi Minh with his future revolutionaries. On the third floor, the art is much older: porcelain pots, statues of Buddha, and Cham, Thai and Khmer sculpture as well as *objets d'art* from the 10th to 20th century.

BELOW:
Ben Thanh market.

REUNIFICATION EXPRESS

Thong Nhat, or the Reunification Express, a misleading title in every sense, refers to the train that crawls along at an average speed of 48 km (30 miles) per hour during the 30- to 41-hour journey between Hanoi and Ho Chi Minh City for 2,000 km (1,243 miles). It's not that the trains are slow, but rather that there is only one track in poor condition, damaged in the north by American bombing and in the south by Viet Cong sabotage. There are few places where trains in opposite directions can pass; if the northbound train is running hours late, so too will the southbound be late.

The Reunification Express first ran on 31 December 1976 after a massive reconstruction effort that repaired 1,334 bridges, 158 stations, and 27 tunnels. Increasingly, the trains on the Hanoi-Ho Chi Minh City stretch are being upgraded by **Vietnam Railways** (www.vr.com.vn) but there are some relics which date from the French colonial era. The express trains are the fastest and have air-conditioned soft sleeper compartments. In contrast, the hard seats on the slower trains are uncomfortable and crammed with food vendors squatting in the aisles. Tireless vendors descend on the train at each and every stop, and petty theft is a problem.

Near the museum, on Le Cong Kieu, is the city's antique street. Here, two dozen or so shops sell old clocks, silver, glass and ceramics: much of it once belonged to wealthy Saigonese who fled the country after 1975. There is quite a bit of junk for sale here, too, but also some valuable furnishings. Down Nguyen Thai Binh, near the corner of Yersin Street, is the **Cho Dan Sinh**. In the back of this market, a few stalls sell "old" US Army jackets, combat boots, gas masks, and fake dog tags.

To the south on Duong Nguyen Tat Thanh, in Quan (District) 4 and near where the Kinh Ben Nghe, a tributary, enters Song Sai Gon, there is a salmon-coloured memorial to Ho Chi Minh, **Bao Tang Ho Chi Minh** ⓫ (Ho Chi Minh Museum; open Tues–Sun 7.30–11.30am and 1.30–5pm; admission fee), also known as Nha Rong (Dragon House). Documents and pictures relating to Ho's life and revolutionary activities are displayed here. The house dates from 1862 and was originally used as the head office of a French shipping company. It was from this place that Ho Chi Minh, then going under his given name of Nguyen Tat Thanh, left Vietnam in 1911 as a cook on a French merchant ship.

Northeast of downtown

As another sign of Saigon's desire to reinvent and modernise itself, the newly erected **Saigon Trade Centre** ⓬ – an office complex with the no-doubt-temporary honour of being the tallest building in Vietnam at 33 floors – stands just off Le Duan on Ton Duc Thang.

At the end of Le Duan is **Thao Cam Vien** ⓭ (Botanical and Zoological Gardens). The gardens were established in 1864 by two Frenchmen – one a botanist, the other a veterinarian – as one of the first projects the French

Map on page 288

TIP

Visitors can opt to take a leisurely cruise up the Song Sai Gon to the Bin Quoi Tourist Village, in Binh Thanh district. Largely a tourist trap, it offers a dinner programme and songs and dances from a traditional wedding ceremony.

BELOW: city girls.

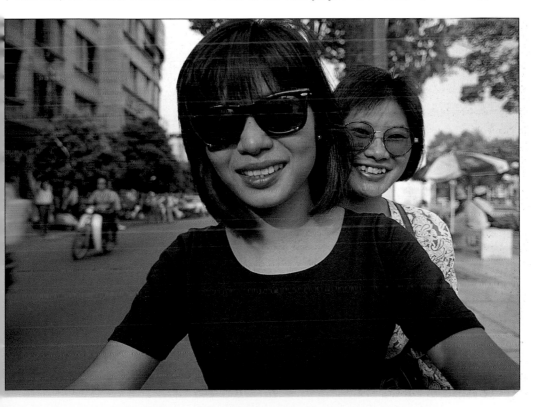

embarked upon after they established their new colony. Recent renovations have brought about improvements to the gardens and animal enclosures. The gardens constitute one of the more peaceful places in Ho Chi Minh City. Feeding times and special events are posted at the entrance.

Bao Tang Lich Su ⓮ (History Museum; open Tues–Sun 8–11am and 1.30–4.30pm; admission fee), located just within the entrance of the Botanical and Zoological Gardens, was built by the French in 1927. It documents the evolution of Vietnam's various cultures, from the Dong Son bronze-age civilisation and the southern Chinese Funan (Oc-Eo) civilisation, through to the Cham, Khmer and Vietnamese. Among the exhibits in the museum are many stone and bronze relics, stelae, bronze drums, Cham art and ceramics, and a display of the traditional costumes of ethnic minorities. There are also valuable relics from Cambodia's Angkor Wat. Behind the building, on the third floor, is a research library that is closed to the general public except by special permission. It houses an interesting and quite extensive collection of French, English and Russian books from the colonial era. Just opposite the museum is the **Den Hung**, a temple dedicated to the ancestors of Hung Vuong, the founding king of Vietnam.

At 2 Le Duan, across from the zoo entrance, is the recently renovated **Bao Tang Chien Dich Ho Chi Minh** ⓯ (Museum of Ho Chi Minh City Campaign; open Sun–Fri 8–11.30am and 1.30–4.30pm; admission fee) displays American, Soviet and Chinese military hardware, including the tank that crashed through the gates of Reunification Palace in 1975. There is little of interest inside, actually, except perhaps some of the old photographs and original film footage of the military campaign to take Saigon.

BELOW: National History Museum.

Northern suburbs

The small Sino-Vietnamese **Phuoc Hai Tu** ⓰ (Tortoise Pagoda) or Chua Ngoc Hoang (Emperor of Jade Pagoda), at 73 Mai Thi Luu and on the northern extents of the central city, was built by Cantonese Buddhists in 1909 and is one of the city's most colourful pagodas. A haze of heady incense and candle smoke envelops a fascinating array of weird and wonderful wooden statues, some Buddhist, others Daoist-inspired. The elaborately robed Daoist Jade Emperor surveys the main sanctuary. Just to his right, the triple-headed, 18-armed statue of Phat Mau Chau De, mother of the Buddhas of the Middle, North, East, West, and South, looks out in three directions from her encasement.

A door off to the left of the Jade Emperor's chamber leads to the Hall of Ten Hells, where carved wooden panels portray, in no uncertain detail, the fate that awaits those sentenced to the diverse torments found in the 10 regions of hell. Next door is a small room containing figurines of 12 women, said to represent the range of human characteristics.

The more recent Buddhist pagoda of **Chua Vinh Nghiem** ⓱ on Nam Ky Khoi Nghia, Quan 3 and west of Phuoc Hai Tu, is the newest and largest of the pagodas in the city. Built with aid from the Japanese Friendship Association, this Japanese-style pagoda was begun in 1964 and finished in 1973. Each stage of its 7-storey tower contains a statue of Buddha. In the huge main hall stands a large statue of Buddha surrounded by his disciples. Behind are altars consecrated to the dead, where tablets and photographs of the deceased are placed for the first 100 days after their death. The temple's screen and large bell were made in Japan. The bell, a gift from Japanese Buddhists, was presented during the Vietnam War as the embodiment of a prayer for an early end to the conflict.

Map on page 288

Detail from Emperor of Jade Pagoda.

BELOW: altar of the Emperor of Jade pagoda.

Chinese sausages in Cho Lon.

The large 3-storey funeral tower behind the main temple holds ceramic burial urns containing the ashes of the dead. There are 45 monks in residence here and a Buddhist college for nuns. The pagoda becomes the scene of great vivacity and colour during the Buddhist Ram Thang Gieng festival, which takes place on the 15th day of the first lunar month.

Cho Lon

Ho Chi Minh City's Chinatown, **Cho Lon**, was formerly a separate sister city but is now in the city's Quan 5, thanks to the outward growth of the suburbs. As the name (lit. big market) indicates, Cho Lon remains a thriving commercial centre. With a population of around a million Hoas – Vietnamese of Chinese origin – Cho Lon has come a long way since 1864 when it was home to just 6,000 Chinese (mostly shopkeepers or traders), 200 Indians, and 40,000 Vietnamese. Today, countless small family businesses operate in this area. Day and night, Cho Lon's streets, markets and restaurants are scenes of noisy animation and much activity. On Hau Giang, between Thap Muoi and Ben Phan, is Cho Lon's main market, the large **Cho Binh Tay** ⑱, offering the usual plethora of goods and fresh produce.

East of here, at the end of Dai Lo Tran Hung Dao, is **Nha Tho Phanxico Xevie** ⑲ (Cham Tam Church), where Pres. Ngo Dinh Diem was captured and shortly afterwards executed along with his brother in the November 1963 coup d'état. The church was built around the start of the 20th century.

One of the largest churches in the city is the **Cho Quan Church**, at 118 Tran Binh Trong. Built in 1896 by the French, it has a belfry with an excellent view, although the climb up is hard work as the stairs are steep and have not been well-

BELOW: avenue in Cho Lon, and public transport in a downpour.

maintained. The neon halo that glows around the head of the statue of Jesus is glaringly late 20th-century.

As fast as the French, and later the Americans, were embedding their ways in Saigon, the Vietnamese were retaliating with the many pagodas, shrines and temples that sprung up all over the city – Buddhist, Indian, Muslim. The small **Cho Lon Mosque**, at 641 Nguyen Trai, was built by Tamil Muslims. (The larger Indo Mosque on Dong Du in District One was built on the site of an older mosque by southern Indian Muslims in 1935. Only a handful of Indian Muslims remain, since most fled the country after 1975.)

The many richly decorated Chinese temples and pagodas found in Cho Lon are distinctly different from their Vietnamese counterparts, and they are best visited in the morning if you wish to see the faithful at their prayers. At number 710 Nguyen Trai is **Chua Thien Hau** [20], temple of the Goddess Protector of Sailors and more commonly known as Chua Ba (Women's Pagoda). This Chinese temple was built by Cantonese Buddhists at the end of the 18th century in thanksgiving for having been safely delivered from their perilous sea journey as "boat people" from China.

The temple is frequented mostly by women, who bring their offerings to the altar of the Heavenly Lady with its three statues of Thien Hau located at the back of the temple. Votive paper offerings are burnt in the big furnace just inside the entrance. Large coils of slow-burning incense hang over the main sanctuary, creating a heady atmosphere. Among the other altars is one dedicated to the protection of women and newborn babies, and yet another to sterile women or mothers who have no sons.

At 678 Nguyen Trai is Chua Ba's counterpart, **Chua Ong**, the men's pagoda.

Many Vietnamese and Chinese temples are not actually Buddhist, but instead are dedicated to the worship of certain legendary or national heroes from history.

BELOW: Binh Tay market, and betting at the races.

Map
on page
288

(Its official name is Nghia An.) An intricately carved wooden boat hangs over the entrance. A statue of Quan Cong with red face, long black beard, and ornate regalia presides over the main altar. Today's worshippers come to pray, not surprisingly, for peace, happiness and prosperity in business.

North of Cho Lon

Northwest of Cho Lon in Quan 11, the smaller Buddhist **Chua Giac Vien** ㉑, on Lac Long Quan, was built in 1803. It was formerly known as Chua Ho Dat (Earth Pit Pagoda) due to the vast amounts of earth required to fill in the site before its construction. Some 153 beautifully carved wooden statues are housed within the pagoda. A statue of founder Hai Tinh Giac Vien stands near the rear of the temple's second chamber. Due to its remote location, few foreign travellers make it out here.

Chua Giac Lam ㉒, in Tan Binh district and about 3 km (2 miles) north of Cho Lon, is a pagoda that dates 1744 and is thought to be the oldest in the city. It is also an ancestral temple. Reconstruction work was last carried out on it from 1906 to 1909. Carved wooden pillars within the main building bear gilded inscriptions in Chinese characters. Portraits of monks of previous generations adorn the left wall. The main sanctuary houses many beautifully carved, gilded, jackwood statues of Buddha, reincarnations of Buddha, judges and guardians of hell, and Quan Am, the goddess of mercy. As is typical in many Vietnamese pagodas, there is also an object resembling a Christmas tree, with 49 light bulbs symbolising the 49 days the Sakyamouni Buddha meditated under the bodhi tree to attain enlightenment. The pagoda has a 7-storey tower with an excellent view of sprawling Ho Chi Minh City. ❑

BELOW: an official of the former South Vietnam who was sent to the "re-education" camps.
RIGHT: urban boulevard.

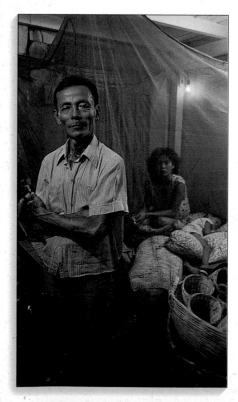

A FRENCH MAN'S CONQUEST

Charles Rigault de Genouilly was a naval officer who led the French invasion of Vietnam in 1858. Rigault de Genouilly entered the navy in 1827 and in 1847 he participated in an attack upon the port of Da Nang, ostensibly to protect the French Catholic mission there. Rigault de Genouilly later took command of French naval forces in China and Cochinchina.

The following year he attacked Da Nang under strict orders that there would be no negotiations with the Vietnamese. Following the fall of Da Nang, he started towards Hue but his armada was turned back by the shallow river. So he headed south instead and attacked Saigon in 1859 with the help of mercenary Spanish troops. But disease and the heat, combined with low supplies and no reinforcements, thwarted his efforts to consolidate his conquests or subjugate the Vietnamese. The following October he was relieved of his post at his request and he returned to France.

In 1867, after a stint as senator, he was named minister of the marine and of the overseas colonies. In the 1870 war between France and Germany, he refused his appointment as commander in chief of an expedition to the Baltic Sea and retired to Spain instead.

BEYOND HO CHI MINH CITY

The highways leading out of Ho Chi Minh City lead to some fascinating sites, including tunnels of the Viet Cong, the Cao Dai temple and some glorious tropical coastal beaches

Map on pages 266–7

To see the city of **Ho Chi Minh** ⓭ and the suburbs beyond from a different perspective, take a boat trip on the **Song Sai Gon** (Saigon River). From the river one sees a downtown skyline dominated by construction cranes and modern high-rises. At the same time, industrial development and overcrowding have forced an expansion into outlying areas. Just south of Ho Chi Minh City, whole satellite cities are being built complete with residential areas, parks, and universities on what was once swamp land. Less affected by urban renewal, some of the other suburbs make for fascinating side trips. Beyond are numerous options of interest and allure.

To the north of Ho Chi Minh City

Located 60 km (36 miles) to the northwest of Ho Chi Minh is the town of **Cu Chi** ⓮, made famous during the Vietnam War for its extensive network of underground tunnels. The tunnels at Cu Chi, which ran three levels deep, were first used by the Viet Minh against the French in the 1940s, then later became hideouts for the Viet Cong, who at one point had even tunnelled under the Mekong Delta headquarters of the US Army's 25th Division. Guerrillas and villagers often lived for months underground, surviving on tapioca and breathing with the help of an ingenious and elaborate ventilation system. From these hiding places, Viet Cong were often able to spring surprise attacks on their enemies. In fact, by the mid-1960s, nearly 250 km (150 miles) of tunnels laced the region around Cu Chi.

The ground through which the tunnels burrowed is of red clay and above the water table, both factors advantageous for tunnel digging. But what to do with the removed earth without alerting the enemy? It was often used to fill in bomb craters or dumped into the Song Sai Gon (Saigon River). Visitors will note that the Cu Chi tunnels open to foreign tourists today have been enlarged for the Western frame. Some tunnels were just 80 cm (30 inches) in diameter. A tunnel complex could have up to four levels with elaborate ventilation, clinics, toilets and meeting rooms. Surgery was performed in the rustic medical clinics; blood was collected from the patient and pumped back into him with tubing and bicycle pumps. Needless to say, morale could be a problem under such conditions, and living conditions within the tunnels were almost unbearable.

The Americans often used trained dogs to sniff out the tunnels, but the Viet Cong would deflect them with pepper at entrances and vents. It is said that the VC would even use the same soap as Americans so as to confuse the dogs. Numerous tactics were used by the Americans to eliminate the tunnels' effectiveness,

PRECEDING PAGES: street barber. **LEFT:** boatwoman on the Saigon River. **BELOW:** unloading a boat, Vinh Long.

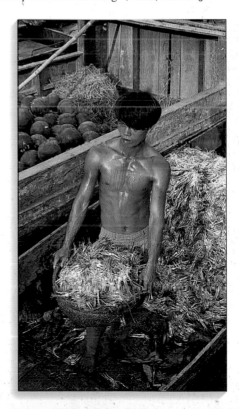

but with little long-term effect until B52s began extensive carpet bombing.

Although the Americans eventually destroyed much of the subterranean network, it was a temporary and Pyrrhic victory. The tunnels had already fulfilled their function by giving the Viet Cong not only the advantage of surprise but also the control of many villages. The Cu Chi tunnels are a vivid testament to the ingenuity and perseverance of the Vietnamese that eventually helped them win the war against their American foes and are definitely worth a visit. Visitors can shudder at the specially designed booby traps used by the guerrillas as well as crawl through a small section of tunnel, which has actually been enlarged and "improved" for the benefit of tourists. Re-forested eucalyptus trees attest to the area's recovery from the ravages of chemical defoliants and large-scale carpet bombing.

Further to the northwest, Tay Ninh Province shares a border with Cambodia. The province's main river, Vam Co Dong, separates Vietnam from Cambodia. From the 7th to the 14th century, Tay Ninh belonged to the powerful Funan empire. Later, it became part of the Chen La kingdom, the forerunner of the Champa kingdom. In the early 18th century, the Nguyen lords defeated the last remnants of Champa and established the province of Gia Dinh, which integrated and administered Tay Ninh.

During the war against the French, Tay Ninh was a hot bed of anti-colonial resistance, and in the 1950s, bearing the standard of the Cao Dai religious sect, a hero of the armed resistance forces conducted his efforts against the central government in the Nui Ba Den (Black Lady Mountain) area.

Tay Ninh's greatest attraction is found approximately 100 km (60 miles) northwest of Ho Chi Minh City, in the township of **Tay Ninh** ⑮ itself. Here,

TIP

Photography was once restricted within the Cao Dai temple, but nowadays the taking of photographs is readily accepted, and flash can be used without problems.

BELOW: Cao Dai believer and the temple exterior.

resplendent in all its glory, stands the holy see of the Cao Dai religious sect. Founded in 1926 by Ngo Minh Chieu, the Cao Dai religion is an amalgamation of Buddhism, Daoism, Confucianism and Christianity, with a bit of Islam, animism, and ancestral worship melded in for diversity. Despite the competing influences in the religion, adherents believe in one ultimate deity and practise meditation and vegetarianism. (There are an estimated 2½ million Cao Dai followers in Vietnam.)

This surreal temple has to be seen to be believed. The best time to arrive is before the daily ceremony at noon, though there are also daily ceremonies at 6am, 6pm, and midnight. On the outside, a large eye symbolising the religion guards the entrance. The interior is like something out of fantasyland with a blue, star-studded vaulted ceiling and dragon-entwined pillars. Followers in their colourful ceremonial gowns of azure, yellow and white cut striking figures in their procession towards the altar.

The most outstanding natural feature in the province, **Nui Ba Den** – the Black Lady Mountain – overshadows the town of Tay Ninh. At 986 metres (3,235 ft) high, the mountain is dotted with many temples and pagodas, and it shelters a statue of a Brahman goddess, the Bhagavati protectress of the region. More than 1,500 steps – almost a 400-metre (1,300-ft) climb – lead up to **Chua Linh Son** half way up the mountain, from where a splendid view takes in the region and the Mekong Delta beyond. For the less athletically inclined, an effortless cable car travels the same route. The Black Lady Mountain Festival takes place here during the spring months, from February through May. At the foot of the mountain is a monument to the soldiers killed in the fierce fighting in the province during the Vietnam War.

Map on pages 266–7

The single eye is the symbol of the Cao Dai religious sect.

BELOW: two field workers outside of Ho Chi Minh.

Children are often essential for the harvest of crops.

To the east

Leaving Ho Chi Minh City via the east-northeast exit, the road passes through **Ba Chieu**. The **Lang On Ba Chieu**, a temple dedicated to Le Van Duyet, the ancient viceroy of Cochin China under Gia Long's reign, is here. Quite a story surrounds this historical figure, who loomed even larger than life after his death. According to numerous records, this respected person is said to have manifested his presence throughout the Mekong Delta area after his death, performing miracles. This caused quite a stir, as might be expected, not only amongst the Vietnamese but also amongst the equally superstitious Chinese community, particularly in Ho Chi Minh's Cho Lon district. And anyone who perjured an oath that was made before the tomb of this revered individual could expect impending death.

The temple and Le Van Duyet's tomb are set in a park. Emperor Minh Mang destroyed the tomb after Le Van Duyet was posthumously tried and found guilty of treason. Later, Emperor Tu Duc repaired the injustice and restored the marshall's tomb and standing through a royal decree. The temple is easily recognised from a distance by its large triple entrance gate. Inside the temple are several altars dedicated to various cults. A portrait of Le Van Duyet in full court costume hangs over the central altar. During the Tet festivities, thousands of Vietnamese and Chinese pilgrims visit the temple for their horoscopes. The temple is most crowded on the anniversary of Le Van Duyet's death, which falls on the 30th day of the seventh lunar month.

From Ba Chieu, the road continues to the market town of **Thu Duc** ⑯, 20 km (12 miles) northeast of the city. Thu Duc is a rapidly growing suburb that is congested with truck traffic along the main road leading to Vung Tau. The area

BELOW: cycling schoolgirls.

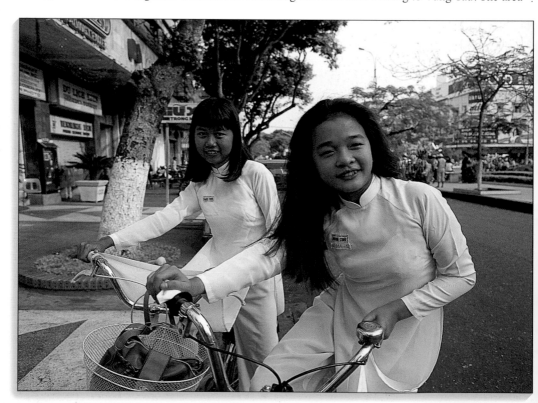

was popular with South Vietnam's leaders; former Pres. Nguyen Van Thieu had a weekend retreat here that he reached by helicopter. Today's new elite – wealthy entrepreneurs – are turning the area into a haven for the rich, complete with a golf resort and the south's first water park.

Song Dong Nai (Dong Nai River) marks the boundary between Ho Chi Minh City and Dong Nai Province to its east. Originating in the Central Highlands far to the north, the river flows through the province for 290 km (120 miles). Once a rural area growing a variety of agricultural crops like sugar cane, maize, coconut palms and peanuts, Dong Nai Province is quickly transforming itself into a loud, boisterous, dusty industrial zone.

The highway leading through the province and the provincial capital, **Bien Hoa** ⑰, is lined with new factories. There is a large concentration of Catholics here, too, evidenced by the number of Catholic churches lining the highway. Many of the people originally migrated from Hanoi and elsewhere in the north in 1954 when Viet Minh forces defeated the French colonialists and the communists came to power. The province also had a large number of refugees who tried to flee as part of the "boat people" exodus to Hong Kong, Malaysia and elsewhere in Asia during the 1970s and 1980s.

The town of Bien Hoa is an important industrial centre 30 km (20 miles) from Ho Chi Minh City, on the banks of the Dong Nai. In the 17th century, Bien Hoa was a focal point for Chinese emigration. One of their leaders, Tran Thuong Xuyen, built a fort on **Cu Lao Pho**, an island in the Dong Nai, though nothing remains of the fort today. Trinh Hoai Duc – the minister that Emperor Gia Long sent to China to negotiate the country's change of name to Viet Nam – was buried on the island.

BELOW: let faces near Can Tho.

Map on pages 266–7

Markets ooze smiles and entrepreneurial energy in the south.

Towards the wharf, on the left bank of the river, stands a temple dedicated to Nguyen Huu Canh, who founded Saigon in 1698. In true Vietnamese fashion, this national hero, better known in southern Vietnam as Chuong Binh Le, has acquired the status of a saint and is venerated by the population as their protector. Several times a year, notably on the general's birthday, and during the spring and autumn seasons, festivities are held at the temple. During the Vietnam War, Bien Hoa and neighbouring Long Ben were the site of a large US army base. Nowadays, few tourists make it out here.

About 50 km (30 miles) to the northeast, the **Cat Tien** ⑱ nature reserve lies in an area adjacent to the three provinces of Dong Nai, Binh Phuoc and Lam Dong. This primeval forest, covering an area of roughly 10,000 hectares (25,000 acres), is the habitat of some rare and unusual creatures, including species of pythons and crocodiles, and the highly endangered Vietnamese Javan rhinoceros.

South to the coast and Vung Tau

Just before Bien Hoa, Highway 51 heads southeast into the coastal province of Ba Ria-Vung Tau. Before reaching the Vung Tau peninsula, a separate road leads east to **Long Hai**, a coastal district with beautiful scenery. With nice, as yet unspoiled beaches stretching for several kilometres, Long Hai is developing into a more attractive alternative to venerable Vung Tau.

Some ancient pagodas stand near the mount of Minh Dam, not far from the beach. **Dinh Co**, near a stretch of beach used by fishermen, is dedicated to a young lady who, as the story goes, was carrying a letter to Emperor Quang Trung when huge waves sank her boat. Local people reputedly built the temple in memory of this patriotic girl.

BELOW: Vung Tau, the Bay of Boats.

The road between Long Hai and **Vung Tau ⑩** (Bay of Boats) passes many salt fields and shrimp hatcheries. Vung Tau is located on a peninsula 125 km (80 miles) southeast of Ho Chi Minh City. In the 15th century, after Le Thanh Tong had conquered the kingdom of Champa, Portuguese merchant ships were already anchoring in the bay of Vung Tau. Known as Cap Saint Jacques under the French, this popular seaside resort has grown increasingly commercialised and has lost much of its old charm. This seaport and economic centre also has a thriving oil-and-gas industry. There is a small community of Russians here who arrived in the late 1970s to work in the oil industry. Its claim as the finest beach resort has also been usurped by Phan Thiet and Mui Ne *(see page 277)*. In an effort to reclaim the tourist trade, further development is being planned: a cable car system that will take visitors up to the mountains, an enclosed port for private pleasure boats, and luxury resorts.

There are a number of Buddhist pagodas and temples. Typical of temples found in Vietnamese fishing villages, the **Lang Ca Ong**, or the Whale Temple, is dedicated to a whale cult. Built in 1911, the temple's most frequent visitors are fishermen who revere the whale as humanity's saviour from the perils of the high seas. Skeletons of whales that have been beached on the shores in the region are kept in huge cases, some of them 4 metres (13 ft) long and dating from 1868. The Vietnamese adopted the whale cult from the people of Champa, who worshipped the whale deity. Every year, on the 16th day of the eighth lunar month, fishermen gather at the temple to make offerings to the whales. Indeed, numerous anecdotes occur in Vietnamese folklore about whales as saviours.

To the northeast of the peninsula, a winding, bumpy road leads inland across **Nui Lon**, or Large Mountain, to **Thich Ca Phat Dai**, the Pagoda of the Buddha,

Map on pages 266–7

BELOW: coastline of Vung Tau.

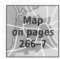

Map on pages 266–7

a site popular with domestic tourists. Built in 1961 and inaugurated in 1963, the pagoda has an enormous white statue of the Grand Buddha sitting on a pedestal. Nearby is a bodhi tree, and further on there is a large stupa with four urns placed at its four corners. These are said to contain lumps of earth taken from the four places in India relating to Buddhism: Buddha's birthplace and his places of enlightenment, preaching, and attaining *nirvana*.

Set in lovely grounds of frangipani, bougainvillaea and rare trees on the Nui Lon hillside, **Villa Blanche** (White Villa) commands a superb view over Vung Tau. It was built by French Governor-General Paul Doumer as his summer residence, but he never spent a single day here because by the time the villa was completed, he had been dispatched back to France. Instead, King Thanh Thai was held here for a few years before he was packed off in exile to Reunion Island, where his son King Duy Tan was also sent in 1916. Later the villa became the seaside residence of two of South Vietnam's presidents, Diem and Thieu. Today it houses ceramics from a shipwreck that took place off the coast. The ship was originally bound for Holland. As if giving a sermon on the mount, a 30-metre (100-ft) statue of Jesus with arms outstretched looks out across the South China Sea at the peninsula's southern point. The statue was erected by the Americans in 1971.

Inland from **Bai Dua** is the most celebrated of Vung Tau's pagodas, **Niet Ban Tinh Xa**. *Niet ban*, Vietnamese for nirvana, is symbolised in the pagoda's long, reclining Buddha, who, having attained *niet ban*, can lie back and enjoy it. The statue is made of concrete overlaid with marble. Each of the Buddha's 12 metres (40 ft) represents one of the 12 stages of reincarnation, all of which are engraved on the Buddha's feet. The goddess Quan Am is also represented here. The statues

BELOW: chairs for hire, Vung Tau.
RIGHT: interior of the White Villa.

standing at the entrance gate are those of Than Thien, the good deity, and Than Ac, the evil deity, both of whom are believed to guard the entrance to nirvana. A two-headed dragon also stands guard. Made entirely out of broken ceramic dishes, it has a Dutch windmill painted on one piece, just behind its right ear, a testimony to the trade between East and West.

From Vung Tau, a one-hour flight from Ho Chi Minh City with Vasco Airlines or a 12-hour boat trip due south links the mainland with the **Con Dao** ⑳, an archipelago comprised of 14 islands that boast unspoiled beaches, coconut groves, corals and clear waters. Sea turtles laboriously make their way onto the beaches to lay their eggs. In 1995 a sea turtle conservation project was launched to protect these endangered creatures.

Dense virgin forest, rich in precious woods, covers the islands' interiors. Today's image of unspoiled natural beauty is a far cry from that of the dreaded penitentiary of **Poulo Condore** (Devil's Island), run by the French on the main island of **Con Son** for almost a century and later by the South Vietnamese regime as a prison for communist sympathisers. Reminders of the island's less attractive past are present in the remains of the penal colony. The few residents on the island today raise peanuts and teakwood, amongst other crops, dive for pearls, or fish the local waters. ❏

MEKONG DELTA

Cuu Long, the river of nine dragons and known in the West as the Mekong, is one of the world's mightiest rivers. In the south, the river enriches and nourishes the land as it enters the ocean

Map on pages 266–7

T he Mekong's Vietnamese name, **Cuu Long**, means Nine Dragons, as the river branches into nine mouths that empty into the sea. The vast delta of the Cuu Long (Mekong River) is formed by the alluvium deposited by the multiple arms and tributaries of the river. The river descends from its source high in the Tibetan plateau and follows a 4,500-km (2,800-mile) course through China, Burma (Myanmar), Laos, Thailand, Cambodia and southern Vietnam before emptying into the South China Sea.

The delta, an ancient Khmer territory, was an area of marshlands and forest before the first European colonisers arrived by sea in the 16th century. During the rule of the Nguyen lords (1802–1945), great expanses of marshlands were reclaimed and a network of small canals was built. By the end of the 18th century, two huge canals – the Thai Hoa, which linked Rach Gia and Long Xuyen, and the Vinh Te, linking Chau Doc and Ha Tien – were in use. The region is still populated by a large percentage of Khmer, Chinese and Chams, as well as Vietnamese. Among them are followers of diverse religions, including Buddhism, Catholicism, Islam and sects of Cao Dai and Hoa Hao.

There is an adequate road network serving the delta's 12 provinces – Long An, Dong Thap, An Giang, Kien Giang, Tien Giang, Ben Tre, Vinh Long, Tra Vinh, Can Tho, Soc Trang, Bac Lieu and Ca Mau. Up to recently, more than 100 ferries also served these areas, but now, only a few are left, because development, in the form of bridges and four-lane highways, has caught up. The condition of the roads vary from paved highways serving the larger cities to pothole-riddled mud tracks in rural areas. The comprehensive waterway network carries a busy and greatly varied flow of traffic. Unless travelling by river, travel is slow and less than efficient.

The region has greatly recovered from the ravages of the chemical defoliants and bombs dropped on it during the 1960s. The markets in the region are abundantly supplied with fish and a variety of produce yielded by the delta's rich alluvial soil: rice, sesame, peanuts, cashews, pineapples, pumpkins, tangerines, melons, cabbages, dragon fruits and durians. (For fruit lovers, April is a good month to visit and sample the rich variety of fruits in season.) The area is known as Vietnam's bread basket, or more aptly, rice bowl, because the region produces much of the country's rice. In many places there are three full harvests during the year.

That increasing modernisation will change life in the delta is a fact. But visitors to the region will still find a way of life that is as closely tied to the laws and moods of nature, or in this case, of the Mekong, as it is to the region's rich if turbulent history.

PRECEDING PAGES: Can Tho floating market. **LEFT:** loading boat at rice factory. **BELOW:** rice harvest.

Delta rice field.

Southward from Ho Chi Minh

The province of Long An, which stretches from the Cambodian border in the west straight across the country to the east coast, is more of historical than scenic significance. It was here, at **Nhat Tao** on the Song Vam Co Dong, that the French battleship *l'Espérance* was completely burnt by the Vietnamese, led by national hero Nguyen Trung Truc in 1861. This decisive battle cost the life of everyone on board and forced the French out of the south, at least temporarily.

The northern part of Long An is slightly hilly, although most of the province occupies a level plain a few metres above sea level. The Vam Co Dong, Vam Co Tay and Sai Gon rivers flow through the province, bringing rich alluvial silt to the extensive rice fields. Travellers may notice the occasional burial tomb in the rice fields. Many farmers believe that burying the dead on home soil helps discourage outsiders from buying their land. The town of **Go Den** in the southern part of the province is famous for producing the best rice wine in the Mekong Delta.

South from Ho Chi Minh on Highway 1, Tien Giang Province represents one of the country's main rice-growing areas. Land reclamation began in this extremely fertile region during the 17th century. This ancient Khmer territory was colonised by the Vietnamese towards the end of the 17th century, then taken over by the French in 1861. Major rivers such as the Tien, Go Cong, Ca Han and Bao Dinh flow through the province. Combined with the extensive canal network, these provide excellent waterway access to Ho Chi Minh and Phnom Penh. The sites of Rach Gam and Xaoi Mut, by the Song Tien, are where the peasant hero Nguyen Hue won his first victory in an historic river battle that claimed the lives of 40,000 Siamese troops in 1785.

BELOW: rambutan vendor, and floating market.

My Tho **㉑**, the provincial capital with a population of 200,000, lies on the left bank of the **Song My Tho**, the northernmost branch of the Mekong. Founded in 1680 by political refugees from Taiwan, the city is easily reached from Ho Chi Minh, 70 km (40 miles) away, by a one-and-a-half-hour bus journey or six-hour trip by river ferry. The old Saigon–My Tho railway, the earliest built in Indochina in 1883, was last used in 1958, but the province has a more-than-adequate road network.

The busy central market is located on Trung Trac and Nguyen Hue streets and is closed to vehicles. The Catholic church here was built at the end of the 19th century, and there is still a large Catholic congregation numbering more than 7,000 followers. The **Vinh Trang**, the largest pagoda in the province, is an eclectic mix of French, Chinese, Vietnamese, and Khmer architectural styles. A dozen or so monks live here, performing charitable works in the area.

From My Tho, a boat can be taken to one of the nearby islands, an interesting and enjoyable excursion. **Con Phung**, or Phoenix Island, lies in the Song Tien Giang a few kilometres from My Tho and can be reached by hired boat. Other islands in the Tien Giang include Con Qui (Turtle Island), Con Lan (Unicorn Island), visited for its extensive fruit gardens, and Con Long (Dragon Island).

Con Phung was the home of the Coconut Monk, Ong Dao Dua, a charismatic character who founded a religion known as Tinh Do Cu Si, a synthesis of Buddhism and Christianity, with Jesus, Buddha and the Virgin Mary forming a challenging triumvirate. Born Nguyen Thanh Nam in 1909, the future Coconut Monk studied physics and chemistry in France between 1928 and 1935 before returning to Vietnam, where he married and had a daughter. In 1943, he left his family to live the life of a monk and for three years is said to have sat on a

Map on pages 266–7

BELOW: Vinh Trang pagoda, near Vinh Long.

Bonsai in Vinh Long.

stone slab beneath a flag pole meditating and eating only coconuts. His philosophy advocated peaceful means of reunifying his country.

This concept did not go down at all well with the South Vietnamese governments, in whose prisons he was a frequent guest. During the Vietnam War, the Coconut Monk gained many new followers, a number of whom were reportedly trying to avoid conscription. He died in 1990, a prisoner of the communist regime that arrested him for anti-government activities. After his arrest, his band of followers dispersed. The island boasts the remnants of a bizarre open-air sanctuary where the Coconut Monk addressed his following. Today, its faded dragon-entwined columns, multi-tiered tower with a great metal globe atop, and Apollo rocket set stand forlorn and neglected and are not worth the entrance fee required.

Twelve km (7 miles) to the west of My Tho is a snake farm at **Dong Tam**, where the snakes yield a variety of medical substances used in traditional medicines. Their flesh is believed to be an effective remedy against a number of ailments ranging from mental disorders to rheumatism and paralysis. Snake gall combined with other drugs is used to treat coughs and migraine. An excellent alcoholic tonic is obtained by steeping three special varieties of snake in alcohol. Some men also believe snake to be a virility enhancer.

Despite My Tho's attractions, it must be said that the Tien Giang People's Committee (the local communists) is reputedly one of the most corrupt in Vietnam, with a stranglehold on all things connected with tourism. The result is that travellers have to contend with high prices and poor facilities and service. Consequently, many tourists either avoid My Tho entirely or visit as part an organised day-tour from Ho Chi Minh.

BELOW: snakes in alcohol are said to assure virility.

To the south, Ben Tre Province lies between the My Tho and Co Chien rivers. More coconut palms are grown here than in any other province in the country, contending for agricultural space with the province's extensive rice fields. The provincial capital, **Ben Tre** ㉒, is located on the Ham Luong tributary. The temple of **Nguyen Dinh Chieu** here is dedicated to a poet of the 19th century who was born in nearby Ba Tri.

A boat trip along the Ba Lai–Ham Luong waterway provides the visitor with an opportunity to become better acquainted with everyday life on the river. Smaller canals lead to bee farms and fruit orchards. Many species of birds can be seen in the bird sanctuary of **Cu Lao Dat**, which covers 30 hectares (74 acres) of forest in the small village of **An Hiep**. Off the main roads, quiet Ben Tre sees few visitors.

West of Ben Tre Province, Vinh Long Province is crisscrossed by canals and has an elevation of just 2 metres (6 ft 4ins) above sea level. Outside the provincial capital, also named **Vinh Long** ㉓, is an interesting pagoda, the Confucian **Van Thanh Mieu**. Boats leave from in front of the Cuu Long Hotel for the An Binh and Binh Hoa Phuoc islands, located in the middle of the Song Tien. The trip is a treat for fruit lovers, as it takes in villages whose gardens and orchards produce a great variety of seasonal fruit such as mangoes, mandarins, rambutans and longans. Visitors can also stroll through well-tended bonsai gardens or stay overnight with local families on the islands.

Southeast of Vinh Long, Tra Vinh Province is bordered by the Tien and Hau rivers. Off the beaten tourist path, Tra Vinh is home to about 300,000 ethnic Khmers. Mostly farmers, these Khmers speak both Khmer and Vietnamese. Top sights in and around the capital of **Tra Vinh** ㉔ include **Ho Ba Om** (Ba Om

Map on pages 266–7

"It became necessary to destroy the town in order to save it".

– U.S. OFFICER ABOUT THE U.S. BOMBING OF BEN TRE DURING THE TET OFFENSIVE, 1968

BELOW: flower seller in boat.

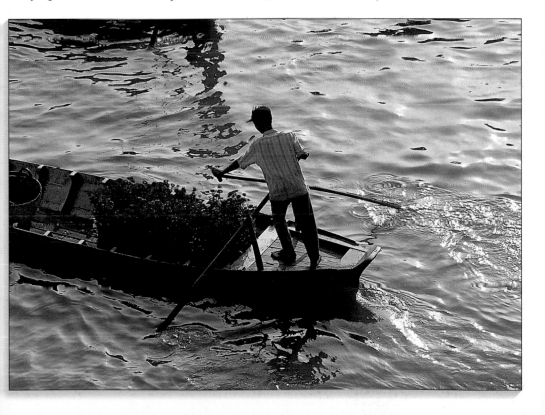

Lake), where a number of important Khmer festivals are celebrated, and **Chua Co** (Stork Pagoda), a Khmer pagoda that shelters hundreds of real storks.

Bordering Cambodia in the north, Dong Thap Province is one of the three provinces lying in the marshy area known as **Dong Thap Muoi**, or the Plain of Reeds. The province takes its name from the 10-storey Thap Muoi tower built long ago in the commune of An Phong. The tower, no longer standing, was used as a lookout by the resistance forces against the French.

The province was formerly inhabited by the ancient Phu Nam kingdom and later the Chan Lap civilisation, a people who in the 1700s exchanged the area of Sa Dec with Vietnam for military aid that restored order to the area. The Chan Lap were subsequently wiped out and assimilated by the Vietnamese, and today the area is populated primarily by people of Chinese, Khmer, Cham and Thai origin.

Interesting sights around the provincial capital **Cao Lanh** 25 include several bird sanctuaries and **Rung Tram**, a forest that harboured an underground Viet Cong camp, **Xeo Quit**, during the war. **Sa Dec**, the former provincial capital, is famous for its many nurseries and flower gardens that cultivate roses.

Booming Delta towns

Can Tho 26, the capital of Can Tho Province, is the largest and most modern city in the Delta and the only one with a university. This important commercial centre and river port, with a population of 350,000, lies on the banks of the Song Hau. Can Tho's university, established in 1966, is involved in valuable agricultural research and development that has contributed substantially to improving production and pest control.

BELOW: village near Can Tho.

As the hub of the Mekong Delta, Can Tho is a booming city. While it has a friendly feel about it, there is not a great deal of sightseeing to be done here. The animated Can Tho market, which spreads out along Hai Ba Trung, with its main building at the intersection of Hai Ba Trung and Nam Ky Khoi Nghia streets, boasts the largest fruit market in the Delta region. Several restaurants along the waterfront serve specialities of the region: frog, turtle, snake and fish.

Of greater interest are boat trips on the Song Hau. Off the main waterways, flimsy bamboo bridges stretch across the smaller canals. These were built for the lighter and more agile Vietnamese and are to be avoided or else negotiated with extreme care unless one wants to end up in the canal, an all-too-easy possibility. At the lively Cai Rang floating market, all manner of boats and sampans gather, their occupants busily engaged in buying or selling a wide variety of fruit, fish and vegetables.

To the west, An Giang Province borders the Cambodian province of Takeo. Here, the Mekong enters the province and splits into two branches, forming the Tien and Hau rivers, which every year deposit millions of cubic metres of alluvium in the adjacent areas. This prosperous region, rich in natural resources and fertile land, produces many varieties of fruit trees and crops of soya bean, tobacco, groundnut and mulberry.

Long Xuyen, the provincial capital located in the east of the province, has a population of about 264,000 people. Its Catholic church, built between 1963 and 1973, can seat 1,000 and is the largest in the Delta. On the northern outskirts of town, an area famous for its incense production, clusters of fuchsia and saffron joss sticks line the roadside, drying in the sun. **Chau Doc ㉗**, not far from the Cambodian border, is situated on the right bank of the **Song Hau Giang**. Chau

Map on pages 266–7

BELOW: floating market on the Han River, Can Tho.

At the water market.

Doc has a population of 100,000. The **Dinh Than Chau Phu** in the township was built in 1926. In this temple, the locals worship Thai Ngoc Hau, the man responsible for the nearby Chau Doc canal, which opens the frontier between Cambodia and Vietnam. He held a high official rank under the Nguyen lords and then later during the Nguyen dynasty.

From the Chau Giang terminal, a ferry crosses the Hau. On the other side is the **Chau Giang Mosque**, which serves the district's Muslim Cham community. Numbering around 20,000 people in the Chau Doc area, many Chams live in stilt houses on the water and make their living from fishing and weaving. From here, travellers can pick up a lift to Tan Chau district, famous throughout southern Vietnam for its silk industry and prosperity. The market there offers many imported goods from Thailand, which are brought into the country through Cambodia.

Chau Doc is also renowned for its floating villages. Living in houses built on empty metal tanks or small boats, many villagers survive on and often prosper from fishing. Metal nets under the houses facilitate the capture of large quantities of fish. Although their living conditions may not reflect it, several fishing families in the area are reputed to be millionaires.

Some 4 km (2½ miles) from Chau Doc is **Nui Sam**, a mountain so named because the surrounding area was once the home to many king crabs, called *sam* in Vietnamese. At 230 metres (755 ft) high, this beautiful site has many Buddhist and Daoist shrines built into the hillside.

BELOW: hill of Chau Doc, with Cambodia in the distance.

Climbing up the south side of the mountain, visitors will find spectacular views of the surrounding countryside greeting them at the summit. On a clear day, even Cambodia is visible. A military outpost at the summit still houses a

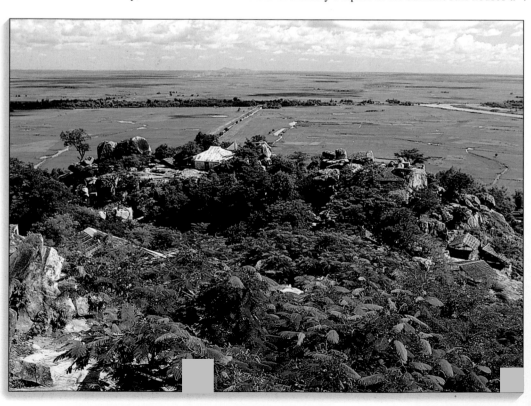

few soldiers, more interested nowadays in their badminton games than in Khmer Rouge incursions, given that the Khmer Rouge army collapsed in the late 1990s. On festival days, vendors and fortune-tellers turn out in force to greet arriving worshippers. At the foot of the mountain, the tomb of Thoai Ngoc Hau holds his remains plus those of his two wives. Also buried here are some of the workers who died during the construction of the Chau Doc canal.

Sharing the base of the mountain are the Indian-style **Tay An**, a pagoda that dates from 1847 and is famous for its many finely carved religious figures, and **Mieu Ba Chua Xu** (Temple of Lady Chua Xu), where a granite statue of Lady Chua Xu is worshipped. Bales of colourful cloth donated by worshippers from Cho Lon are stored here.

This temple is reputed to be the richest temple in Vietnam – worshippers including many Chinese from Ho Chi Minh City, Hong Kong and Taiwan flock here bearing money and gifts. Every year on the 22nd day of the fourth lunar month, a large procession of religious followers begins a week-long series of festivities and ceremonies to celebrate their pilgrimage. One special ritual involves the washing of Lady Chua Xu's statue by three virgins. Thus made holy, the bath water is then dispensed to the waiting crowds.

About 40 km (25 miles) west of Chau Doc lies Vietnam's killing fields, **Ba Chuc**. In April 1978, Khmer Rouge forces massacred 3,157 civilians in the commune of Ba Chuc. Many of the victims were tortured to death. A pagoda built in 1991 contains the skulls and bones of 1,155 victims, and on display in the temple are some graphic photos depicting the aftermath of the slaughter. Due to the poor condition of the roads, few visitors make it out here, even though a visit is well worthwhile, though not for the faint of heart.

Map on pages 266–7

Lady Chua Xu is in fact a statue of stone, reputedly discovered on the slopes of Nui Sam some time during the 19th century.

BELOW: pagoda at Tay An.

Phu Tan, a village in the north of the province, is the birth place of Huynh Phu So, founder of the Hoa Hao religious sect. Its male followers are easily identified by their long beards and equally long hair tied into a bun. Adhering to simplicity, Hoa Hao followers reject the need for altars, temples, or any other intermediaries between them and a supreme deity.

Ancient civilisation

Some 40 km (25 miles) southwest of Long Xuyen, in the hilly area of Ba The, are the ruins of **Oc Eo** ㉘, which was a major trading port during the first centuries AD. Oc Eo lay submerged for centuries until it was rediscovered in the 1940s. Remnants of architectural structures and other finds made by researchers here indicate that it was a city closely linked with the ancient Chinese kingdom of Phu Nam (Funan), which dates back to the 1st century AD and reached its peak in about the 5th century.

Most of what we know about this ancient civilisation – gleaned from excavations at Oc Eo – reveals evidence of contact with the Roman Empire, Persia, China, Thailand, Malaysia and Indonesia; in addition, there are the written accounts of Chinese travellers and emissaries referring to the site. Oc Eo's elaborate and intricate canal system was used not only for irrigation but also for transportation.

It is difficult but possible to visit the ruins themselves; however, during the rainy season the area tends to be flooded The artefacts have been moved to museums throughout Vietnam and a canopy covers the few remaining bricks.

Not far from here are the long irrigation canals of the district of Tri Ton, where a significant percentage of the population is now Khmer, including the

Oc Eo, ringed by a protective moat, has been linked to the extensive trade that plied between Asia and Europe, as evidenced by the ancient Roman, Egyptian, Indian, Persian, and Chinese artefacts uncovered at the site.

BELOW: Khmer Buddhist monk.

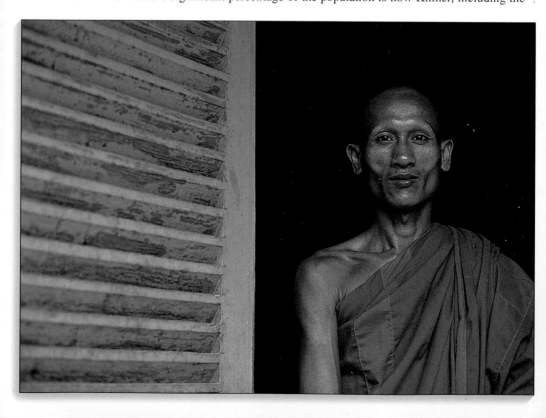

many thousands of refugees who poured into the area during the late 1970s as they fled Pol Pot's vicious Khmer Rouge forces in Cambodia.

Along the coast

Kien Giang Province, in the southwest of the Delta, shares a common border in the northwest with Cambodia and in the west is washed by waters from the Gulf of Thailand. Forests, plains, offshore islands and a 200 km- (125 mile-) long coastline contribute to Kien Giang's rich scenic diversity.

The journey up the coast begins in the provincial capital, **Rach Gia 29**, an active fishing port with a population of around 220,000. It is bordered by marshlands, much of which have been drained for rice cultivation.

The town has quite a number of interesting temples and pagodas. The large Khmer **Chua Phat Lon** (Big Buddha Pagoda) was established about two centuries ago. **Hoi Tuong Te Nguoi Hoa** (Ong Bac De), on Nguyen Du in the town centre, was built by the local Chinese community over a century ago. The central altar is occupied by a statue of Ong Bac De, the reincarnation of the Jade Emperor of Heaven. To his left is Ong Gon, the guardian spirit of happiness and virtue, and on his right is Quan Cong.

Nguyen Trung Truc, a temple at 18 Nguyen Cong Tru, is dedicated to Nguyen Trung Truc, who led the resistance campaign against the French during the 1860s, including the attack on the French ship *l'Espérance*. Although the French repeatedly tried to capture him, it wasn't until 1868 that they succeeded, after taking his mother and a number of civilians hostage. Truc eventually gave himself up and was executed by the French in the Rach Gia marketplace. Many Vietnamese consider this brave nationalist and pious son to be a deity, and

Map on pages 266–7

BELOW: labourer in a Delta rice paddy.

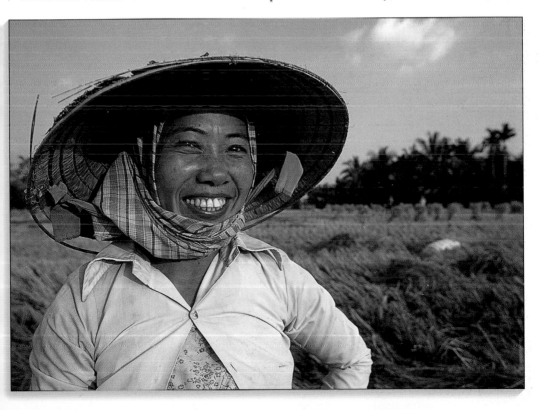

worshippers from all over the Mekong Delta flock to this temple annually to observe the anniversary of his death in October.

Rach Gia is well known for its seafood, and it has a good selection of restaurants serving both Chinese and Vietnamese food, as well as specialities such as eel, turtle, snake, frog legs, deer and cuttlefish.

The road from Rach Gia to the town of Ha Tien in the northwest corner of the province is good, and it passes many small farms and villages and provides an interesting look at life on the canal. About 80 km (50 miles) from Rach Gia and 20 km (12 miles) from Ha Tien, a detour off the main road leads to the seaside town of **Hon Chong** ㉚. Unlike much of the pancake-flat Mekong Delta, this area is studded with impressive, towering limestone formations. Unfortunately, as a prime source of quality limestone for the cement factories near Hon Chong, increasingly these mountains are being blasted with dynamite and denuded, if not levelled entirely.

For now, however, Hon Chong remains relatively peaceful and beautiful. The best beach in the area is **Bai Duong**, which takes its name from the *duong* (casuarina) trees growing beside it. Its white, clear water and picturesque surroundings make it an ideal spot to break the journey with a swim. Looking out to sea, you will see the famous Father and Son Rocks, whose grottoes are a favourite haunt of sea swallows.

A toll gate leads to **Chua Hang** (Grotto Pagoda), next to the beach. The grotto is entered from behind the altar of the pagoda, which is set back into the base of the hill. Small, tastefully-lit shrines line the cave, and you can walk through to the beach on the other side. For a small fee, the tour boats take you on a 20-minute cruise around the three islands, locally known as mini Halong Bay.

BELOW: successful fisherman.

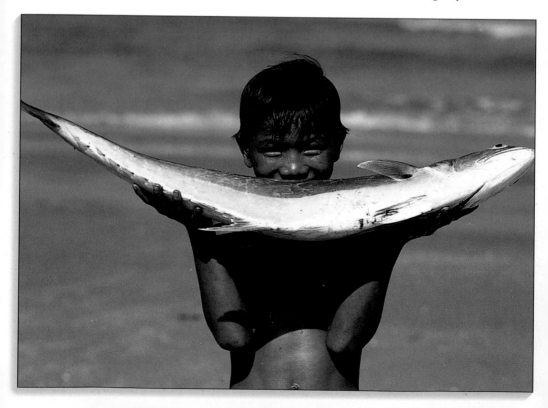

About 25 km (15 miles) from Ha Tien in the **Hang Tien** (Coin Grotto), which takes its name from the zinc coins found buried within it by Nguyen Anh – the future Emperor Gia Long – and his troops, who camped here while battling the Tay Son rebels. About 17 km (10 miles) from Ha Tien and 3 km (2 miles) from the main road is **Hang Mo So**. During the wet season, this grotto is accessible only by boat, but for the rest of the year it can be reached on foot. A torch and a local guide will come in handy when exploring the labyrinth of tunnels beyond the three main caverns.

A floating toll bridge completes the last watery stretch of the journey to **Ha Tien** ❸. Nestling in a cove formed by the **Song Gian Thang**, Ha Tien has a population of 120,000 and is located only about 10 km (6 miles) from the Cambodian border. This charming town of Chinese origin was founded around 1670 by Mac Cuu, a Chinese immigrant from Guangzhou (Canton) who arrived here after the fall of the Ming dynasty in 1644. He refused to serve the Manchu rulers and instead explored the South Seas with his men. After procuring the agreement of the Cambodian kings and the Vietnamese Nguyen lords, he and his men installed themselves at Ha Tien, transforming it in no time into a prosperous principality equipped with a maritime port.

In 1714, Ha Tien was given to Nguyen Phuc Chu, a lord from Hue, who compensated Mac Cuu with the title *generalissimo* of Ha Tien. The principality prospered with the revenue accumulated from a gambling house and a tin mine. His only son, Mac Thien Tu, continued his father's work in improving the town's development. He organised an army equal to the task of repelling the Cambodian and Siamese invasions, and also founded an academy of arts, known as the Chieu Anh Cac (Pavilion of Quintessential Welcome).

Map on pages 266-7

TIP

With its reasonably flat terrain, the countryside around Ha Tien lends itself nearly perfectly to bicycle touring. Several of the hotels in Ha Tien rent bicycles at modest rates by the day.

BELOW: beach at Hon Chong.

BELOW: Thac Dong
Thon Van – Grotto
That Swallows
the Clouds.

Ha Tien's natural beauty attracts many visitors. To the east of Ha Tien, scenic **Ho Dong** (East Lake) greets the arriving visitor. The town has several temples dedicated to the Mac family and an even greater number of tombs that rest on the eastern flank of **Binh San**. These are built of bricks and contain the remains of both Mac Cuu and his relatives. His own tomb, built in 1809, is the largest and is decorated with finely carved figures of the traditional Blue Dragon and White Tiger.

Tam Bao, a pagoda at 328 Phuong Thanh, was founded by Mac Cuu in 1730. A statue of Quan Am atop a lotus stands in front of the pagoda. Nearby is the **Phu Dung**, a pagoda founded by Mac Cuu's second wife, Nguyen Thi Xuan, in 1750. Her tomb is built on the hillside behind the pagoda's main hall. The pagoda contains some interesting statues. In the centre of the main hall is one of the newborn Sakyamuni Buddha, in the embrace of nine dragons; on the main dais in a glass case is a bronze Chinese Buddha.

Ha Tien does a lively trade in items handcrafted from the shells of sea turtles, which are domestically reared in pools along the coastline. It is also famous for its seafood and black pepper. There are a number of beaches around Ha Tien that are popular with locals, such as Mui Nai and Bai No. Don't expect pristine white sand or crystalline turquoise waters, however. The beaches are also full of pushy vendors, which hardly makes for a quiet, relaxing time.

One of the main attractions located a few kilometres from town on Mac Tu Hoang is **Thach Dong Thon Van**, the Grotto That Swallows the Clouds. The grotto shelters a Buddhist sanctuary and funerary tablets; altars to Quan Am and to Ngoc Hoang, the Jade Emperor of Heaven, are contained in several of its chambers. Exploring the grotto can yield breathtaking views of the surrounding rice fields and smaller offshore islands. Near the grotto is a mass grave where 130 people, victims of a massacre by Pol Pot's Khmer Rouge troops in 1978, are buried. To the left of the sanctuary's entrance is a stele known as Bia Cam Thu – the stele of hatred – that commemorates the victims.

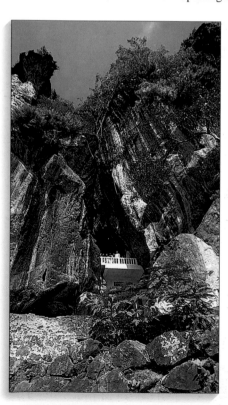

The island of **Tien Hai** lies about 15 km (9 miles) off the coast of Ha Tien and can be reached by boat. It has a lovely and quite secluded beach.

Phu Quoc island

Vietnam's largest island, **Phu Quoc** ㉜, is located about 40 km (25 miles) west of Ha Tien. This inverted tear drop-shaped island is 50 km (30 miles) long and covers some 1,300 sq km (500 sq miles). In the 18th century, Ngyuen Anh (who later became Emperor Gia Long) was sheltered here from the Tay Son rebels by French missionary Pigneau de Behaine, who himself used the island as a base between the 1760s and 1780s. The French later used the island as a prison.

Phu Quoc is renowned for its bountiful fishing grounds, its black pepper trees and its high-quality quality *nuoc mam* (fish sauce). These days, however, it's the island's near continuous chain of spectacular white sand beaches – like Bai Dai and Bai Thom in the north, Bai Truong (or Long Beach) in the west and Bai Khem in the south – that are attracting visitors. Several resorts have already opened up along the 20 km (12½ mile) Bai Truong coastline stretching south from the 'capital' Duong Dong. Roads are dusty, potholed affairs, but not for long. Massive US$3-4 billion worth of investment is planned for the development of the island, including a golf course to lure international hoteliers. Phu Quoc can be accessed by a 2 hour boat ride from Rach Gia or Ha Tien or the daily Vietnam Airlines flight from Ho Chi Minh City or Rach Gia.

Phu Quoc National Park was established in 2001 in the hilly northeastern part of the island. Chua Mountain, the highest of the 99 peaks in the island in found within the park. Little, however, is yet known about the biodiversity of the park's 37,000 ha (91,427 acres) of lowland evergreen forest, which covers almost a third of the island.

To the south of the island is the **An Thoi Archipelago**, a group of 15 islands which is popular with divers and snorkellers. The surrounding waters are home to the endangered dugong as well as Leatherback and Hawksbill turtles, although underwater enthusiasts are more likely to see a huge variety of small, colourful reef and coral fish, many of which are endemic to Vietnamese waters.

The deep south

About 35 km (20 miles) southeast of Can Tho is Soc Trang Province. About 300,000 Khmer people live here. Its capital **Soc Trang** ㉝ has a number of interesting Khmer temples and pagodas. Of note is the striking **Kh'leng**. Originally built more than 400 years ago, this pagoda was rebuilt in 1907. Typical of Khmer pagodas, this one is richly decorated on the outside with carved griffins, snakes and statues of dancing maidens. Inside, a gilded bronze statue of Sakyamuni, flanked by marble statues of two of his first disciples, presides over

Map on pages 266-7

Recognising the importance of Phu Quoc Island as key nesting grounds for the endangered Leatherback and Hawksbill turtles, the World Wildlife Foundation (WWF) has plans to start a turtle tagging and protection scheme in the near future.

BELOW: Phu Quoc Island is blessed with white sand beaches and swaying palms

Map on pages 266–7

the main altar. There are about two dozen monks in residence and 170 monks attending the Buddhist college on the premises. Also here is a 25 metre- (80 ft) long *ghe ngo*, or long-boat. During the Oc Om Boc Festival – on the 15th day of the 10th lunar month – the Khmer community turns out to watch long-boat races on the Soc Trang river. Opposite the pagoda is a Khmer museum.

Not far from here on 68 Mau Than is the fascinating **Chua Dat Set**, built in 1906. Made of clay, this Chinese pagoda houses statues and figurines that are also made of clay. An intricately sculpted Bao Thap tower is remarkable for having a little Buddha figurine on every lotus petal. Also here are six giant paraffin candles, two of which have been burning since 1970 when they were first made. The second pair will be lit at the end of 2005 in honour of the architect of this pagoda, Ngo Kim Tong.

On the outskirts of town is **Chua Doi**, or the Bat Pagoda. Less ornate than the Kh'leng pagoda, this Khmer temple is more famous for the several thousand screeching fruit bats residing in its gardens. It is said that while these bats may attack the fruit trees in other orchards, they know not to eat from the trees that shelter them. Colourful murals depicting scenes from Buddha's life adorn the inside of the temple.

As the newest province in Vietnam, Bac Lieu was carved from the former Minh Hai Province in 1997. During French rule, the area saw a rise in the number of wealthy landlords. Much of the land was confiscated by the government after 1978, although it was eventually returned in the mid-1980s. Nevertheless, a majority of the population here is still landless and quite poor, and many of the locals make a living through fishing. **Bac Lieu** ❸ today is mostly a rest-stop for travellers on their way to Ca Mau.

The southernmost province of Vietnam, the peninsula of Ca Mau is not best described as a tourist destination. **Ca Mau** ❸, the largest town, lies 180 km (110 miles) south of Can Tho on the Song Gan Hao, in the heart of an immense, submerged plain covered in mangroves and rich in fishing.

Ca Mau marks the extreme southernmost tip of Vietnam. It is a shifting tip and peninsula, however, as the continual deposit of silt from the Mekong and its tributaries is actually extending the shoreline by up to 80 metres (260 ft) a year. Moreover, the average elevation of the Ca Mau peninsula is just 2 metres (6 ft 7 ins) above sea level.

Until World War II, most of the peninsula lacked any vehicular roads at all. During the French years following World War II, the peninsula was held by the Viet Minh, and during the Vietnam War with the Americans, it was a refuge and base of operations for the Viet Cong guerrillas.

The mangrove forest at **U Minh**, just outside of Ca Mau and the largest of its kind in the world outside of the Amazon Basin, was seriously damaged by defoliants dropped by the Americans during the Vietnam War. Still, the dense and swampy undergrowth is home to numerous varieties of venomous snakes, leeches, unidentifiable things and mosquitoes. Locals catch the snakes and breed them, selling them for pharmaceutical products and for food. ❑

BELOW: Muslim men of the south. **RIGHT:** boats at Ben Tre.

® INSIGHT GUIDES
Travel Tips

CONTENTS

Getting Acquainted

Name: Socialist Republic of Vietnam.

Area: 329,556 sq km (127,242 sq miles), half the size of Texas or slightly larger than Italy.

Location: Vietnam forms the eastern edge – meeting the South China Sea – of the area formerly called Indochina. Due north is China. On the country's western border are Laos and Cambodia. Directly east, across the South China Sea, are the Philippines.

Population: 83.5 million. Some 87 percent of the people are indigenous Vietnamese or Kinh, 2 percent are ethnic Chinese and the rest comprise Khmer and Cham people and the hill-tribe minorities.

Language: Although numerous hill-tribe languages pepper the country, Vietnamese is the national language. Amongst older people, French is sometimes spoken. In the south, especially, English is quite widely spoken.

Religion: Mahayana Buddhism predominates. Catholicism is fairly common (about 10 percent of the population), along with elements of Taoism, Confucianism, Hinduism and Islam.

Time Zones: Vietnam, like Laos, Cambodia and Thailand, is +7 hours GMT.

Currency: Vietnamese *dong*.

Weights & Measures: Vietnam uses the metric system.

Literacy: Estimated at 92 percent.

Life Expectancy: 68 years.

Dialling Codes: Vietnam's country code is 84. For the complete list of area codes, see page 344.

The Economy

Vietnam is essentially an agricultural country, with rice cultivation accounting for 45 percent of the GNP and employing 70 percent of the population. Other major crops include tea, coffee, maize, bananas, manioc, cotton, tobacco, coconut and rubber.

Industry represents over 30 percent of the country's GNP output. Electricity, steel, cement, cotton fabrics, fish sauce, fisheries, wood, paper, and the growing petroleum exploration and production industry represent Vietnam's major areas of industrial production. Ho Chi Minh City has a small oil refinery and has become Vietnam's economic capital, accounting for 30 percent of the national industrial production.

The country's standard of living ranks amongst the lowest in the world. Despite a protracted effort to revive the rural economy, disastrous economic policies, coupled with the drain of more than 50 percent of the country's budget on supporting its occupation forces in Cambodia and Laos in the late 1970s, have had devastating effects on the economy.

In an effort to revive the ailing economy the country has recently opened its doors to encourage foreign investment and tourism, while further reform policies have been geared to re-establish a market economy and encourage production in the private sector, agriculture and light industry. However, foreign investment levels have waxed and waned with the frequent economic policy changes by the Communist government.

Although annual growth rates for the past few years have hovered at 8 percent, the average per capita income is only US$500. In Ho Chi Minh City and Hanoi, however, the figure is double that.

In both Ho Chi Minh City and Hanoi, there is a burgeoning consumerism reflected in the number of motorcycles, electronics and Western clothes for sale. In these two cities, an estimated 95 percent of households now own TVs. Outside of these cities, however, poverty is rampant.

Government

Vietnam is a socialist republic ruled by the Vietnamese Communist Party since the fall of Saigon in 1975, and the country's subsequent reunification in 1976. Vietnam's domestic policy is shaped primarily by the party and its Secretary General. The Prime Minister presides over drafting of laws and day-to-day governing. The President oversees state policy, the military and internal police apparatus.

The government is nominated by the National Assembly, proposed by the party and theoretically elected by the people. Although the National Assembly has in the past been something of a rubber-stamp operation, recently it has become more aggressive in challenging government functions, implementing laws, debating policy, and holding government ministers accountable.

The republic is divided into 53 administrative areas: three cities – Hanoi, Ho Chi Minh City and Hai Phong – and 61 provinces. Traditionally provincial officials maintain some level of independence in implementing state policy. All candidates are screened for their suitability, although not everyone is a member of the Communist Party – in 2004, 40 percent of officials elected were not members. Vietnam has generally avoided major upheavals within its power structure. When high-level officials retire, they still maintain important advisory roles.

If there is any crisis in leadership in Vietnam today, it is that there does not appear to be a younger generation of leaders ready to step in and take the reins of power. Thus there is considerable speculation that the current leadership will most likely continue in their positions instead of retiring as was earlier expected.

Party leaders emphasise that there is no room for political pluralism at this point and that the Communist Party will maintain its hold on power.

Climate/When to go

Given Vietnam's length – it stretches 1,650 km (1,000 miles) from north to south – its topography and the effect of the monsoon tropical climate, temperatures and rainfall patterns can vary widely from one region to another. In the north the thermometer can dip as low as a frosty 10°C (50°F) and with a biting winter wind that can feel a lot colder. In the south, however, it is hot all year round and subject to the monsoon weather patterns.

The south has two seasons; wet and dry. The rains arrive in May and leave in November. Between these months it rains fiercely for 20 or 30 minutes a day normally in the afternoon or early evening. Late February to late April are the hottest months, with temperatures well into the mid 30s (C) and high humidity levels. The dry season runs from December to April.

The north experiences four seasons. The summer months from May to September are almost always hot and humid, with the most rainfall during this period. Winter, from late December to early March, is grey, drizzly and cool.

Central Vietnam from Danang to Nha Trang has its own weather patterns due to the monsoons: the dry season is from January to September, with the rainfall from October to mid-January.

It is also best to avoid all travel during the Vietnamese Lunar New

Best Time to Visit

It's near impossible to find a time of the year when both the north and south have equally good weather but the safest bet – if you're travelling the length of Vietnam – is between October and November. The rains will be abating in the south, humidity levels will drop, and it will be relatively cool and dry in the north. However, you may get some rain in the centre, depending on when the monsoons hit.

Year or Tet (see below) in January or February (depending on the lunar calendar). As the celebrations begin the week before the actual festivities, roads, trains and planes become clogged with local and overseas Vietnamese rushing home for their family reunions. It may be difficult to arrange transportation and book hotels during this period.

Public Holidays

The most important celebration of the year in Vietnam is Tet, or **Lunar New Year** (see page 87), which falls either in late January or early February each year, on the day of the full moon between the winter solstice and the spring equinox. Officially, there are three public holidays but in reality almost all of Vietnam shuts down for an entire week.

The dates of nearly all festivals vary from year to year because they adhere to the lunar calendar. By counting the days from a new moon, it's fairly easy to determine when, say, "the third day of the second lunar month" falls on the familiar Gregorian calendar. It's easier to consult a Vietnamese calendar, which always come with both systems. Following is a list of "fixed" public holidays in Vietnam.

Official Public Holidays
New Year's Day: 1 January
Tet: January/February *
Liberation Day: 30 April
International Labour Day: 1 May
National Day/Independence Day: 2 September
* Exact date varies depending on lunar calendar.

Planning the Trip

Visas and Passports

It used to be incredibly difficult for independent travellers to gain entry to Vietnam in the past. Today, it is fairly straightforward to get a visa. Most travellers get a one-month single-entry visa that costs US$30 (multiple-entry ones cost US$125–200, depending on duration of stay and where you are applying for it).

The easy way of getting a visa is to use the travel agent from whom you buy your air ticket. There will be a commission charge on top of the usual visa processing fee paid to the visa office of the Vietnamese embassy or consulate. In addition to the application form, you must submit a valid passport and two passport-size photos. Allow 5–7 working days for approval.

Individual travellers may also apply for a visa directly with the Vietnamese embassy or consulate in their home country but this might prove tedious. For a list of Vietnamese foreign missions overseas, check the **Vietnamese Ministry of Foreign Affairs** website at www.mofa.gov.vn.

Many travellers who stop over in Bangkok make arrangements to have their visas issued there. Travel agents in Bangkok offer attractive round-trip flight and visa packages.

Other types of visas available include business, press, family visit and official visit. To enter Vietnam on business, you must contact your Vietnamese sponsor, who will then submit an application form and letter to the embassy. Such visas allow for multiple-entry and are valid for up to six months. This process can often take weeks, so apply early.

It is wise to obtain a visa well in

advance because Vietnamese embassies in the past have abruptly suspended issuing visas for short periods of time due to domestic political reasons. The most recent instance was in the summer of 1998, when visas were suspended to halt foreigners from attending inaugural ceremonies marking year-long celebrations at the Catholic pilgrimage site of La Vang. Similar restrictions are expected for similar celebrations in the future.

Certain Vietnamese companies have the connections to have visas issued on arrival in Hanoi and Ho Chi Minh City for US$50. If you do enter Vietnam without a visa in hand, and there is a problem with immigration, remain calm. Usually the worst thing that will happen is you'll be put in the airport hotel for a night while your host hopefully secures your visa.

Most visas must be used within one month of their issue. Note that the period of your visa begins on the date you specify – not on the date in which you actually enter the country; postponing your visit by two weeks means that your month-long visa will only be valid for two weeks.

You will be given a copy of your landing card on your arrival. This, along with your visa, must be kept with you at all times and handed back on your departure. Even with a proper visa in hand, you may encounter popular airport scams.

Extension of Visas

It is currently fairly easy to extend a visa for one month; the government prefers that travel agencies handle tourist extensions, for which the total cost should be about US$30. But the government has been known to change such policies with no notice. Foreigners who enter on tourist visas and conduct business or government activities can be deported when caught. They may also be fined.

Visa extensions may also be granted for foreigners working in joint-venture companies and in foreign representative offices.

Police Registration

Internal travel permits are no longer required for visiting major tourist areas in Vietnam. In 1993, Hanoi eased its internal travel policies and opened all provinces to tourists. However, each province has its own regulations. Many tourists have reported being arrested by provincial police in the Central Highlands and Mekong Delta for travelling in restricted areas. Occasionally innocent tourists walk unknowingly into sensitive border areas and military installations unaware that they are breaking the law. In Vietnam, ignorance of the law is no excuse. Regulations change daily and some provinces completely ignore directives from Hanoi. The best advice is to play it safe in remote areas and always contact the police. It may end up costing a few

Big Brother

Visitors should keep in mind that there is a comprehensive registration procedure for all foreigners, and that their movements may be monitored by security police.

Some tour guides have been told to report the activities of their clients, while some private tour companies, and certainly state-owned ones, have members of the country's internal security apparatus working for them.

While visitors will not notice a heavy police presence, and although it has been said of late that the police have reduced the intensity of their surveillance, places frequented by tourists and expatriate residents, including bars and pubs, may still be monitored.

Persons suspected of engaging in criminal or politically sensitive activities will also be closely watched. So don't put your new Vietnamese friends in jeopardy – leave your political views at home.

dollars, but it beats spending your holiday under house arrest.

Tourists staying in hotels and guesthouses outside of Hanoi and Ho Chi Minh City do not need to register with the police directly. When you check in at reception the staff will take your passport to the police for registration. They will return it to you the next morning. In Hanoi or Ho Chi Minh City, they may only require your landing card, from which they will fill in details in a book and then return it. In other places, the staff may insist on holding your passport for your entire stay. This is probably a sign that police keep a very close watch on foreign visitors.

Note that procedures and policies change constantly and often without warning.

If you must turn over your passport, make sure that the correct one – and the landing card – are returned to you. Hotel staff are prone to misplacing passports; don't wait until a half-hour prior to departure to request the return of your passport.

If you plan on staying with family or friends you may want to visit the local police station to avoid any late night visits by the police, as nosey neighbours often report suspicious foreigners. Although you may consider this a nuisance, you will be saving your hosts quite a bit of trouble from authorities. Consider what impact your visit and contact may have on your friends who will be living and working in Vietnam after you have gone home.

Customs

Entry Formalities

Visitors to Vietnam are required to fill in a detailed customs declaration in duplicate upon arrival. Customs may inspect your luggage to verify that you have made a correct declaration. Although it is unpleasant to say this, authorities seem to cause more problems for overseas Vietnamese than for other foreigners. At times this is probably justified, as many overseas

Vietnamese return loaded down with boxes and bags. The volume of baggage, as much as the nationality, may account for the extra scrutiny.

Currency, as well as most electronics items – cameras, computers, video cameras – must be declared. Books, reading material and videos are supposed to be declared, but it doesn't seem expected. Your items may be inspected to check for anything considered culturally or politically sensitive.

You must keep a copy of the customs declaration form to show to customs officials upon leaving Vietnam. They may check to see if you are leaving with the items declared, such as computers and cameras.

Exit Formalities

Official authorisation from the Ministry of Culture is required to export or take out antiquities. Visitors are not allowed to take ancient artefacts, antiques or items of value to Vietnamese culture. An antique is defined as anything more than 30 years old. Travellers have reported problems in trying to leave with items that appear to be antiques, even if they are reproductions. It is a good idea to take a detailed receipt from the shop with a description of the item.

When leaving Vietnam, you may be stopped to have film, video and reading materials inspected. Usually this is just an annoyance, but if you are a journalist, your film or tapes will be seized unless you have permission to take them out from the government's Foreign Affairs Press Department.

Health and Insurance

Vaccines and Malaria Protection

The only vaccination required is for yellow fever, for travellers coming from Africa. Immunisation against hepatitis (A and B), Japanese encephalitis and tetanus are strongly urged.

It is a good idea to consult a physician a month to six weeks before departing to leave enough time to obtain the immunisations.

Malaria is widespread in Vietnam, especially in the Central Highlands and the Mekong Delta. The best protection is prevention. Always sleep under a mosquito net when visiting rural areas, use a high concentrate DEET repellent, and wear long sleeves and pants from dusk to dawn when malaria carrying mosquitoes are active.

Lastly, consult with a knowledgeable doctor to determine what anti malarial drugs are best suited for your travels. Opinion is divided about using prophylactics for malaria. Some doctors argue against taking anti-malarial drugs because of the potential side effects, which can also mask symptoms of other illnesses. In addition, new malarial strains have developed over the years that have become resistant to the drugs.

For more information check the website of the **Centre for Disease Control** (CDC) in Atlanta, United States: www.cdc.gov.

Food and Water

Caution should be taken when eating, because food is often prepared in insanitary conditions. Doctors advise abstaining from shellfish, especially shrimp. Fruit and vegetables should be peeled before eating. Cooking them is a better idea. Some doctors advise avoiding even raw vegetables like the herbs and lettuces served with *pho*, Vietnamese noodle soup, and spring rolls. If you must, make sure

Drinking Water

Do not drink tap water unless it has been boiled properly and avoid ice in drinks, especially in the countryside. Imported bottled water is available in most cities, but beware of bottles that are refilled with tap water. Check to make sure the bottle has a seal.

All large hotels provide free thermoses of boiled water (while some provide kettles) and you can usually ask for a free refill.

you eat in restaurants that are crowded. Because most places do not have refrigeration, food is thrown away at the end of the day. If a place is crowded, it is a good sign that the establishment serves freshly cooked food. Avoid the usual suspects: mayonnaise and eggs that have not been cooked thoroughly, for example.

Emergencies

Should you have an accident or an emergency health problem in Vietnam, you may want to consider evacuation to Singapore or Bangkok for treatment. Vietnam has no shortage of well-trained doctors, but hospital services and supplies are in very short supply. Visitors to Vietnam should therefore have health insurance that includes repatriation (or at least travel to Bangkok or Singapore for emergency treatment).

Medication

Imported pharmaceutical drugs are available in Hanoi and Ho Chi Minh City, but it is best to bring a small supply of medicine to cope with diarrhoea, dysentery, eye infections, insect bites, fungal infections and the common cold.

What to Wear/Bring

The main thing to consider is the weather, as it can be freezing cold in the mountainous north and at the same time hot and humid along the central coast. If you are travelling in the north or the Central Highlands during the winter months definitely bring jeans and a warm coat or sweater. It seems that it is always raining somewhere in Vietnam, so lightweight rain gear is essential.

In the hot months, dress cool but conservative. Many Vietnamese cannot understand why foreigners insist on wearing shorts, tank tops and sleeveless T-shirts when they have the money to dress well. For the Vietnamese, appearance is very important, so if you are dealing with an official of any rank make sure you are dressed appropriately.

It is best to travel light in Vietnam. One medium-sized bag and a daypack will provide more than enough room to carry everything you'll need to survive and enough space for the things you'll buy in Vietnam. There is an extensive black market for smuggled consumer goods in both Hanoi and Ho Chi Minh City, so don't worry about running out of something important.

However, it is difficult to find earplugs. It is difficult to get access to news in Vietnam, so you may want to bring a small short-wave radio. Film is available in cities; check the expiry date.

Money Matters

Vietnam's unit of currency, the dong (pronounced *dome*), currently circulates in bank notes of 500,000, 100,000, 50,000, 20,000, 10,000, 5,000, 2,000, 1,000, 500, 200 and 100 and coins of 5,000, 2,000, 1,000, 500 and 200 denominations. The larger notes are now made of polymer plastic, which ensures a longer life span and fewer copies. The dong's value against the dollar has remained stable in the past few years: at just over 15,000 dong per US$1. Care should be taken when exchanging money or receiving change. The 20,000 dong notes and the 5,000 notes – both widely used – are the same size and colour (blue) and easily confused.

All transactions are supposed to be conducted in Vietnamese dong; in practice, a dual-currency system is in effect. That is, most purchases can be made in US dollars as well as Vietnamese dong. However, often shops, restaurants and taxi drivers insist on a lower conversion rate – such as 15,000 dong to US$1 – when using dollars. To avoid haggling, it is better to carry some Vietnamese dong.

Another potential problem is the quality of the notes themselves. Although the Vietnamese dong notes are often ripped, faded and crumpled, Vietnamese are reluctant to accept US dollars that are not crisp and new. Before taking US dollars from a bank, you should inspect them to make sure they have no stray marks or tears, or appear old, as some people may refuse damaged notes.

Exchanging Money

Vietnam's black market for US dollars isn't what it used to be. The difference between the street rate and the bank rate is very small – if there is any difference at all.

Changing money on the street is a foolish proposition. Because the dong notes are the same size and in same or similar colours, you can easily be given the wrong denomination. As the old saying goes, you get what you pay for. It's best to stick to a bank *(see page 346)* or currency exchange booth, of which there are many in all the major cities.

Apart from banks, hotels, travel agencies, restaurants and cafés catering to foreigners will also exchange dollars at bank rates. It is also possible to change dollars at almost any jewellery or gold shop; sometimes the rate is slightly higher than the bank rate. Look for a shop with the sign *Vang* (gold). They are easily identifiable because their signs usually have bright, gold-coloured letters.

Be prepared to be offered two exchange rates: one for denominations of 50 and 100 US dollars, and a lower rate for smaller denominations.

Some banks will also exchange Vietnamese dong for other currencies: Euro, Japanese yen, Australian dollars, for example but it's better to bring US dollars.

Note: the Vietnamese currency is not convertible so you cannot legally bring in or take out dong as a foreigner.

Travellers' Cheques and Credit Cards

Travellers' cheques in US dollars are accepted in most banks and in major hotels, but not in shops and not in smaller hotels and restaurants. Major credit cards are becoming widely accepted. A fairly high commission – 3 percent is standard – is tacked on to your bill when using credit cards, however.

Cash advances can be withdrawn from major credit cards (again with the 3 percent commission) from major banks, including Vietcombank. Vietcombank will also provide cash dollars for US dollar travellers' cheques – for a 2 percent charge.

Price Differences

Because of low income levels among the Vietnamese, a state subsidy scheme for Vietnamese nationals has given rise to a two-tiered price system for some goods and services, setting one price for nationals and another for foreigners. Hotel rooms are subject to the dual pricing system and there is little you can do about this, although the law is set to abolish this in the near future.

Internet Research

Vietnam National Administration of Tourism
www.vietnamtourism.com
Vietnam Airlines
www.vietnamairlines.com
Hotel booking agencies
www.asiatravel.com/vietnam
www.asia-hotels.com
www.vietnamrooms.com
Vietnam Investment Review
www.vir.com.vn
WWF Indochina
www.wwfindochina.org
Ministry of Foreign Affairs
www.mofa.gov.vn

Getting There

BY AIR

The easiest and quickest way of getting to Vietnam is by air. International flights to Hanoi and Ho Chi Minh City are available, and direct flights to Da Nang are now also available.

On leaving Vietnam, travellers have to pay an international departure tax of US$12 (HCMC) and US$14 (Hanoi).

Ho Chi Minh City

Ho Chi Minh City is connected via international flights to Bangkok, Beijing, Busan, Dubai, Frankfort, Guangzhou, Hong Kong, Kaohsiung, Kuala Lumpur, Macau, Manila, Melbourne, Moscow, Nagoya, Osaka, Paris, Phnom Penh, Seoul, Singapore, Sydney, Taipei, Tokyo, Vienna, Vientiane and Zurich.

From the Airport

Ho Chi Minh City's **Tan Son Nhat Airport** in Tan Binh District is located 7km (4½ miles) from the city centre. Most of the big hotels offer shuttle services but this has to be arranged ahead of time. Bus 152 takes you to the Pham Ngu Lao area past the Reunification Hall, for 2,500 dong. A taxi into town should cost around US$5. Even in a metered taxi, agree on the price beforehand as taxi drivers have been known to take long circuitous routes through heavy traffic.

Airline Offices in Ho Chi Minh City

Air France, 130 Dong Khoi, District 1, tel: 08-829 0981, www.airfrance.com/vn.
Asiana Airlines, 34 Le Duong, District 1, tel: 08-822 2622, www.flyaisana.com.
British Airways, 114A Nguyen Hue, District 1, tel: 08-930 2937, www.britishairways.com.
Cathay Pacific Airways, 115 Nguyen Hue, District 1, tel: 08-822 3203, www.cathaypacific.com.
China Airlines, 132-134 Dong Khoi, District 1, tel: 08-825 1388/89, fax: 08-825 1390, www.china-airlines.com.
China Southern Airlines, 21-23 Nguyen Thi Minh Khai, District 1, tel: 08-823 5588, fax: 08-829 68/010, www.cs-air.nl.
Eva Air, 19 Nguyen Hue, District 1, tel: 08-822 4488, fax: 08-821 7215, www.evair.com.
KLM Royal Dutch Airlines, 130 Dong Khoi, tel: 08-823 1990, fax: 08-822 0537, www.klm.com.
Korean Airlines, 34 Le Duan, District 1, tel: 08-824 2878 www.koreanair.com.
Lao Airlines, 93 Pasteur, tel: 08-822 6990, fax: 08-822 6990, www.laoairlines.com.
Lauda Air, 1 Dong Khoi, District 1, tel: 08-829 7117, www.laudaair.com.
Lufthansa, 25 Nguyen Hue, District 1, tel: 08-829 8529, fax: 08-829 8537, www.lufthansa.com.
Malaysia Airlines, 116 Nguyen Hue, District 1, tel: 08-842 4950/829 2529, www.malaysiaairlines.com.
Qantas, 37 Ton Duc Thang, District 1, tel: 08-910 5373, fax: 08-910 5376, www.qantas.com.
Siem Reap Airways International, 132 Dong Khoi, District 1, tel: 08-823 9289, www.siemreapairways.com.
Singapore Airlines, Suite 101, Saigon Tower Building, 29 Le Duan, District 1, tel: 08-823 1588, www.singaporeair.com.
Thai Airways, 65 Nguyen Du, District 1, tel: 08-829 2810, www.thaiairways.com.
United Airlines, 17 Le Duan, District 1, tel: 08-823 4755 www.unitedairlines.com.vn.
Vietnam Airlines, 116 Nguyen Hue, District 1, tel: 08-832 0320, www.vietnamairlines.com. Open Mon–Sat 7.30am–6pm, Sun and holidays: 8.30am–12.30pm.

Hanoi

Hanoi is served by direct flights from Bangkok, Beijing, Berlin, Dubai, Frankfort, Guangzhou, Hong Kong, Kuala Lumpur, Kunming, Moscow, Paris, Phnom Penh, Seoul, Siem Reap, Singapore, Sydney, Taipei, Tokyo and Vientiane.

From the Airport

Hanoi's **Noi Bai Airport** is 35km (21 miles) form the city centre. There are bus and taxi services from the airport into central Hanoi. There is a designated taxi rank outside the arrival hall. Official metered taxis to the city cost US$10. Do not use unlicensed taxicabs.

Airport minibuses depart directly for the city; tickets cost US$2, terminating at 2 Quang Trung Street. Air-conditioned buses (No. 7) also depart for the city (2 hours); tickets cost 25,000 dong.

Airline Offices in Hanoi

Aeroflot Russian Airlines, Daeha Business Center, 360 Kim Ma, tel: 04-771 8718, fax: 04-771 8522, www.aeroflot.ru.
Air France, 1 Ba Trieu, tel: 04-825 3484.
Asiana Airlines, 4 Da Duong, tel: 04-822 2671.
British Airways, 25 Ly Thuong Kiet, tel: 04-934 7239.
Cathay Pacific, 49 Hai Ba Trung, tel: 04-826 7298.
Malaysia Airlines, 15 Ngo Quyen, tel: 04-826 8820.
Singapore Airlines, 17 Ngo Quyen, tel: 04-826 8888.
Thai Airways, 44B Ly Thuong Kiet, tel: 04-826 6893.
United Airlines, Main floor, Hilton Hanoi Opera, 1 Le Thanh Tong, tel: 04-933 3183, fax: 04-933 3186.
Vietnam Airlines, 1 Quang Trung Street, tel: 04-832 0320.

BY SEA

Though Ho Chi Minh City has a bustling port, few visitors choose to arrive here by boat. While the occasional cruise ship may dock here for a short stay, there is no ongoing regular service. Visitors who do arrive on cruise ships often find themselves shunted off on strictly regimented tours, all organised by the government-run monopoly Vietnam Tourism.

BY ROAD

It is possible to enter Vietnam from China (and vice versa) at the Lang Son and Lao Cai border crossings.

A few travellers travel overland from Laos to Vietnam by bus via the Lao Bao border crossing in Central Vietnam. Although definitely not common practice it is becoming more popular among budget travellers. Travellers also can enter Vietnam by crossing the border with Cambodia at Moc Bai, which is only a few hours by road from Ho Chi Minh City or at Vinh Xuong, located about 30 km (18 miles) north of Chau Doc.

Practical Tips

Media

Vietnam News is the only national daily English-language newspaper in circulation. The weekly newspaper *Vietnam Investment Review* and the monthly magazine *Vietnam Economic Times* are both products of joint ventures between foreign companies and Vietnamese government entities; they carry eminently less propaganda than the wholly state-run periodicals, which are published in Vietnamese, English and French.

The Review and The Times publish supplements – the weekly *Timeout* and the monthly *Guide*, respectively; these are useful guides to entertainment and events in both Hanoi and Ho Chi Minh City.

Ho Chi Minh City

There is a newsstand called Lao Dong on Nguyen Hue Street in Ho Chi Minh City, across from the Rex Hotel near City Hall. In Ho Chi Minh City, though, one doesn't need to look far to find foreign-language newspapers and magazines; in heavily touristed areas, such as Pham Ngu Lao Street, vendors stroll through restaurants. If they don't have a title you want, ask – they will often be able to secure it within a few minutes. In addition, all the big hotels have newsstands that sell a range of international newspapers and magazines.

Hanoi

In striking contrast with Ho Chi Minh City, finding decent reading material in Hanoi or anywhere else in Vietnam is difficult. A few pavement vendors on Trang Tien Street sell foreign newspapers and there is a bookstore, near the corner of Ngo Quyen, and sometimes a pavement newsstand, but your best bet is one of the big hotels for the *Asian Wall Street Journal*, *International Herald Tribune* and *Financial Times* as well as English-language newspapers from Bangkok, Hong Kong and Singapore. They arrive at least a day late. Most hotel shops also sell French newspapers and fashion magazines and English-language news weeklies, such as *Time*.

Radio & Television

The Voice of Vietnam, the official radio station, broadcasts twice a day. Two stations transmit worldwide from Hanoi and Ho Chi Minh City in 11 languages: English, French, Spanish, Russian, Mandarin/Cantonese, Indonesian, Japanese, Khmer, Lao and Thai.

International stations can be received on a shortwave receiver.

Many hotels, even smaller ones, now have satellite dishes that beam in BBC and CNN in addition to Star TV, which broadcasts a healthy dose of old and new American TV shows and a sports channel. Vietnam TV has nightly broadcasts in English and French.

Telecommunications

International telephone connections are quite clear from Vietnam but the cost of calling overseas still ranks among the highest in the world. Direct calls can be placed from hotels, post offices and residences. Reverse charges are not allowed for foreigners, however. Expect to pay up to US$3 a minute to call the United States, Europe, or Australia. Hotels will add a surcharge that can make calls about US$5 a minute.

Domestic calling is still haphazard. The circuits between Hanoi and Ho Chi Minh City tend to be quite busy, so calling from one city to another can take awhile – so be patient.

When calling a city in Vietnam from overseas, dial the country code 84, followed by the area code but drop the prefix zero. When making a domestic call from one province or city to another in Vietnam, dial the area code first (including the prefix zero). Note: local calls within the

Cheap Calls

To make an international direct dial call from Vietnam, dial the international access code: 00, followed by the country code, the area code and the local telephone number. To save on hefty international call charges, however, dial the prefix 171 or 178 before the international access code 00. These codes can also be used to call long distance within Vietnam. Alternatively, use an international calling card to call home.

Many internet cafés now have internet-assisted calls at very low rates. SIM cards for your overseas mobile phones are also available at the main post offices or the many mobile phone shops.

same province/city do not require the area code.

Area Codes: Cities

Vietnam's country code is 84

Buon Ma Thuot	050
Chau Doc	076
Can Tho	071
Da Lat	063
Da Nang	511
Hai Phong	031
Hanoi	04
Ho Chi Minh City	08
Hoi An	0510
Hue	054
Long Hai	064
My Tho	073
Nha Trang	058
Phan Thiet	062
Quy Nhon	056
Rach Gia	077
Vinh	038
Vung Tau	064

Area Codes: Provinces

Ben Tre	075
Binh Dinh	056
Can Tho	071
Chau Doc	076
Ha Tien	077
Ha Tinh	039
Hoa Binh	018
Khanh Hoa	058
Lai Chau	023
Lao Cai	020

Quang Nam Da Nang	0511
Quang Tri	053
Rach Gia	077
Soc Trang	079
Son La	022
Tay Ninh	066
Thai Binh	036
Thanh Hoa	037
Thua Thien-Hue	054
Tien Giang	073
Vinh Long	070
Vinh Phu	021
Yen Bai	029

Mobile Phones

Most mobile phone users with a roaming facility will be able to hook up with the GSM 900/1800 network that Vietnam uses. The exceptions are users from Japan and the North America (unless they have a tri-band phone). Check with your service provider before leaving.

To save on expensive mobile phone charges, consider using a local prepaid phone card which will give you a local number to use in Vietnam. These are available at Vina Phone and Mobi Phone shops in Ho Chi Minh City and Hanoi.

Note: all mobile phone numbers in Vietnam begin with the prefix 090, 091, 095, 098.

Faxes

Fax machines are available in post offices and hotels. Be warned that the cost is quite high. A one-page fax overseas costs about US$1.50. Hotels will charge even more.

Postal Services

Post offices are open every day from 7am to 8pm. Every city, town and village has a post office of some sort, and the service is remarkably reliable and fast. Within the country, mail reaches its destination within three days, sometimes faster. There is also an express mail service that promises overnight delivery for about US$10. Overseas mail delivery however is neither reliable nor very fast.

For the philatelist, a stamp shop (Buu Dien Tem Choi) at 14 Trang Hung Dao sells Vietnamese stamps from the days of Indochina (1946)

to the present. Many post offices now have meter machines so stamps are no longer necessary.

Telegram and telex services are available 24 hours a day in larger cities. Most post offices in major cities also have fax machines where messages can be sent or received.

Central Post Offices

Hanoi, 75 Dinh Tien Hoang, tel: 04-825 2730.
Ho Chi Minh City, 2 Cong Xa Paris, tel: 08-823 2541, 827 1173.
Hue, 8 Hoang Hoa Tham.
Da Nang, 45 Tran Phu.
Can Tho, Hoa Binh Street.
Nha Trang, 4 Le Loi, tel: 073-828 000. There is a branch office on Le Thanh Ton Street just east of Tran Hung Dao Street, tel: 073-823 866.
Da Lat, 14–16 Tran Phu Street, tel: 063-822 586, 821 003.
Hai Phong, 5 Nguyen Tri Phuong.
Vung Tau, Ha Long City, Vuon Dao crossroads, tel: 064-852 689.

Internet Cafés

Internet, e-mail and chat services proliferate in the larger cities and are becoming increasingly common in the more out of the way places too. Internet chat rooms are massively popular with young Vietnamese too. Vietnam's two main Internet service providers are FPT and VNN.

Internet cafés abound at major streets in Ho Chi Minh City and Hanoi, and costs range from 100–500 dong a minute. Most big hotels in both cities also provide Internet and e-mail services (although fees are much higher than at the cafés). Post offices are another place where you will find public Internet access. Note that the government firewalls websites it deems objectionable.

Business Hours

Most banks, public services and state-run offices work Monday to Friday, from 7.30–8.30am, closing between 4–5pm. Museums roughly

follow the same hours, but generally close on Monday (sometimes Fridays) and sometimes closed for lunch from 11.30am–1pm. Tourist-orientated shops work a seven-day week from 9am to 7–9pm. Markets open early, winding down by late afternoon. Pagodas and temples open until the evening.

Electricity

The voltage in the cities and towns is generally 220V, 50 cycles, but sometimes 110V in the rural areas. Electric sockets are standard European or American. It is a good idea to bring adapter plugs in case your plugs do not fit the sockets, which sometimes fit two round pins, other times three pins. If you do not have the correct size plug, however, it is easy to buy an adaptor.

If you bring a computer to Vietnam, you must use a surge suppressor to protect your circuits. Taiwanese-made voltage regulators can be bought at computer stores in Vietnam to give greater protection.

Tipping

Tipping is generally not part of the culture although many waiters, bar staff and especially taxi drivers can get annoyed if they are not tipped by foreigners. Major hotels include a 5 percent service charge on their bills. As with anywhere, if you receive particularly good service tip 5–10 percent or 10,000–20,000 dong or so, but avoid giving excessive amounts. At times taxi drivers, cyclos and motorbike taxi drivers will claim they have no change, but this is often a ruse. Depending on your mood and generosity you might be inclined to let it go and get on with your day. This annoyance tends to be more prevalent in Hanoi than in Ho Chi Minh City.

Medical Services

While Vietnam has ably trained medical professionals, it may not have adequate equipment and facilities to treat all emergencies. Make sure that you have comprehensive medical cover in case you have to be airlifted to Bangkok or Singapore for treatment.

Ho Chi Minh City

International SOS, 65 Nguyen Du, District 1, tel: 08-829 8424; emergency 24 hours, tel: 08-829 8424, fax: 08-828 8551, www.internationalsos.com.
Columbia Saigon 24-hour clinic, 8 Alexandre de Rhodes, District 1, tel: 08-823 8888, fax: 08-823 8454. Western doctors on duty 24 hours a day.
International Medical Centre, 1 Han Thuyen, District 1, tel: 08-827 2366; emergency 24 hours, tel: 08-827 2366, fax: 08-827 2365, www.vietnam-medical.org.

Hanoi

International SOS, Central Building, 31 Hai Ba Trung, tel: 04-934 0666; emergency 24 hours, tel: 04-934 0555, www.internationalsos.com.
Hanoi Family Medical Practice, Van Phuc Diplomatic Compound, Kim Ma Road, tel: 04-843 0748, fax: 04-846 1750, www.vietnam medicalpractice.com. Run by Westerners. 24-hour emergency.
Vietnamese French Hospital, 1 Phuong Mai Street, tel: 04-574 0740; emergencies tel: 04-574 1111; www.hfh.com.vn. International standard hospital, with French and Vietnamese doctors. Facilities include 24-hour accident and emergency ward, and dental clinic.

Fake Drugs

Medicine of almost every kind can be bought at pharmacies – *nha thuoc* – but there is a problem of fake drugs being sold.

Banks

There are several foreign banks now in operation in Hanoi and Ho Chi Minh City. It is possible to receive cash advances on a major credit card (usually with a commission of 3 percent) and to open bank accounts. Money can also be wired into bank accounts from overseas banks.

To exchange money or cash travellers' cheques, it is advisable to go to a Vietnamese bank rather than a branch of an international bank group, as the Vietnamese government requires foreign banks to charge higher fees.

Ho Chi Minh City

Several banks are located on or near Chuong Duong Street, which runs parallel to the Saigon River.

Many of the larger hotels offer foreign exchange services *(see page 342)* but often at lower rates. Though there are an increasing number of foreign banks in Ho Chi Minh City, you'd do well to check with the individual bank beforehand as to the exact services they offer. Many have ATMS. Some can only cash travellers' cheques issued by their bank. Others are not licensed to conduct foreign exchange. To cash travellers' cheques or to receive cash advances on a major credit card, it is best to stick to one of the government-run banks like Vietcombank.
ANZ Bank, 11 Me Linh Square, District 1, tel: 08-829 9319.
Calyon, 21–23 Nguyen Thi Minh, District 1, tel: 08-829 5048.
Citibank, 15th Floor, 115 Nguyen Hue, District 1, tel: 08-824 2118.
HSBC, 235 Dong Khoi St, District 1, tel: 08-829 2288.
Vietcombank, 29 Ben Chuong Duong, District 1, tel: 08-823 0310.

Hanoi

ANZ Bank, 14 Le Thai To, tel: 04-825 8190.
Calyon, 49 Hai Ba Trung, 5th Floor, tel: 04-825 8102.
Citibank, 17 Ngo Quyen, tel: 04-825 1950.
Standard Chartered Bank, 27 Ly Thai To, tel: 04-825 8970.
Vietcombank, 78 Nguyen Du, tel: 04-826 8039.

Tourist Information

Vietnam's tourism industry lags behind other Asian countries (and for some travellers this may be a good thing). Even in the capital, you won't find official tourist information kiosks giving out impartial free information.

The official representative for Vietnam's tourism – domestically and overseas – comes under the government-operated **Vietnam National Administration of Tourism** (VNAT; www.vietnamtourism.com). It is more involved in the construction of new hotels and infrastructure development rather than in providing tourist services. State-run "tourist offices" under the VNAT (or local provincial organisations) are merely tour agents out to make money and are not geared towards meeting travellers' requirements. For tours, car hire and information, you are better off with privately-run tour agencies, but be sure to use established, reliable outfits.

Travel Agencies

Ho Chi Minh City

Sinh Café, 246-248 De Tham, District 1, tel: 08-836 7338, e-mail: info@sinhcafevn.com, www.sinhcafevn.com. Overwhelmingly popular among budget travellers, Sinh Café offers, in addition to the usual travel services and inexpensive guided tours to the Mekong Delta and the Cu Chi Tunnels, the popular option of an "Open Tour" ticket on their daily bus between Ho Chi Minh City and Hanoi with stops at Da Lat, Nha Trang, Hoi An and Hue, all for under US$30. Travellers have given the agency mixed reviews for uneven level of service so proceed with caution.
Ann Tours, 58 Ton That Tung Street, District 1, tel: 08-833 4356, e-mail: info@anntours.com, www.anntours.com. A classy professional outfit, Ann Tours is a private agency offering everything from ticket booking to organising tours throughout the country. Friendly service and knowlegeable guides, all at competitive prices.
Dana Tours, 77 Nguyen Cuu Van, Ward 17, tel: 08-840 8288, fax: 08-898 0191, www.danatourvietnam.com. Dana Tours specialises in small groups.
Exotissimo, Saigon Trade Centre, 37 Ton Duc Thang, District 1, tel: 08-825 1723, e-mail: vietnam@

exotissimo.com, www.exotissimo.
com. Main office of one of the
leading tour operators in the
Mekong region – handling groups,
incentives, adventure, nature and
special-interest travel. With offices
in Vietnam, Cambodia, Laos,
Myanmar and Thailand.
FidiTourist, 127–129A Nguyen Hue
Street, District 1, tel: 08-914 1414,
e-mail: fidi@fiditourvietnam.com,
www.fiditourvietnam.com. One of
the better high-end Vietnamese-run
tour operators. It has over 200
affiliates around the world and can
organise anything from tours
covering the regular sights to
adventure treks.
Peace Tour Co, 60 Vo Van Tan
Street, District 3, tel: 08-930 3325,
e-mail: peacetour@hcm.vnn.vn,
www.peacetour.com.vn. This
company works under the auspices
of the Vietnam Women's Union. It
organises cultural tours and treks in
the Mekong Delta. Has 80 multi-
lingual guides and offices in Da
Nang and Hanoi.
Saigon Tourist, 49 Le Thanh Ton,
District 1, tel: 08-829 8914,
e-mail: sgtvn@hcmc.netnam.vn,
www.saigon-tourist.com. Operating
since 1975, government-owned
Saigon Tourist is the oldest tour
provider in Vietnam, but not
neccessarily the best. It has a wide
array of tours, although for what you
get the price is high compared with
other private outfits.
Vietravel, 190 Pasteur Street,
District 3, tel: 08-822 8898, fax:
08-829 9142, www.vietravel-vn.com,
c-mail: victravel@fmail.vnn.vn. A
wide range of mid-priced and higher-
end tours including golfing, scuba
and cruising tours.

Da Lat
Dalattourist, 35 Tran Hung Dao, tel:
063-822 520, www.dalattourist.com,
e-mail: dalattour@dalattourist.com.
Tailormade trips and package tours
to Dalat and beyond. Has branch
offices in Hanoi and HCMC.
Dalat Holidays, 42B Le Dai Hanh
Street, tel: 063-829 422, e-mail:
langbian@hcm.vnn.vn. Reliable
operator that organises tours with a
strong eco theme. Its adventure

Out Of Bounds Areas

Vietnam for the most part is open
to tourism, yet some areas in the
country remain closed to tourists
and even to the Vietnamese
themselves. Some areas in the
Central Highlands around Daklak
and Pleiku are occasionally
closed to foreigners due to local
unrest. The north's high plateau
region is occasionally off limits;
Cao Bang and Lang Son in the
north on the Chinese border and
Cam Ranh Bay in the centre.
However it is not impossible to
visit these areas "unofficially",
although it's not advisable to
tempt fate too far. Any area can
suddenly become sensitive these
days due to the growing
discontent with the present
system, and if your request to
visit an area is stonewalled, this
may be the reason.

tours that combine mountain biking,
treks to hill-tribe villages and
abseiling are tops.

Nha Trang
Khanh Hoa Tourist, 1D Tran Hung
Dao, tel: 058-822 753. This
provincial tourism office also
organises a variety of tours but
prices are on the high side.
Sailing Club Divers, 72 Tran Phu, tel:
058-813 788, fax: 058 527 006,
www.sailingclubvietnam.com.
The Sailing Club offers a variety of
up-market dive packages as well as
diving courses.
Sinh Café, 10 D Biel Thu, tel:
058-811 981, e-mail: sinhcafent@
dng.vnn.vn. Branch office of the
famous Sinh Café in Ho Chi Minh
City, this mainly caters to the
budget traveller.

Hanoi
Sinh Cafe, 25 Hang Be Street, tel:
04-836 4212, fax: 04-756 7862,
www.sinhcafevn.com. The Hanoi
branch of this popular budget travel
agent. Can organise just about
everything at a decent price. The
bargain "Open Tour" bus which
services the length of the country is
very popular.

Ann Tours, 18 Duong Thanh Street,
Hoan Kiem District, tel: 04-923
1366, e-mail: info@anntours.com,
www.anntours.com. The northern
branch of this popular and efficient
tour operator.
Buffalo Tours, 9–13 Hang Muoi, tel:
04-828 0702, fax: 04-826 9370,
e-mail: info@buffalotours.com,
www.buffalotours.com. Highly
recommended agency with tailor-
made and package tours, including
kayaking around Halong Bay and
mountain biking in the northern
mountains.
Exotissimo, 26 Tran Nhat Duat
Street, tel: 04-828 2150, fax:
04-928 0056, www.exotissimo.
com. This is a reliable agency that
offers quality tailor-made and
scheduled tours, travel services
and adventure trips.
Explore Indochina, Rm. 500, Tuoi
Tre Hotel, 2 Tran Thanh Tong Street,
Tel: 091 352 4658 (mobile),
www.exploreindochina.com. Expert,
expatriate Minsk riders with in-depth
regional knowledge, run tailor-made,
off-the-beaten track Minsk
motorbiking tours in the north.
Handspan Adventure Travel,
80 Ma May, tel: 04-926 0589,
fax: 04-933 2378, e-mail:
handspan@hn.vnn.vn,
www.handspan.com. This adventure
travel company applies an "eco-
ethos" concept to tourism in
Vietnam with tailor-made tours
involving adventure kayaking,
mountain biking, 4WD's, trekking
and also more sedate journeys.
Hidden Hanoi, tel: 091 225 4045
(mobile), e-mail: anhiddenhanoi@
yahoo.com, www.hiddenhanoi.com.
In-depth, small-group cultural and
culinary tours of Hanoi (including
walking tours in more unusual city
areas) led by local experts.
Rainbow Tours, 80 Tran Nhat Duat,
tel: 04-928 3040, fax: 04-928
3041, www.holidaysvietnam.com.
A wide range of prices and options
for package tours. Caters for mainly
small groups.

Hue
Hue Tourist Co, 18 Ly Thuong Kiet
Street, tel: 054-821 626, fax: 054-
825 814.

Huong Giang Tourist Company, 2 Nguyen Cong Tru, Hue, tel: 054-826 070, e-mail: hgtourist@dng.vnn.vn, www.huonggiangtourist.com. An old stalwart operating since 1976. Offers trips around the Hue area and beyond including Bach Ma National Park and Phu Vang with its hot water springs.

Da Nang

Danatours, 76 Hung Vuong Street, Danang, tel: 0511-825 653, e-mail: danamarie@dng.vnn.vn, www.danatourvietnam.com. Another state-run tour operator and one of the few operating out of Danang. It can arrange onward transport, individual and group travel, but service may not be as good as some competitors.

Quang Nam – Danang Tourist Co., 92A Phan Chu Trinh, Da Nang, tel: 0511-822 112, fax: 0511-821 560.

Hoi An

Hoi An Tourist Service Co, 6 Tran Hung Dao, Hoi An, tel: 0510-861 362, fax: 0510-861 636.

Hoi An Travel Agency, www.hoianworldheritage.org. Tickets for Hoi An Old Town are sold here.

Sinh Café, 18B Hai Ba Trung, tel: 0510-863 948, e-mail: sinhhoian@dng.vnn.vn, www.sinhcafevn.com

Embassies & Consulates

Embassies in Hanoi

Australia, 8 Dao Tan Street, Ba Dinh District (beside the Daewoo Hotel), tel: 04-831 7755, fax: 04-831 7711, www.ausinvn.com.

Canada, 31 Hung Vuong Street, tel: 04-734 5000, fax: 04-734 5049, www.dfait-maeci.gc.ca/vietnam.

Cambodia, 71 Tran Hung Dao, tel: 04-942 4788, fax: 04-942 3225.

Denmark, 19 Dien Bien Phu Street, tel: 04-823 1888, fax: 04-823 1999, www.ambhanoi.um.dk.

France, 57 Tran Hung Dao, tel: 04-943 7719, fax: 04-943 7236, www.ambafrance-vn.org.

Germany, 29 Tran Phu, tel: 04-843 0245, fax: 04-845 3838, www.hanoi.diplo.de.

Italy, 9 Le Phung Hieu, tel: 04-825 6246, fax: 04-826 7602, www.embitalyvietnam.org.

Laos, 22 Tran Binh Trong, tel: 04-942 4576, fax: 04-822 8414.

Netherlands, 360 Kim Ma, tel: 04-831 5650, fax: 04-831 5655, www.netherlands-embassy.org.vn.

New Zealand, 63 Ly Thai To, tel: 04-824 1481, fax: 04-824 1480, e-mail: nzembhan@fpt.vn.

Singapore, 41-43 Tran Phu, tel: 04-823 3966, fax: 04-825 1600, www.mfa.gov.sg/hanoi.

Sweden, 2 Nui Truc, tel: 04-726 0400, fax: 04-823 2195, www.hanoi.embassy.ud.se.

Switzerland, 44B Ly Thuong Kiet, tel: 04-934 6589, fax: 04-934 6591.

Thailand, 63-65 Hoang Dieu, tel: 04-823 5092, fax: 04-823 5088.

United Kingdom, 31 Hai Ba Trung Street, tel: 04-936 0500, fax: 04-936 0561, www.uk-vietnam.org.

United States, 7 Lang Ha, tel: 04-772 1500, fax: 04-772 1510, http://usembassy.state.gov/vietnam.

Consulates in Ho Chi Minh City

Australia, 5-B Ton Duc Thang, District 1, tel: 08-829 6035, fax: 08-829 6035.

Canada, 235 Dong Khoi, District 1, tel: 08-824 5025, fax: 08-829 4528.

Denmark, 115 Nguyen Hue, District 1, tel: 08-821 9375, fax: 08-821 9371.

France, 27 Nguyen Thi Minh Khai, District 1, tel: 08-829 7231, fax: 08-829 1675.

Germany, 126 Nguyen Dinh Chieu, District 3, tel: 08-822 4385, fax: 08-823 1919.

Italy, 203 Dong Khoi, District 1, tel: 08-829 8721, fax: 08-829 8723.

Laos, 93 Pasteur, District 1, tel: 08-829 7667, fax: 08-829 9272.

Netherlands, Saigon Tower, 29 Le Duan, District 1, tel: 08-823 5932, fax: 08-823 5934.

New Zealand, 235 Dong Khoi, District 1, tel: 08-822 6907, fax: 08-822 6905.

Singapore, Saigon Centre, 8th Floor, 65 Le Loi, District 1, tel: 08-822 5173, fax: 08-914 2938.

Thailand, 77 Tran Quoc Thao, District 3, tel: 08-932 7637, fax: 08-932 6002.

United Kingdom, 25 Le Duan, District 1, tel: 08-823 2604, fax: 08-829 5257.

United States, 4 Le Duan, District 1, tel: 08-822 9433, fax: 08-822 9434.

Security & Crime

In general, Vietnam is a safe country to travel in and violent crimes against foreigners are very rare. However, there are dangers. In Ho Chi Minh City, tourists are increasingly becoming the victims of pickpockets, snatch and grab thieves and hotel burglars. Always leave valuables in a hotel safe, and when you must carry cash, put it in a money belt inside your clothes. When walking, or travelling in a cyclo, keep one hand firmly on handbags and cameras.

Be careful of pavement vendors selling maps, books and souvenirs or people begging for money, especially in Hanoi and Ho Chi Minh City. They can easily distract you while a friend slips a hand into your pocket, grabs your wallet and is gone before you know it. Watches are easy prey, too, and even glasses are ripped off by passing motorcyclists. Pickpocketing often involves children and women with babies as well.

Daylight travel is pretty safe on Vietnam's highways and trains. There are isolated cases of highway robbery and hijacking, but foreigners are rarely the targets of these attacks. When travelling on buses or trains always stay with your bag. If you intend on taking the train, bring a cable lock to secure your bags to your bed frame when you are sleeping.

The Vietnamese are extremely friendly and generous, but caution must be taken when making casual acquaintances. On Vietnamese buses and trains, foreigners have been knocked out by drugged food and drink offered to them by fellow passengers. Vietnam also has its fair share of con men, who hustle everything from Cambodian gems to "genuine" bones of missing American servicemen.

Etiquette

Arguing in a loud and aggressive manner will get you nowhere very fast in Vietnam. Complaining about bad service in an international standard hotel is fine, but will fall on deaf ears at a humble guesthouse in the northern provinces. The very notion of service is alien to the majority of the Vietnamese and vociferous complaining doesn't help. On the other hand, a smile can go a long way, open doors and win favours. The Vietnamese prefer a co-operative approach to just about everything. However, be careful as some Vietnamese "co-operate" more out of self interest than for the sake of helping you.

As with many other parts of Asia, Confucian attitudes remain strong and seniority demands respect whatever the circumstances. The eldest male member of any group is invariably "in charge". At any party it is the eldest who gets served first, gets to eat and sing first and generally dictates the course of events. In the larger cities Western-style short dresses, sleeveless tops and shorts are common. However, it is best to dress conservatively as the Vietnamese stake a great deal upon first impressions. Generally speaking, the grubby backpacker look won't win you any friends.

Single Women Travellers

Women should take extra precautions when travelling alone, as some Vietnamese men can be very aggressive. Their behaviour ranges from following you to your hotel room to physically touching you (usually after being egged on by their male friends).

Also, Vietnam can be a very difficult country for an Asian woman, or a woman of Asian descent, travelling with a white male companion. Some Vietnamese men mistakenly assume such women to be Vietnamese and prostitutes, and can often be verbally abusive.

Women staying alone in budget hotels may want to consider using an extra lock on the door at night. Women, especially, should be careful late at night. The streets tend to be deserted, giving a sense of false confidence to many travellers. In fact it is in such situations that a cyclo or xe om driver is more likely to hassle a woman. This is most likely in Ho Chi Minh City, Da Nang and Nha Trang. It is a good idea to travel in groups or to arrange transportation ahead of time. A good driver can steer you clear of trouble; paying a little extra to have a driver wait for you is better than having to find a way of getting home late at night.

What a Racket

Bring earplugs. Vietnam is a noisy country and the noise starts when Vietnamese arise – usually by 5.30am.

Villages and small towns offer no respite because it is here tourists will be wakened by early-morning loudspeaker broadcasts of martial music, calisthenics and economic victories. While these broadcasts sometimes start at 6am and only last half-an-hour, a 4.30am kickoff is not unknown and a two-hour blast, as in Sa Pa, is common.

The latest noise development is karaoke. Nearly every hotel has a karaoke lounge and many villages have a karaoke shack. Fortunately, performances are usually over by 10pm.

Travelling with Children

The Vietnamese love children and "foreign" looking kids, especially the blonde, blue-eyed variety, get a lot of attention wherever they go. Although the cities may not be the most comfortable places to travel around with the little ones, it isn't all that bad. Taxis are inexpensive and journeys are generally short within cities, and there is plenty to see and do. Travel between cities can be more of a strain and long distance bus or car travel can be extremely tiring, not to say harrowing. It is probably best to break the journey at regular intervals and try to use the plane when you need to cover long distances.

Disabled Travellers

With the traffic, the scarcity of lifts, clogged pavements and the sheer amount of people out and about on the streets, disabled travellers do not have an easy time in Vietnam. The roads are extremely treacherous and people don't tend to stop even for disabled Vietnamese people, especially in the major cities. But it's not impossible for adventurous disabled people with an easy-going attitude to get by. Make sure you plan well ahead and find out about hotel access. Generally the bigger hotels have wheelchair access, toilets and lifts for the disabled.

Gay Travellers

Travel in Vietnam is a relative breeze for gay people. Legally there is no law against homosexuality but Vietnamese people tend to be frown upon homosexual behaviour. Fortunately they are far too polite, shy or scared to say anything negative to you directly. Same-sex couples will not be questioned about sharing the same hotel room.

However, it is quite common to see open affection between the same sexes in cafés or on the street among the Vietnamese. Men can often be seen holding hands together and women too even though they are probably not homosexual at all. On the other hand, it is quite rare to see open affection between men and women.

In 2002, Vietnamese writer Bui Anh Tan won a literary prize for his novel A World Without Women, which tackles the issue of homosexuality in Vietnam. However, the fact that one of the novels main characters is suddenly "cured" of homosexuality and becomes attracted to women makes the whole premise of the novel somewhat laughable. Still, the very fact that a novel like this was published at all in Vietnam shows a measure of progress in attitudes.

Getting Around

By Air

Domestic flights are operated by **Vietnam Airlines** (www.vietnam airlines.com) to the following destinations: Buon Ma Thuot, Da Lat, Da Nang, Dien Bien, Hai Phong, Hanoi, Hue, Nha Trang, Phu Quoc, Pleiku, Quy Nhon, Rach Gia, Tuy Hoa and Vinh. A second domestic carrier **Pacific Airlines** (www.pacific airlines.com.vn) flies only from Hanoi to Ho Chi Minh City (and vice versa) and from the latter to Da Nang.

Vasco Airlines, 114B Bach Danh, tel: 08-844 5999 to Ca Mau in the deep south and Con Dao Island.

Flying is by far the best way to travel if you intend to visit only a few cities in Vietnam. A Vietnam Airlines flight from Hanoi to Ho Chi Minh City costs under US$200. Vietnam Airlines also flies to places that are very time-consuming to get to by other means, like Phu Quoc Island and Pleiku. The major problem with flying is getting seats. Popular flights fill up a few days before departure, so it is imperative to book flights early.

You can use credit cards to buy airline tickets in Hanoi and Ho Chi Minh City, but in other cities you may be asked to pay cash. Tickets are sold by most travel agents in the big cities (see pages 346–8), or book directly with the airline office at Ho Chi Minh City and Hanoi (see page 343). Note that the domestic departure tax is included in the ticket price.

For information on transport from the Ho Chi Minh City and Hanoi airports to the respective city centres, see page 343.

By Train

Train travel, operated by **Vietnam Railways** (www.vr.com.vn) in Vietnam is very slow. Due to the existence of only one track along the coast, train travel in Vietnam is subject to frequent delays. The fastest express train from Hanoi–Ho Chi Minh City (called the Reunification Express) covers 1,730 km (1,073 miles) in 30 hours, with the slower ones up to 41 hours because of the numerous stops they make. If you need to get somewhere fast you can forget about the train. However, if you want to leisurely soak up the Vietnamese countryside the train has a lot to offer including spectacular mountain passes, ocean views, tunnels,

City Transport

• Cyclo

No trip to Vietnam is complete without a ride in a cyclo (three-wheeled trishaw). Vietnam has thousands of cyclo drivers who can be hired by the kilometre or the hour. Expect to pay at least 8,000 dong for a short ride or 30,000 dong for an hour. It is essential to bargain with cyclo drivers beforehand. And make sure you carry enough small change as drivers often claim they cannot change anything larger than a 10,000 dong note. As a rule, halve their first offer and work up. Most cyclo drivers in the south are former ARVN soldiers and speak a little English. Cyclo drivers are indispensable as guides, sources of historical information, and as the procurers of hard-to-find items.

• Motorcycle Taxis

A faster way to get around town in Hanoi and Ho Chi Minh City is a motorcycle taxi, called a xe om (say-ohm) or Honda om, which literally means "hugging taxi" as

passengers grab onto the driver's waist. You don't need to look for xe om; they will find you. Fares are actually cheaper than on cyclos, and of course the ride is quicker. Some of the drivers navigate the roads badly, however, so be careful. If a driver seems unsafe, tell him to stop, get off, and pay him. Find another driver. Some women travellers have reported problems with xe om drivers getting too friendly; be especially careful travelling late at night.

• Bicycles

Bicycles can be rented for as little as US$1 per day from tourist cafés in Hanoi and Ho Chi Minh City. If you plan on staying in one city for a month or two, consider buying one, as prices are very reasonable. If you have a mechanical problem or a tyre puncture, don't worry: there are stands set up on practically every street corner (most repairs will cost a few thousand dong). New cheap Chinese-made bicycles are very common and cost about US$25.

• Taxis

Air-conditioned metered taxis are common in the major cities and fares are cheap. Make sure you travel with a clearly marked company taxi as unmarked taxis do patrol the streets, overcharge and can cause problems for you especially after dark. There are different flag fall rates and per kilometre charges so check with your hotel reception.

• Buses

There are more city buses on the roads these days and services are improving. However, most Vietnamese prefer to use their own transport. One company (Saigon Star Bus, tel: 08-864 2762) operates routes within Ho Chi Minh City. Fares are low, about 3,000–5,000 dong. However the service is not really geared up for tourists. Timetables either do not exist or are out of date and bus stops are often difficult to locate. Save yourself uneccessary headaches and use taxis, cyclos or motorbike taxis.

Romantic Train Travel

If you don't want to be herded with the masses on Vietnam's public trains, opt for style and luxury on board the comfortable **Victoria Express** train car which travels from Hanoi to Lao Cai, the jump-off point for trips to the Sa Pa highlands. There are four trips a week and journey time is about 8 hours. Both twin and four berth cabins are available and prices are cheaper when purchased as part of a room package at the Victoria Sa Pa Hotel. For more information, call the Ho Chi Minh City office at tel: 08-837 3031 or check www.victoriahotels-asia.com.

French-era bridges and an opportunity to get to know the Vietnamese up close and personal.

There are five classes of train travel in Vietnam: hard seat, soft seat, hard sleeper, soft sleeper, and soft sleeper with air-conditioning – this last option available only on certain trains. Expect to pay at least US$60 for a berth in a four-person compartment on the fastest express train from Hanoi to Ho Chi Minh City (or vice versa). There are two express trains every day and berths are reserved fast, so try to make reservations two days in advance. There is a kitchen car on most trains, and waitresses serve food, or you can buy snacks from the many vendors that service the train at local stops.

There are also local train services on the Hanoi–Ho Chi Minh City line that branch out to various coastal cities. Lines also run from Hanoi northwest to Lao Cai, east to Hai Phong, and north to Lang Son.

Ho Chi Minh City

Trains leave Ho Chi Minh City for the northern coastal towns from the Railway Station, which is located at 1 Nguyen Thong Street, District 3 (tel: 08-823 0105). The ticket office is open daily 7.15–11am and 1–3pm. Book at least 2–3 days in advance for sleepers. Alternatively, many travellers find it worthwhile to pay extra to have a travel agency purchase the tickets.

Hanoi

Hanoi's Railway Station is at 120 Le Duan Street, tel: 04-825 3949 (located at the far Western end of Tran Hung Dao Street). The ticket office is open daily from 7.30–11.30am and 1.30–3.30pm.

By Bus

If you are planning to travel long distance by bus, it is probably best to use one of the modern, comfortable tourist bus services. Although more expensive than the local buses, at least you are guaranteed a seat to yourself, there is no livestock on board and space to stretch your feet. The bus will pick you up from your hotel and send you to your hotel of choice, or the one the travel agency recommends. The buses often work in partnership with sister travel agencies and hotels, but there is no undue pressure to stay at the recommended hotels. Visit the offices of Sinh Café in Hanoi or Ho Chi Minh City (see below) to book your tickets. Alternatively, your hotel can probably make all the arrangements for a small fee.

If you're feeling adventurous, you could take local buses. However, you will almost certainly be overcharged (at three or four times the local rates) and be stuck in an overcrowded deathtrap with a suicidal driver. It might be authentic, but the fun can very soon wear thin if you have a 10-hour journey ahead of you.

Ho Chi Minh City
Private Buses

A highly popular option is to buy an "open ticket" on an air-conditioned private bus as this allows you to get on or off anywhere along the route with few restrictions. With a Ho Chi Minh City–Hanoi ticket costing less than US$30, this is certainly one of the cheaper ways of getting around. Travelling this way does reduce the opportunity to interact with locals or to get off the beaten path, but realistically, this is the price one pays for hassle-free travelling in Vietnam.

The easiest way is to book with one of the agencies in the Pham Ngu Lao area or contact **Sinh Café**, 246-248 De Tham, District 1, tel: 08-836 9420, www.sinhcafevn.com.

Public Buses

From Ho Chi Minh City, public buses serve all the major cities in the Mekong Delta:

My Tho (72 km/45 miles)
Can Tho (169 km/105 miles)
Ben Tre (86 km/53 miles)
Vinh Long (136 km/85 miles)
Soc Trang (231 km/144 miles)
Bac Lieu (276 km/172 miles)
Ca Mau (344 km/214 miles)
Tra Vinh (194 km/121 miles)
Long Xuyen (184 km/114 miles)
Rach Gia (280 km/174 miles)
Ha Tien (360 km/224 miles).

Both express and local buses, as well as mini-buses, leave from Mien Tay Station, which is at 137 Hung Vuong in Binh Chanh District. In addition, there is an express bus service to My Tho that departs from the Cho Lon Bus Station. Getting to many destinations in the Delta often requires a combination of bus journey and ferry crossings.

Road Conditions

The road network has improved greatly in the past 5 years. In the southern delta, the romantic ferries crossing the various tentacles of the Mekong have almost disappeared. From Ho Chi Minh City north to Hanoi, paved roads range from four-lane and single-access toll roads to two lanes through the centre of towns. The northern circle route, from Hanoi to Dien Bien Phu and Sapa, is also in excellent condition, although off the main highway, one still needs a Russian jeep or the hardy Minsk motorbike.

Hanoi
Private Buses

The popular "open ticket" on a private air-conditioned bus operates from Hanoi to Ho Chi Minh as well. Contact the Hanoi branch of **Sinh**

Café at 25 Hang Be Street, tel: 04-836 4212, fax: 04-756 7862, www.sinhcafe.com.

Public Buses

Hanoi has four main bus stations. For the northwest, **Kim Ma station** is on the corner of Nguyen Thai Hoc and Giang Vo. **Gia Lam station** serves the northeast (and China). Southern buses leave from **Giap Bat station** on Giai Phong road. (7 km or 4 miles south of the train station) and **Son La station** on Nguyen Trai road has buses to Dien Bien Phu and west of Hanoi.

By Car & Minivan

In Hanoi and Ho Chi Minh City it is possible to hire good Japanese cars and minivans to go on day trips or week-long excursions. Hiring a driver and vehicle in Vietnam is good value if your travelling party is large enough to spread out the cost. Ask to go for a test ride before committing to a driver to see if the

Road Warriors

A few adventurous (some would say foolhardy) souls have managed to see Vietnam with cars and motorcycles that they have unofficially purchased or rented in Hanoi and Ho Chi Minh City. Second-hand motorcycles are slightly cheaper. In the north, the Belarus-made Minsk is best for tackling the mountainous areas. Contact the **Minsk Club** in Hanoi online at e-mail: minskclub@crosswinds.net, or www.minskclubvietnam.com to see where you can buy a Minsk. Or visit **Cuong's Adventure Biking Shop** in Hanoi at 1 Luong Quyen, tel: 0913-518 772.

In Dalat, **Easy Riders** (e-mail: wingstours@hotmail.com) offer custom-made tours to the Central Highlands. **Explore Indochina** (www.exploreindochina.com) offers small-group motorcycle adventures to exotic destinations throughout Vietnam's spectacular northern mountains.

car is running properly. Expect to pay a minimum of US$40 a day for a comfortable car (with driver) from a reputable tourist agency. Car costs can be expensive, but it is always a good idea to negotiate.

Sometimes drivers from one part of the country are reluctant to drive into another. Drivers from Ho Chi Minh City, for example, are hesitant to drive to Hanoi. Licence plates on cars denote what province the car is from, and drivers fear police will give cars from out of the region trouble. A driver in Ho Chi Minh City might agree to take you as far as Da Nang, for example, and then help you find another driver to take you further.

If you plan to drive yourself, something few people in their right minds would recommend in Vietnam, take note that recent changes in the law require foreigners to have a Vietnamese driving licence and that any bike over 50cc must have wing mirrors. However, laws are vague for visiting tourists. The Vietnamese also recognise international driving permits issued by the Automobile Association. However, more than one foreigner has been arrested for driving without a licence. Bao Viet is the largest insurance company supplying the required accident insurance but often, in an accident, the Vietnamese will hold you until you have reimbursed the other party – even if it wasn't your fault.

Given the road conditions and the absence of traffic rules, you are better off hiring a car with a driver.

Boats

To reach the more remote areas in the Delta, local boats have to be hired. A popular daily hydrofoil service between Ho Chi Minh City and Can Tho was discontinued at time of press due to several accidents, some of them fatal.

The hydrofoil service from Ho Chi Minh City to Vung Tau however is still is operation and is the easiest way of getting there. There are 16 trips daily. In Ho Chi Minh City, travellers can purchase hydrofoil tickets at the port (Ben Bach Dang, tel: 08-825 3880) across from the Majestic Hotel.

Where to Stay

Booking a Room

In the recent past, Vietnam's hotel infrastructure, particularly in the north and centre, was far from international standard. Rooms were often under-equipped or equipped with fixtures and appliances that don't work, and power cuts were frequent. Room rates were also quite high, often more than the standard of accommodation warranted, especially in contrast with other poor Asian countries.

A few years ago, demand outstripped supply, but following a hotel boom in the mid-1990s in Ho Chi Minh City and Hanoi, the reverse is true today. Hotel development in the country is flourishing and visitors are spoiled for choice. International chains, with international services and prices, can be found in all major cities. They include business centres, high-speed Internet access, in-house tour agencies and spas. Hotel staff is friendly and helpful. In smaller towns, family-run guesthouses offer the personal touch, and you may even be invited to have dinner with the family.

The easing of restrictions on joint venture developers has been rewarded with a boom in luxury resorts with private beaches and five-star restaurants. Some maps being sold in book stores will show resorts and casinos that are just being planned and not yet in existence – a testimony to the unflagging optimism of the Vietnamese.

When booking your accommodation, it is always a good idea to ask for a discount. Also, hotels offer better rates for corporate clients, repeat customers and people booked by a travel agent. Thus, all of the published rates listed here should only be taken as a guide.

As disposable income increases, more and more Vietnamese are travelling. During the school holidays, the beaches are full and at Tet in late January or early February, buses and trains are packed with domestic travellers. On days that the lunar calendar indicates as auspicious for weddings, you'll also find many honeymooners flocking to Dalat. If you are making a trip during any of these times, it would be a good idea to book ahead.

Note: Higher-end hotels usually charge an additional tax of about 10 percent and a service charge of about 5 percent.

Price Categories

Below US$50:	$
US$50 to US$100:	$$
US$100 to US$150:	$$$
More than US$150:	$$$$

South Vietnam

HO CHI MINH CITY

Note: all the hotels listed in this section are found in the prestigious District 1 city centre.

Caravelle Hotel
19 Lam Son Square
Tel: 08-823 4999, Fax: 08-824 3999
www.caravellehotel.com
With a prime city centre location, this one-time favourite with journalists has been thoroughly renovated and expanded into yet another modern high-rise. The roof of the Caravelle offers a great view of Central Saigon. With 335 rooms, including suites and service apartments as well as several restaurants and bars, it's possible to believe you never left home. Very popular downtown hotel. **$$$–$$$$**
Renaissance Riverside Hotel
8-15 Ton Duc Thang Street
Tel: 08-822 0033, Fax: 08-823 5666
www.renaissancehotels.com/sgnbr

International-class 21-storey hotel with nice views of the Saigon River. The hotel offers 329 tastefully appointed rooms and 20 suites (including a club floor), café, restaurant, business centre and fitness centre with a huge swimming pool. Not least of all, the hotel has a central location. **$$$–$$$$**
Saigon Prince Hotel
63 Nguyen Hue Boulevard
Tel: 08-822 2999, Fax: 08-824 1888, Reservations: 08-822 5666
www.duxton.com
This modern, spacious hotel complete with fountains and wide, curving staircases right in the heart of downtown attracts mostly business executives and tour groups. Serves Vietnamese, Singaporean, Japanese and Western cuisines. **$$$–$$$$**
Sheraton Saigon
88 Dong Khoi Street
Tel: 08-827 2828, Fax: 08-827 2929
www.sheraton.com/saigon
The vast 5-star Sheraton is the latest addition to the Saigon skyline boasting the highest bar in town and four restaurants to boot. Sumptuous rooms and restaurants and located on the hippest shopping street in Ho Chi Minh City. **$$$–$$$$**
Sofitel Plaza Saigon
17 Le Duan Boulevard
Tel: 08-824 1555, Fax: 08-824 1666
www.accorhotels.com
This posh 5-star hotel is a joint venture project with Hong Kong and Singapore investors. Opened in September 1998, it has friendly staff, tasteful rooms, full facilities including Western and Asian restaurants serving a variety of cuisines, and a rooftop pool offering great city views. **$$$–$$$$**
Bong Sen Hotel
117-123 Dong Khoi Street
Tel: 08-829 1721, Fax: 08 829 8076
www.hotelbongsen.com
Conveniently located in the middle of the Dong Khoi shopping district and in close proximity to a number of excellent Vietnamese and French restaurants, this is a reliable, unpretentious favourite with many guests. The Saigon Health Club is on the 6th floor. **$$–$$$**

Continental Hotel
132-134 Dong Khoi Street
Tel: 08-829 9201, Fax: 08-829 0936
www.continental-saigon.com
Built in 1880 and last renovated in 1989, this legendary French Colonial-style hotel with Chinese-style furniture tries hard to evoke a bygone era when Graham Greene haunted its corridors in the 1950s, and journalists sipped beers on the terrace during the war. Though facing stiff competition from a spate of newer hotels, the Continental's pleasant frangipani garden and excellent Vietnamese, Chinese and Italian restaurants still make it one of the more popular hotels in town. **$$–$$$**
Kim Do – Royal City Hotel
133 Nguyen Hue
Tel: 08-822 5914, Fax: 08-822 5913
www.kimdohotel.com
A Vietnamese standard '3 Star' hotel with fitness centre and jacuzzi suites. The rooms are comfortable enough and the hotel is close to all the downtown action and a stroll from the riverfront. **$$–$$$**
Legend Hotel
2A-4A Ton Duc Thang Street
Tel: 08-823 3333, Fax: 08 823 2333
Located along the Saigon waterfront and harbour offering great views along the river. There's an outdoor swimming pool as well as a jacuzzi and fitness centre. The hotel also houses three restaurants and a bar, with live music every weekend. **$$–$$$**
Majestic Hotel
1 Dong Khoi Street
Tel: 08-829 5514/7, Fax: 08-829 5510, www.majestic-saigon.com
Originally built in 1925, this old classic has since undergone numerous renovations, the last in 1995. Overlooking the Saigon River, the hotel offers splendid suites and the usual full facilities, including restaurants, bars and a fitness centre with a swimming pool. **$$–$$$**
New World Hotel
76 Le Lai
Tel: 08-822 8888, Fax: 08-823 0710
www.newworldvietnam.com
One of the largest hotels in town, the New World is of late looking a

little lacklustre on the outside. It offers the usual modern conveniences, five restaurants and full facilities including an outdoor pool, tennis courts and a golf driving range. Caters to many business travellers and Japanese tour groups. **$$–$$$**

Norfolk Hotel
117 Le Thanh Ton
Tel: 08-829 5368, Fax: 08-829 3415
This pleasant 3-star hotel is located near the business and shopping districts and offers comfortable rooms. A monthly "Second Friday" social allows business people to exchange ideas. The hotel caters to business people and journalists. Health club and business centre. **$$–$$$**

Oscar Saigon Hotel
68A Nguyen Hue Boulevard
Tel: 08-829 2959, Fax: 08-829 2732
www.oscarsaigon.com
Formerly the Century Saigon Hotel, this Hong Kong joint venture is located in the central business district. The hotel has a rather bland air about it, with 109 adequate but unspectacular rooms. Health club, conference rooms, business centre, and the requisite disco and karaoke rooms. **$$–$$$**

Rex Hotel
141 Nguyen Hue Boulevard
Tel: 08-829 2185, Fax: 08-829 6536
www.rexhotelvietnam.com
That this hotel is still a popular choice has less to do with its garish mix of Eastern and Western decorative styles than with its colourful history of having once housed US military officers. Great location with full facilities. The popular rooftop garden with singing birds provides 24-hour dining as well as excellent views of bustling downtown Saigon. **$$–$$$**

Palace Hotel
56-66 Nguyen Hue Boulevard
Tel: 08-824 4236, Fax: 08-824 4230
www.palacesaigon.com
Restaurant, bars, disco, video, swimming pool, souvenir shop, money changing facilities and laundry. Convenient location on one of the busiest shopping boulevards and the restaurant offers a great view over the city. **$$**

Windsor Saigon Hotel
193 Tran Hung Dao Street
Tel: 08-836 7848, Fax: 08-836 7889
www.windsorsaigonhotel.com
Located less than a kilometre from downtown Saigon, this boutique hotel with balconies and wide arched windows has 64 spacious rooms and caters to many Europeans as well as long-term business travellers. Pleasant ambience, full facilities, excellent restaurant and bakery. **$$**

Giant Dragon Hotel
173 Pham Ngu Lao Street
Tel: 08-836 1935, Fax: 08-836 4759
e-mail: giantdragonhotel@1saigon.net
Located near the heart of backpackers' quarters, this mid-range hotel offers 34 rooms with air-conditioning, phones and satellite TV. Restaurant on premises serves Western and Asian cuisine. Friendly staff. Easy access to travellers' cafés. **$–$$**

Que Huong – Liberty 2 Hotel
129-133 Ham Nghi Boulevard
Tel: 08-822 4922, Fax: 08-823 0776
www.quehuonghotel.com
The second in a string of four Liberty Hotels, this one is centrally located near the Ben Thanh Market. Rooms are basic. Breakfast is included. A restaurant on the 10th floor affords a panoramic view of the city. **$–$$**

Price Categories

Below US$50:	**$**
US$50 to US$100:	**$$**
US$100 to US$150:	**$$$**
More than US$150:	**$$$$**

LONG HAI

Anoasis Beach Resort
Domain Ky Van, Long Hai,
Baria-Vung Tau
Tel: 064-868 227, Fax: 064-868 229
www.anoasisresort.com.vn
This is so far the nicest resort in still-developing Long Hai. Set around 32 acres (16 hectares) of tropical parkland and overlooking the ocean with a private beach, this secluded hotel offers accommodation in thatched cottage bungalows. Facilities and services include a business centre, conference rooms, a swimming pool, beach sports, a golf range, and even helicopter service. **$$$–$$$$**

Thuy Duong Hotel
Phuoc Hai Village, Long Dat District, Baria-Vung Tau
Tel: 064-886 215, Fax: 064-886 180
e-mail: tranchauld@hcm.vnn.vn
This modest resort nestled between the hills and the beach offers accommodation in a variety of bungalows and cottages. In addition to the usual resort amenities, a swimming pool, tennis courts, Jacuzzi, sauna, karaoke and billiards can be found here. **$**

VUNG TAU

Palace Hotel
1 Nguyen Trai Street
Tel: 064-856 265, Fax: 064-856 878
e-mail: palacevt@hcm.vnn.vn
www.palace.oscvn.com
Located a block from Front Beach, this hotel, which has 120 guest rooms, appears to be popular with Western and Asian tour groups. The rooms are somewhat tacky but the staff is friendly. In-house restaurants serve a la carte Vietnamese, Asian and European cuisines. **$$**

Royal Hotel
36 Quang Trung Street
Tel: 064-859 852, Fax: 064-859 851
The Royal Hotel overlooks Front Beach. All 53 guest rooms are equipped with IDD telephone, satellite TV, mini-bar and safe deposit box. Full business and entertainment facilities. **$$**

Cap Saint Jacques Hotel
169 Thuy Van Street
Tel: 064-859 519, Fax: 064-818 026
e-mail: csjhotel@hcm.vnn.vn
Formerly the Phuong Dong Hotel, this modern complex on Back Beach boasts 109 comfortable rooms, some with great sea views. Facilities include 2 restaurants serving Western and Asian cuisines, a swimming pool, tennis court, gymnasium, nightclub and karaoke. **$–$$**

Rex Hotel
1 Le Qui Don Street
Tel: 064-852 135, Fax: 064-859 862
e-mail: rex.osc@hcm.vnn.vn
Centrally located on Front Beach,
this 8-storey hotel has 75 average
rooms, 3 restaurants serving Asian,
European and seafood specialities,
health club, sauna, karaoke,
souvenir shops and a very nice
pool. Bears no relation to the Rex
Hotel in Ho Chi Minh City. **$–$$**

Grand Hotel
2 Nguyen Du
Tel: 064-856 469, Fax: 064-856 088
Right on Front Beach, this low-rise
offers two separate wings, 70
rooms, and all the entertainment
facilities you could want. **$**

MEKONG DELTA

Can Tho
Golf Can Tho Hotel
2 Hai Ba Trung
Tel: 071-812 210, Fax: 071-812 282
e-mail: golfcanthohtl@hcm.vnn.vn
This hotel has 101 river view
rooms, a business centre, pool and
sunset dinners in the 10th floor
restaurant. **$$–$$$**

Victoria Can Tho Hotel
Cai Khe Ward, Can Tho City
Tel: 071-810 111, Fax: 071-829 259
www.victoriahotels-asia.com
Opened in October 1998, this is
the most luxurious hotel in the
whole Delta. Located on its own
promontory on the banks of the
Hau River several kilometres from
the centre of town, this resort has
88 tasteful rooms and 8 suites.
With full facilities, business centre,
conference rooms, swimming pool,
and its own jetty. Hotels has plans
to develop ecotourism in the area
as a way of attracting guests.
Restaurant offers Western and
Asian cuisine. **$$–$$$**

Phuong Dong Hotel
62, 30 Thang 4, Can Tho
Tel: 071-812 199, Fax: 071-820 133
www.phuongdonghotel.com
Has 40 spacious rooms and the
ubiquitous combination of sauna,
massage and karaoke facilities.
$–$$

Saigon Can Tho Hotel
55 Phan Dinh Phung Street
Tel: 071-825 831, Fax: 071-823 288
www.saigoncantho.com
A flashy modern hotel with 46
rooms. Facilities include a business
centre, conference room, fitness
centre with sauna and massage,
and billiard and karaoke rooms. The
restaurant serves Western, Chinese
and Vietnamese food. **$–$$**

My Tho
Rang Dong Hotel
25, 30 Thang 4
Tel: 073-874 400
One of the nicer places in town, this
mini-hotel next to the river has 22
rooms with air-conditioning,
telephones and hot water. **$**

Song Tien Hotel
101 Trung Trac
Tel: 073-872 009, Fax: 073-884 745
Located in the centre of town, this
8-storey hotel is the largest in My
Tho, with 40 rooms and a view of
the city from the hotel's terrace.
Rooms with fans run at US$6,
those with air-conditioning range
from US$6 to 20. **$**

Long Xuyen
Dong Xuyen Hotel & Restaurant
9A Luong Van Cu
Tel: 076-942 260, Fax: 076-942 268
e-mail: dongxuyenag@hcm.vnn.vn
360 rooms from US$25. Currently
the largest hotel in town. **$**

Long Xuyen Hotel
19D Nguyen Van Chung
Tel: 076-841 927, Fax: 076-842 483
e-mail: longxuyenhotel@hcm.vnn.vn
Both air-conditioned rooms and fan-
cooled rooms available. **$**

Chau Doc
Victoria Chau Doc Hotel
32 Le Loi, Chau Doc
Tel: 076-865 010, Fax: 076-865 020
www.victoriahotels-asia.com
93 well-appointed rooms in a stylish
setting going for between
US$40–120. Located on the banks
of the Bassac River. Not the most
popular of the Victoria chain of
hotels in Vietnam, but worth
checking out if you are passing
through. **$$**

Ben Da Nui Sam Resort
Quoc Lo 91
Tel: 076-861 745, Fax: 076-861 530
e-mail: bendanuisam@hcm.vnn.vn
New hotel offering 62 rooms and a
large restaurant. Also has disco,
health club and tennis courts.
$–$$

Trung Nguyen
86 Bach Dang
Tel: 076-866 158, Fax: 076-868 674
e-mail: trunghotel@yahoo.com
This new mini hotel is clean and
fitted with air-conditioning in every
room and private balconies
overlooking the busy street. **$**

Vinh Long
Cuu Long Hotel
1, 1 Thang 5
Tel: 070-823 656, Fax: 070-823 848
e-mail: cuulonghotelvl@hcm.vnn.vn
This hotel is in need of renovation.
53 rooms in total. Located on the
riverfront with facilities including
restaurant, bar, laundry and
karaoke rooms. **$**

Tai Nguyen
60/12 Duong Mau Than Phuong 3
Tel: 070 827 235, Fax: 070-830 829
Located outside the city centre, this
is the newest and by far the best
hotel in town. **$**

Ben Tre
Dong Khoi Hotel
16 Hai Ba Trung
Tel: 075-822 240, Fax: 075-822 410
Basic rooms in the centre of town
going for US$20–25. **$**

Trade Union Hotel
36 Hai Ba Trung Street
Tel: 075-825 082
14 rooms from US$6–12 just down
the road from the Dong Khoi Hotel. **$**

Rach Gia
1 Thang 5 Hotel
137 Nguyen Hung Son Street
Tel: 077-862 103, Fax: 077-866 917
18 air-conditioned rooms – when
the electrics are working. The
plumbing is also very
temporamental. Very basic
accommodation at US$10–15. The
food, however, is good. **$**

Diamond Hotel
95 Nguyen Trung Truc
Tel: 077-877 667, Fax: 077-923 035

e-mail: toanphatkg@hcm.vnn.vn
A basic hotel that caters to travellers taking the speed boat to Phu Quoc. **$**

Palace Hotel
243 Tran Phu Street
Tel: 077-863 049, Fax: 077-867 423
Probably the nicest, most modern hotel in town. Usual entertainment and karaoke facilities. **$**

Ha Tien

Ha Tien Hotel
36 Tran Hau
Tel: 077-851 563, Fax: 077-951 102
e-mail: khachsanhatien@vnn.vn
Located centrally across from the docks and next to the market, this hotel has 32 rooms, with prices ranging from $20–$50. **$**

Hai Yen
15 To Chau
Tel: 077-851 580, Fax: 077-851 889
This adequate hotel is clean and has the usual services and facilities. **$**

Phu Quoc Island

Cassia Cottages
Ba Keo Beach
Tel: 077-848 395
www.cassiacottage.com
This villa offers a range of rooms, from family-sized cottages to rooms for singles or twin-share. Also available is an in-house restaurant and a new swimming pool, which faces the sea. Transfers from the airport are provided. **$–$$**

Tropicana Phu Quoc Resort
Duong Tho
Tel: 077-847 127, Fax: 077-847 128
www.tropicanavietnam.com
Comfortable bungalows and rooms

Dong, Not Dollars?

Officially, hotels are now required to accept payment only in Vietnamese dong. However, many still accept US dollars. Small ones prefer US dollars and will always quote rates in dollars. Many establishments, large and small, will now take major credit cards. Some charge a commission so make sure you ask first.

in this attractive, landscaped resort with its own beach 10 minutes south of Duong Dong Town. Organises fishing and snorkelling trips to the An Thoi islands. **$–$$**

Bo Resort
Ong Lang Beach
Tel: 091-364 0520 (mobile)
www.boresort.com
This new guesthouse consists of fisherman's cottages re-constructed on a hillside. If peace, quiet and absolute privacy are what you crave, Bo Resort is for you. **$**

Thang Loi Bungalows
(contact Rheinhard Mueller)
Tel: 077-0918 073494 (mobile)
Fax: 077-846 144
www.phu-quoc.de
This pleasant resort run by a German couple is set far from all the other resorts in a coconut and cashew nut plantation with a pleasant, although rocky beach. There are 10 basic wooden bungalows with shower and toilet. The one biggest complaint is the amount of insects. Access is by motorbike taxi. **$**

PHAN THIET

Bamboo Village Resort
36 Nguyen Dinh Chieu
Tel: 062-847 007, Fax: 062-847 095
www.bamboovillageresortvn.com
This resort offers a pleasant all-bamboo environment. For accommodation, take your pick from 20 thatched-roof lodges, 3 newly-designed villas, and 20 hexagonal bamboo bungalows. There is an in-house restaurant serving Western and Asian cuisines. Also available are volleyball courts and a children's playground. **$$–$$$**

Blue Ocean Resort
54 Nguyen Dinh Cheiu
Tel: 062-847 322, Fax: 062-847 351
www.blueoceanresort.com
36 pleasant rooms. The resort has a swimming pool, decent bar and the restaurant serves Asian and European food. **$$–$$$**

Coco Beach
58 Nguyen Dinh Chieu
Tel: 062-847 111, Fax: 062-847 115

www.cocobeach.net
34 bungalows all with sea views. Tastefully designed landscaped gardens. The restaurant has a fantastic evening seafood grill buffet and all-day service to guests lounging on the beach. **$$–$$$**

Novotel Ocean Dunes Resort
1 Ton Duc Thang
Tel: 062-822 393, Fax: 062-825 862
www.accorhotels-asia.com
This large Club Med-style hotel with 123 rooms is surrounded on three sides by the 18-hole Ocean Dunes Golf Course. Facilities include two pools, a private beach, tennis courts, conference rooms. **$$–$$$**

Phu Hai Resort
Km 8, Ham Tien
Tel: 062-812 799, Fax: 062-812 797
www.phuhairesort.com
44 standard rooms and 19 deluxe villas and a large swimming pool. Located right on the beach. **$$–$$$**

Rach Dua Tropico Resort
68 Nguyen Dinh Chieu, Km 19, Ham Tien, Mui Ne
Tel: 062-847 001, Fax: 062-847 153
www.asiarachduaresort.com
This resort has 25 comfortable air-conditioned bungalows designed in traditional Vietnamese style. **$$–$$$**

Saigon Mui Ne Resort
55 Nguyen Dinh Chieu
Tel: 062-847 324, Fax: 062-847 307
www.saigonmuineresort.com
A series of bungalows and low-rise apartments set in a coconut palm-strewn resort with central swimming pool and jacuzzi. The food is not the greatest but the setting more than makes up for that. **$$–$$$**

Victoria Phan Thiet Resort
Km 9 Phu Hai
Tel: 062-813 000, Fax: 062-813 007
www.victoriahotels-asia.com
One of the more luxurious resorts in Mui Ne, the Victoria features 50 cottages, either with sea or garden views. Family cottages are also available. Full facilities, conference room, bike and car rentals, private beach, freshwater pool and Jacuzzi, it's all here. Restaurant serves Western, Asian and local cuisine but the food can be disappointing. Transfer to and from Ho Chi Minh City can be arranged. **$$–$$$**

Sailing Club Resort
24 Nguyen Dinh Chieu, Ham Tien
Tel: 062-847 442, Fax: 062-847 441
www.sailingclubvietnam.com
One of the newer resorts in Mui Ne.
The Sailing Club has landscaped
gardens and deluxe ocean view
villas and bungalows with nice
bathrooms. The resort has a
swimming pool and a full range of
watersports activities on offer. **$$**

The Beach
18 Nguyen Dinh Chieu Street
Tel: 062-847 626, Fax: 062-847 336
e-mail: thebeach@hcm.vnn.vn
The latest addition to the Mui Ne
beachfront with outdoor swimming
pool, jacuzzi and sauna, beachfront
parasols and deck chairs. Located
10 minutes from the Ocean Dunes
Golf Club. 40 rooms with garden
views. **$$**

Doi Duong Hotel
403 Le Loi, Phan Thiet
Tel: 062-822 108, Fax: 062-825 858
e-mail: doiduonghotel@hcm.vnn.vn
www.binhthuantourist.com
76 comfortable rooms located in
the town of Phan Thiet. Restaurants
serving Asian and European
cuisine. **$–$$**

Chez Nina
86 Nguyen Dinh Chieu
Tel: 062-847 177, Fax: 062-847 002
www.chezninaresort.com
For a glance back at what used to
be in Mui Ne, before the resorts
arrived, book a room at Chez Nina.
This small, charming, family-run
hotel on the beach has three
bungalows and two rooms in the
main house. Friendly and efficient
service. **$**

DA LAT

Sofitel Da Lat Palace
12 Tran Phu Street
Tel: 063-825 444, Fax: 063-825 666
www.accorhotels-asia.com
The only 5-star hotel in Da Lat, this
magnificent sprawling palace
overlooking Xuan Huong Lake is one
of the top luxury hotels in Vietnam.
Renovated in classic French colonial-
style, the hotel boasts 43 tastefully
furnished rooms, a gourmet French
restaurant, the usual full facilities,

as well as 2 tennis courts and easy
access to the 18-hole Da Lat Golf
Course. **$$$–$$$$**

Novotel Da Lat
7 Tran Phu Street
Tel: 063-825 777, Fax: 063-825 888
www.accorhotels.com
Formerly the Du Parc Hotel, this
hotel was renovated in 1997 and
is now managed by the same
company that manages its
neighbour the Sofitel Da Lat Palace.
Elegant rooms are the feature here,
but the one disadvantage of this
Novotel Da Lat is that it shares
many of its facilities, including the
restaurants and bar, with the Sofitel
Da Lat Palace, all of which are
located on the latter hotel's
premises. **$$$**

Price Categories

Below US$50:   **$**
US$50 to US$100:   **$$**
US$100 to US$150:   **$$$**
More than US$150:   **$$$$**

Golf 3 Hotel
4 Nguyen Thi Minh Khai Street
Tel: 063-826 042, Fax: 063-830 396
www.vietnamgolfhotel.com
This newly opened hotel in the
centre of the city is a good mid-
range choice. With 7 floors and 78
posh rooms, a restaurant serving
Asian, European and local food, the
usual entertainment facilities, and
the open-air Sky View Café on the
top floor. **$$–$$$**

Empress Hotel
5 Nguyen Thai Hoc Street
Tel: 063-833 888, Fax: 063-829 399
www.empresshotelvn.com
Located on the edge of picturesque
Xuan Huong Lake. Accommodation
comes in the form of 18 chalet
style rooms, and there is a small
restaurant serving international
cuisine. There is also a terrace bar
overlooking the lake. **$$**

Golf 2 Hotel
114, 3 Thang 2 Street
Tel: 063-826 031, Fax: 063-820 532
e-mail: golf2hot@hcm.vnn.vn
37 guest rooms and restaurant in the
centre of Dalat. Serves Vietnamese
and European cuisine. **$$**

Lyla Hotel
18 Nguyen Chi Thanh
Tel: 063-820 151
lylahotel@hcm.vnn.vn
Lyla is a friendly-family hotel with
clean, basic rooms. **$**

Minh Tam Villas
20A Khe Sanh
Tel: 063-82 2447
Located 3 km from the town centre,
this basic but comfortable hotel is
located on the grounds of a large
and well-kept flower garden and has
48 rooms. So popular is the garden
that it is now on the usual tourist
route. **$**

NHA TRANG

Ana Mandara Resort
Beachside, Tran Phu Boulevard
Tel: 058-829 829, Fax: 058-829 629
www.six-senses.com/ana-mandara
Nha Trang's nicest and most
luxurious beachside hotel and spa
is located in the southern part of
Nha Trang. There are 68 rooms and
16 villas. Full facilities, including a
watersports centre, diving school
and private beach, are featured.
Open-air restaurant serving
Vietnamese and international
cuisine. **$$$–$$$$**

Que Huong Hotel
60 Tran Phu
Tel: 058-825 047, Fax: 058-825 344
www.nhatrangtourist.com.vn
One of the newer, and therefore
nicer, government-run hotels, the
Que Huong is up to the
international standards of a 3-star
hotel. Rooms are comfortable and
equipped with satellite TV and IDD
phones. The usual entertainment
facilities, swimming pool and tennis
courts. Popular with Western tour
groups. **$$–$$$**

Yasaka Saigon Nha Trang Hotel
18 Tran Phu Boulevard
Tel: 058-820 090, Fax: 058-820 000
www.yasanhatrang.com
Newly opened, located opposite the
beach. There are 174 ocean view
rooms, swimming pool, fitness
centre and tennis courts. **$$–$$$**

Nha Trang Lodge Hotel
42 Tran Phu
Tel: 058-810 500, Fax: 058-828 800

www.nt-lodge.com
This Malaysian deluxe joint venture on the beachfront boasts 14 floors and 132 tasteful rooms, each one with an ocean view. Seafood restaurant with Asian and European dishes. Full facilities, business centre, and a swimming pool and tennis courts shared with the Vien Dong and Hai Yen hotels. **$$**

Bao Dai's Villa
Cau Da, Vinh Nguyen
Tel: 058-590 147, Fax: 058-590 146
www.vngold.com/nt/baodai
One of the last remaining examples of French colonial architecture, built in 1923. There are 48 rooms and five original villas together with two sea-view restaurants. Rooms are fairly basic, but you pay for the history of the place. **$–$$**

Ban Me Hotel
3/3 Tran Quang Khai
Tel: 058-829 499, Fax: 058-810 035
e-mail: banmehotel@dng.vnn.vn
New hotel located in the centre of the city within walking distance of the beach. Clean and comfortable, but basic airconditioned rooms. IDD and Internet service downstairs along with massage and sauna services. **$**

Hai Yen Hotel
40 Tran Phu
Tel: 058-822 828, Fax: 058-821 902
This mid-range option by the beach offers 107 unremarkable but adequate rooms and the usual facilities, including a seafood restaurant, dance hall, conference rooms, karaoke, massage, sauna, beauty parlour and shared swimming pool. Credit cards accepted. **$**

Thanh Thanh Hotel
98A Tran Phu
Tel: 058-824 657, Fax: 058-823 031
e-mail: thanhthanhhotel@dng.vnn.vn
Located somewhat inconveniently on the southern edge of town, this no-frills mini-hotel nevertheless gets good reviews from travellers for its clean rooms, many of which come with balconies and ocean views, friendly service and proximity to the beach. Rooms are from US$18 for a double, and US$15 for a single. A good choice if you don't mind being a little further from town. **$**

Whale Island Resort
Tel: 058-845 8096
Fax: 058-844 0205
www.whaleislandresort.com
An island hideaway off the coast of Nha Trang, this resort consists of 19 bungalows and a hilltop dormitory overlooking an empty sandy beach. Restaurant, snorkelling, scuba diving, and windsurfing. It is necessary to boook early. **$**

Central Vietnam

HUE

Century Riverside Inn
49 Le Loi Street
Tel: 054-823 390, Fax: 054-821 426
e-mail: cenhotvn@dng.vnn.vn
Recently remodelled, the Century commands a stunning view of the Perfume River. Breakfast in the restaurant is excellent. **$$**

Lang Co Beach Resort
Lang Co Town, Phu Loc District, Thua Thien
Tel: 054-873 555, Fax: 054-873 504
www.huonggiangtourist.com
This beach-side resort 50km from Hue airport has 60 comfortable rooms and serves traditional food from the Hue region. The bar offers a pleasant spot overlooking the Huong river. **$$**

Phu Xuan Hotel
9 Ngo Quyen Street
Tel: 054-823 278, Fax: 054-828 372
e-mail: pxhotel@dng.vnn.vn
Imposing hotel located right in the centre of Hue. 65 well appointed rooms and two restaurants serving local and international food. **$$**

Saigon Morin Hotel
30 Le Loi
Tel: 054-823 526, Fax: 054-825 155
www.morinhotel.com.vn
Originally built by French businessman Mr. Morin in 1901, this hotel still retains a touch of its colonial past although it was extensively renovated in 1997. Discounts are available for bookings via its website. **$$**

Thanh Noi Hotel
57 Dang Duong
Tel: 054-522 478, Fax: 054-527 209
www.viehotel.com/thanhnoihotel

Located near the citadel with 55 rooms, restaurant and pool. **$$**

Thuan Hoa Hotel
7 Nguyen Tri Phuong
Tel: 054-822 553/576
Fax: 054-822 470
e-mail: t_hoahtl@dng.vnn.vn
80 rooms – 44 air-conditioned, with fridge and telephone. Restaurant, terrace café, small boutique. **$–$$**

Dong Duong Hotel
2 Hung Vuong Street
Tel: 054-823 866, Fax: 054-825 910
e-mail: indochine-hotel@dng.vnn.vn
Close to the Perfume River, this hotel has 66 standard rooms and a restaurant serving local specialities. **$**

Green Hotel
2 Le Loi
Tel: 054-822 323, Fax: 054-824 527
This centrally located town hotel features 164 comfortable rooms. Along with the ubiquitous karaoke and massage services, the hotel can also organise adventure travel trips into the Hue environs and beyond. **$**

DA NANG

Royal Hotel
17 Quang Trung Street
Tel: 0511-823 295
Fax: 0511-827 279
e-mail: royalhotel@dng.vnn.vn
Four-storey hotel with 28 rooms located in the city centre, just 15 minutes from the airport and 45 minutes from the ancient city of Hoi An. Small but stylish rooms and the usual facilities. **$$**

Bamboo Green Harbourside Hotel
177 Tran Phu Street
Tel: 0511-822 722
Fax: 0511-824 165
e-mail: bamboogreen@dng.vnn.vn
50 comfortable rooms opposite the Catholic church. Restaurant serves Vietnamese, Chinese and European food. **$–$$**

Daesco Hotel
155 Tran Phu Street
Tel: 0511-892 808
Fax: 0511-892 988
e-mail: daescohotel@dng.vnn.vn
This hotel has the look of a cold, communist, concrete carbuncle, but

the rooms are spacious and comfortable with views along the river. **$–$$**

Datraco Hotel
6 Le Loi
Tel: 0511-894 501
Fax: 0511-823 470
e-mail: datracohotel@dng.vnn.vn
Central location at the northern end of Le Loi street and only 3km from the airport. This six-storey modern hotel has 52 pleasant enough rooms and a garden restaurant in a quiet location. **$**

CHINA BEACH

Furama Resort
68 Ho Xuan Huong
Tel: 0511-847 888
Fax: 0511-847 666
www.furamavietnam.com
Luxury resort located right on the beach. Elegant landscaped gardens with two swimming pools, private beach and well-appointed rooms and chalets. Fully equipped fitness centre and excellent restaurants.
$$$–$$$$

MY KHE BEACH

My Khe Beach Hotel
My Khe Beach
Tel: 0511-836 125
Fax: 0511-836 123
Features 45 well-furnished rooms and an in-house restaurant. **$**

HOI AN

Victoria Hoi An Resort
1 Cua Dai Beach
Tel: 0510-927 040
Fax: 0510-927 041
www.victoriahotels-asia.com
This is a charming hotel that's located right on a white sand beach and only 5km away from Hoi An. There are several accommodation options, with French, Vietnamese and Japanese inspired decor. Also features a large swimming pool and restaurants. The hotel also operates a shuttle bus into Hoi An.
$$$–$$$$

Price Categories

Below US$50:	**$**
US$50 to US$100:	**$$**
US$100 to US$150:	**$$$**
More than US$150:	**$$$$**

Hoi An Beach Resort
Cua Dai Beach
Tel: 0510-927 011
Fax: 0510-927 019
e-mail: hoianbeachresort@dng.vnn.vn
Located 5km from the old town of Hoi An. This resort is located opposite Cua Dai beach and is popular with well-to-do Vietnamese tourists. Delicious seafood, including snapper, crabs, clams and lobsters is served in the evenings at its restaurant. **$$–$$$**

Hoi An Hotel
6 Tran Hung Dao Street
Tel: 0510-861 373
Fax: 0510-861 636
www.hoiantourist.com
120 rooms. Located in the centre of town this old favourite is starting to look a bit tired next to the newer competition. However, the rooms are comfortable enough and there is a swimming pool and tennis courts. **$$–$$$**

Hoi An Riverside
Cua Dai Road
Tel: 0510-864 800
Fax: 0510-864 900
www.hoianriverresort.com
This resort has 60 rooms in 15 villas, which are set in landscaped gardens overlooking the river. The restaurant serves great Vietnamese food, but as a resort this is probably the least impressive of the selection in the Hoi An area.
$$–$$$

Vinh Hung Hotel
143 Tran Phu
Tel: 0510-861 621
Fax: 0510-861 893
www.vinhhunghotels.com
This old Chinese house-cum-hotel certainly has the atmosphere of old Hoi An from the outside. But it is only in the more expensive rooms that the ancient Chinese theme is continued. A comfortable homely place. **$–$$**

Vinh Hung II Hotel
Nhi Trung
Tel: 0510-863 717
Fax: 0510-864 094
e-mail: quanghuy.ha@dng.vnn.vn
This hotel is larger than its older namesake and has a swimming pool. Located on the edge of the old town, which means you don't quite wake up in the heart of things, but it's comfort at an affordable price. **$–$$**

Hai Yen Hotel
22 Cua Dai Street
Tel: 0510-862 445
Fax: 0510-862 443
e-mail: kshaiyen@dng.vnn.vn
On the beach road just outside the centre of town. This hotel has 31 basic, but comfortable rooms and a restaurant. **$**

North Vietnam

HANOI

Sofitel Metropole Hanoi
15 Ngo Quyen Street
Tel. 04-820 0919, Fax: 04-826 6920
www.accorhotels-asia.com
The former Metropole dating back to 1901 is the ultimate hotel in Vietnam. Major renovations by the French Sofitel company in 2005 kept its colonial-era atmosphere intact while improving vastly on its comfort levels. Kings, princes, presidents, and famous writers and film directors have all stayed here in the past. Has 232 luxury rooms and two restaurants (Spices Garden and Le Beaulieu), three bars and a swimming pool. **$$$$**

Daewoo Hotel
360 Kim Ma
Tel: 04-831 5000, Fax: 04-831 5010
www.hanoi-daewoohotel.com
Immense complex in western Hanoi with every conceivable facility for the international traveller. Large and comfortable rooms. Great view over Hanoi from the upper floors and an excellent Chinese restaurant. **$$$–$$$$**

Hilton Hanoi Opera
1 Le Thanh Tong
Tel: 04-933 0500, Fax: 04-933 0530
www.hanoi.hilton.com
Superb location and an architecturally impressive building

which aims to compliment the neighbouring French-built Opera House. Excellent facilities and the elegant facade provides a popular backdrop for Vietnamese wedding photographs. **$$$–$$$$**

Nikko Hotel
84 Tran Nhan Tong
Tel: 04-822 3535, Fax: 04-822 3555
www.hotelnikkohanoi.com.vn
A favourite with Japanese tourists. This elegant hotel has one of the better swimming pools in town, a superb Cantonese restaurant and the finest Japanese dining in Vietnam in the Benkay restaurant. Book a room high up for a commanding view over Hanoi. **$$$–$$$$**

Sheraton Hanoi Hotel
K5, Nghi Tam, 11 Xuan Dieu Road
Tel: 04-719 9000, Fax: 04-719 9001
www.sheraton.com/Hanoi
Hanoi's newest five-star, the Sheraton lies in landscaped gardens on West Lake. Facilities include lakeside swimming pool, floodlit tennis courts, conference facilities, function rooms, bars and restaurants. All rooms are tastefully appointed and have spacious bathrooms with separate shower.

Hanoi Hotels

Hanoi has a glut of hotel rooms of all standards the whole year-round. Feel free to bargain. The hotels listed above typically post rack rates of about US$100 for a single room; negotiating a 50 percent discount should not be difficult. Most welcome has been the explosion of countless "mini-hotels" in the Old Quarter and other areas close to Hoan Kiem Lake. Rather like European pensions, many are family-run and located in appealing colonial-style buildings but lack restaurants. A top-end room in a mini-hotel costs about US$30 and includes a bathroom with hot shower, air-conditioning, balcony, refrigerator, telephone and Vietnamese-language TV. The atmosphere is charming, but with the charm comes noise.

The more expensive rooms have lake views. **$$$–$$$$**

Hanoi Horison Hotel
40 Cat Linh Street
Tel: 04-733 0808, Fax: 04-733 0888
www.swissbelhotel.com
An imposing five-star hotel that rises somewhat pyramid-like over the skyline. Very comfortable, attractive rooms. All the usual amenities plus a great health club and swimming pool. Located adjacent to the British Council. **$$$**

Melia Hanoi
44B Ly Thuong Kiet Street
Tel: 04-934 3343, Fax: 04-934 3344
www.meliahanoi.com
Located in the business and diplomatic district, this glitzy affair has 308 rooms, restaurants, bar and pool. Serves excellent Spanish food including an authentic paella. Also features a helipad on its rooftop. **$$$**

Sofitel Plaza Hanoi
1 Pho Thanh Nien
Tel: 04-823 8888, Fax: 04-823 9388
www.accorhotels-asia.com
The Plaza dominates the skyline at the edge of West Lake (Tay Ho). Recently renamed the Sofitel Plaza, this hotel houses the best indoor/outdoor swimming pool in the city and is home to the popular Wave nightclub. **$$$**

Dan Chu Hotel
29 Trang Tien Street
Tel: 04-825 4937, Fax: 04-826 6786
e-mail: danchuhotel@hn.vnn.vn
This hotel looks a little depressing from the street, but the rooms are quite nice in this one-time French-owned hotel. **$$**

De Syloia Hotel
17A Tran Hung Dao
Tel: 04-824 5346, Fax: 04-824 1083
www.desyloia.com
A small but international quality hotel, with an excellent restaurant (Cay Cau) and gym. Situated only a few minutes away from the French Quarter and the city centre. Its 33 rooms are spacious and comfortable. Airport transfer is also available upon request. Excellent value for money. **$$**

Hoa Binh Hotel
27 Ly Thuong Kiet
Tel: 04-825 3315, Fax: 04-826 9818

www.hoabinhhotel.com
A small but elegant and centrally located colonial hotel. 102 guest rooms and 3 restaurants serving Vietnamese and French cuisine and is situated just a stone's throw from Hoan Kiem Lake. **$$**

Hoa Thuy Tien Hotel
1C Tong Dan
Tel: 04-824 4775, Fax: 04-824 4784
Newly built with modern facilities on a street nicely located near the centre of town and near the Old Quarter. **$$**

Moon River Retreat
Bac Cau 3, Ngoc Thuy Village
Long Bien District
Tel: 04-871 1658
Fax: 04-871 3665
New riverside retreat in a tranquil village setting, 5km (3 miles) from central Hanoi. Features traditional Asian architecture in tropical gardens, with comfortable en-suite guestrooms and a fine-dining restaurant in authentic timber houses. **$$**

Asia Hotel
23 Nguyen Cong Tru Street
Tel: 04-821 2045, Fax: 04-821 5872
e-mail: asia@bdvn.vnmail.vnd.net
49 well appointed rooms in this eight-storey hotel furnished in Oriental style. Has a large restaurant with an international menu. **$–$$**

Green Park Hotel
48 Tran Nhan Tong
Tel: 04-822 7725, Fax: 04-822 5977
www.hanoi-greenpark-hotel.com
Close to Lenin Park. This comfortable hotel overlooks a lake to the south of the centre of town. **$–$$**

Heritage Hotel
80 Giang Vo Street
Tel: 04-834 4727, Fax: 04-835 1458
e-mail: her.htl@bdvn.vnmail.vnd.net
62 comfortable guest rooms located away from the main tourist attractions, but within easy reach by 5-minute cyclo ride. **$–$$**

Royal Hotel
20 Hang Tre
Tel: 04-824 4230, Fax: 04-824 4234
e-mail: royaljv@hn.vnn.vn
This is one of the oldest of the "new wave" Hanoi hotels built in the early 1990s. It is located conveniently

close to the Old Quarter and features its own restaurant and nightclub. **$–$$**

Bodega Café & Guesthouse
57 Trang Tien Street
Tel: 04-826 7784, Fax: 04-826 7787
This place is always full, but if you can get a room expect it to be good value, clean and tidy. **$**

Prince Hotel
78 Hang Ga
Tel: 04-828 1332, Fax: 04-828 1636
www.princehotelhanoi.com
Centrally located in the old town for an easy stroll to and from the hectic action in the narrow streets, this hotel features comfortable, basic en-suite rooms with aircon and IDD. **$**

CAT BA

Cat Ba Sunrise Resort
Cat Co 3 Beach, Cat Ba Island
Tel: 031-887 360, Fax: 031-887 365
www.vietnamtourism.com.vn
Cat Ba Sunrise Resort is situated on a private beach with a health club, restaurants, conference centers and a beautiful view over Halong Bay. **$$$**

Sunflower Hotel
Cat Ba town, on the waterfront
Tel: 031-888 215, Fax: 031 888 451
e-mail: sunflowerhotel@hn.vnn.vn
Located near the ferry terminal, this hotel offers clean rooms with television, refrigerator as well as en-suite hot showers. Breakfast is included. **$**

HAI PHONG

Harbour View Hotel
4 Tran Phu Street
Tel: 031-827 827, Fax: 031-827 828
www.harbourviewvietnam.com
127 tastefully decorated rooms make up Hai Phong's only international standard hotel. There is a restaurant and a fitness centre. **$$$–$$$$**

Huu Nghi
60 Dien Bien Phu
Tel: 031-823 244, Fax: 031-823 245
e-mail: huunghihotel@hn.vnn.vn
This hotel features 162 rooms with a fitness centre, swimming pool

and international restaurant. Offers top-quality accommodation at high prices, but lacking the period charm of the Hotel du Commerce. **$$–$$$$**

Hotel Du Commerce
62 Dien Bien Phu
Tel: 031-842 706, Fax: 031-842 560
Colonial-style accommodation redolent of the French era. recently refurbished; friendly staff. 40 rooms available. **$**

Price Categories

Below US$50:	**$**
US$50 to US$100:	**$$**
US$100 to US$150:	**$$$**
More than US$150:	**$$$$**

HA LONG BAY

Halong Plaza Hotel
8 Halong Road
Tel: 033-845 810, Fax: 033-846 867
e-mail: plaza.qn@hn.vnn.vn
www.halongplaza.com
200 guests rooms, swimming pool, tennis courts and bay front-view. **$$$$**

Heritage Halong Hotel
88 Ha Long Road
Tel: 033-846 888, Fax: 033 846 999
e-mail: heritagehl.qn@hn.vnn.vn
Centrally located, 101 comfortable rooms with sea views. Chinese restaurant, swimming pool, tennis courts and even has a disco. **$$$–$$$$**

Bach Dang Hotel
2 Ha Long Road
Tel: 033-846 330, Fax: 033-845 892
e-mail: bachdanghotelqn@hn.vnn.vn
www.baohdanghotel.com
Seven storey hotel with 82 rooms with another spurious 3 stars. Good views from the upper floors. Rooms are spacious and comfortable. It is conveniently located in the centre of Halong city. **$$**

Ha Long 1 Hotel
Ha Long Road, Bai Chay
Tel: 033-846 320, Fax: 033-846 318
23 rooms overlooking the bay in this renovated colonial hotel. **$–$$**

Vuon Dao Hotel
Ha Long Road
Tel: 033-846 427, Fax: 033-846 287

www.vichotel.com/vuondaohotel
A simple hotel with 3 Vietnamese stars, but don't confuse that rating system with the international one. Conveniently located within easy reach of the main restaurant areas and departure points for tours of Halong Bay. Reasonably priced air-conditioned rooms. **$$**

Halong 2 Hotel
Ha Long Road
Tel: 033-846 320, Fax: 033-846 318
Another budget hotel overlooking the bay. This one was recently renovated and has pleasant enough standard rooms. **$**

SA PA

With the exception of the Victoria Sa Pa, Sa Pa's accommodation consists of guesthouses and small hotels. The rate for a single room is typically in the US$7–20 range, whether there are one, two or three occupants. Rates may be increased by one-third on summer weekends when tour groups from Hanoi descend.

Victoria Sa Pa Hotel
Sa Pa, Lao Cai Province
Tel: 020-871 522, Fax: 020 871 539
www.victoriahotels-asia.com
The only luxury hotel in Sa Pa. It's starting to look a little faded, but still offers a comfort zone in the mountains. There are 76 rooms, all of which come with heaters, IDD telephones, satellite TV, swimming pool. Room rates start at US$135. **$$$**

Auberge Dang Trung Hotel
7 Muong Hoa
Tel: 020-871 243, Fax: 020-871 666
e-mail: sapanow@yahoo.com
Known for its cuisine, including wildlife entrees. It features 28 elegantly appointed rooms with views of Fansipan mountain when the mist clears. **$–$$**

Cat Cat
Sapa, Lao Cai Province
Tel: 020-871 946, Fax: 020-871 282
www.catcathotel.com
There are 36 rooms from US$6–US$20, with spectacular views and an excellent rooftop restaurant. **$**

Where to Eat

General

Vietnamese cuisine offers the visitor a wide variety of fine dishes, delicately flavoured with fresh herbs, spices and *nuoc mam* (fish sauce), usually accompanied by *nuoc cham*, a condiment sauce of *nuoc mam*, lime juice, a little grated carrot, chilli, garlic and sugar. Steamed rice *(com)* and soup are eaten at every meal. Different regional specialities lend even more variety to this varied menu. Ask the locals for recommendations and they will be very happy to initiate you.

Due to the highly inflated price of meat, seafood and river fish play an important part in the Vietnamese menu, particularly in the south. The lobsters, flower crabs and oysters, in particular, are excellent. Pork, chicken, beef, duck and pigeon also feature widely on the menu, plus a wide variety of vegetables and tropical fruit. A leftover from the colonial era, French bread is available throughout the country. Baguettes with local pate and salad make an excellent snack.

The famous national dish, *cha gio* is made from crab and pork, mushrooms, prawns, rice vermicelli and bean sprouts, rolled in a thin rice pancake then deep-fried. These delicious crisp rolls are eaten wrapped in a lettuce leaf with fresh herbs and dipped in sauce. *Go cuon*, another national favourite, is made without pork and eaten raw. Look out for *chao tom*, a dish made of minced prawn rolled onto a stick of sugarcane and grilled, and served with vermicelli, vegetables and coriander leaves.

Another celebrated dish is *cha ca* – fish marinated with *nuoc mam*

and *saffron* then barbecue grilled and served with rice vermicelli, herbs, grilled peanuts and a special sauce. One of Hanoi's oldest streets is named after this delicious speciality.

For the more adventurous some speciality restaurants serve turtle, snake, eel, bat and wild game. Numerous restaurants specialise in French and Chinese food. Note that Vietnamese restaurants often do not list prices next to menu items. Always determine the price first – it doesn't hurt to go as far as writing the figure down and ensuring the waiter's agreement.

Where to Eat

Ho Chi Minh City and Hanoi's large hotel restaurants offer both Vietnamese specialities and Western dishes, particularly French, but be sure to check on the opening hours and book in advance if you're not a hotel guest. Wherever you are in the country, don't hesitate to frequent the small local eating places serving a variety of Vietnamese dishes at any hour; you will be in for some delicious surprises.

The price categories which appear below are for a meal for two people wihout drinks.

Price Categories

Below US$10:	**$**
US$10 to US$20:	**$$**
More than US$20:	**$$$**

HO CHI MINH CITY

Vietnamese
Ben Thanh Night Market
Some of the best, cheap and cheerful Vietnamese standards including *banh xeo* (beansprout pancakes) and *cha gio* (spring rolls) are served until late just outside of Ho Chi Minh City's Ben Thanh market. **$**

Binh Quoi Tourist Village
1147 Xo Viet Nghe Tinh Street, Ward 28, Binh Thanh
Tel: 08-899 1831
www.binhquoiresort.com.vn
Take a boat or a taxi to this

Floating Restaurants

At the end of Dong Khoi Street on the Saigon River, boats pick up passengers every evening for a slow two-hour dinner cruise on the Saigon River.

riverside spot to feast on some 70 traditional dishes in a delightful setting. An all-in meal ticket costs just US$6. There's even "grilled field rat" for the adventurous. **$**

Bo Tung Xeo Restaurant
31 Ly Tu Trong Street, District 1
Tel: 08-825 1130
Though the menu (available in English) is extensive, the speciality here seems to be barbecue, Vietnamese-style. A popular favourite with locals. Even if grilled frog legs, deep-fried scorpions or "jumping prawns" aren't to your liking, come and soak in the always festive, sometimes raucous atmosphere, especially on weekend nights or when the power goes out. **$$**

Lemon Grass
4 Nguyen Thiep Street, District 1
Tel: 08-822 0496
A consistent favourite for delicious and inventive Vietnamese food. The chicken salad is especially good. The tasteful Vietnamese decor is not bad either. Special luncheon menus afford a chance to sample different items. **$$–$$$**

Mandarin
11A Ngo Van Nam Street, District 1
Tel: 08-822 9783
Fine Vietnamese dining in a traditional setting. Popular with tourists. **$$**

Nam Phan
64 Le Thanh Ton Street, District 1
Tel: 08-829 2757
A lovely high-end Vietnamese eatery housed in a restored old villa decorated with silks and antiques. Run by the owner of Khaisilk so expect sophistication. **$$$**

Pho 24
89 Mac Thi Buoi
Tel: 08-825 8325
This popular eatery now has 7 outlets and is expanding fast. Traditional noodle soup is served in a clean, bright setting. **$**

Quan An Ngon
138 Nam Ky Khoi Nghia
Tel: 08-829 9449
Recreation of a street stall eatery with style. Vast array of excellent traditional Vietnamese standards to try and all very reasonably priced. One of the city's most popular lunchtime eateries. **$**

Song Ngu Seafood Restaurant
70-72 Suong Nguyet Anh Street, District 1
Tel: 08-832 5017
Come here for some of the best seafood dining in the city: crabs in tamarind sauce, crispy squid with onion and herbs, and "drunken" prawns marinaded in wine.

Tan Nam
60-62 Dong Du, District 1
Tel: 08-829 8634
Delicious Vietnamese fare in a French colonial setting just off Dong Khoi Street. Cosy candle-lit atmosphere. **$$**

Vietnam House
93-95 Dong Khoi, District 1
Tel: 08-829 1623
Moderately-priced favourite with tourists. Serves over 70 traditional dishes; has a set menu option. **$$**

Asian

Ashoka
17/10 Le Thanh Ton, District 1
Tel: 08-823 1372
A popular place for authentic Indian cuisine. **$$**

Asian Reflections
Caravelle Hotel, 19 Lam Son Square, District 1
Tel: 08-823 4999
Cutting-edge Asian fusion cuisine – like Sichuan pepper beef salad and macadamia-crusted softshell crabs – plated Western-style. Stylish atmosphere and excellent service. **$$$**

Chao Thai
16 Thai Van Lung Street, District 1
Tel: 08-824 1457
This is the best Thai restaurant in Vietnam. Piquant papaya salad, luscious *laab* (sausage) and delicious curries. Good service too. **$$**

Saigon Indian Restaurant
73, Mac Thi Buoi, 1st Floor, District 1
Tel: 08-824 5671

Latest Indian offering in town. The fact that it's popular with Indian expats says it all. Serves South and North Indian cuisine and tandoori dishes. **$–$$**

Seoul House
37 Ngo Duc Ke, District 1
Tel: 08-829 4297
A popular Korean restaurant serving all the traditional dishes. **$$**

The Sushi Bar
2 Le Thanh Ton, District 1
Tel: 08-823 8042
Value-for-money Japanese with 45 varieties of sushi in between sips of warm *sake*. **$$**

Totoya
15E Le Thanh Ton, District 1
Tel: 08-823 5089
This restaurant is filled with Japanese expatriates and tourists. Small private rooms for groups are also available upon request. **$$**

International/Western

Au Manoir De Khai
251 Dien Bien Phu Street, District 3
Tel: 08-930 3394, Fax: 08-933 0583
High-class French cuisine in a renovated manor. Fanatical attention to detail – rose petals are strewn in the toilet bowl and are changed after each flush. Advance bookings are essential. **$$$**

Au Parc
23 Han Thuyen
Tel: 08-829 2772
Massively popular lunchtime eatery. The biggest range of sandwiches in Saigon and delicious salads. **$**

BiBi
8A/8D2 Thai Van Lung, District 1
Tel: 08-829 5783
Fine French and Mediterranean cuisine in this popular restaurant. **$$**

Ciao Café
40 Ngo Duc Ke, District 1
Tel: 08-829 1491; and
21-23 Nguyen Thi Minh Khai Street, District 1
Tel: 08-822 9796
Popular place serving a variety of reasonably priced sandwiches, pastas and excellent pizzas. Finish by choosing from a selection of desserts and ice cream. **$**

Java Coffee Bar
38-42 Dong Du Street, District 1
Tel: 08-823 0187

Multitude of coffees available in this hip café. Great selection of bagels, pastries and lips-smacking cakes. **$–$$**

Pomodoro
79 Hai Ba Trung, District 1
Tel: 08-823 8957
Friendly Italian with wood-fired oven pizzas. Great service and home made specials daily. The owner makes his own wonderful grappa and also serves some of the best Italian espresso in Saigon. **$$**

Sheridan's Irish Bar
17/13 Le Thanh Ton Street
Tel: 08-823 0793
Marvellous Sunday roast dinner, the best fish 'n' chips in Saigon and a live Irish band every weekend. **$**

Skewers
8A/1/D2 Thai Van Lung Street, District 1
Tel: 08-829 2216
www.skewers-restaurant.com
Mediterranean restaurant, café and bar serving a wide range of dishes, including skewered meat, hence the name. Serves a wonderfully aromatic Greek sausage. Good wine list, friendly owner and a relaxed setting. **$$**

Soup Specialities

Most localities have their particular noodle soups, which vary in the noodles and meat used and the use of spices and herbs. The most celebrated dish in the north is *pho*, a delicious soup of rice noodles, beef stock, and ginger, to which beef, bean sprouts, fresh coriander, basil, and mint are added at the very last minute. This is one of those universally hearty meals.

In the south, an excellent soup, *hu tieu*, is enjoyed, which is often made with prawns or crabmeat and pork. Another very popular soup is *bun bo*. Rich and spicy, it is eaten with mint, bean sprouts, and a twist of lime.

People from Hue make their own version of this. One of their favourite soups is *canh chua*, made with fish, pineapple, star fruit, okra and fresh herbs.

The Hideaway
41/1 Pham Ngoc Thach, District 3
Tel: 08-822 4222
www.hideawaycafe-saigon.com
Tucked away in an alley far from the
hustle and bustle, The Hideaway
has free wi-fi access and live music
during weekends. **$$**

Tib
187 Hai Ba Trung, District 1
Tel: 08-829 7242
Vegetarian dishes inspired by Hue-
style Central Vietnamese cuisine in
this quiet restaurant down an alley
off Hai Ba Trung Street. Probably
the best veggie joint in town. Has a
set menu of eight dishes. **$**

HANOI

Every large hotel has a restaurant
where a variety of Vietnamese and
Chinese dishes are served. Hanoi
is famous for its delicious *pho*. This
is most evident at breakfast time,
when many pavement restaurants
serve it.

Vietnamese

Brother's Café
26 Nguyen Thai Hoc Street
Tel: 04-7333 866
Charming Vietnamese restaurant set
in a colonial villa and serving
authentic dishes buffet-style. Both
indoor and outdoor seating available.
Excellent value for money. **$$**

Bun Cha
20 Ta Hien Street
Fantastic lunch time dish of noodles
and grilled pork served all over
Hanoi. This tiny place serves one of
the best versions in town. **$**

Cay Cau
De Syloia Hotel, 17A Tran Hung Dao
Tel: 04-933 1010
Excellent Vietnamese food that is
popular among people in the know.
The pomelo salad, crabs in
tamarind and pork-stuffed egg plant
are all highly recommended. **$$**

Cha Ca La Vong
14 Cha Ca Street
Tel: 04-825 3929
The name means fried freshwater
fish and that's what it serves. Ten
years ago, this was one of the few
restaurants in town. It has been

substantially refurbished, but it's
questionable whether the quality
has kept pace with prices. But try it
anyway as it's a Hanoi-must. **$$**

Emperor
18b Le Thanh Tong
Tel: 04-826 8801
Upmarket Vietnamese dining in a
superb setting. The food tries hard to
keep pace with the atmosphere but
is of uneven quality at times. **$$$**

Highway 4 Bar/Restaurant
54 Mai Hac De Street, tel: 04-976
2647; 5 Hang Tre Street, tel: 04-
926 0639
Specialises in authentic rice wine
liquors and Northern Vietnamese
cuisine, particularly steamboat,
fish, spring rolls (try the catfish
spring rolls with wasabi-based dip)
and earthen pot dishes. **$**

Le Tonkin
14 Ngo Van So Street
Tel: 04-943 3457
Set in a century-old restored French
villa, you can dine inside or in the
garden courtyard. The beautifully
presented Vietnamese cuisine has
been tailored to suit Western
tastes. Good value. **$**

Quan Com Pho
29 Le Van Huu
Tel: 04-943 2356
This comfortable restaurant serves
great, affordable Vietnamese. Well
located in what is "street food
central" Le Van Huu street. Very
popular for its lunchtime set menu.
Serves a vast array of dishes. **$**

Seasons of Hanoi
95B Quan Thanh
Tel: 04-843 5444
Classic Vietnamese cuisine in a
beautiful French-style villa
decorated with antiques. **$$**

Spices Garden
Sofitel Metropole Hanoi,
15 Ngo Quyen Street
Tel: 04-826 6919
If you cannot bear the thought of
eating street food, head for this
stylish establishment, where
traditonally-garbed Vietnamese
women dish out street food to
order. Noodles, salads, fried rice,
grilled chicken and spring rolls are
part of a 40-item menu that are
served in genteel surroundings for
lunch and dinner. **$$$**

Nguyen Van Duc's Restaurant
Le Mat Village, Gia Lam
Tel: 04-827 2891
Local snake meat aficionados
swear by this place. You'll get to
see the slaying should you so
choose, drink the blood, swallow
the live heart and eat grilled,
steamed, stewed and fried snake,
snake rice, ground snake bones,
snake soup... you name it and,
within reason, the chefs here can
do it. Each table comes with a very
interesting selection of *ruou*
(traditional wines). Particularly
recommend is *ruou ong* (bee
wine). Not for the faint of heart. **$$**

Asian

Bangkok Hanoi Restaurant
52A Ly Thuong Kiet Street
Tel: 04-934 5598
A bit further along Ly Thuong Kiet
Street, staff here wear Thai
costumes and serve delicious (and
spicy) Thai food. **$**

Tandoor
24 Hang Be
Tel: 04-824 2252
Hanoi's premier curry house.
Extensive menu, including
favourites like chicken jalfrezzi and
lamb curries. Order some *naan* or
pilau rice to go with the spicy fare.
Reasonable prices. **$$**

Tao Li Restaurant
Nikko Hotel, 84 Tran Nhan Tong
Tel: 04-822 3535
Serves excellent Cantonese fare,
including dim sum. **$$**

International/Western

Al Fresco's
23L Hai Ba Trung
Tel: 04-826 7782
If you miss home, this place serves
a variety of steaks, pizzas, pastas
and fresh salads plus great fish and
chips. **$$**

Cyclo Bar and Restaurant
38 Duong Thanh
Tel: 04-828 6844
Favourite with the French, but all
nationalities are welcome. Duck
liver is superb but the steaks can
be a little chewy. **$$**

La Salsa
25 Nha Tho
Tel: 04-828 9052
Fabulous tapas, good atmosphere and friendly staff draw large expatriate crowds here. Does a mean paella as well. **$$**

Price Categories

Below US$10:	**$**
US$10 to US$20:	**$$**
More than US$20:	**$$$**

Le Beaulieu
Sofitel Metropole, 15 Ngo Quyen
Tel: 04-826 6919
You wouldn't come all the way to Vietnam to dine on French food, but if you did, Le Beaulieu is the place. Every morning sees a large breakfast buffet featuring freshly baked croissants and baguettes. Lunch and dinners are more elaborate affairs. Its lavish Sunday brunch is an institution among Hanoi's well-heeled. **$$$**

Luna d'Autunno
11b Dien Bien Phu
Tel: 04-823 7338
The best Italian food in Hanoi. Great pasta and pizza and friendly staff. Particular highlights are Scampagnata pizza and the Quattro Formaggi pizza. **$$**

Moca Café
14-16 Nha Tho Street
Tel: 04-825 6334
More Covent Garden than Hanoi. Stylish but reasonably priced eatery and drinks venue right in the centre of Hanoi's shopping district. The delicious eggs benedict has helped ease many a Hanoi hangover. **$**

Restaurant Bobby Chinn
1 Ba Trieu Street
Tel: 04-934 8577
Restaurateur and chef Bobby Chinn serves a gourmet blend of Asian-Californian cuisine. This fabulously opulent restaurant features a stylish bar, contemporary art and silk drapes. **$$**

Tamarind Café
80 Ma May Street
Tel: 04-926 0580
Imaginative and contemporary vegetarian cuisine, with an Asian

twist. All-day breakfasts, spring rolls and quesadillas are recommended. Best fruit juice bar in town. **$**

Vine Wine Boutique Bar and Café
1a Xuan Dieu Street
Tel: 04-719 8000
Canadian Donald Berger runs this intimate and stylish restaurant and bar near the West Lake area. World-class wines complement the eclectic menu of delicious global "comfort food", including gourmet pizzas and Thai-inspired spaghetti. The cellar also doubles as an intimate dining room. **$$**

HUE

Am Phu Restaurant
35 Nguyen Thai Hoc
Tel: 054-825 259
Serves reasonably priced Hue specialities. **$**

Club Garden
8 Vo Thi Sau
Tel: 054-826 327, Fax: 054-849 836
Tables are set in a quiet garden or air-conditioned dining rooms. Their speciality is Hue food. **$**

Tinh Gia Vien
7K/28 Le Thanh Ton
Tel: 054-522 243, Fax: 054-522 243
Set menus for US$10 or $12 in an open-plan house overlooking a lovely garden. **$$**

DA NANG

Apsara
222 Tran Phu
Tel: 0511-561 409
Specialties of the central region and the elegant décor are evocative of the Cham royal court.

Café Indochine
Furama Resort, 68 Ho Xuan Huong
Tel: 0511-847 333;
Fax: 0511-847 220
Great sea views, atmospheric restaurant and good food. A little out of town though. **$$**

Mau
35 Do Thuch Tinh Street Khue Trung
Tel: 0511-846 615
This is the place for Vietnamese specialities in Da Nang including rice paper wrap dishes. **$**

HOI AN

Brothers Café
27 Phan Bui Chau
Tel: 0510-914 150
Fax: 0510-923 012
Upmarket colonial villa setting and fine Vietnamese dining by the riverside. Good range of wine and cocktails on offer too. **$$**

Café des Amis
52 Bach Dang
Tel: 0510-861 616
Still going strong after many a year at the top of the favourites list of many travellers. There are other restaurants of similar quality nearby, but this is the original Hoi An seafood restaurant. Lovely riverside setting. **$**

Cargo Club
107-109 Nguyen Thai Hoc
Tel: 0510-910 489
Charming French-owned café with some of the best sandwiches, cakes and pastries in Hoi An. At night, the upper floor opens up and serves both Vietnamese and Western fare.**$**

Good Morning Vietnam
34 Le Loi Street
Tel: 0510-910 227
Hearty pizzas and pastas in a casual street-side café. Has daily specials on the board apart from the regular menu. **$**

Hai's Scout Café
98 Nguyen Thai Hoc
Tel: 0510-863 210
This eco-friendly café supports many environmental causes and has a basic menu. Their cooking classes are well known. **$**

Mermaid Restaurant
2 Tran Phu Street
Tel: 0510-861 527
Delicious Vietnamese fare served in homely surroundings. Try its typical Hoi An dishes like cao lao rice noodles and the "white rose" – steamed shrimps in rice paper. **$**

NHA TRANG

Bombay Indian
15 Biet Thu
Tel: 058-524 399
The original and best Indian restaurant in Nha Trang and

probably the only place you can find lamb on the menu in town. **$**

Chieu Anh
6 Ngo Thoi Nhiem
Tel: 058-510 429
Very popular with Vietnamese diners and serves some of the best seafood in Nha Trang. **$**

Mecca
16 Tran Quang Khai
Tel: 058-827 030
Superb fresh and live seafood, including lobsters, prawns, crabs and clams, can be found here. Dine In a very pleasant outdoor setting. Good selection of Australian and French wines. **$$**

Price Categories

Below US$10:   **$**
US$10 to US$20:   **$$**
More than US$20:   **$$$**

Night Market (Cho Dem)
Across from 98 Tran Phu is a group of beachside food stalls serving great seafood. It is the place to dine al fresco, as is evident by the numbers of Vietnamese families who eat here. Open 6–11pm. **$**

Sailing Club
72 Tran Phu
Tel: 058-826 528
Popular upscale late night restaurant serving Indian, Italian, International and Japanese foods. **$–$$**

Same Same But Different Café
111 Nguyen Thien Thuat
Tel: 058-524 079
The usual travellers fair here including some Thai and vegetarian dishes. **$**

DA LAT

Café de la Poste
12 Tran Phu
Tel: 63-825 777, Fax: 63-825 888
This triangular building across from the Cathedral has styled itself as a café of the 1950s, when Dalat was popular with the elite from Saigon. **$$$**

Dalat Palace Golf Club Restaurant
Phu Dong Thien Vuong

Tel: 063-821 201
Some of the best food in Dalat and not only popular with golfers. Has an international menu. **$$**

Empress
5 Nguyen Thai Hoc
Tel: 063-833 888
For pizza, pasta and Italian wine head here. Reasonable prices and good food have made this place a hit with tourists. **$–$$**

Le Rabelais
Sofitel Dalat Palace, 12 Tran Phu
Tel: 063-825 444
High-end French dining in the flashiest hotel in Dalat. **$$**

Thanh Thuy – Bluewater Restaurant
2 Nguyen Thai Hoc
Tel: 63-531 668, Fax: 63-531 606
This quiet location on the lake is ideal if the idea of having a pre-dinner drink while watching the sun set over the hills is appealing to you. **$**

PHAN THIET

Champa
Coco Beach Resort, Km 12.5
Tel: 062-847 111
Slightly pricey restaurant with an excellent seafood grill and decent soups. **$–$$**

Hanh Café
Km 13.5 Ham Tien
Tel: 062-847 347
Traveller's restaurant serving pancakes, sandwiches, soups and fried rice dishes. **$**

Hot Rock
Km 12.1 Ham Tien
The service can be sloppy here, but you do get to cook the food on a "hot rock" hence the name. **$**

Sailing Club
24 Nguyen Dinh Chieu
Tel: 062-847 440
One of the newest and also most popular dining spots along the Mui Ne beach front. Serves Vietnamese and Western dishes in a tropical garden. **$–$$**

Sherdian's Irish House
54 Nguyen Dinh Chieu
Tel: 062-847 322
Popular bar and snack restaurant serving decent Western food. **$**

Nightlife

General

The polarity between rural and urban lifestyles in Vietnam is nowhere more glaringly obvious than when it comes to nightlife. In a country where people habitually rise at 5am, it is no surprise that a drink at 9.30pm may be construed as a late night out. In the big cities, where incomes are rising and foreign influences felt, this attitude has all but disappeared. Bright lights come on, CD players are spun and cocktails are served in increasing quantities. The night is coming to life.

At weekends, youth culture in Ho Chi Minh City and Hanoi parades itself in glorious technicolour. Cruising down Ho Chi Minh's fashionable Dong Khoi Street or around Hanoi's Hoan Kiem Lake on a motorcycle and enjoying the more liberal atmosphere is now de rigueur for the city's outgoing youth.

Although *bia hoi* establishments exist in other large cities, they are most popular in Hanoi. These small, downmarket bars cater exclusively to men – though there would be no objections to a Western woman sitting down for a drink – serving fresh beer without preservatives at amazingly low prices. Vietnamese high society is scarcely likely to patronise these bars, but ordinary Vietnamese workers often stop by for a glass on the way home. They can be good places to meet the locals, but usually run out of beer early and close by 8 or 9pm.

Cafés everywhere stay open reasonably late and are filled with couples chatting or just listening to music. Vietnamese generally tend not to drink coffee late at night, and you will probably be offered tea.

Karaoke bars are very popular with the Vietnamese. If you are lucky enough to wrangle an invitation to somebody's home karaoke get-together, you will get a very different insight into the Vietnamese side of this addictive diversion.

Old-fashioned dances like the waltz and mambo are alive and kicking at traditional dance halls. But, there are also modern discos where ravers bop to the latest house music.

Bars and Clubs

HO CHI MINH CITY

Carmen
8 Ly Tu Trong, District 1
Tel: 08-829 7699
Distressed brickwork and flamenco dances in a candlelit cavern. Extensive cocktail list.

Catwalk International Tourist Club
76 Le Lai, District 1
Tel: 08-824 3760
This disco is very popular with Korean and Japanese tourists. There are several karaoke rooms, a large dance floor and many very glamorous hostesses.

Hoa Vien Brauhaus
28B Mac Dinh Chi, District 1
Tel: 08-825 8605
Authentic Bavarian beerhall and micro-brewery serving the best beer in Vietnam. Also dishes up hearty East European fare including deep fried cheese and a range of Vietnamese staples.

Lion Brewery and Restaurant
11C Lam Son Square
Tel: 08-823 8514
This is a vast 700-seater drinking den next to the Caravelle Hotel, serving decent pilsner and dark draught beer from their microbrewery. Tries to copy the Hoa Vien Brauhaus, but it is still worthwhile stopping off here.

Maya Bar
6 Cao Ba Quat, District 1
Tel: 08-829 5180
This is a very stylish and trendy joint that offers free drinks on "Ladies Night" for the fairer sex every Wednesday.

Number 5 Bar
5 Ly Tu Trong Street, District 1
Tel: 08-825 6300
Friendly service and popular with football fans. Pool table, draught beer and a basic bar snack menu.

Q Bar
7 Lam Son Square, District 1
Tel: 08-823 5424
Despite competition from other bars, this is still one of the coolest places for the hip to see and be seen. With an extensive selection of drinks and a good jazz collection.

Saigon Saigon Bar
Caravelle Hotel, 19 Lam Son Square, District 1
Tel: 08-823 4999
Has become a staple drinking haven because of the view. This pleasant place offers bar food, drinks, decent cocktails and live music from the in-house band.

Tropical Rainforest
5-15 Ho Huan Nghiep, District 1
Tel: 08-825 7783
Themed to look like the Amazon (well, nearly). Very popular among young Vietnamese.

Underground
Lucky Plaza Basement, 69 Dong Khoi, District 1
Tel: 08-829 9079
One of the few live music venues opened till late on weekends. Also serves great burgers, nachos, Middle Eastern food and salads.

Vasco's Bar
16 Cao Ba Quat, District 1
Tel: 08-824 3148
Outdoor/indoor bar and disco. Live bands every Friday. Very popular expatriate hangout which doesn't start filling up until 11pm.

HANOI

Cheo Theatre
15 Nguyen Dinh Chieu (see page 99)
You may not understand the songs or the dialogue but there's no mistaking the slapstick antics of the characters. There are traditional musicians to serenade you as well. The programme is scheduled every Friday, Saturday and Sunday night at 8pm; costs only 30,000 dong (US$2).

Funky Monkey Bar
15B Hang Hanh
Tel: 04-928 6113
Narrow bar, popular with a younger crowd with boisterous DJs and pool room.

Hanoi Cinemateque
22A Hai Ba Trung
Tel: 04-936 2648
Nightly screenings of foreign and Vietnamese movies, accompanied by English subtitles. The courtyard café serves drinks and light meals from 5pm daily.

Jazz Club
31 Luong Van Can
Tel: 04-828 7890
www.minhjazzvietnam.com
Popular jazz club in the Old Quarter. Other type of bands play too including some young Vietnamese rock bands.

New Century
10 Trang Thi
Tel: 04-928 5285
The most favoured nightspot for young and affluent Vietnamese. Huge dance floor, lightshow, go-go dancers and DJs.

R & R Tavern
47 Lo Su
Tel: 04-934 4109
A Hanoi institution, Jay's R & R has rock and roll and "Open Mic Saturdays", so bring your guitar.

Relax Bar
60 Ly Thuong Kiet
Tel: 04-942 4409
Has a charm all of its own. Simple bamboo and brick affair on a street corner; can get cold in the winter.

Spotted Cow
23C Hai Ba Trung
Tel: 04-824 1028
Very popular expat drinking den with a dart board and pool table.

The Terrace Bar
Press Club, 59A Ly Thai To
Tel: 04-934 0888
Happy Hour on a Friday. Has a wide selection of drinks and live music. Very popular with expats and locals.

The Wave Bar & Club
Sofitel Plaza Hanoi, 1 Thanh Nien
Tel: 04-823 8888
Party lovers will enjoy the loud music, large dance floor and big screen video at this popular weekend night spot on the edge of Ho Tay (West Lake).

Culture

Museums

HO CHI MINH CITY

Reunification Hall (Dinh Thong Nhat), Nam Ky Koi Nghia Street at Le Duan; visitors can enter from 106 Nguyen Du or from 133 Nam Ky Hoi Nghia, tel: 08-822 3652. Open daily 7.30–11am and 1–4pm. Admission: 15,000 dong or about US$1. A fascinating look at the official residence of the former Presidents of South Vietnam. Guided tours in English and French will take you from underground war-planning and communications rooms to cavernous banquet rooms and reception halls, to grand sitting and dining rooms, libraries, a theatre, finally landing you on the rooftop helipad complete with non-working helicopter.

War Remnants Museum (Bao Tang Chung Tich Chien Tranh), 28 Vo Van Tan, District 3, tel: 08-930 5587. Open daily 7.30am–noon and 1.30–5pm. Admission: 10,000 dong (less than US$1). One of the most visited museums in Saigon, this place offers a sobering, if somewhat one-sided view of the legacy of the Vietnam War. On display here are American military hardware including tanks and fighter planes, pictures of American war atrocities, graphic exhibits of the effects of Agent Orange, an original French guillotine, and tiger cages from the prison island of Con Son.

Fine Arts Museum (Bao Tang My Thuat), 97-A Duc Chinh Street, District 1, tel: 08-821 0001. Open Tuesday–Sunday 9am–4.45pm. Admission: 10,000 dong. Features ancient Cham and Khmer relics, Revolutionary-era art and sculpture,

and contemporary Vietnamese paintings.

History Museum (Bao Tang Lich Su), 2 Nguyen Binh Khiem Street, District 1, tel: 08-829 8146. Open daily 8–11.30am and 1.30–4.30pm. Admission: 10,000 dong. This museum houses a good collection of artefacts tracing the evolution of Vietnam from the Bronze Age Dong Son Culture through the ancient Oc Eo culture to the coming of the Chams, Khmers and Vietnamese. Also on display here is a collection of Buddhas from different Asian countries.

Museum of the Ho Chi Minh City Campaign (Bao Tang Chien Dich Ho Chi Minh), 2 Le Duan, District 1, tel: 08-822 9387. Open daily except Saturday 8–11.30am and 1.30–4.30pm. Admission: 10,000 dong. Exhibits include American, Soviet and Chinese military hardware as well as the tank that crashed through the gates of Reunification Palace in April 1975.

Ho Chi Minh Museum (Bao Tang Ho Chi Minh), 1 Nguyen Tat Thanh Street, District 4, tel: 08-825 5740. Open daily except Monday, 7.30–11.30am and 1.30–5pm. Admission: 10,000 dong. Documents, letters and photographs charting Ho Chi Minh's life and rise to power are all displayed in this salmon-coloured edifice. Originally a customs house, this was where the young revolutionary set sail from Vietnam in 1911 as a cook on a French ship.

Ho Chi Minh City Museum (Bao Tang Thanh Pho Ho Chi Minh), 65 Ly Tu Trong, District 1, tel: 08-829 8250. Open daily 8–11.30am and 1–4.30pm. Admission: 10,000 dong. Formerly the Gia Long Palace and most recently renovated in 1998, this museum houses photographs, maps and relics from the French and American wars. There are also underground tunnels here leading all the way to the Reunification Palace.

HCMC Botanical and Zoological Gardens (Thao Cam Vien), 2 Nguyen Binh Khiem, tel 08-829 1425, fax: 08-822 8309,

www.saigonzoo.org. Open daily 7am–10pm. Admission: 8,000 dong adult/4,000 dong children. The cool gardens are a respite from the heat and noise of the city. Check at the gate for special events as well as feeding times.

HANOI

Military History Museum (Bao Tang Lich Su Quan Su), 28A Dien Bien Phu, tel: 04-823 4264. Closed Monday and Friday 8–11.30am and 1.30–4pm. Admission: 15,000 dong. From the crumpled metal of a B-52 shot down over Hanoi to a pistol belonging to former South Vietnamese President Nguyen Van Thieu, the Army museum displays a range of war souvenirs from Vietnam's battles against the French and Americans. No mention of the 1979 war with China or the invasion of Cambodia.

Fine Arts Museum (Bao Tang My Thuat), 66 Nguyen Thai Hoc, tel: 04-846 5081. Open Tuesday, Thursday, Friday, Sunday 8.30am–5pm; Wednesday and Saturday 8.30am–9pm. Admission: 15,000 dong. Beginning with 10,000-year-old Dong Noi stone carvings, includes Cham statues, dinh house carvings, lacquer Buddha statues and the Impressionism and Post-Impressionism of the present day. Along with the History Museum, for information and quality of exhibits, this is Hanoi's best museum.

Geology Museum (Bao Tang Dia Chat), 6 Pham Ngu Lao, tel: 04-824 1659. Open Monday–Saturday, 8am–noon and 1.30–4.30pm. Admission: 15,000 dong. Details the processes behind many of Vietnam's unique geological features.

History Museum (Bao Tang Lich Su), 1 Trang Tien, tel: 04-825 3518, e-mail: btlsvn@hn.vnn.vn. Open Tuesday–Sunday 8–11.30am and 1–4.30pm. Admission: 15,000 dong. Exhibits cover every era of Vietnam's fascinating and complex history. The archaeological collection dates from the Paleolithic

"Hanoi Hilton"

Hoa Lo Prison, 1 Hoa Lo, tel: 04-934 2253. Open daily 8–11.30am and 1.30–4pm. Admission: 5,000 dong. Built in 1896, Hoa Lo was the prison home and execution site for many revolutionaries under the French. After 1954, it was used by the Vietnamese state to 'imprison legal violators'. It was dubbed the 'Hanoi Hilton' by US prisoners-of-war held here during the American war. In the mid-1990s, virtually the entire prison was torn down to make way for the construction by foreign capitalists of an enormous, curtain-glass, imperialist-style shopping-office-hotel complex. The 'historic relic' consists of a few cells, stocks, and a guillotine employed by the French and vintage rhetoric.

and Neolithic eras, including relics from the era of the Hung kings, Neolithic graves, bronze age implements, the beautiful bronze drums of Ngoc Lu and Mieu Mon, Cham relics, stelae, statues, ceramics, and an eerie sculpture of the goddess Quan Am with her one thousand eyes and arms. One room features an ornate throne, clothes and artefacts belonging to the thirteen kings of the Nguyen Dynasty. This and the Fine Arts Museum are the best two museums in town, even if history stops at 1975. Originally the museum of the French School of the Far East, the 1930 structure is a blend of East and West.

Ho Chi Minh Mausoleum (Lang Chu Tich Ho Chi Minh), Ba Dinh Square, near Hung Vuong Street, tel: 04-845 5124. Open daily except Monday and Friday, 8.30–11.30am. Admission: free. Often closed from September to December.

Ma May Restored House, 87 Ma May, tel: 04-928 5604. Open daily 8am–5pm. A restored "tube" house, it's an excellent example of the traditional housing, showing how people in the area used to live.

Ho Chi Minh Museum (Bao Tang Ho Chi Minh), 19 Ngoc Ha Street, tel: 04-846 3757. Open daily except Saturday, 8–11am and 2–4pm. Admission: 5,000 dong. Its reputation as a truly bizarre museum is not exaggerated.

Revolutionary Museum (Bao Tang Cach Mang), 216 Tran Quang Khai, tel: 04-825 4151. Open daily 8–11.30am and 1.30–4pm. Admission: 10,000 dong. The museum documents the struggles of the Vietnamese people from 2,000 years ago until 1975. Among the exhibits are some of the long wooden stakes used to cripple the Mongol fleet during the battle of Bach Dang in Ha Long Bay and an enormous bronze war drum dating from 2,400BC.

Temple of Literature (Van Mieu), Quoc Tu Giam Street, between Van Mieu and Ton Duc Thang streets, tel: 04-845 2917. Open daily, 8–5pm. Admission: 2,000 dong. Tablets engraved with the names of scholars from Vietnam's Confucian era are the highlight of this ancient temple in a pleasant, outdoor park setting.

Vietnam Museum of Ethnology (Bao Tang Dan Toc Hoc), Duong Nguyen Van Huyen, tel: 04 824 5117. Open daily 8am–5pm. Admission: 10,000 dong. Built with French funds, this is Vietnam's newest, most modern museum. Behind the museum are hill tribe houses, a water puppet theatre and gardens. The reception has a list of special events. Videos, full-scale models, crafts and musical instruments are impressive, but relatively few of the 54 ethnic groups are represented.

Women's Museum (Bao Tang Phu Nu), 36 Ly Thuong Kiet. Open Tuesday–Sunday, 8am–4pm. Admission: 15,000 dong. Interesting 4th-floor exhibit of the female dress of various ethnic groups.

Festivals

Traditional Festivals

Many traditional and religious festivals take place in Vietnam, particularly in the north and around Hanoi during Tet. Dates, unless otherwise stated, fall in the first lunar month (either January or February).

Dong Ky Festival, a firecracker competition festival, held on the 15th in Dong Ky village, Tien Son District. One of the largest and most spectacular festivals. Tape recordings take the place of the real thing since the government banned firecrackers in 1995.

Mai Dong Festival, which takes place from the 4th to 6th at the Mai Dong Temple in Hai Ba Trung District, Hanoi, is held in honour of Le Cham, the Trung Sisters' brave female general who fought against the Chinese in the first century.

Dong Da Festival, held on the 5th, in Hanoi's Dong Da District, commemorates King Trung Quang's victory at Dong Da and those who died in this battle against the Tsing in 1789.

An Duong Vuong Festival occurs between the 6th and 16th, in the temple of the same name in Co Loa village near Hanoi. Held in memory of King Thuc An Duong Vuong, one of the founders of ancient Vietnam who built the Co Loa Citadel.

Le Phung Hieu Festival, on the 7th, at the temple of the same name in Hoang Hoa district, Thanh Hoa Province.

Lim Festival, held on the 13th in the Lim village pagoda, Ha Bac Province. Features singing and a wide range of cultural and artistic activities.

Ha Loi Festival, on the 15th at Ha Loi Temple in the Me Linh suburb of Hanoi. Commemorates the Trung Sisters.

Den Va Temple Festival, dedicated to Tan Vien, God of the Mountain, held in the Bat Bat suburb of Hanoi on the 15th.

Ram Thang Gieng, the most important Buddhist festival, takes place on the 15th.

Van Village Festival, celebrated in Hanoi's Viet Yen District from the 17th to the 20th.

Khu Lac and Di Nau Festival, occurs on the 7th and 26th in Tam Thanh District, Vinh Phu Province.

Lac Long Quan Festival, from the 1st to 6th days of the third lunar month, at Binh Minh village, Ha Tay Province. Dedicated to Lac Long Quan, the quasi-legendary ancestor of the Vietnamese people. Features traditional music, elders dressed in traditional silk robes, firework displays, and a stunning display of young ladies carrying altars laden with fruit and flowers through Binh Minh's narrow streets.

Huong Tich Festival, held throughout the Spring in the spectacular Huong Son mountains west of Hanoi in Ha Tay Province. This festival can be visited at the same time as Lac Long Quan Festival.

The Buffalo Immolation Festival, held during Spring in the Tay Nguyen Highlands.

Tay Pagoda Festival, held from the 5th to 7th day of the 3rd lunar month in Quoc Hai, Ha Tay Province, is dedicated to To Dao Hanh, a revered Buddhist monk and teacher. An excellent opportunity to see the traditional water puppet theatre in an historical and idyllic setting. Also features rowing contests and mountain climbing.

12th March, the Den Festival takes place at the site of the ancient capital of Hoa Lu in Ha Nam Ninh Province. The festival commemorates King Dinh Bo Linh and General Le who fought against the Sung invaders.

16th March, De Tham Festival in Hanoi's Yen The district.

8th April, the Dau Pagoda festival in Thuan Thanh.

Easter, this is celebrated more in the south than in the north of the country.

12th April, the anniversary of Vietnam's first King, Hung Vuong.

15th May, Buddha's birth, enlightenment and death, celebrated in pagodas, temples, and private homes throughout the country.

July/August, on the first day of the 7th lunar month. Offerings of food and gifts are made in homes and temples for the wandering souls of the dead.

September/October, the Mid-Autumn Festival on the day of the full moon in the 8th lunar month. Celebrated with sticky rice mooncakes filled with lotus seeds, salted duck egg yolks, peanuts and melon seeds. Brightly coloured lanterns depicting all manner of things, including dragons, boats and butterflies, are carried by children in evening processions.

The Kiep Bac Temple Festival, held in Hai Hung Province on the 20th day of the 8th lunar month, commemorates the national hero Tran Hung Dao who wiped out the invading Mongol forces in the 13th century.

25th December, Christmas.

Shopping

What to Buy

Traditional Vietnamese handicrafts offer a wide variety of wares to choose from. These include lacquerware, mother-of-pearl inlay, ceramics, pottery, precious wood, tortoise shell, embroidery, silk paintings, bamboo and wickerware, baskets, sculpture, wood, marble and bone carvings, jewellery, jade, engraving, silk and brocade. You may like to add a *non la*, the famous Vietnamese conical hat and an *ao dai*, the traditional costume worn by the Vietnamese fairer sex, to your wardrobe. Green pith helmets, worn by soldiers during the war and by cyclo drivers and labourers today, are sold.

Heavy taxation has discouraged the sale of antiquities and export is strictly controlled. Goods illegally exported can be confiscated at border crossings and airports. Strict controls on the export of wood products are also in place. A reputable dealer will obtain export papers and the necessary receipts and ship your purchase with little trouble. Copies of bronze statues, old porcelain and objects used by ethnic minorities are for sale in the old quarter in Hanoi, and Le Cong Kieu or Dong Khoi streets in Ho Chi Minh City.

Where to Buy

HO CHI MINH CITY

Antiques/Lacquerware/Handicrafts

Butterfly, 26B Le Thanh Ton, District 1, tel: 08-822 1162. Wide range of handicraft goods on offer.

Celadon Green, 51 Ton That Thiep, District 1, tel: 08-914 4697. Selling

pottery, much of it from the north.
Huynh Mai, 32 Le Cong Kieu, District 1, tel: 08-822 4316. Glass and crystal ware
Indochine House, 27 Dong Du, District 1, tel: 08-822 7318. Arts, crafts and furnishings on offer.
Kim Phuong, 125 Le Thanh Ton, District 1, tel: 08-827 7091. This is one of three galleries with exceptional hand embroidery on silk and linen.
Lucky, 309 Huynh Van Banh, Phu Nhuan District, tel: 08-845 9957, Wide range of antiques.
Oriental Home, 2A Le Duan, District 1, tel: 08-910 0194, fax: 08-910 3504. One of the better antique shops in town.
Precious Qui, 29A Dong Khoi, District 1, tel: 08-825 6817. Large shop selling a wide range of furniture.

Fashion/Clothing/Tailors
Cao Minh, 145-150 Pasteur, District 1, tel: 08-822 4298. Men's tailor making high quality suits.
C&C Zakka Fashion, 27 Dong Khoi, District 1, tel: 08-829 8922. There are several of branches of this popular shop on Dong Khoi street.
Khaisilk, 107 Dong Khoi, District 1, tel: 08-829 1146, fax: 08-823 3773, www.khaisilkcorp.com. Very popular large shop carrying a wide range of high-quality silk and cotton clothing as well as home accessories.
Mai Anh, 81 Mac Thi Buoi, tel: 08-829 5367, fax: 08-899 1214. Francophile Mai Anh tailors silk and cotton outfits.
Minh Huong, 85 Mac Thi Buoi, District 1, tel/fax: 08-822 3074. One of the oldest hand embroiderers in Saigon.

Export Permission

Bear in mind that it is forbidden to export certain objects and, in principle, clearance must be obtained before you take antiquities out of the country. Obtaining this permission from officials can take weeks. An antique is defined as any object more than 30 years old.

Tri Tam Silk, 49 Dong Khoi, District 1, tel: 08-8228210. Handmade and ready-made silk outfits.
Viet Thanh Silk, 65 Mac Thi Buoi, District 1, tel: 08-829 7959. Yet more silk at this popular shop.

Jewellers
Anpha Jewellery, 167 Dong Khoi, District 1, tel: 08-825 1918.
Saigon Jewellery, 66 Le Loi, District 1, tel: 08-823 1139.
Therese, Alphana Jewellery, 159 Dong Khoi, District 1, tel: 08-829 7398.

Art Galleries
There are many galleries offering the works of masters and younger Vietnamese artists. Below is just a sampling. In addition, there are also some galleries in the basement of the Fine Arts Museum.
Apricot Gallery, 50-52 Mac Thi Buoi, District 1, tel: 08-822 7962. Southern branch of the same gallery in Hanoi.
Blue Space Gallery, 1A Le Thi Hong Gam, District 1, tel: 08-821 3695.
HCMC Fine Arts Association, 218A Pasteur, District 1, tel: 08-823 0025.
Hien Minh, 32 Dong Khoi, District 1, tel: 08-829 5520.
Particular Art Gallery, Level 3, Kim Do Business Centre, 123 Le Loi, District 1, tel: 08-821 3019. Works by famous Vietnamese artists.
Pho Hoa Art Gallery, 107 Dien Bien Phu Street, District 1, tel: 08-829 6720. Vietnamese contemporary fine arts.
XQ Hand Emroidered Painting, 81 Dong Khoi, District 1, tel: 08-822 2856. Authentic embroidered designs.

Bookshops
Fahasa, Xuan Thu, 185 Dong Khoi, tel: 08-822 4670, fax: 08-822 5795, e-mail: tahasa-sg@hcm.vnn.vn. This branch has the largest collection of English books on Vietnam.

Supermarkets
Citimart, Regency Chancellor Court, 21-23 Nguyen Thi Minh Khai, District 1, tel: 08-824 4818.
Veggy's, 15/A/5 Le Thanh Ton, District 1, tel: 08-823 8526.

Other Shopping Areas
Apart from the popular Dong Khoi Street, the following are worth checking out too.
Ben Thanh Market, at the intersection of Ham Nghi, Le Loi, Tran Hung Dao and Le Thanh Ton streets, is the city's central market, where fruit, vegetables, rice and meat are sold, as well as electronics, clothes, household goods and flowers. There are also some small food stalls selling soup and rice dishes.
Binh Tay Market, Cho Lon's main marketplace located on Hau Giang Blvd. The usual plethora of household goods and food items are on sale here, though there is a significant amount of wholesale business too.
Dan Sinh Market, at the corner of Yersin and Nguyen Thai Binh streets. Once known as the American market, this place now only has a few stalls in the back selling paraphernalia related to the Vietnam War: army fatigues, combat boots, dog-tags (fake, no doubt), gas masks and the like. Most of the other stalls offer items for daily living: housewares, household tools, machinery, clothing and electronics.
Le Thanh Ton Street. Several shops sell embroidery and silk clothes in Western styles. A shop across from the Norfolk Hotel sells modern glass, ceramics, linens and wood items, all made in Vietnam. Near the New World Hotel a shop sells glass, ethnic fabrics and ceramics of good quality.
Le Cong Kieu is Saigon's main antique street. **Dong Khoi Street** also has a number of stores selling everything from old furniture to trinkets. As always, beware of fakes.

HANOI

Antiques and Handicrafts
54 Traditions, 30 Hang Bun, tel: 04-718 2389, 090-320 4144 (mobile). Artefacts of the 54 ethnic minorities, and antique beads and coins designed as modern fashion jewellery, are sold here.

Au Co Street is the extension of Nghi Tham, north of West Lake (Ho Tay). The shops specialise in antiques and reproductions.

Craft Link, 43 Van Mieu, tel: 04-843 7710. Very popular handicrafts shop with a wide range of items made by hill-tribe minorities.

Furniture Gallery, 8B Ta Hien, tel: 04-826 9769. Antique furniture and knick-knacks.

Bookshops

Bookworm, 15a Ngo Van So, tel: 04-943 7226, e-mail: bookworm@fpt.vn. The only English bookshop in Vietnam. Stocks include the latest fiction, children's books and non-fiction.

Trang Tien Street is filled with bookshops displaying books in Vietnamese, English and French, and some current international magazines and newspapers.

Clothing/Tailoring

There are many shops on **Hang Gai Street** and **Hang Bong Street** that sell silk and cotton clothing. Many shops also provide a tailoring service for made-to-measure clothing. Make sure you allow time for one or two fittings.

Khai Silk, 96 Hang Gai Street, tel: 04-825 4237. One of the best places to shop for silk and cotton clothing. Prices are higher than elsewhere but the range and quality are better.

Le Vent, 115 Hang Gai Street. Specialises in modern takes on traditional designs in sheer organza.

Cocoon, 30 Nha Chung Street. Sells taffeta silk with intricate embroidery.

Lacquerware

Lacquerware is another excellent buy in Hanoi. Countless shops sell lacquerware boxes, bowls, photograph albums, vases and trays. Contemporary lacquerware is another good buy; handmade but with a more modern style, sometimes with Japanese-influenced shapes and a matt finish.

Minh Tam, 2 Hang Bong Street. Specialises in black and white eggshell lacquerware.

Home Decor

Particularly around **Nha Tho Street**, near St Joseph's Cathedral, cutting edge and innovative home decor and interior design shops combine Asian flair with contemporary Western designs, using traditional local materials such as wood, silk, buffalo horn, lacquer and bamboo. Quality stores include **Mosaique**, No 22 and Italian-run **LaCasa**, No 12, on Nha Tho Street and **Dome**, 71 Hang Trong Street (also 10 Yen The Street).

Musical Instruments

Wooden percussion instruments, stringed instruments and bamboo xylophones are sold in several shops in the Old Quarter on Hang Non Street.

Fine Art

Hanoi boasts scores of art galleries. Below are some of the finer ones, where works by the contemporary painters that have recently drawn international attention to Vietnam can be found. Beware, though, that there are plenty of poor imitations of the great masters.

Apricot Gallery, 40B Hang Bong, tel: 04-828 8965, fax: 04-828 7304, www.apricotartvietnam.com.

Art Vietnam Gallery, 30 Hang Than Street, tel: 04-927 2349, www.vietnamesefineart.com

Bui Mai Hien Studio, 99 Nguyen Thai Hoc Street, tel: 04-846 9614, www.hienkhanhart.com.

Codo Gallery, 46 Hang Bong, tel/fax: 04-825 8573. Sculptures, ceramics, paintings.

Green Palm Gallery, 110 Hang Gai, tel 04-828 9293, www.greenpalmgallery.com.

Hanoi Art Gallery, 36-38 Tran Tien, tel: 04-943 7192. The city's slickest art space.

Mai Hien–Anh Khanh, 99 Nguyen Thai Hoc, tel: 04-846 9614, fax: 04-823 0886. This well-known couple run their own gallery.

Mai Gallery, 183 Hang Bong Street, tel: 04-828 5854, www.maigallery-vietnam.com.

Salon Natasha, 30 Hang Bong, tel: 04-826 1387, www.artsalonnatasha.com. Showcases up-and-coming artists.

Language

General

Vietnamese, the national language, is spoken by practically all the population. Variations in dialect, accent and pronunciation exist between the north, south and centre and among the ethnic minorities who have their own dialects. The Vietnamese language has its origins in the Austro-Asiatic languages and has been influenced by the Sino-Tibetan Tai language. Through the centuries of Chinese occupation the Vietnamese adopted the Han characters. In the 13th century they developed their own written language – Nom. In the 17th century, on the initiative of a French Jesuit priest, Alexandre de Rhodes, missionaries translated the language into its Romanised form, Quoc Ngu, which was first used by the Catholic church and the colonial regime's administration. Gradually its use spread, replacing the old written form in the 20th century. Variations of spelling, particularly noticeable in place names, are common. The languages of Vietnam's ethnic minority groups are drawn from the many Southeast Asian linguistic groups of Austro-asiatic, Austronesian or Malayo-Polynesian, Tibeto-Burman, Kadai and Miao.

Pronunciation

Vietnamese is not an easy language to pronounce. The syllable is the language's base unit. Most syllables have their own particular meaning and each syllable can be pronounced in six different tones to convey six meanings. They bear no relationship to one another, either.

In the Romanised written form these tones are expressed by five diacritical accents and one atonic, where the syllable has no accent. For example the syllable "bo" can mean a children's toilet, father, lover, to chop, impolite, or a government ministry. Obviously that leaves much room for confusion for any novice and anyone on the receiving end of a beginner's efforts. (You might accidentally call someone's father his lover, for example, or worse yet, his toilet.)

French is still spoken by many of the older, educated generation in Vietnam. English is spoken by more and more young people, and a fair amount of middle-aged people, particularly in the south.

Greetings

The basic hello – *chao*, is always followed by another word that varies depending on the age and sex of whom you address.
for an old lady/*Chao ba*
for a young lady/*Chao co*
for an older lady/*Chao chi*
for an old man/*Chao ong*
for a young man/*Chao anh*
for an older man/*Chao bac*
for a young person/*Chao em*
goodbye/*Tam biet*
See you again/*Hen gap lai*
I am sorry/*Xin loi*
please/*Xin moi*
thank you/*cam on*
yes/*da*
no/*khong*
My name is .../*Toi ten la ...*
What's your name?/*Ten ong la gi?* (pronounced zee)
How are you?/*Bac co khoe khong?*
Fine thank you/*Cam on binh thuong*
I/*toi*
a little/*it*
how much?/*bao nhieu?*
today/*hom nay*
tomorrow/*ngay mai*

Asking For Directions

O dau? – where?, comes at the end of the sentence directly after the noun. For example if you want to ask for the Post Office – *Buu dien, Buu dien o dau?*

Further Reading

Non-Fiction

A Dragon Apparent – Norman Lewis, Eland, London, 1982. Travels through Indochina in the waning days of the French Empire.
Fire in the Lake – Frances Fitzgerald. Vintage Books, New York, 1972. A classic on Vietnam War.
Free in the Forest: Ethnohistory of the Vietnamese Central Highlands, 1964–1976 – Gerald C. Hickey. Yale University Press, New Haven, 1982. One of many volumes by a top expert on ethnic minorities.
Hanoi Stories – Pamela Scott. New Holland Publishers, London, 2004. Tales of people and everyday life in Hanoi.
The Refused – Barry Wain. Simon and Schuster, New York, 1981. Boat people and fellow travellers.
The Smaller Dragon: A Political History of Vietnam – Joseph Buttinger. Praeger, New York, 1958. Pre-history through the French conquest by a pioneering and talented writer.
Vietnam: A Dragon Embattled (Vol 1): From Colonialism to the Vietminh – Joseph Buttinger. Praeger, New York, 1967. A lacerating indictment of the destruction of traditional Vietnamese society and economy.
Vietnam: A History – Stanley Karnow. Viking Press, New York, 1983. Comprehensive account of the American War.
Vietnam Notebook – Murray Hiebert. Review Books, Hong Kong, 1996. An insightful collection by a Vietnamese-speaking journalist, among the first Westerners in Hanoi after the onset of *doi moi*.
Vietnam: Revolution in Transition – William J. Duiker. Westview Press, Boulder, 1995. Politics, economics, culture since 1975. Very academic.
Vietnam, Now: A Reporter Returns – David Lamb. Public Affairs, 2003. A journalist in the south from 1969

to 1975, David returned to Vietnam in 1999 to open the peacetime office for the *L.A. Times*. His experiences with the two Vietnams – the embattled and the post war – are recounted in depth and with great sensitivity.

Vietnamese Authors

Behind the Red Mist – Ho Anh Thai. Curbstone Press, Connecticut, 1998. Translated by Nguyen Qui Duc and Wayne Karlin, VK Van Hoa, 2004. Contemporary short stories about postwar life in Vietnam.
Dumb Luck: A Novel, Vu Trong Phung. The University of Michigan Press, Ann Arbor, 2002. Written by arguably the greatest Vietnamese writer of the 20th century, this book is newly translated by Nguyen Nguyet Cam and Peter Zinoman. It is a hilarious tongue-in-cheek satire of hip Hanoians in the 1930s who want to be "modern" (read: French).
Novel Without a Name, Paradise of the Blind – Duong Thu Huong. Morrow (US English-language edition), New York, 1995. The writer has been imprisoned for her writings that included veiled criticisms of the government.
The Sorrow of War – Dao Ninh. Pantheon (US English-language edition), 1995. A North Vietnam war veteran who writes one of the first realistic novels from a northern soldier's perspective.
The Tale of Kieu – Nguyen Du. English translations sold in Vietnam bookstores.
A Vietcong Memoir – Truong Nhu Tang. Harcourt, Brace, San Diego, 1985. The voyage of a scion of the Saigon bourgeoisie to the jungle, to the National Liberation Front, to victory and finally to escape as a boat person.
The Will of Heaven – Nguyen Ngoc Ngan. Dutton, New York, 1981. Memoir by survivors of Communist re-education camps.
A World Without Women – Bui Anh Tan, 2000. Written by a former crime journalist, this book tackles the issue of homosexuality. It won a literary competition in Vietnam in 2002.

ART & PHOTO CREDITS

David Henley/CPA 147, 238
Dieulefils, Pierre 18/19, 36/37, 39, 40, 78, 79
Dinh Duc, Trinh 41
Dugast, Jean-Leo 107, 140, 143, 158, 209, 304/305
Exotissimo 181
Evrard, Alain 177, 330
Farnay, Rachel 110L, 113
Holmes, Jim spine, front flap top, back cover right, back flap top, 54, 60, 65, 88, 101, 124, 134, 146M, 148M, 148, 153M, 164M, 170, 180M, 198, 200, 202M, 208M, 208, 211, 224M, 224, 225, 231, 236, 240M, 242M, 245M, 254M, 256M, 256, 257, 258, 261, 264, 270, 272M, 273, 276M, 279, 280M, 280, 281M, 284M, 285, 289, 292L/R, 293L, 294M, 295M, 300L/R, 301L, 306, 310M, 315, 320M, 322M, 326M, 336
Julian Abram Wainwright/APA 150, 153
Karnow, Catherine 8/9, 12/13, 17, 22/23, 43, 48, 50, 52, 53, 58/59, 61, 64, 66/67, 71, 72, 89, 94/95, 96, 106, 114, 120/121, 122, 123, 125, 128/129, 138/139, 145, 149, 150M, 151, 152, 155M, 155, 156M, 156, 157, 163, 164, 165, 166, 167L/R, 168, 171M, 171, 176, 180, 182M, 182, 183, 184M, 184, 185, 188/189, 191, 194, 195, 196, 204, 206, 214/215, 216, 218, 219, 220, 221, 222, 223, 226, 227, 228, 232/233, 242, 244, 245, 252, 254, 262/263, 268/269, 286/287, 290, 291M, 291, 293R, 295, 296M, 301R, 302, 303, 308R, 318, 322

Lynch, Joseph front flap bottom, 6/7, 68, 69, 70, 80/81, 84L, 91, 100, 116, 210, 230, 298, 308L, 312, 313, 314, 320L, 326, 327, 331, 332
Naylor, Kim back cover centre, 20, 62L, 84R, 169R, 174, 203, 229, 237, 241, 253, 272, 274, 275, 277, 282, 283, 311, 324
Page, Tim 25, 30L, 49, 56/57, 74, 75, 77L/R, 82, 83, 85L/R, 87, 90, 169L, 172, 173, 175, 179, 192, 193L/R, 197, 199, 201, 217, 243, 246, 247, 250/251, 255, 259, 278, 284, 334, 335
Photobank 10/11, 24, 26, 51, 55, 98, 105, 115, 127, 190
Robert Harding Picture Library/Alamy 333
Rutherford, Scott 109, 111, 112
Thoma, Zdenka 126
Turnnidge, Brenda 99
Van Cappellen, Wim 14, 202, 205
VPA Images 132/133
Wassman, Bill back cover bottom, 62R, 130/131, 146, 159, 207, 239
Westlake, Martin back flap bottom, 73, 86, 154, 238M, 294, 296, 297, 299M, 299, 300M, 307, 309M, 309, 310, 312M, 316/317, 319, 320R, 321, 323, 325, 328, 329
New York Public Library Picture Collection 38
Plum Blossoms Gallery 102/103, 104, 110R
U.S. National Archives 21, 42, 46L/R, 76
Vietnam News Agency 44, 45, 47, 144
Vietnam Tourism 63, 97, 160/161, 240

Picture Spreads

Pages 92/93: Top row from left to right: Jim Holmes; Jim Holmes; Liba Taylor; Jim Holmes. Bottom row from left to right: Trip/Viesti Collection; Jim Holmes; Jim Holmes; Jean-Leo Dugast; Jean-Leo Dugast.
Pages 118/119: Top row from left to right: Jim Holmes; Jim Holmes; Trip/R Nichols; Jim Holmes. Centre row from left to right: Trip/W Jacobs; Jean-Leo Dugast. Bottom row from left to right: Tibor Bognar; Jim Holmes; Tibor Bognar; Trip/R Nichols.
Pages 208/209: Top row from left to right: Jim Holmes; Jean-Leo Dugast; Jim Holmes; Panos Pictures. Centre row from left to right: Trip/J Sweeney; Panos Pictures. Bottom row from left to right: Jim Holmes; Jean-Leo Dugast; Peter Barker; Jim Holmes.
Pages 244/245: Top row from left to right: Jim Holmes; Jim Holmes; Trip/W Jacobs; Trip/R Nichols. Bottom row from left to right: Tibor Bognar; Tibor Bognar; Jean-Leo Dugast; Trip/W Jacobs; Trip/B Vikander.

Maps Cosmographics
© 2006 Apa Publications GmbH & Co. Verlag KG (Singapore branch)

INSIGHT GUIDE
Vietnam

Cartographic Editor **Zoë Goodwin**
Production **Caroline Low**
Design Consultants **Carlotta Junger, Graham Mitchener**
Picture Research **Hilary Genin**

Index

INSIGHT GUIDES
The classic series that puts you in the picture

INSIGHT GUIDES
www.insightguides.com

Hanoi

0 — 500 m
0 — 500 yds

N

H o n g (R e d)

Ho Tay
(West Lake)

Chua Phu Tay Ho
Yen Phu
Au Co
Nghi Tam
Chua Kim Lien
An Thanh I
An Thanh II
An Duong
Thanh Nien
Ngu Xa

Chua Tran Quoc
(Pagoda)
Chua Ngu Xa
Ho Truc Bach
(White Silk Lake)

Duc Chinh
Nghia Dung
Tam Ap
Yen Phu
Pham Hong Thai
Nguyen Truong To
Duc Chinh

Cau Long Bien

Hai Phong

Den Quan Thanh
(Temple)
Quan Thanh
Chua Hoe Nhai

Thuy Khue
Hoa Nhai
Tran

Bao Tang Dan Toc Hoc Vietnam
(Vietnam Museum of Ethnology)
Hoang Hoa Thiem

CONG VIEN
Phu Chu Tich
(Presidential Palace)
Nha San Bac Ho
(Ho Chi Minh House)
Lang Chu Tich Ho Chi Minh
(Ho Chi Minh Mausoleum)
Ngoc Ha

BACH THAO
Phan Dinh Phung
Hang Dau
Gam Cau

Cua Bac
Nguyen Bieu
Tri Phuong
Cao Chan
Ng.
Hoang Van Thu

36 PHO PHUONG
Cho Dong Xuan
(Market)
(OLD QUARTER)

BA DINH
Ngo Ngoc Ha
Lang Hoa Ngoc Ha
(Flower Village)
Doi Can

Chua Mot Cot
(One Pillar Pagoda)
Bao Tang Ho Chi Minh
(Ho Chi Minh Museum)
Hung
Chua Mot Cot
P
Le Hong ng

Ba Dinh Square
OLD CITY
Bac Son
Hoang Dieu

CITADEL
Di Tich Hau Lau
(Ladies Pagoda)
Di Tich Dien Kinh Thien
(Heavenly Palace)
Hanoi Ancient Capital
Cua Dong
Cot Co
(Flag Tower)

Cha Ca La Vong
Den Bach Ma
Independence Museum
Nha Hat Chuong Vang
Hang Bac

Ly Nam De
H. Cot
Hang Ga
Thuoc Bac
Hang Bo
H. Chai
H. Quat
L. Van Can
Cau Go
Hang Trong
Hang Bong

HOAN KIEM
Roi Nuoc Thang Long
(Water Puppet Theatre)
Lo Su
Cho Cau
Nha Hat Kim Dong
Ham Tu Quan
Tran Quang Khai
Bach Dang

Voi Phuc
Kim Ma
Son Tay
Bao Tang Lich Su Quan Su
(Military History Museum)
Lenin
Tran Phu
Dien Bien Phu
Bao Tang My Thuat
(Fine Arts Museum)
Thai Hoc

Nguyen
Phung Hung
Bat Dan
H. Da
Hang Bong

Den Ngoc Son
Ho Hoan Kiem
Chua Ba Da
(Pagoda)
Dinh Tien Hoang
Le Thai To
Le Lai
Le Thach

Giang Vo
G.V.
Cat Linh
Trinh Hoai Duc
Van Mieu
Van Mieu
P. Nguyen Khuyen
Quoc Tu Giam
Ng. Si Lien

Nha Tho Lon
(St Joseph's Cathedral)
Thu Vien Quoc Gia
Ga Ha Noi
(Station)

Ngo Hoa Nam
Ngo Thinh Hao 1
Ton Duc Thang
N. Van Huong
Tran Quy Cap
Chua Quan Su
(Ambassadors' Pagoda)
Hoa Lo
(Prison)
Ly Thuong Kiet
Hai Ba Trung
Tho Nhuom
Pham Bo Chau
Quang Trung

Metropole Hotel
Bao Tang Cach Mang
(Revolutionary Museum)
Bao Tang Lich Su
(History Museum)
Nha Hat Cong Nhan
Ba Trieu
Hang Bai
Hue
Nha Hat Lon
(Municipal Theatre)
Ngo Huyen
Ly Thuong Kiet
Phan Ngu Lao
Tran Thanh Tong

Ngo Hao Tho 1
La Thanh
Nguyen Luong Bang
Cung Van Hoa Huu Nghi
(Cultural Palace)

Le Duan
Yet Kieu
Binh Tong
Tran Quoc Toan
Tran Nhan Tong
Nguyen Du
Tran Hung Dao
Ham Long
Lo Duc
Bach Dang

Dai Hoc Tong Hop Ha Noi
(University)

DONG DA
Ngo Xa Dan
Cho Kham Thien
Kham Thien
Tien Huong
Ng. Thuong Hien
Ho Thien Quang
Ngo Si Lien

Nha Hat Rap Xiec
(Circus Theatre)
CONG VIEN TONG NHAT
(REUNIFICATION PARK)
Nha Hat Cheo
Bun Cha
Nha Hat Dai Nam
Nha Hat Tuoi Tre
Den Hai Ba Trung

Go Dong Da
De La Thanh
Nguyen Du
Ba Trieu
Binh Khiem
Tran Xuan Soan
Tue Tinh
Hoa Ma
Le Thanh Tong

Tay Ninh